Edited by Anne Marie Morgan and A. R. "Pete" Giesen, Jr.

Governing Virginia

Pearson Learning Solutions, 501 Boylston Street, Suite 900, Boston, MA 02116
A Pearson Education Company
www.pearsoned.com

Printed in the United States of America

1 2 3 4 5 6 7 8 9 10 V092 16 15 14 13 12 11

000200010270789334

CG/LD

ISBN 10: 1-256-42606-7
ISBN 13: 978-1-256-42606-6

TABLE OF CONTENTS

Acknowledgments   vii

Contributors   viii

Introduction: The Diffusion of Knowledge   1
Anne Marie Morgan and Pete Giesen

Part I: Virginia's Metamorphosis   5

1   **Virginia in the Vanguard**   7
Frank B. Atkinson

2   **Virginia Transformed:
The Election that Made History**   14
Hon. L. Douglas Wilder

3   **The Six Constitutions of Virginia**   19
A. E. Dick Howard

4   **The Emergence of Modern Virginia Politics:
From the "Byrd Machine" to Two-Party Competition**   35
Hon. A. R. "Pete" Giesen, Jr.

5   **Commemorating the Anniversary of Public
School Closings in Virginia**   48
Hon. Henry L. Marsh, III

Part II: The Legislative Branch   52

6   **The Virginia General Assembly
and the Process of Making State Laws**   56
Jeffrey A. Finch, B. Scott Maddrea, and John McE. Garrett

7   **Virginia's Budget Process:**   76
        Following the Money
        Hon. Vincent F. Callahan, Jr.

8   **A Lady's Place is in the House (of Delegates):**   85
        Virginia Women and Politics, 1909-2009
        Sandra G. Treadway

9   **From the Front Lines:**   91
        Virginia's Longest-Serving Delegate
        Anne Marie Morgan

10 **The Lieutenant Governor:**   97
        Presiding Over the Virginia Senate
        Hon. William T. Bolling

11 **Lobbying in Virginia:**   101
        Making a Case for Policies
        Eldon James

        A Closer Look: 107
        The Role and Ethics of the Lobbyist
        David Bailey and Tom Hyland

Part III: The Executive Branch   **112**

12 **The Governor and His Cabinet**   115
        Bernard L. Henderson, Jr.

13 **A Choice for Innovation and Investment**   129
        Hon. Gerald L. Baliles

14 **On Our Virginia Renaissance:**   131
        Expanding Opportunity with Reform
        Hon. George F. Allen

15 **A Time for All Virginians**   136
        Hon. James S. Gilmore, III

16 **Virginia Leading the Way**   143
        Hon. Timothy M. Kaine

17 **The Path to Jobs and Prosperity:** 146
Economic Development in Virginia
Hugh D. Keogh

18 **The Attorney General:** 154
Virginia's Chief Legal Officer
Hon. Jerry W. Kilgore and Christopher R. Nolen

Part IV: The Judicial Branch 159

19 **Selecting Virginia's Judges** 160
Hon. David B. Albo

20 **Virginia Courts in Brief** 168
Office of the Executive Secretary,
Supreme Court of Virginia

Part V: The Fourth Estate 177

21 **The State Capitol News Media:** 179
Eyewitnesses to Important Events
Tyler Whitley

22 **The Broadcast Perspective** 184
Adam Rhew

Part VI: Local Governments in Virginia: A Unique Arrangement 187

23 **Virginia's Counties: Governing Close to Home** 189
James D. Campbell

24 **Virginia's Municipal Governments:** 202
Independent Cities—or Are They?
Mary Jo Fields

Part VII: Elections and Politics   212

25 **Voting in Virginia:**   214
       Ensuring Integrity of Elections
       Nancy Rodrigues

26 **Money in Virginia Politics**   221
       David Poole

27 **Political Parties in Virginia:**   224
       Organizing to Win Elections
       Charles E. Judd

Epilogue: The Virginia Way   229
       Hon. John Chichester

Bibliography   234

The Constitution of Virginia: 252
       Table of Contents

Endnotes   256

Acknowledgments

We would like to extend our deepest appreciation to all of the contributors who donated their invaluable time and expertise to create this textbook on Virginia government. From the outset of this project, we envisioned the book as the work of "practitioners"—who love Virginia and have spent many hours on Capitol Square in the trenches, laboring diligently to leave the Commonwealth even better than they found it. When they write on these subjects, they know what they are talking about because they have lived what they describe.

We want to give special thanks to photographer extraordinaire Bob Brown of the *Richmond Times-Dispatch*, who donated a large number of his photos to illustrate this book, as well as to the managers of the *Richmond Times-Dispatch* for their generosity. We would also like to express our gratitude to Michaele White, the talented photographer to Virginia governors who also shared her work with us. Additionally, David Bailey and Bonnie Atwood provided enormous assistance in getting this project off the ground.

And finally, we could not do much at all without the love, support, and patience of our spouses, Mike and Pat, and our children. We are especially grateful to Mike for all of his help and IT expertise. Thank you for *all* you do.

Everyone who worked on this textbook can attest to the wise counsel of James Madison—the 4th President of the United States, Father of the Constitution and the Bill of Rights, and, above all, Virginian: "Knowledge will forever govern ignorance; and a people who mean to be their own governors must arm themselves with the power which knowledge gives." It is our hope that this book will be helpful in arming readers to be enlightened, self-governing Virginians who are worthy of the legacy of Madison and our other inimitable Founding Fathers.

Anne Marie Morgan and Pete Giesen

Contributors

The Honorable David B. Albo is a Member of the Virginia House of Delegates, representing the 42nd District since 1994. He is Chairman of the House Courts of Justice Committee and a member of the Virginia State Crime Commission.

The Honorable George F. Allen served as U.S. Senator from 2001-2007, Governor of Virginia from 1994-1998, Member of Congress from 1991-1993, and Member of the House of Delegates from 1982 to 1991. He is currently the founder and Chairman of the American Energy Freedom Center and President of George Allen Strategies.

Frank B. Atkinson is the Chairman of McGuireWoods Consulting LLC and a partner in the McGuireWoods LLP law firm in Richmond, Virginia. He served as counselor and director of policy for Virginia Gov. George Allen, senior counsel and deputy chief of staff to the U.S. Attorney General under Pres. Ronald Reagan, and as chairman of the federal Jamestown 400th Commemoration Commission.

David Bailey is the publisher of *Virginia Capitol Connections* news magazine, a lobbyist at the Virginia General Assembly, and the founder of David Bailey Associates.

The Honorable Gerald L. Baliles served as Governor of Virginia from 1986-1990, Attorney General from 1982 to 1985, and Member of the House of Delegates from 1976-1982. He is currently the Director of the Miller Center of Public Affairs at the University of Virginia.

The Honorable William T. Bolling served his first term as Lieutenant Governor from 2006-2010 and was re-elected to a second term, which will expire in 2014. He serves as Virginia's Chief Jobs Creation Officer and as a member of the Governor's Cabinet. He previously served as a State Senator from 1996-2005 and Member of the Hanover County Board of Supervisors from 1992-1995.

Bob Brown is Senior Photographer for the *Richmond Times-Dispatch*. He has covered Virginia and national politics since 1970 and has been honored three times as the Virginia News Photographer of the Year. He is a winner of the Miley Award, the highest honor given by the Virginia News Photographers Association and is the first photojournalist inducted into the Virginia Communications Hall of Fame. He is also the author of *Capitol Comics*, a humorous look at the Virginia General Assembly.

The Honorable Vincent F. Callahan, Jr., represented Fairfax County in the House of Delegates from 1968 to 2008, and was a member of the Appropriations Committee from 1972 to 2008, Co-Chairman from 1998 to 2002, and Chairman from 2002-2008. He was also a member of the Joint Legislative Audit and Review Commission and its Chairman from 2000-2002.

James D. Campbell, AICP, CAE, has 40 years of service to local governments in Virginia, including more than 20 as the Executive Director of the Virginia Association of Counties.

The Honorable John Chichester represented the 28th District in the Virginia Senate from 1978-2007. He served as President *Pro Tempore* of the Senate and as Chairman of the Senate Finance Committee.

Mary Jo Fields is Director of Research at the Virginia Municipal League. She is a VML lobbyist and also coordinates program planning for the league's annual conferences, mayors institutes, and conferences for newly elected officials.

Jeffrey A. Finch is the Deputy Clerk for Legislative Operations with the Virginia House of Delegates and has worked for the Virginia General Assembly since 1981.

John McE. Garrett is the Chief Deputy Clerk of the Senate of Virginia and has worked in various capacities for the Commonwealth of Virginia since 1973.

The Honorable A. R. "Pete" Giesen, Jr., represented the 10th, 15th, and 25th Districts in the House of Delegates from 1964-1996. He is the Vice President of Academic Affairs and an adjunct Professor of Political Science at James Madison University.

The Honorable James S. Gilmore, III, served as Governor of Virginia from 1998-2002, Attorney General from 1994-1997, and Henrico County Commonwealth's Attorney from 1987-1993. He is currently the President and CEO of the Free Congress Foundation.

Bernard L. Henderson, Jr., served for 30 years in Virginia government, including as Director of the Department of Commerce under Gov. Charles Robb, Director of the Department of Health Professions during the Administrations of Govs. Gerald Baliles and Douglas Wilder, and the Senior Deputy Secretary of the Commonwealth for Govs. Mark Warner and Timothy Kaine.

A. E. Dick Howard is the White Burkett Miller Professor of Law and Public Affairs at the University of Virginia. He served as executive director of the commission that wrote Virginia's current Constitution and is an expert in constitutional law, comparative constitutionalism, and the Supreme Court.

Tom Hyland is a former Virginia lobbyist and career local, state, and federal government official.

Eldon James is the President of Eldon James & Associates, Inc., a consulting firm that specializes in public policy, project, and program management. The firm primarily assists local governments and nonprofits. He worked 17 years in state and local government in Virginia before founding Eldon James & Associates, Inc., in 1994.

Charles E. Judd is the Chairman of the State Board of Elections. He served as Executive Director for the Ohio Republican Party, Deputy Director for the Republican National Committee, and Executive Director for the Republican Party of Virginia. He previously held elective office and is currently an active instructor in campaign schools and workshops around the country.

The Honorable Timothy M. Kaine served as Governor from 2006 to 2010 and Lieutenant Governor from 2002-2006. He also served as Mayor of the City of Richmond and Richmond City Councilman. He is the past Chairman of the Democratic National Committee.

Hugh D. Keogh was the President and CEO of the Virginia Chamber of Commerce from 1992-2010 and Director of the Virginia Department of Economic Development from 1987-1992.

The Honorable Jerry W. Kilgore served as Virginia Attorney General from 2002-2005 and Secretary of Public Safety from 1994-1998. He is a partner with McGuireWoods LLP and a Senior Advisor with McGuireWoods Consulting LLC.

B. Scott Maddrea serves as Deputy Clerk of Committee Operations for the Virginia House of Delegates and has worked for the Virginia General Assembly since 1986.

The Honorable Henry L. Marsh, III, is a member of the Virginia Senate, representing the 16th District since 1992. He is Chairman of the Senate Courts of Justice Committee and member of the Virginia State Crime Commission. He previously served on the Richmond City Council.

Anne Marie Morgan has worked as a broadcast journalist for many years and is the State Capitol Bureau Chief for Virginia Public Radio. She teaches an array of courses as an adjunct Professor of Political Science at the University of Richmond School of Professional and Continuing Studies, where she was presented with the Distinguished Faculty Award. She also served as a Member and Chair of the State Board for Community Colleges, governing 23 Virginia colleges on 40 campuses.

Christopher R. Nolen served as Special Counsel to the Attorney General from 2002 to 2003 and as Chief Counsel from 2003-2005. He is a partner with McGuireWoods LLP and a Senior Vice-President with McGuireWoods Consulting LLC.

The Office of the Executive Secretary of the Supreme Court of Virginia provides administrative support for all of the courts and magistrate offices within the Commonwealth.

David Poole founded and is the Executive Director of the nonprofit Virginia Public Access Project. He worked as a newspaper reporter from 1983 to 1997, including as a state capital correspondent for *The Roanoke Times* and *Virginian-Pilot*.

Adam Rhew was the State Capitol Bureau Chief and chief political reporter for WVIR-TV, the NBC affiliate in Charlottesville, Virginia.

Nancy Rodrigues served as Secretary of the State Board of Elections and Virginia's Chief Election Officer from 2007 to 2011.

Sandra Gioia Treadway has served as director of the Library of Virginia since 2007. She is co-editor of several volumes on Virginia and women's history topics and serves on numerous state boards, commissions, and advisory groups. She also is the former President of the Southern Association of Women Historians.

Tyler Whitley is a political writer and reporter who worked at the *Richmond Times-Dispatch* and the former *Richmond News Leader* for 50 years. He has written about politics since 1980 and the General Assembly since 1972. He also covered 14 national political conventions and nine governors.

Michaele White is the Photographer for the Office of the Governor and has worked for four consecutive gubernatorial administrations.

The Honorable L. Douglas Wilder served as Governor of Virginia from 1990-1994 and was the first African-American to be elected Governor in the United States. He also served as Mayor of the City of Richmond from 2005 to 2009, Lieutenant Governor from 1985 to 1990, and State Senator from 1970 to 1985. He is currently Distinguished Professor at the L. Douglas Wilder School of Government and Public Affairs at Virginia Commonwealth University, where he has served since leaving the office of Governor.

Introduction
The Diffusion of Knowledge

I t is not uncommon for authors who write about the Commonwealth of Virginia to begin with a sagacious observation by that most iconic of Virginians, Thomas Jefferson. But in this case, it is decidedly appropriate. This is a textbook about what happens in and around the State Capitol Building, designed by Jefferson to serve as the seat of Virginia's government in Richmond.

Without question, Jefferson and the other Founders who conceived of the American Republic believed that the people must be both educated and well-informed in order to govern and preserve the nation. Jefferson wrote about this on many occasions, but his views are epitomized in state legislation that he proposed in 1778 to establish public schools, entitled: "A Bill for the More General Diffusion of Knowledge":

> Whereas it appeareth that however certain forms of government are better calculated than others to protect individuals in the free exercise of their natural rights, and are at the same time themselves better guarded against degeneracy, yet experience hath shewn, that even under the best forms, those entrusted with power have, in time, and by slow operations, perverted it into tyranny; and it is believed that the most effectual means of preventing this would be, to illuminate, as far as practicable, the minds of the people at large, and more especially to give them knowledge of those facts...[1]

Virginia's Capitol Square. Photo by Bob Brown, *Richmond Times-Dispatch.*

A view of the Capitol's South Portico. Photo by Bob Brown, *Richmond Times-Dispatch.*

That is what this book seeks to do: teach the facts about how Virginia is governed to equip readers with the information they need to be discerning participants rather than passive bystanders. But instead of being the customary work of academicians who observe from a distance, this textbook is the handiwork of *practitioners* who have labored intensely in the realms of state or local government. Thus, it is more than mere theory. This varied collection incorporates expertise and first-hand accounts that make it a unique and valuable contribution to the existing corpus of literature on the subject.

We have often considered it a privilege to work on Capitol Square, with its remarkable statuary and architecture renowned for their beauty and republican symbolism. Some of the greatest minds in American history walked on those grounds, and Capitol Square itself is a constant reminder of the principles they espoused.

As Chapter 1 points out, these were ideals that would change the world—a fact that occurred to another prominent revolutionary Virginian, George Washington: "Our cause is noble; it is the cause of mankind!"[2] In this chapter, our author traces the legacy of Virginia's contribution to the United States and, ultimately, to the world. He also uses a broad brush to paint the history of how Virginia's governing principles were momentous, but their execution was flawed. These failures cast a dark cloud over a state that had been a beacon of freedom and representative government. This essay and the other chapters in Part I, *Virginia's Metamorphosis*, also outline the changes that took place over the centuries as the Commonwealth slowly, arduously began to correct its mistakes. These transitions culminated in the victory at the polls of the first elected African-American governor in the United States, L. Douglas Wilder, who also tells his profound story here. Additionally, this section describes the revisions made to the state Constitutions, the emergence of Virginia's atypical habit of fiscal discipline, and the birth of its vigorous two-party political system.

Part II describes the origins of the oldest representative legislature in the New World nearly 400 years ago and the intricate process of making laws in today's Virginia General Assembly. This includes the extensive vocabulary of legislating, the pathways that bills may take, and the strategic role of the governor. The earlier theme of fiscal discipline is illustrated in an account of how the state budget is made today, written by a former Appropriations Committee chairman who was one of the longest-serving members of the General Assembly. This section also describes the office and role of the lieutenant governor, as well as how lobbyists make a case for or against proposed laws. A contribution that is unique to this compendium—and rarely seen in other textbooks on Virginia government—relates the painstaking progress that women have made in winning election to the General Assembly. Additionally, the section features an eyewitness account by a delegate who served in the legislature during the last half-century, who recounts some of the ways that the General Assembly's processes, members, and ways of governing have significantly changed throughout those decades.

Virginia's executive branch is covered in Part III. The initial chapter in this section is a comprehensive narrative about the fundamentals of serving as governor and the workings of the chief executive's cabinet. As the author explains, although the configuration of this branch has changed over the years, the Commonwealth has a record of competent administration during the modern era. In this section, four of Virginia's former governors chronicle their own policy priorities. These preeminent Virginians provide positive perspectives of their administrations, and we invite the readers to delve further into their records and the news accounts of the day to form opinions of their leadership. Although these chief executives represent different political parties, it is evident that they also pursued common goals, such as economic development, a business-friendly environment, and job creation. That's one reason that we also feature a chapter that depicts the critical importance of economic development as a paramount executive function and a path to jobs and prosperity. The policy choices made by governors and the General Assembly have made a profound difference in the perception of Virginia as an attractive state for business. Additionally, many may be surprised to learn that the attorney general is a member of the executive branch. In this chapter, a former attorney general describes for us the growing significance of that office.

The judicial branch and how Virginia selects its judges are described in Part IV. It is a process that is very different from nearly all other states, and a veteran of this legislative activity explains the rationale behind the Commonwealth's approach, the classifications of judges who are elected, and the various scenarios that can arise in the General Assembly. This account is followed by a description of our state courts system, the functions of each type of court, and an illustration of the system's hierarchy and route of appeal.

The news media are an integral component of the political and governmental landscape in Virginia. Part V focuses on the function of the fourth estate in communicating timely information about the daily developments and significant events on Capitol Square. These eyewitnesses have played a strategic role in keeping Virginians informed. But as our two authors report, many news outlets no longer have State Capitol Bureaus, prompting political observers to wonder how the public will know what's happening—and to speculate about the implications for a democratic republic. "New media" consisting of bloggers, on-line videos, and social networking sites could help keep Virginians informed, but questions remain about their efficacy if fact-checking and objective standards of journalism are not followed.

In Part VI, our two experts provide narratives about Virginia's local governments. The Commonwealth has a unique arrangement with cities that are governed independently of counties. Local governments provide many services that citizens need close to home, such as public safety and schools, but they are subject to state authority under the Dillon Rule and are required to carry out mandates over which they have little control. The state also strictly supervises how localities may fund these services.

The dynamics of electoral politics are featured in Part VII. This section examines how elections are conducted to ensure their fairness, the way Virginia regulates the use of money in campaigns and the resulting trends, and the vital role of political parties in waging electoral contests.

4

Our book concludes with an Epilogue by a veteran state senator who expounds on the remarkable "Virginia Way"—an approach that combines fiscal prudence, careful policymaking, strategic investments, and political courage. Those who work at the Capitol have observed this mindset in action. Readers will want to learn about it, too.

Virginia's Bill of Rights proclaims that "all power is vested in, and consequently derived from, the people."[3] But to exercise that sovereign authority wisely, Virginians must be knowledgeable. We believe *Governing Virginia* can play a small part in achieving that goal. After all, as another renowned Virginian, James Madison, reminds us, "... a well-instructed people alone can be permanently a free people ..."[4]

Anne Marie Morgan and Pete Giesen
Editors

"Thus Always to Tyrants": Virginia's state seal is featured prominently on the floor of the State Capitol. Photo by Bob Brown, *Richmond Times-Dispatch*.

PART I: VIRGINIA'S METAMORPHOSIS

The Commonwealth has undergone profound changes over the centuries, and Part I, *Virginia's Metamorphosis*, provides a general overview of its political growth—*and* growing pains. This section is not a comprehensive history, but it briefly outlines the story of Virginia as it led the nation in establishing the first representative legislature and in crafting an intellectual foundation on which a great polity could be built.

As Chapter 1 relates, this was Virginia's legacy to America. And when Thomas Jefferson explained to the world in the Declaration of Independence why the 13 colonies were rebelling against the Crown, he settled on reasons that extended far beyond the violations of the established political rights of Englishmen; instead, he invoked the inalienable, universal rights to which all men are entitled and which no government has the right to take away. That Declaration, which is one of the most famous political documents in history,[1] incorporated consequential concepts that are merely a portion of Virginia's legacy to the world. But Chapter 1 also provides an account of how the Commonwealth paradoxically failed to honor its own political ideals when it deprived many of its residents of their natural rights. In his seminal work, *Democracy in America*, the French political thinker Alexis de Tocqueville shared his insight into the root cause: "The colony was scarcely established when slavery was introduced; this was the capital fact which was to exercise an immense influence on the character, the laws, and the whole future of the South."[2] After a fratricidal war and many agonizing political struggles, Virginia found its way back to its profound ideals.

Chapter 2 features one of the most significant outcomes of that rebirth as the first elected African-American governor in the United States, L. Douglas Wilder, personally tells his remarkable story. Wilder writes about what life was like in racially segregated Virginia, his own ideals and goals, and the changes that ultimately took place which culminated in his history-making electoral victory. Some did not expect Wilder to win or to succeed, but he describes what transpired and how Virginia became the "best-managed" state in America.

Using his extensive knowledge of the subject, Virginia's leading state constitutional scholar surveys the history of the Commonwealth's Constitutions in Chapter 3. Unlike the U.S. Constitution, which has been amended but never revised, Virginia's fundamental law underwent five revisions—at least once nearly every generation—after it was first written in 1776. One portion that did not undergo wholesale redrafting was the first six sections of Article 1, the Bill of Rights, which was written predominantly by George Mason and which provided inspiration for both Jefferson and the U.S. Bill of Rights.[3] It still exists today in Article 1. Nevertheless, other alterations were sweeping and significant. A.E. Dick Howard, who served as the director of the Commission that drafted Virginia's current Constitution, relates how and why the changes were made—which followed the societal and political transformations that were taking place in the Commonwealth.

One significant change was how Virginia was governed and the transition from its one-party system that discriminated against many of its citizens and violated their right to vote to a vibrant, two-party system that guarantees equal rights. Written by legislators, one former Republican member of the House of Delegates and one current Democratic member of the State Senate, Chapters 4 and 5 bring the authors' personal observations and experiences to bear on one of the flawed periods of Virginia's history and the story of its political evolution. These changes, which occurred during the 20th century, did not come easily and required a larger electorate, determined advocates, and extensive legal challenges. The Republican author, former Del. Pete Giesen, was elected to the House as the power of the political organization headed by then-U.S. Sen. Harry F. Byrd, Sr., began to wane, and he took part in building a "New Dominion." But his mother, Del. "Pinky" Giesen, served in the House before he did and was the first Republican woman elected to that body. She was a member during the turbulent period of Massive Resistance, when she opposed the Byrd Organization's decision to close public schools rather than comply with a U.S. Supreme Court order to integrate them. The section's Democratic author, Sen. Henry Marsh, worked for a law firm that challenged Virginia's discriminatory laws and practices through the courts. The reader can relate these chapters back to the story of Doug Wilder's election as governor. It is fascinating when told by those who lived and participated in this period of Virginia's dramatic metamorphosis.

The dome of the State Capitol's Rotunda towers over The Houdon statue of George Washington. Photo by Bob Brown, *Richmond Times-Dispatch*.

CHAPTER 1
Virginia in the Vanguard

By Frank B. Atkinson[1]
Partner, McGuireWoods LLC

On a cold, damp evening a few days before Christmas in 1606, three small ships bearing 104 hearty men and boys slipped from their berths just down-river from London and began a journey that would change the world. Their destination was Virginia and a settlement they would call "Jamestown." Varied dreams of fortune and fame accompanied those and other early voyagers who risked all for the promise of a new world. Among their purposes—identified by one of their number in the earliest recorded indigenous Virginia poem—was this: *"We mean to plant a Nation where none before has stood."[2]*

Against all odds, the planting at Jamestown took root—and not just a nation, but a community animated by a republican ideal, flowered. Today, four centuries later, that nation is the world's oldest enduring republic and sole superpower. From Athens to Rome, from Magna Carta to the American Constitution, the story of *democracy* in its various forms occupies an exceedingly small quarter in the vast expanse of human history. Many in our time would find this surprising, so accustomed have we become to seeing representative government ascendant around the world, springing forth even in war-ravaged lands thanks to a Pax Americana that keeps hostile forces and ideologies largely in check. Yet, democracy and the liberty it enables are improbable developments. *Without America, their remarkable advance would not have occurred. And, without Virginia, America as we know it would not exist.*

A nation of refuge for freedom-seekers since its earliest days, America in the 20th century stood abroad as a bulwark against powerful totalitarian threats to democratic principles. With the collapse of Soviet Communism and the lightning-fast advance of technology and telecommunications at the turn of the century, the tide of freedom has flowed in much of the world. In the early 1970s, there were 40 democratic nations; by the end of the last century, that number had tripled to 120. Yet, the world is a big place with many still-darkened corners; traditions and conditions in many lands do not readily lend themselves to enlightened self-rule; and the enemies of democracy have many faces and startling new methods. The sobering truth is that totalitarianism—with religious extremism as its latest handmaiden—already has claimed more casualties on American soil in this new century than did a parade of despicable despots in the previous one. It is all the more significant, then, that not just the defense of American interests, but the active promotion of democratic principles worldwide, remains the policy of the United States. Together with our democratic allies, America still *means to plant free nations where none before have stood.*

During the four centuries since the settlement of Jamestown in 1607, Virginians have been central players in the remarkable story that is the rise of the United States of America and the worldwide advance of democracy. Even before the Pilgrims set foot on the North American continent, representative government—though rudimentary and selective—had blossomed at

Statue of George Washington in the State Capitol. Photo by Bob Brown, *Richmond Times-Dispatch.*

Jamestown. For 17th-century Britons, all America was "Virginia"—an idea as much as a place, literally a new world of discovery, adventure, and opportunity that encompassed lands as far flung as present-day New England, the Great Lakes region, and the Southeast. Though her geographic bounds were successively narrowed as other colonies and then other states were forged from her lands, Virginia remained, as Thomas Jefferson expressed it, the "blessed mother of us all." From the arrival, survival, and perseverance of the 17th century settlement to the miraculous winning of independence and inspired framing of the nation's charter in the 18th century, people from Virginia played pivotal roles in the seminal developments that forged America's national institutions and character. The freedom today blithely assumed in the Western world, celebrated in emerging democracies, and coveted elsewhere, gained its foothold in our age largely through the soul and sword of George Washington, the fiery breath of Patrick Henry, the elegant quill of Jefferson, and the extraordinary vision of George Mason, James Madison, and John Marshall—*Virginians all.*[3]

For much of the 19th century and part of the 20th, however, Virginia's voice was heard mostly in dissent. When North and South collided in the convulsion of a horrendous civil war, Virginians cast their lot with the Confederacy and proceeded to lead her through battle. Recovered eventually from the ravages of war and reconstruction, the politically cohesive South came to dominate the Congress in the mid-20th century, and Virginia's Senator Harry Flood Byrd and his venerable lieutenants—at one point, with a combined congressional seniority of more than a century—chaired the key committees. From there, the Virginians and their Southern brethren endeavored with mixed success to impede developments they deemed detrimental to individual freedom and the public interest: creation of the federal welfare state; the rapid multiplication of federal spending and debt; and the growth of central government power at the expense of state prerogatives. They also stood out among the nation's stoutest defenders against the international Communist threat. Yet, they placed themselves on the wrong side of history—and morality—by sacrificing civil rights on the altar of states' rights and seeking at length to preserve a racially discriminatory social and political order that was irreconcilable with America's most cherished values. It was because of fearless private citizens like Oliver Hill and Spottswood Robinson and the imposition of federal law, not through the efforts of Virginia's elected leaders, that Jefferson's promise of liberty finally began to be realized by African-Americans—and by other ethnic minorities, including Virginia's Indian peoples[4]—in the middle decades of the 20th century.

For nearly a hundred years—from the civil war through the Second World War—Virginia aptly could be described as a "political museum piece."[5] The cataclysmic civil conflict cast a long political shadow over the Old Dominion[6] and the other states of the Old South. The region languished as a one-party political backwater, continually out of sorts and outside the lively mainstream of American politics. But the winds of economic, social, and political change began to blow briskly across the Virginia landscape during World War II and its aftermath, setting in motion a series of events that would revitalize the state's economy, reinvigorate its democratic processes, and realign its politics before the century was out. From a one-party Democratic state—a conservative Camelot under the deft domination of Sen. Byrd and his political organization—Virginia evolved into a two-party competitive system under no party's and no person's thumb. The advent of competition paralleled the resuscitation and resurgence of the Virginia Republican Party, a long-moribund political entity that sprang to life in the second half of the century behind the lead of dynamic figures like Theodore Roosevelt ("Ted") Dalton, Richard Obenshain and, later, George Allen. The transition to a competitive state brought the Virginia political parties largely into accord philosophically with their counterparts at the national level, and paralleled completion of the long post-bellum march from Southern ostracism to Southern prominence in American politics.

If the prodigal Commonwealth of Virginia had merely rejoined the Union in the latter 20th century, its belated return to the national fold would merit little note. But today Virginia is once again in the vanguard of American politics and society, its place of prominence marked by dramatic economic gains and technological advances, barrier-shattering political accomplishments and ground-breaking policy innovations, unparalleled cultural diversity and dynamic two-party competition. To be sure, shortcomings exist and formidable challenges remain. But if competitive politics and creative governance are the business of democracy, then the once-shuttered Old Dominion clearly is open for business again.

The signs of dynamism are everywhere. In the economic arena, Virginia easily outpaced the nation during the last three decades of the 20th century. The United States economy grew rapidly during that time, but Virginia's economy grew nearly 30 percent faster. Inflation-adjusted per capita income in Virginia increased by nearly 50 percent from 1969 to 1999, a rate of improvement eclipsing that in all but a handful of states and placing the Commonwealth among the wealthy elite. Before the economic bubble burst late in the first decade of the new century, Virginia's growth rate exceeded nearly every other state's—a product not only of post-September 11, 2001, federal spending on homeland security but of a burgeoning high-tech sector centered in Northern Virginia and extending to other fast-growing areas of the state. As the information revolution transformed the world at the turn of the century, much of the data—more than 50 percent of the world's Internet traffic—passed through Virginia, and computer memory chips supplanted cigarettes as the state's leading manufactured export.[7]

While technological progress plainly powered Virginia's economic renaissance, the state's pre-recession economic gains were broad-based and diverse, and they appeared at least partly to be fruits of longstanding and deeply ingrained economic and fiscal policies. With a pro-business regulatory and legal liability environment, comparatively restrained levels of state and local taxation, a balanced budget, modest debt, and—beginning in the 1990s—a "rainy day" fund to cushion economic downturns, Virginia perennially remained among the handful of states to earn the prized AAA bond rating and routinely received national accolades as one of the best fiscally run states and one of the best states in which to live and conduct business.

Governance is typically easier (though not necessarily better) when there is plenty of money to spend, and state government spending in Virginia grew rapidly as the economy expanded in the closing decades of the twentieth century. Indeed, government spending growth in Virginia, as in most states, easily eclipsed even the robust rate of personal income growth throughout the period. Despite spirited debates in which Republicans routinely derided Democrats for profligacy and urged tax relief while Democrats complained of populist GOP shortsightedness and pressed for increased investment in public infrastructure and programs, the statistical evidence seemed largely to belie both arguments. Virginia's ranking among the states for spending growth was influenced by the way it coped with the occasional downturns that beset the national economy, but otherwise that ranking varied little even as the state was undergoing an extended period of intense political competition and transition from the 1970s through the 1990s. For example, the state legislature's research arm reported in 2004 that Virginia's ranking among the states for per capita spending was the same in 2000 as it had been in 1981—36th.[8] Virginia thus maintained one of the *lowest* rates of per capita state spending while enjoying one of the *highest* rates of personal income growth—circumstances that were not easily dismissed as coincidental and that seemed to justify the state's reputation as a moderate-conservative, pro-growth state.

Where Virginia stood out in the late 20th century, however, was not in the size or growth of its government, but in its readiness to innovate and in its ability to conceive and implement innovations. Long identified with adherence to tradition, the Old Dominion suddenly seemed to break out of its bonds, becoming a policy proving ground in the years just before and after the turn of the century. It came at a time in the nation's journey when the focus of domestic policymaking was shifting back to the state capitals. Virginia's innovators passed ground-breaking educational accountability measures that were on the leading edge of a national academic reform movement. They charted new territory with initiatives on international trade, technology, and economic development. They accomplished a wholesale restructuring of adult and juvenile correctional systems and social service delivery (i.e., "welfare") systems, supplying models that would be emulated by other states and even other countries. In developing needed public infrastructure of various kinds, they led the nation in facilitating innovative public-private partnerships as an alternative to traditional financing approaches. And they passed a succession of reforms that enabled Virginia's widely heralded higher education system, already one of the most decentralized and diverse, to become even more so.

Some of these innovations were initiated through consensus; others were commenced through forceful demands for change; but all ultimately came to enjoy broad, bipartisan support. (In a state with a competitive political system and a single, four-year term limit on governors' service, such innovations could only be sustained from conception to implementation through bipartisan consensus.) Of course, more beneficial reform could have been accomplished on more fronts; more, in fact, was accomplished than is recounted here; and many more challenges remain. Structural features that seem rooted in tradition more than practicality—for example, Virginia's independent cities and counties, the one-term limit on gubernatorial service, and a host of others—remain as obstacles to change and objects for reform. But what stands out about public policy in Virginia at its four-century mark is the renewed spirit of discovery, experimentation, innovation, and improvement—the spirit of *leadership*—that animates the state's governance.

The vibrancy of Virginia's communities is also worthy of comment. When three peoples—Native Americans, Europeans, and Africans—came together at Jamestown under the most divergent of circumstances and trying of conditions, the cultural diversity that would uniquely define America was born. Today, the Virginia that helped found a nation of immigrants is itself one of the most ethnically diverse states in that nation. Populous Northern Virginia is home to more varied immigrant populations, its people practice more faiths, and its schools teach children who speak more languages, than almost any other area of the country. And Virginia's diversity is not merely ethnic or religious. There is a long distance, figuratively at least, between cosmopolitan Northern Virginia and rural Southwest and Southside Virginia, and between the Commonwealth's fast-growing, prosperous suburban areas and its landlocked, struggling central cities. Virginia spends much of its time and energy coping with these differences, and it will need to spend more. Yet, there is much unity amid all this diversity, and the state seems to retain a distinctive culture. Values of faith, family, and freedom are not a source of embarrassment for most nor the province of a single party, faction, or movement. There is a sense of community and of shared destiny even while there is a strong spirit of individualism, entrepreneurship, and personal accountability.

Politically, the Commonwealth has become a frequent harbinger of national trends, increasingly examined for clues about the direction of politics and governance in other competitive states and in the nation as a whole. Since the turbulent, transforming period of the late 1960s and early 1970s, Virginia politics has tended to foreshadow national political trends. The conservative coalition assembled by Virginia Republicans in the 1970s presaged the shift of "Reagan Democrats" into the GOP column nationally in the 1980s. The centrist positioning of the successful Virginia Democrats in the 1980s anticipated the Clinton-led national Democratic resurgence in the 1990s. The populist, reform-oriented appeal of George Allen's Virginia GOP during the 1990s found parallels in state capitols across the country and in the White House as the new century opened. And Virginia's moderate Democrats, led by Mark Warner, claimed midway through the first decade of the 21st century to have found a "sensible center" that could hold for Democrats in national contests as well. Even Gov. Robert F. McDonnell's landslide win in 2009 seemed to foretell the sweeping electoral gains that Republicans would make in the midterm contests following President Obama's historic election. A sure correlation or cause-and-effect relationship between Virginia's leading-edge politics and the course of national events is, of course, impossible to prove. But with its off-year elections and competitive politics proximate to the nation's capital, Virginia has become—in the words of one noted national commentator—a "test bed for political change in the country as a whole."[9]

Whether that means a Virginian will play the central role on that stage anytime soon is another question altogether. Dubbed the "Mother of Presidents" because of her sons' dominance of the highest office in the nation's first decades, Virginia has rarely been with child since. An alcove in the rotunda of the State Capitol awaits the bust of the ninth president from Virginia. (The likeness of an honorary Virginian, the Marquis de Lafayette, has been keeping the spot warm in the meantime, and Lafayette's place has long seemed secure.) Yet, with Virginia's sudden return to political prominence, some of its contemporary leaders have been thrust into the national limelight. A succession of one-term Virginia governors—Charles Robb, Douglas Wilder, George Allen, James Gilmore, and Mark Warner—have been touted as potential presidential aspirants at various points in the last two decades, but only two of them (Wilder and Gilmore) actually took the plunge, and the results were not impressive.

White House aspirations aside, however, leading Virginia politicians in both parties have exerted unusual influence on national affairs in recent years. Before his 2009 retirement after 30 years in the United States Senate, Virginia's John W. Warner broadly shaped American military and defense policy as the powerful chairman of the Senate Armed Services Committee. Warner was just one of several members of the Virginia congressional delegation to chair important committees or subcommittees or play other key leadership roles just before or after the turn of the century. With the Republican recapture of a majority in the U.S. House of Representatives in 2010, Seventh District Congressman Eric Cantor gained the highest congressional leadership post held by any Virginian in modern times—House Majority Leader. On the political scene, Virginia governors gained the top posts in both national parties—Gilmore as chairman of the Republican National Committee early in the new century, and Gov. Timothy Kaine as Democratic National Committee chief at decade's end. Though their tenures were not especially happy ones, the high-profile political roles attested to the competitive Commonwealth's importance as a swing state in a politically deadlocked country.

For national significance, though, these and other Virginia developments still pale in comparison with the election of Douglas Wilder as governor in 1989. The birthplace of American liberty, Jamestown, also saw the first institution in America of the greatest affront to liberty—human slavery. So when a majority-white Virginia electorate elevated a grandson of slaves to its highest elective office, the event drew a fitting symbolic close to a supremely tragic chapter and reaffirmed Virginians' commitment to the founding promise of individual liberty. Yet, Wilder's triumph was but a fleeting moment in an ongoing struggle to make the promise of freedom real for all people at home and abroad. And, since freedom begets opportunity and not entitlement, it was of superseding importance that Wilder overcame adversity and claimed his distinctive electoral prize mainly through his own initiative and perseverance. Wilder also helped open the door for others, and it is notable that the first Democrat to carry Virginia for President in a half century was a figure destined for even greater prominence in the history books—Barack Obama—in 2008.

Through more than half a century of dynamic change in the Old Dominion, much has remained the same. The Commonwealth's sudden, often surprising, political twists and turns have masked a more gradual and logical political, social, and economic evolution. A substantial partisan realignment has occurred; an era of vigorous two-party competition has arrived; Virginians have assumed important roles on the national stage—and, through it all, many of the tenets that long have guided political behavior in Virginia have emerged intact.

For Virginians mindful of their past, there remains an abiding conviction that their Commonwealth possesses something unique and well worth preserving. As the fresh breeze of freedom whistles across the dunes on distant shores, there is a sense that what began when pioneers first set foot on Virginia's Atlantic sands is profoundly good, but far from perfect—and still unfinished. In his Second Inaugural Address, Gov. Mills Godwin placed responsibility for the future where it inevitably must lie. During a time of promise yet challenge not unlike today, he said, "Let us abandon the hunt for someone or something we can blame for whatever offends or aggrieves us. Where the people govern, no citizen can hold himself completely blameless if government be found wanting."[10]

Freedom is God's gift to mankind, Virginia's legacy to America, and America's mission in the world. As a new generation steps forward to lead Virginia in its fifth century, striving to preserve the Commonwealth's distinctive heritage while adapting to the brisk winds of change, the challenges no doubt will be formidable. Political conflict, partisan and otherwise, will be sharp. But in this process the venerated tenets of individual freedom and responsibility, limited government, religious liberty, free enterprise, equal opportunity, public integrity, and private charity will find new expression. And

Virginians will remind the nation again of the timeless wisdom in their state Constitution: "That no free government, nor the blessings of liberty, can be preserved to any people, but ... by frequent recurrence to fundamental principles ...."[11]

Frank B. Atkinson is the chairman of McGuireWoods Consulting LLC and a partner in the McGuireWoods LLP law firm in Richmond, Virginia. His published works include "The Dynamic Dominion" and "Virginia in the Vanguard." He served as counselor and director of policy for Virginia Gov. George Allen and as senior counsel and deputy chief of staff to the U.S. Attorney General under Pres. Ronald Reagan. His public service also includes commissions, not-for-profit boards, and the chairmanship of the federal Jamestown 400th Commemoration Commission.

CHAPTER 2
Virginia Transformed:
The Election that Made History

By L. Douglas Wilder
Governor of Virginia, 1990-1994

Any history of government and politics in this nation has to include Virginia, where the first permanent English settlement in America was founded in 1607. In his book, *The River Where America Began*, Bob Deans captures that essence in describing the James River. He writes: "It was into these waters we first waded—red, white, and black—and from them emerged as one. It is here, in that sense, our national story begins."[1]

I like to think that the beginning of our national story does not have an ending, and it shouldn't. America is an experiment in democracy and Virginia's participation in that experiment is ongoing.

The role that slavery played in shaping our political history cannot be overstated, for it was that issue of slavery that led to the beginning of the Civil War. The conclusion of that war framed the context for politics in Virginia, and indeed the South, for the next 100 years thereafter.

One dozen years after the landing on Jamestown Island, Africans (19 in number) were among those who came to these shores seeking new ways to develop as free people. They were indentured servants, not slaves, and sought to work and pay off that bonded indebtedness so that they could breathe their first breath of freedom. Sadly, for most of them and their progeny, that was not to be the case. And those who brought them to this country to assist them in their pursuit of liberty codified the law and forged the shackles and chains that bound them to a life of hell that seemed to far surpass the hell preached by those who spoke of eternal damnation for those non-believers in the faith embraced by those colonists.

Photo courtesy of L. Douglas Wilder.

What happened in Virginia since that landing in 1619 is the story of the building of America and the denouement of the superior race theory (that whites were better than people of African descent and other ethnic populations) that was practiced and enjoyed in the Commonwealth.

It is this tragic history that made the election of a grandson of slaves to Virginia's highest office in 1989 so remarkable—but also a fulfillment of our highest ideals.

Being entrusted with the governance of the Commonwealth is a privilege unrivaled, save by those who have been chosen to lead our nation, and there are some who question even that. It suffices to say that I feel privileged, beyond any expectation, to have been so chosen.

I won't here dwell on the seeming incongruity of that occasioning in my lifetime, but I want to reference why, to me, it did not appear to be so out of the ordinary.

All schoolchildren in the Commonwealth are required to read and recite the Declaration of Independence, penned in 1776 by a Virginian who also became governor, Thomas Jefferson. I always found great strength and comfort in the words of that document, so much so that I questioned whether it could possibly include me among those who were "created equal, and endowed by their Creator with certain inalienable rights." I posed that question to my mother, whom I considered a font of knowledge, although only having a high school education, and she never, ever, disabused me of that notion that I was indeed as equal as anyone else.

I pause to speak of that early introduction to the world outside of the friendly and warm confines of my household where I was raised with seven siblings, six sisters, and one older brother. By law, racial segregation had been the policy of the Commonwealth for decades. Going to a segregated elementary school, segregated high school, and having all white principals and all teachers of African descent likewise had an effect. We had outdoor toilets in some schools, no cafeterias, no auditoriums, no libraries, second-hand books in all schools, and yet the most dedicated teachers in the world, exacting and demanding of us that we excel. In spite of those aforementioned facility shortcomings, they made no excuses for underachievement and accepted none from us.

Those teachers made us believe that there was nothing we could not achieve.

So, it was my world, within, that served as the winds beneath my wings. For I was surely met with every discouragement and disillusionment from the outside, which could have had more negative effects.

There was no television at that time or competing news sources in mainline media reporting. When I was in college and upon graduation, there was a steady stream of negativism from the media sources to which I was exposed.

I was drafted into the Army shortly after graduation from college and that was an eye-opening experience for me. It didn't add up to me that my country would send me to fight for the freedom of Koreans when those same freedoms would be denied me when I returned home. Pres. Harry S. Truman had integrated the races in the armed services—not by an Act of Congress, nor any decision by any court, but by Executive Order.

Though I experienced total integration when I was serving in the military, once I returned home, it was the same old enforcement of segregation. That was until the *Brown v. Board of Education* decision by the U. S. Supreme Court in 1954 outlawing racial segregation in the public schools. It was such a tonic to me that though I had graduated with a degree in Chemistry from Virginia Union University, I knew that I wanted to be a part of the social machinery to help fashion the change in our society. I applied for and was accepted at the Howard University School of Law.

Though I was not intending to be involved with politics, I was drawn into it. Upon entering the practice of law, I found the continuous denouncement of that decision to outlaw segregation challenging enough to make a reassessment.

Having grown up seeing the signs at the department stores: "colored" and "white" on all the restroom doors, on the street cars and the buses, and knowing that hotels, restaurants or places of public accommodation were not open to all persons, I was not content to refrain from being critical and a part of change.

It was those searing images that could become so engrained in a child's mind that he might eliminate the possibility of high attainment. The state told a swath of its citizens that they were second-class, if that.

I was reminded of that on a daily basis, just by reading the daily newspaper. Its editor, James J. Kilpatrick, had adopted as his personal mantra, and that of his newspaper, to write, say, and do everything possible to keep the fires of segregation burning.

On occasion, I would write letters to the editor rebutting his outlandish justifications for racial discrimination. Virginia's influence was so vast among the Southern states, chiefly because of the seniority of its political leaders in the U. S. Congress. But the newspaper was also highly respected and followed and copied with almost religious adherence as to political philosophy.

Kilpatrick's fiery rant caused countless millions of taxpayers' dollars to be wasted on the second "lost cause" of the Confederacy. (And the indelible stain on that newspapers' credibility continues to this day as far as its reputation for equity and fair play, justifiably or not.)

I knew that I had to be more directly involved with the decision-making process of this state and nation. I knew that to do so, one had to be a part of the polity.

Whenever one is called upon to reflect on what it was that he did when performing certain duties, I find it best to dwell upon what others have had to say; it is more objective and removes the tendency to "color" the factual accounting.

In his book, *Virginia's Native Son*, J. L. Jeffries writes about my election and administration. I will give direct attribution to some of his observations and freely quote from his book. In his analysis, Jeffries describes the complex electoral environment at the time that I ran for governor:

> As far as statewide politics is concerned in the South, an accommodating or race-neutral strategy is pragmatic. A black statewide candidate can only win with the aid of white votes. Coalition politics is the most important tool for blacks in their struggle to gain more political offices. Alliances with whites are vital and are seen as the most viable method to get and maintain black political offices. Nevertheless, several students of black and urban politics took exception to Wilder's political campaign strategy. They argued that Wilder's platform was not merely an electoral strategy, but an agenda-setting platform. Those who argued this point believed that Wilder had "sold out" either his black heritage or his once-liberal reputation to get ahead. Those who may have thought that Wilder had forgotten his roots needed only to pay attention to Wilder's first days in office. In the chief executive office, hangs the portraits of Virginia's first governors, Thomas Jefferson and Patrick Henry. A new governor gets to add a third. Wilder's choice: George Mason (who had never been a gŏvernor), a Virginia patriot who refused to sign the constitution because it had no language abolishing slavery.[2]

While getting elected to that office was a significant challenge, so, too, was governing. I have said on many occasions that there is a one-word definition for politics: money. I steadfastly believe this. My administration was met head-on with having to deal with that politically and actually.

As Jeffries explains,

Any examination of Wilder's tenure as governor must be placed in the context of Virginia's severe budget crisis. The Wilder administration began under a cloud of fiscal crisis more severe than any since the end of World War II. Not surprisingly, Wilder's number one priority during his first year was the budget. Unfortunately, the budget would continue to be a concern over the next three years. Over a two-and-a-half-year period Virginia suffered a loss of $2.5 billion in revenues. Former Gov. Mills Godwin blamed the state's fiscal woes on Wilder's Democratic predecessors for their excessive spending.[3]

Even before I took my hand off the Bible and assumed the office of governor on Inauguration Day, the previous decade's economy had begun to cool. On day one, we did not yet know just how bad things would get—but it was obvious that the people of Virginia would need to become reacquainted with the meaning of the word "austerity." Perhaps I should say that it was obvious to me, at least, that the buzz word of the next couple of years would be austerity.

As it turned out, the economy softened at an alarming rate and we had some tough choices to make in Richmond.

Virginia has a reputation of being a fiscally conservative state, and when compared to many of our sister states, it is. But when times are good, even politicians steeped in a legacy of tight-fisted, "pay as you go" policies aren't immune from an ironclad rule of government: When politicians have other people's money, they'll spend it—then demand more. Be they from the left or the right, liberal or conservative, urban, suburban or rural, politicians can't resist the intoxicating allure of the public trough. Even in Virginia, officials had spent too much and saved too little.

As we headed into those difficult economic days, I had more than a few people tell me that the definition of "tough choices" was some variation of higher taxes. And as the nation's first elected governor of African descent and a Democrat, many people—both friends and one-time political opponents—expected me to stumble down a path of higher spending, more taxes, and more burdensome government regulations.

The people who thought such things didn't know me.

First and foremost, I am a Virginian, a grandson of slaves, and a child of the Great Depression. Not only as a legislator had I never been comfortable with negligent, free-spending and high-taxing policies, but I also had not grown up in an environment where pennies were wasted. My father, our family's sole bread winner, never earned more than $50 a week. Even with that meager income he built the family home, modest but comfortable, and the only home my family ever knew. But no member of the Wilder family went without the necessities, either. I learned how to make a dollar out of 15 cents early and from masters—my parents, Robert and Beulah.

So I followed my instincts during those days and began the process of right-sizing Virginia's budget. We funded necessities over niceties, and we avoided increasing taxes. The people of Virginia were hurting economically, and I wasn't about to lead the charge to have their dreams dashed and their financial house collapse because government decided to spend more and more.

We made tough choices all right—some still haven't acknowledged what we did and how we did it—but every square inch of Virginia is better off because we decided to tackle our fiscal emergency responsibly.

Jeffries further points out that "Wilder established several budget reduction policies":[4]

1. Virginia would not enact any general tax increases or defer any planned tax relief.
2. The state would preserve programs that provided direct aid to individuals and other essential public services.
3. They would preserve local government programs.
4. They would emphasize permanent on-going reductions to one-time budget actions.
5. Reductions would be targeted rather than across the board to protect high priority programs.
6. Maximum flexibility would be provided to state agencies to determine where cuts would be made.[5]

Once we finished, Virginia was leaner and more efficient, plus it finally had a savings account for rainy days. It also was twice recognized as America's best-managed state. These were the first such recognitions for Virginia.

One can never capture all that transpired during an administration nor should one be expected so to do. Even expressing the essence of the same is problematic. The caveat that hovers throughout the attempt is leaving out and putting in nonessentials.

I have been asked many times if I ever thought that I would be elected as governor of Virginia. I never thought of it as a child, or even as a young man, because I really had no interest in politics.

The development of the high possibility of the individual had been instilled in me at home, and drilled into me academically in the segregated public schools that I attended and at Virginia Union University and the Howard University School of Law. The seeds of expectation were planted by my mother's confidence that the inalienable rights of "life, liberty, and pursuit of happiness" did, indeed, apply equally to me.

From that early assurance, as a child, I never felt that there was anything that I could not accomplish if I performed my task sufficiently. It is a profound lesson for all of us.

I still regard myself as a "son of Virginia." And in serving as the 66th governor of the Commonwealth, I have had no higher honor.

L. Douglas Wilder served as the 66th Governor of Virginia from 1990-1994 and was the first African-American to be elected Governor in the United States. He also served as Mayor of the City of Richmond from 2005 to 2009, Lieutenant Governor from 1985 to 1990, and State Senator from 1970 to 1985. He is currently Distinguished Professor at the L. Douglas Wilder School of Government and Public Affairs at Virginia Commonwealth University, where he has served since leaving the office of Governor.

CHAPTER 3
The Six Constitutions of Virginia

By A. E. Dick Howard
White Burkett Miller Professor of Law and Public Affairs, University of Virginia.

Long before events brought them to the drafting of their own constitution in 1776, Virginians had had a wealth of constitutional experience. That heritage of constitutionalism had begun to accumulate even before the first Englishmen landed at Jamestown. The first Charter of the Virginia Company of London, granted in 1606, was, like other early colonial charters, a rather practical document, reflecting the essentially commercial nature of the enterprise about to be launched in the New World. Yet—likely as an inducement to those who might settle in the new colony—the first Virginia charter carried language that had in it the seeds of later libertarian stirrings on the American shore:

> Alsoe wee doe, for us, our heires and successors, declare by theise presentes that all and everie the parsons being our subjects which shall dwell and inhabit within everie or arne of the saide severall Colonies and plantacions and everie of their children which shall happen to be borne within the limitts and precincts of the said severall Colonies and plantacions shall have and enjoy all liberties, franchises and immunities within arne of our other dominions to all intents and purposes as if they had been abiding and borne within this our realme of Englande or anie other of our saide dominions.[1]

The guarantee to an Englishman who emigrated to Virginia that, once there, he would enjoy the same "liberties, franchises and immunities" that would have been his in England set the English colonist apart from colonists of other countries. The Spaniard who settled in a colony of Spain, for example, did not enjoy the benefits of the laws and privileges he might have had in his homeland. But, by the terms of the charter of 1606, the English colonist would carry with him the protections and privileges that the common law would have accorded him in England. The Virginia charter's guarantee, or language having like import, became standard in the charters granted for later colonies in English America, for example, the Charter of Massachusetts Bay of 1629.[2] A constitutional precedent was being established which would have telling effect when the colonists confronted imperial policies in the latter half of the eighteenth century.

Other charter provisions encouraged colonists in Virginia and her sister colonies to look to English laws and customs as their patrimony. The second Charter of Virginia, that of 1609, required that all "statuts, ordinannces and proceedinges as neere as convenientlie maie be, be agreable to the lawes, statutes, government and pollicie of this oure realme of England."[3] Like provisos were found in the third Virginia Charter (1612) and in charters of other colonies.[4] Moreover, later colonial charters often contained other devices that sought to ensure that colonial laws would be in accord with those of England, including the transmission of enacted statutes to England for approval or disapproval, appeals to England of certain judgments of colonial courts, and requirements that colonial oaths of office conform to English practice.[5]

In the first few years of the Virginia colony, the settlers were more concerned with sheer survival than with the liberties or rights they might enjoy as Englishmen. The winter of 1609-1610—aptly called the "starving time"—left but sixty settlers alive of the original five hundred. But the tiny colony survived, and others followed, beginning with the landing at Plymouth in 1620. It was not long before some of the laws and institutions of England began to take root in the New World.

Representative government was among the first of those institutions. In 1618 the Instructions to Governor Yeardley directed him, on his arrival in Virginia, to convene a general assembly.[6] Yeardley did so, and in 1619 the first representative legislative assembly in the New World met at Jamestown.[7] Virginians quickly became accustomed to self-government. In the Cromwellian era, after the Virginia Assembly had declared its loyalty to the Crown, the Puritan Commonwealth determined to subdue Virginia, by force if necessary. After some negotiations, Virginia agreed to submit, but the articles of submission explicitly guaranteed that Virginians should enjoy "such freedomes and priviledges as belong to the free borne people of England" and that representative government should continue in Virginia.[8]

A century later the doctrines implanted in the first decades of settlement emerged with new vigor. In the years leading up to the American Revolution, Virginians had ample opportunity to sharpen their sense of constitutional argument. When the Privy Council in Britain disallowed Virginia's Two-Penny Act, passed in 1758 to allow debts payable in tobacco to be paid in money (because the value of tobacco had risen), Richard Bland published *The Colonel Dismounted*, a statement of the right of the Virginia Assembly to enact such laws as it pleased for Virginia's self-government.[9] Soon thereafter, when England enacted the Revenue Act of 1764 in an effort to pass on to the American colonies a part of the cost of the Seven Years' War (much of it fought in British America), the colonists were quick to protest. In December 1764 Virginia's Assembly passed three resolutions—a petition to the King, a memorial to the House of Lords, and a remonstrance to the House of Commons. All three protests asserted the right not to be taxed without consent. The Virginians rested this claim squarely on the grant in the colonial charters of the "rights of Englishmen": "As our Ancestors brought with them every Right and Privilege they could with Justice claim in their Mother Kingdom, their Descendents may conclude they cannot be deprived of those Rights without Injustice."[10]

A sharper clash lay ahead. Even the Revenue Act had levied only an external tax, in the form of customs duties. In 1765 Parliament enacted the Stamp Act—the first direct, internal tax ever levied by Parliament on the American colonies. The colonists were outraged. In May 1765 Patrick Henry rose in the Virginia Assembly to declare, "Tarquin and Caesar each had his Brutus, Charles the First his Cromwell and George the Third"—at which there were cries of "Treason" from the chamber—"may profit by their example. If this be treason, make the most of it."[11]

The House adopted four resolutions. The first declared that Virginia's original settlers brought with them and transmitted to their posterity the "Liberties, Privileges, Franchises, and Immunities" enjoyed by all Englishmen. The second recalled that James I, by royal charter, had formally confirmed this right. The third proclaimed the right not to be taxed without representation. And the fourth submitted that this right of internal self-government had regularly been recognized in Great Britain.[12]

Passed but two months after the passage of the Stamp Act, the Virginia resolutions were widely imitated throughout the colonies. Other colonies passed their own resolutions, and responding to the prompting of Massachusetts, the colonies sent delegates to a congress in New York—the Stamp Act Congress. That assemblage passed resolutions similar to those of the individual colonies, asserting the

Surrounding the base of the George Washington Equestrian Monument on Capitol Square are statues of six Virginia leaders that depict Virginia's role in the Revolution and each patriot's contribution: from left, Patrick Henry—Revolution; George Mason—Bill of Rights; Thomas Jefferson—Independence; and Thomas Nelson—Finance. Photo by Anne Marie Morgan.

right not to be taxed without consent and the right to trial by jury (cases arising under the Stamp Act being vested in courts of admiralty, which sat without juries).[13]

At the local level, manifestations of opposition to the Stamp Act included the action of the justices of Stafford County, Virginia, who resigned in a body rather than enforce the Stamp Act, a measure which they declared to be in conflict with Magna Carta.[14] The Northampton County Court declared that the Stamp Act "did not bind, affect, or concern the inhabitants of this colony, inasmuch as they conceive the same to be unconstitutional...."[15] Since there was no actual case before the court, its pronouncement was not a holding in any technical sense. But such a declaration was nonetheless a statement of the principle that a court could declare a legislative act unconstitutional—the theory of judicial review later enunciated under the Federal Constitution by Chief Justice John Marshall in *Marbury v. Madison*.[16]

General prosperity in the colonies and the repeal of the Stamp Act brought a lull to the feud between colonies and mother country, but in 1773, in protest of the Townshend duties that had been retained on tea, came the Boston Tea Party. When the Sons of Liberty dumped tea of the East India Company into Boston Harbor, Parliament reacted by passing the Boston Port Act and other measures that the colonists called the "Coercive" or "Intolerable" Acts. These measures placed Boston under a kind of blockade until it would pay reparations for the jettisoned tea, made provision for the commandeering of private houses to quarter British troops, and provided for the appointment of the Governor's Council by the King rather than by the more popular Assembly.[17]

In May 1774, a few days before the punitive statutes were to take effect, the Virginia House of Burgesses voiced its concern about the "hostile invasion" of Boston and set aside a day of fasting and prayer. Governor Dunmore thereupon dissolved the Assembly.[18] The Burgesses then met at the Raleigh Tavern, formed a committee, and agreed upon a resolution for united action by the colonies. Eighty-nine members of the dissolved house signed the resolution, which recommended that each colony appoint delegates to meet in a general congress.[19] The other colonies, as well as scores of counties, towns, and localities, passed similar resolutions.

The resolutions of 1774 argued the rights of the colonists, sometimes drawing on theories of natural rights, sometimes on colonial charters, sometimes on the British Constitution, often on all three.[20]

No resolution was more articulate in its discussion of the colonists' constitutional rights than the resolves of the freeholders and inhabitants of Fairfax County, drafted by George Mason—two years later to be the chief architect of Virginia's first Constitution. At a meeting chaired by George Washington, the people of Fairfax County began their resolutions with the following declaration:

> RESOLVED, that this Colony and Dominion of Virginia can not be considered as a conquered Country, and if it was, that the present Inhabitants are the Descendants not of the Conquered, but of the Conquerors.
>
> That the same was not settled at the national Expence of England, but at the private Expence of the Adventurers, our Ancestors, by solemn Compact with, and under the Auspices and Protection of the British Crown; upon which we are in every Respect as dependant, as the People of Great Britain, and in the same Manner subject to all his Majesty's just, legal, and constitutional Prerogatives. That our Ancestors, when they left their native land, and settled in America, brought with them (even if the same had not been confirmed by Charters) the Civil Constitution and Form of Government of the Country they came from; and were by the Laws of Nature and Nations, entitled to all its Priviledges, Immunities and Advantages; which have descended to us their Posterity, and out of Right to be as fully enjoyed, as if we had still continued within the Realm of England.[21]

The words that the colonists had brought with them in 1606 still echoed at the eve of the American Revolution. Events in the span of over a century and a half between settlement and revolution had only served to strengthen the heritage of constitutionalism that Virginians and other colonists considered their own.

It is obvious that when the Virginia Convention of May 1776 assembled in Williamsburg, the break with the mother country imminent, the delegates were not writing on a clean constitutional slate. The delegates included the colony's best talent, save for those who—Thomas Jefferson and Benjamin Harrison among them—were sitting with the Congress in Philadelphia. Uppermost in the minds of the delegates at Williamsburg was the question of independence, and on May 15 the Convention adopted a resolution calling on Virginia's representatives in Congress to declare the United Colonies free and independent states.[22]

The move toward independence logically entailed a plan for self-government. Therefore, as a companion to the resolution calling for independence, the Convention passed a resolution creating a committee to prepare a declaration of rights for Virginia and "such a plan of government as will be most likely to maintain peace and order in this colony, and secure substantial and equal liberty to the people."[23]

Several plans for a constitution for Virginia were brought to the attention of the Convention. They ranged from a rather democratic plan drawn up by Massachusetts's John Adams and favored by Patrick Henry to a quite aristocratic document attributed to Carter Braxton and modeled after the British Constitution in the form it had taken after the Glorious Revolution of 1688. From Philadelphia, Thomas Jefferson sent drafts of a constitution for Virginia, but by the time they reached Williamsburg, the Convention's work was sufficiently advanced that only parts of Jefferson's plan were adopted.[24]

The chief architect of the Virginia Constitution of 1776 was George Mason. Well steeped in the principles of the British Constitution,[25] Mason proposed a bill of rights which contained most of the provisions that appeared in the final document. On June 12 the Convention gave its approval to the Virginia Declaration of Rights. In good part the Declaration of Rights was a restatement of the basic principles of the English liberty documents, such as Magna Carta, the Petition of Right, and the Bill of Rights. To this English heritage were added statements of natural rights philosophy: that power derives from the people, that men have certain inherent rights which they retain in civil society, and that a majority of the people have the right to alter or abolish an existing form of government.[26]

The frame of government agreed to by the Convention owed less to the British heritage than did the Declaration of Rights; indeed, in some ways the plan of government was a reaction against such things as strong executives, which the colonists had come to fear and distrust. The Constitution of 1776 created a General Assembly with virtually no explicit limits on its power to legislate, and a dependent Governor, elected by the two houses of the Assembly and able to act only with the advice of a Privy Council, also chosen by the Assembly. Suffrage, as in the colony, was limited, being tied to the ownership of land. Representation in the Assembly bore no relation to population; in the lower house, for example, each county was entitled to two delegates, regardless of the county's population.

Many Virginians were dissatisfied with the Constitution of 1776. The most articulate voice for reform was that of Thomas Jefferson. In his *Notes on the State of Virginia*, first printed in 1785, Jefferson leveled particular attack against the Constitution's provisions concerning suffrage and legislative apportionment. Of the restricted suffrage, Jefferson said, " The majority of the men in the state, who pay and fight for its support, are unrepresented in the legislature ..." Of the malapportioned Assembly, Jefferson observed that the County of Loudoun, with 1746 fighting men, had no more representation than did Warwick, with only one hundred, so that one man in Warwick had as much influence in the government as 17 men in Loudoun.[27]

Jefferson also objected to the Constitution's failure to make reality of its theoretical proclamation of the separation of powers. "All the powers of government, legislative, executive and judiciary," Jefferson submitted, "result to the legislative body. The concentrating these in the same hands is precisely the definition of despotic government."[28] Perhaps Jefferson's most basic objection to the Constitution of 1776 was that the 1776 Convention had no mandate to establish a constitution; therefore the 1776 document was no more than any other statute and could be altered at will by the General Assembly. What was needed, Jefferson concluded, was a constitutional convention.[29]

It was to be fifty years after the adoption of the first Constitution, however, before a convention was to meet to rewrite Virginia's fundamental law. In the meantime, despite Jefferson's complaint that the Constitution of 1776 was of questionable origins, the General Court in 1793 concluded that the 1776 document did have the status of a constitution against which legislative acts could be measured and, if found in conflict, declared unconstitutional.[30] Through general acquiescence, Virginians lived under the Constitution of 1776 as fundamental law, and the arguments focused more acutely on the actual merits of the document and the need for its revision.

Snow settles on Capitol Square, including the State Capitol Building designed by Thomas Jefferson and the George Washington Equestrian Monument. Photo by Bob Brown, *Richmond Times-Dispatch.*

The early decades of the nineteenth century were times of economic and political stress for Virginia. Soil exhaustion, falling land prices, and other factors led to a decline in the economy of the plantation-based eastern areas of Virginia. At the same time the western parts of the State were prospering, and the West's population was growing at a much faster rate than that of the East. Yet the Constitution of 1776 left political power largely where it had been before 1776. East and West quarreled over many things, especially internal improvements, which the West wanted but the East was unwilling to pay for. Hence Westerners grew increasingly restive under a Constitution which so severely limited the vote and which so favored the older counties against the newer.[31]

Efforts to have a convention called to revise the Constitution were frequent during the early years of the nineteenth century.[32] In 1816, delegates from thirty-three counties, mostly western, met at Staunton and adopted a memorial calling on the Legislature to recommend to the people of Virginia the calling of a convention.[33] But the General Assembly, as it had done with previous requests of this kind, voted down the proposal.[34] Western tempers grew shorter, and local resolutions adopted in western counties began to hint strongly at extralegal action if no reforms were forthcoming.[35] At length, the General Assembly agreed to put the question of a convention before the people, who in a referendum in 1828 approved the convention call.

The Convention of 1829-30 was a remarkable gathering.[36] Among the delegates were two former Presidents, James Madison and James Monroe; a future President, John Tyler; the Chief Justice of the United States, John Marshall; the brilliant and eccentric orator John Randolph of Roanoke; seven past, present, or future United States Senators; twenty-six past, present, or future Congressmen; and many other notables. Merrill Peterson has called the 1829-30 Convention "the last of the great constituent assemblies in American history. As an arena of ideological encounter it was unexcelled."[37]

The issues confronting the Convention were clear to most of the delegates. The reformers, mostly from counties beyond the Blue Ridge Mountains, wanted an extension of the suffrage, apportionment of seats in the Legislature based on white population, a Governor elected by the people, provision for future reapportionment, and provision for future amendments to the Constitution.[38] As James M. Mason, of Frederick County, summed it up, the overriding object was "to place the Government where of right it ought to be, in the hands of the majority of the political community ...."[39]

Conservatives at the Convention preferred the status quo or, at least, as little change as possible. John Randolph, surely the most colorful speaker at the Convention, protested the "lust of innovation" and declared "change is not reform." In particular Randolph wanted no part of popular sovereignty and majority rule: "I would not live under King Numbers. I would not be his steward—nor make him my taskmaster."[40]

As it turned out, on most issues the conservatives largely had their way. After debating whether representation in the Assembly should be based on white population or on some mixed basis reflecting property, slaveholdings, or tax payments as well as population, the Convention ultimately adopted a plan which reflected no basis at all but which arbitrarily apportioned legislative seats. Under this plan representation was more equitable than it had been previously, but the East retained a majority in both houses of the Assembly. The Legislature was to reapportion its seats decennially, beginning in 1841, but the share of each of the State's four "great districts" (into which the House was divided) and its two "great divisions" (into which the Senate was divided) could be changed only upon the vote of two-thirds of the members of each house.[41]

On the question of suffrage, the reformers failed in their objective of securing universal white manhood suffrage or, at the least, suffrage for all who paid taxes.[42] The action taken by the Convention—adding householders to the franchise—was only a modest extension of the suffrage.

The reformers were no more successful in their effort to introduce popular control of the executive branch of government. Efforts to abolish the Executive Council and to have the Governor elected by the people failed, and the Governor remained elected by the General Assembly.[43] Similarly, efforts to reform the county court system failed. Self-perpetuating local governing bodies with legislative, executive, and judicial powers, the county courts had been condemned by Thomas Jefferson as "the most afflicting of tyrannies,"[44] but the Convention voted to retain constitutional status for the county courts.[45]

For all the expectation that the calling of the 1829-30 Convention had aroused, it made little substantive change in the existing order. Their power largely undisturbed, the older counties voted heavily for the new Constitution. Sussex County, for example, went for the 1830 Constitution by a vote of 259 to 2. Western counties were as strongly opposed. Harrison County, for example, went against the new Constitution by a vote of 1,112 to 8. Valley counties were more divided. Augusta and Frederick counties, for example, were each almost evenly split in their respective votes. Statewide, the Constitution of 1830 was approved by a total vote of 26,055 to 15,563.[46]

Adoption of the Constitution of 1830 failed to quiet western demands for reform. Only two of the twenty-six trans-Allegheny counties had voted for the Constitution, and after 1830 the tension between

East and West mounted further as the population and wealth of the West continued to outpace that of the older regions. By 1840 the population of Virginia's transmontane regions had surpassed that of the East; in the East, slaves outnumbered whites.[47] Differences over internal improvements continued to divide East and West, and other issues arose to accentuate the division. Slavery, especially after the Nat Turner slave uprising in 1831, became a point of contention,[48] as did such state issues as education (the East being unreceptive to the West's desire for state-supported free schools) and such national issues as nullification, tariffs, and banks (the West supporting President Andrew Jackson against South Carolina, favoring tariffs, and wanting more banks).[49]

The General Assembly that met in 1841-42 failed to act on legislative reapportionment as directed by the Constitution, and although western protests mounted during the ensuing years, the Assembly, on sectional votes, year after year defeated calls for another constitutional convention. At the 1849-50 session of the Assembly, a bill was adopted putting the question of calling a convention to the people, but the act apportioned convention delegates so that those from the East would be in the majority.[50] At referendum, all but two eastern counties voted for calling a convention. Statewide, the convention call was approved by a vote of 46,327 to 20,668.[51]

The question of representation dominated the Convention of 1850-51.[52] Not counting time spent on procedural items, four of the first six months of debate were spent on this issue. Ultimately, the Convention adopted a plan giving the West a majority in the House and the East a majority in the Senate and deferring further reapportionment until 1865. On other questions, most of the reforms so fruitlessly sought at the 1829-30 Convention were attained in the Constitution of 1851. Sentiment even in the East had shifted markedly since 1830 on the question of suffrage, and the Convention of 1850-51 voted by a heavy margin to give the vote to white male citizens twenty-one years of age who had resided for two years in Virginia and for one year in the county, city, or town and who were not disqualified on enumerated grounds such as being of unsound mind or a pauper.

A notable feature of the Constitution of 1851 was that the Governor, for the first time, was to be elected by the people, as were other state officers, including the Lieutenant Governor and the Attorney General. The increase in power thus implied in the executive branch was matched by new restrictions on the power of the legislative branch—including a ban on binding the State for the debts or obligations of private companies, a prohibition on the emancipation of slaves, transfer of certain functions judicial in nature to the courts, and biennial rather than annual legislative sessions. The Constitution of 1851 also reorganized and strengthened the judiciary and took steps to bring local government more nearly under the control of local people, notably by making the county courts and other county offices elective by the people.

Although eastern reaction to the new Constitution was divided, the document apparently was seen as giving adequate protection to eastern interests, especially in slaves and other property. The West was highly pleased with the reforms achieved in the new Constitution. It was overwhelmingly approved by a vote of 75,748 to 11,063. Only five counties, all eastern, voted "no".[53]

Sectional feelings in Virginia subsided for a time after the adoption of the Constitution of 1851, rather as North-South animosities on the national scene abated somewhat by virtue of the Compromise of 1850.

But just as the American North and South found that their differences were not to be settled short of civil war, sectional feelings reemerged in Virginia and resulted ultimately in the division of the State.

The Convention that met in Richmond in February 1861 is best known for its vote to have Virginia secede from the Union. Delegates to the Convention included members from the forty northwestern counties that later seceded from Virginia to form West Virginia. When the Convention

The statue of Confederate General Robert E. Lee stands in the old House of Delegates Chamber. Photo by Bob Brown, *Richmond Times-Dispatch.*

voted, on April 17, 1861, to take Virginia out of the Union, the vote was 88 to 55 for secession, but the vote of delegates from the northwestern counties was two-to-one against secession.[54] On May 24, the people of Virginia voted to ratify the secession ordinance, and later in the year the Convention reassembled to revise Virginia's Constitution. A new Constitution was submitted to the voters but was rejected by a slim margin, 13,911 to 13,233.[55]

In June 1861 disenchanted western Virginians called a convention at Wheeling, where they established a "restored government" for Virginia with Francis H. Pierpont as its first Governor.[56] In 1862 the legislature of the restored government passed an act consenting to the formation of a new state out of Virginia's western territory,[57] and in June 1863 West Virginia was admitted to the Union. Governor Pierpont thereupon moved the restored government to Alexandria, from which he governed in a sense those parts of Virginia— Alexandria, Fairfax, Eastern Shore, and some territory around Norfolk—under the control of federal troops. In February 1864 a constitutional convention called by the restored government of Virginia met in Alexandria to draft a new Constitution for the State. The seventeen delegates drafted a Constitution which abolished slavery, levied a poll tax for the support of public schools, and reduced the period of residence required for voting in Virginia. Only 500 votes were cast for ratification; there is no record of negative votes.[58] Given the circumstances under which it was drafted, the legal effect of the Constitution of 1864 has always been dubious.

After the fall of the Confederacy, President Johnson issued an executive order nullifying the Confederate state government at Richmond and declaring the Pierpont government to be the legitimate government of Virginia.[59] Governor Pierpont moved his government to Richmond, elections were held, and a conservative majority was returned to the General Assembly. In Congress, however, radical sentiment was on the rise, and on March 2, 1867, Congress enacted legislation dividing the South into five military districts; Virginia became Military District No. 1. The Reconstruction Act required each "Rebel State" to form a state government conforming with the Federal Constitution, to extend the franchise to all male citizens twenty-one years of age resident for one year in the state (the same electorate to elect delegates to the state constitutional convention), and to ratify the proposed Fourteenth Amendment to the Federal Constitution. Only then could the state have representation in Congress.[60]

Two further acts of Congress prescribed test oaths which barred large numbers of ex-Confederates from serving in a reconstruction convention or voting for delegates to the convention.[61] Of the 105 members of the Virginia Convention of 1867-68, the majority, 72, were radicals, (of these 25 were blacks), and 33 were conservatives.[62] The Convention named as its president John Curtiss Underwood, a New Yorker who had lived in Virginia until shortly before the war and who later, as federal district judge, presided over the treason trial of Jefferson Davis. The Convention wrote a Constitution which was characterized by some notable innovations. The document provided for the creation of a statewide system of public education supported by tax money, imported into Virginia the northern concept of townships, for the first time provided a method of amending the Constitution, and save for the classes of ex-Confederates it would have disfranchised, provided essentially for universal male suffrage for those over twenty-one years old.

The most drastic proposals coming out of the 1867-68 Convention were two clauses—the so-called "disenfranchisement" clause and the "test-oath" clause—which would have effectively denied the ballot and public office to the vast majority of white Virginians who, because of their earlier political activities, might otherwise have exercised political power in Virginia. Conservatives, under the leadership of Alexander H. H. Stuart, formed a Committee of Nine and went to Washington to consult with President Grant and Congress. They proposed that Virginia would accept the Constitution and black suffrage in return for the opportunity to vote separately on the two "obnoxious" clauses. General J. M. Schofield, the commander of Military District No. 1, also opposed the two disqualifying clauses and recommended that Congress allow separate votes on them. In April 1869 Congress, on President Grant's recommendation, approved a separate vote.[63] In July 1869 the new Constitution was approved by an overwhelming margin, and the two separate provisions were defeated.[64]

The 1870's saw the emergence in Virginia of the Readjuster movement, which sought to ease the heavy burden of prewar debt made all the more onerous by the impoverishment following the Civil War and Reconstruction. In 1879 the Readjusters won a great victory in elections for the Assembly, and in 1881 a Readjuster, William E. Cameron, was elected Governor of Virginia. The Readjusters had depended heavily upon the African-American vote, and the conservatives, taking the name Democrats, raised the spectre of African-American domination. In 1883 the Democrats gained both houses of the General Assembly, and General Wilham Mahone, the Readjuster leader, now working in coalition with the Republicans, failed to regain power.[65]

Widespread abuses and frauds marked Virginia elections in the 1880's and 1890's. There was abundant evidence of bribery of voters, stuffing of ballot boxes, false counting of votes, and false returns of elections. Between 1874 and 1900 twenty contested election cases were heard in the United States House of Representatives.[66] Since the abuses were often tied to efforts to maintain white supremacy, many people began to think the answer lay in revising the Constitution so as to eliminate, insofar as possible, the black vote. In 1900 the General Assembly voted to put the question of calling a convention to the people, and in a very light turnout the people approved the call by a vote of 77,362 to 60,375.[67] Uppermost in the minds of many of the delegates to the Constitutional Convention of 1901-02 was the disfranchisement of the African-American. As Carter Glass said upon the floor of the

Convention, "Discrimination! Why, that is precisely what we propose; that, exactly, is what this Convention was elected for—to discriminate to the very extremity of permissible action under the limitations of the Federal Constitution, with a view to the elimination of every negro voter who can be gotten rid of, legally ...."[68]

The Convention prescribed temporary qualifications under which voters might register before January 1904 and permanent requirements to be in effect after that date. Virtually the only way blacks could qualify under the temporary qualifications was to demonstrate an ability to understand and explain the Constitution—a requirement which, in the hands of an unfriendly registrar, meant certain rejection. The permanent requirements included the payment of a poll tax, cumulative for three years, by all save Civil War veterans. Altogether, the new provisions were so restrictive that of the estimated 147,000 blacks of voting age prior to the adoption of the 1902 Constitution, only 21,000 remained on the registration list by October 15, 1902. By 1905, after the poll tax had become a voting requirement, it was estimated that less than one-half of that 21,000 had met both poll tax and registration requirements.[69] Many whites, as well, ceased to be voters. The poll tax, the rigors of registration, and a measure of apathy on the part of the populace, including many whites, cut Virginia's voting so heavily that it was 1928 before as many people voted in a general election as had voted in 1888, despite the State's growth in population and the admission of women to the suffrage.

The other principal work for which the Convention of 1901-02 is remembered is the creation of the State Corporation Commission. The decade of the 1890's "was the railroad era in Virginia both economically and politically";[70] the railroads were lavish in their political contributions and in return could count on the Legislature to do little to inhibit their activities. As A. Caperton Braxton said at the 1901-02 Convention, "I ask you if has there been a judge elected in this State, if there has been a legislature elected and in session, if there has been a campaign fought out, in which you do not see the hand of the railroad?"[71] In the face of a history of legislative inaction, the Convention decided therefore to create in the Constitution itself a State Corporation Commission "clothed with all the legislative, judicial and administrative powers necessary for the vigorous and complete execution of its duty to regulate and control the operation of railroads."[72]

Before the Convention of 1901-02 met, it was almost universally supposed that the Convention's product would be submitted to the people for their ratification or rejection. The enabling legislation assumed submission, and the Democratic Convention that had met at Norfolk in May 1900 had resolved that the new Constitution should be submitted to the people.[73] The Constitutional Convention, however, decided to take no chances. A motion to submit the Constitution to the present electorate failed by a vote of 33 to 52; another motion, to submit it to the electorate provided for in the new Constitution, also failed, 24 to 58. The Convention then voted 47-38 to proclaim the Constitution in effect.[74]

The Constitution of 1902 was recognized by the three branches of government, legislative, executive, and judicial, and any doubts about its validity were removed by the ruling of the Supreme Court of Appeals in *Taylor v. Commonwealth*:

> The Constitution of 1902 was ordained and proclaimed by a convention duly called by direct vote of the people of the State to revise and amend the Constitution of 1869. The result of the work of that convention has been recognized, accepted, and acted upon as the only valid Constitution of the State by the Governor in swearing fidelity to it and proclaiming it, as directed thereby; by the Legislature in its formal official act adopting a joint resolution, July 15, 1902, recognizing the Constitution ordained by the convention which assembled in the city of Richmond on the 12th day of June, 1901, as

the Constitution of Virginia; by the individual oaths of its members to support it, and by its having been engaged for nearly a year in legislating under it and putting its provisions into operation; by the judiciary in taking the oath prescribed thereby to support it, and by enforcing its provisions; and by the people in their primary capacity by peacefully accepting it and acquiescing in it, by registering as voters under it to the extent of thousands throughout the State, and by voting, under its provisions, at a general election for their representatives in the Congress of the United States.

The Constitution having been thus acknowledged and accepted by the officers administering the government and by the people of the State, and being, as a matter of fact, in force throughout the State, and there being no government in existence under the Constitution of 1869 opposing or denying its validity, we have no difficulty in holding that the Constitution in question, which went into effect at noon on the 10th day of July, 1902, is the only rightful, valid, and existing Constitution of this State, and that to it all the citizens of Virginia owe their obedience and loyal allegiance.[75]

Several amendments to the Constitution, most of them dealing with questions of local government, were approved by the people in 1910, 1912, and 1920. One of the 1920 amendments, to section 184 of the Constitution, permitted state debt to be incurred for the building of roads. But a proposal to authorize the issuance of $50 million of road bonds was overwhelmingly defeated in November 1923, the opposition being led by Harry F. Byrd. Two years later Byrd was easily nominated and elected Governor. In his quest for more businesslike state government, Byrd took an interest in constitutional revision, and acting on authority given him by the General Assembly in 1926 he appointed a Commission to Suggest Amendments to the Constitution.[76]

Until that time, major revisions of the Constitution had always been undertaken by means of a constitutional convention elected for that purpose. But even though the popular notion of an amendment is a specific change isolated from a general revision, the Constitution has never made such a distinction, and even before 1926 there were instances when it had been proposed to revise the Constitution by having a commission propose changes to the Legislature, which in turn would submit proposed amendments to the people.[77] The Supreme Court of Virginia, in a case decided in 1945, made it clear that either of two vehicles—a constitutional convention or amendments proposed by the Legislature and submitted to the people—may be used to revise the Constitution.[78]

The Commission to Suggest Amendments to the Constitution, chaired by Robert R. Prentis, submitted in 1927 a report which recommended no change at all in well over half the 1902 Constitution's 197 sections and proposed "material" changes in only fifty sections. The Commission expressed its dominant purpose as follows:

The animating purpose of the Commission has been to relax many of the existing restrictions on the powers of the General Assembly, so as to secure to the Commonwealth and to its political subdivisions more elastic forms of government, capable of being adjusted from time to time to new conditions, and, enlightened by experience, to existing conditions. The General Assembly, the House being elected every two years, is closest to the people, and its powers to adapt government in its details to the needs of the people should not be unduly restricted, under a system of government which derives all of its powers from the people.[79]

Those amendments which were twice approved by the General Assembly, at a special session in 1927 and the regular session in 1928, were laid before the people for their approval or rejection in November 1928. Most of the changes, including many of a housekeeping nature, were grouped in a single question on the November ballot. These included a new constitutional section, 184-a, which, replacing the 1920 amendment allowing state bonds to be issued for road purposes, required any state debt to receive approval by the people and limited the total of any such state debt to an amount equivalent to 1 percent of the assessed value of taxable real estate in Virginia.

In addition to the general question on the 1928 ballot, four amendments were listed for separate votes.[80] One proposal segregated real and tangible personal property for taxation by the localities. The other three left to general law the manner of selecting the Commissioner of Agriculture and Immigration, the Superintendent of Public Instruction, and the State Treasurer, all of whom were currently elected by the people. In explaining these last three amendments—the "short ballot" amendments—Governor Byrd said that the Governor "can and should be held responsible for efficient administration, but if he is to be held responsible he must be given sufficient power to select the administrative heads of departments upon whom he must rely for results."[81] All five propositions on the 1928 ballot were approved; the vote was closest on the three short ballot amendments.[82]

Limited conventions to deal with specific matters, not entailing a general revision of the Constitution, were held in 1945 and 1956. In placing the question of calling a convention before the voters in 1945, the enabling legislation passed by the General Assembly provided that the convention was to be limited to the matter of absentee voting by members of the armed forces. Efforts made on the floor of the Convention to enlarge the range of subjects to be considered were rejected. The Convention wrote a new article, Article XVII, and ordained it to be effective May 3, 1945.[83] Subsequently the Supreme Court of Appeals upheld the validity of a limited convention.[84]

Another limited convention, held in 1956, was part of Virginia's reaction to the United States Supreme Court's school desegregation decisions. A legislative effort to give tuition grants to children attending private schools was declared by the Supreme Court of Appeals of Virginia to conflict with section 141 of the Virginia Constitution. A limited convention was therefore called. Meeting in March 1956, the Convention proclaimed an amendment to section 141 to permit public aid to children in private, nonsectarian schools.[85]

In January 1968 Governor Mills E. Godwin, Jr., in his opening address to the General Assembly, noted the effects of the "inexorable passage of time" on Virginia's Constitution and called upon the Assembly to authorize him to create a Commission on Constitutional Revision.[86] The Assembly passed the necessary resolution,[87] and the Governor appointed an eleven-man commission chaired by former Governor Albertis Harrison, Jr., by then a Justice of the Supreme Court of Appeals of Virginia. Among other distinguished members of the Commission were another former Governor, a past president of the American Bar Association (later to be named to the Supreme Court of the United States), the first African-American in modern times to serve on Richmond City Council, and a law school dean later to become a member of the World Court at the Hague.[88]

The Commission divided itself into five subcommittees, availed itself of the assistance of an executive director and of legal counsel, had research memoranda prepared on about 140 subjects, held public hearings at various points in Virginia, deliberated proposed revisions, and in January 1969 submitted a report to the Governor and General Assembly.[89]

FEBRUARY 28, 1969

NOW IS THE TIME

HOLTON
FOR GOVERNOR

Campaign literature for Gov. A. Linwood Holton. The latest revision of Virginia's Constitution took effect during his administration. Photo by Anne Marie Morgan.

The Commission's report reflects the basic assumptions that underlay the body's recommendations. Among the more important principles was the recognition that a constitution "embodies fundamental law. It follows that a constitution is not a code of laws and that unnecessary detail, not touching on fundamental matters, ought to be left to the statute books." Related assumptions were that the Constitution should be brief and to the point, expressed in simple, intelligible language. In particular, the Commission thought that the Constitution ought to make possible "healthy, viable, responsible state government" and, given the pace of social and other changes, to make it possible to deal with future problems as they arise. Throughout, the Commission's report was tempered with an understanding of the need to write, not a "model" or "ideal" constitution, but one suited to the needs and circumstances of Virginia.[90]

Among the more important of the Commission's recommendations were a strengthened Education article committing the Commonwealth to providing a public school system of quality, an enlarged capacity for the Commonwealth to borrow for capital purposes, a new Conservation article, a much simplified Judiciary article leaving most of the particulars of court structure and jurisdiction to statute law, more powers and options for the State's counties and cities, and a tighter Franchise article making the vote less subject to abuse. In addition, the Commission proposed the deletion of obsolete material and detail better left to the statute books and recommended a good deal of reorganization and rewriting in the interests of clarity and coherence.

Called into special session in March 1969, the General Assembly was receptive to the Commission's general philosophy. In particular it grasped and acted on the Commission's distinction between fundamentals that belong in a constitution and less basic matters that ought to be left to legislation. The basic outline of the document as proposed by the Commission was accepted, as was most of the substance. In some instances, the Assembly was not willing to go as far as the Commission suggested. For example, the Assembly rejected the proposal that cities and those counties over 25,000 be allowed to adopt and amend their own charters upon local referenda and that cities and charter counties be allowed to exercise all powers not expressly denied them. It also rejected investing the Governor with authority to initiate administrative reorganization. Although the Assembly concurred in the general proposition that the Commonwealth's power to borrow for capital purposes should be enlarged beyond that permitted by the old Constitution, it decided that all general obligation bonds issued by the Commonwealth (other than certain revenue bonds backed by the State's full faith and credit) must first be approved in referendum.

At the same time, in a number of respects the Assembly went beyond the Commission's proposals. It embraced annual sessions of the Legislature, which the Commission had been unwilling to recommend. The Assembly made the Education article even stronger by imposing on the localities an enforceable duty to put up their share of money for the public schools as decreed by the Legislature. The Conservation article's mandate for environmental quality was strengthened.

Both the Commission and the Assembly were mindful of the importance of how the constitutional revisions were to appear on the ballot. In recent years voters in New York and Maryland had voted down proposed new constitutions that had been presented as a "take-it-or-leave-it" single proposition. Following the approach recommended by the Commission, the Assembly therefore voted to put several questions on the ballot. The first contained the vast majority of the changes; those questions thought more sensitive or controversial were split off to be voted on separately.

The amendments approved at the 1969 special session had to be approved a second time by the Assembly before going on the ballot. At the 1970 regular session, two amendments that had been approved in 1969 were killed. One would have allowed state aid to handicapped children in private schools, including church-related schools. The other would have allowed the General Assembly by special act to alter the boundaries of the Capital City. The four remaining propositions—the main body of the Constitution, a repeal of the constitutional ban on lotteries, and two questions dealing with borrowing by the Commonwealth—were approved at the 1970 session.

The campaign for ratification was undertaken by a private organization, Virginians for the Constitution, using private rather than state funds. This group organized a speakers' bureau, sent out pamphlets and other information, created local city and county committees, and in general undertook a statewide campaign to inform the voters on the purpose and effect of the revisions. Opposition to the new Constitution centered on the charges that it would result in the creation of regional governments, that it would lead to the busing of school children for purposes of racial integration, that it would permit the creation of $1 billion in state debt, and that, because not drafted by a convention, the whole revision was in fact unconstitutional.

In November 1970 the new Constitution was overwhelmingly approved. All four questions passed. The main body of the Constitution received the approval of 72 percent of the voters, while 63 percent voted to delete the constitutional ban on lotteries (understood in Virginia to include pari-mutuel betting). The two bond questions received the affirmative vote of two out of three voters; 67 percent approved the proposal permitting the issuance, subject to referendum, of certain amounts of general obligation bonds, and 66 percent approved the proposal authorizing the Assembly, under certain conditions, to place the State's full faith and credit behind selected revenue bond issues. As provided in the new Constitution's Schedule, a session of the General Assembly was convened in January 1971 to pass implementing legislation. The Constitution of 1971 became effective at high noon on July 1, 1971.[91]

A. E. Dick Howard is the White Burkett Miller Professor of Law and Public Affairs at the University of Virginia. He served as executive director of the commission that wrote Virginia's current Constitution and is an expert in constitutional law, comparative constitutionalism, and the Supreme Court. His published works include "The Road from Runnymede: Magna Carta and Constitutionalism in America," "Commentaries on the Constitution of Virginia," and "Democracy's Dawn." This chapter is reprinted by permission from A.E. Dick Howard, "Commentaries on the Constitution of Virginia" (Charlottesville: University of Virginia Press, 1974).

Editors' Note: Amending the State Constitution

Virginia's Constitution can be amended through a process that it establishes in Article XII. The most common method used in recent decades is by introducing a resolution that must pass by a majority vote in both houses of the General Assembly. Following an intervening election of the House of Delegates, the resolution with identical language must be voted on a second time at another session of the General Assembly. If it again passes both houses by a majority vote, then it is submitted to voters and listed on the ballot at the next general election. If a majority of voters approves the amendment, it becomes part of the state Constitution on the date prescribed by the General Assembly.

The Constitution also may be revised or amended through a convention called by two-thirds of the members of both houses. Any changes proposed by the convention must also be submitted to voters for a decision before they can become part of the Virginia Constitution.

The language of any proposed constitutional amendment is published on the State Board of Elections Website so that voters can read it before the election is held.

Source: The Constitution of Virginia, http://legis.state.va.us/Constitution/Constitution.htm#12S1.

CHAPTER 4
The Emergence of Modern Virginia Politics: From the "Byrd Machine" to Two-Party Competition

By A. R. "Pete" Giesen
Former Member, House of Delegates

"I t is a political museum piece," observed political scientist V. O. Key, Jr., referring to 1949 Virginia. "Of all of the American States, Virginia can lay claim to the most thorough control by an oligarchy. Political power has been closely held by a small group of leaders who, themselves and their predecessors, have subverted democratic institutions and deprived most Virginians of a voice in their government."[1]

In conversations with an array of people, I have heard many express their amazement that such an incongruous situation existed in the mid-20th century in the state where America's political ideals and the New World's first representative legislature were born. They would also speculate: "Where was the two-party system that was supposed to be the foundation of voter choice and vibrant political competition in the United States?" But at this juncture in Virginia's history, it just didn't exist! Today it does. Gradually, as a result of federal laws, population growth, and the actions of prominent political figures, Virginia has evolved into a competitive two-party state. To secure a reasonable understanding of how this happened one needs to review some of Virginia's earlier history.

It started after the Civil War and the period commonly referred to as Reconstruction, when many Virginians still had a great deal of anger about the battles fought between 1861 to 1865. During Reconstruction Virginia was under military rule. Governors who were all of the same party as that Republican President who had caused the war were appointed by the Military Commander. Voting was restricted. Any male who had fought for the Confederacy—and that was 90 percent of the white male population—was not eligible to vote. The Constitutional Convention of 1869 attempted to maintain this restriction, but it was defeated, and the adopted Constitution of 1870 essentially gave voting rights to all males who were at least 21 years of age.

During the next three decades voting fraud ran rampant in the state. Under pressure from the electorate, the General Assembly convened another Constitutional Convention in 1901, and there was no mistaking the purpose of those who assembled to rewrite Virginia's basic document. U.S. Sen. E. C. Glass, a delegate, stated emphatically that their goal was to disenfranchise as many black voters as possible within the confines of the law.[2]

Voter registrars were given extraordinary powers and provisions for collection of poll taxes and literacy tests were enacted. Strict registration procedures were handed to the local registrars, which caused "[t]he African-American voter registration in the Commonwealth to plummet immediately by

36

more than 86 percent, and ... also provided the mechanism for the more gradual exclusion of Republicans and other white voters who refused to support candidates of the dominant Democratic faction."[3]

From the confusion and uncertainty of the late 19th century a man with a very tough political instinct and will, Sen. Thomas S. Martin, emerged as the strong Democratic Chieftain. With the new tools for restricting the electorate, Martin was able to consolidate his power and establish the "Martin Organization," which controlled Virginia's government until Martin's death in 1919.[4] Others tried to take over the organization, but it was not until a decade later that events brought forth the next person with a personality strong enough and the political know-how to become the new Organization Chieftain.

Harry F. Byrd, Sr., left high school at age 15 to rescue his father's debt-ridden newspaper. He proved to be a very shrewd and capable business person and turned the newspaper into a profitable business. During this early career, Byrd developed a horror of debt and developed his "pay as you go" philosophy toward business *and* government finances. It was this attitude toward debt that brought the young state senator from Clark County into the forefront of Virginia politics in 1922. Byrd clashed with the Virginia Highway Contractors Association when he advocated a tax on gasoline as a fair method of raising revenue for road construction and led a fight against using bonded indebtedness to pay for new roads. The courts dismissed the suit which the Association brought against Byrd for critical comments he made about the highway contractors.

The publicity generated by the court proceedings propelled Byrd into a position of prominence within the Democratic Party and helped him to win his election as governor of Virginia in 1925.[5]

During his term as governor[6] from 1926 to 1930, Byrd pushed the General Assembly to authorize a commission to revise the state's Constitution. The amendments proposed by this commission, adopted over-whelmingly by the restricted electorate, streamlined the state government; established the short ballot for Virginia by eliminating the statewide election of all officials except the governor, lieutenant governor, and attorney general; established the principle of "pay as you go" by limiting the issuance of bonds by the state; and made it possible for the state to take over Virginia's secondary road systems.

Byrd recognized the essentials in building a successful political organization. During his early

The statue of Gov. Harry F. Byrd, Sr., stands like a sentinel in front of the General Assembly Building on Capitol Square. Photo by Anne Marie Morgan.

business career he had watched Sen. Martin maintain his organization and knew the key was his contacts and influence with the local courthouse cliques. So, as governor, he curried support from the locally elected officials in most of the counties of the state.

The support of these constitutional officers, particularly the circuit court judges, played a large role in the 1929 struggle within the Democratic Party to select a successor to Byrd. Ultimately, they prevailed, and a long series of hand-picked governors were elected who were loyal to Byrd and his political machine. The Byrd Organization (as it was known) remained the dominant political force in the state for the next three-and-a-half decades.

Byrd controlled the machine from his U.S. Senate position to which he was initially appointed to fill a vacancy—and retained by winning the subsequent interim election and the next six elections for six-year terms. When he retired because of ill health in 1965, his son, St. Sen. Harry F. Byrd, Jr., was appointed to fill the seat.

Keys to the Machine: Frugality, Honesty, and a Restricted Electorate

The organization reflected the elder Sen. Byrd's priorities. Honesty was essential for anyone who would serve in office or be affiliated with his organization. Only slightly less important to Byrd was frugality in government. "Pay as you go" was the necessary practice of those who were elected from the organization if they wanted to stay in favor and retain their position. These two attributes, honesty and frugality, were partially responsible for the machine's long endurance. This was true even though the frugality at the state level meant low spending on public services for decades.

Another major factor in the dominance of the political machine was the way Byrd had constructed the working components of the organization. Under the 1902 Constitution and its later amendments, Byrd created a tight organization of very conservative Democratic loyalists. The cornerstone of this structure, of course, was the restricted electorate. Political participation was abysmal, although women eventually had won the right to vote. "Of the eleven states of the South … at mid-century, Virginia ranked last in average (voter) turnout in gubernatorial primaries." [7]

The flow chart on the next page illustrates how orders were handed down. Gov. Byrd had curried their favor and thus, Circuit Court judges and locally elected constitutional officers became key players in keeping active and budding politicians loyal to the Democratic hierarchy headed, of course, by Byrd.

To Accomplish This Control: Needed a Small Electorate, Well-Known to the Appointed Local Registrars and Elected Constitutional Officers

As one can see from this flow chart, the loyalty of those in charge of registering voters resided with the organization. The poll tax discouraged many citizens even though the cost was only $1.50 per year. But then before a registrar could even consider handing over an application, the potential voter had to prove he had paid his poll tax for the past three years and had done so at least six months prior to the election for which he was registering. He then was given a literacy test to make sure he was capable of voting intelligently.

The literacy test could be anything (within certain limits) that the registrar wanted it to be. The questions might direct one to write down on a blank piece of paper all of the requirements to vote in the Virginia Constitution. Or perhaps a more creative registrar might ask one to list the Bill of Rights in the state Constitution. The possibilities were endless.

CHART 1: THE BYRD MACHINE: HOW THE POLITICAL MACHINE OPERATED AND KEPT LOCAL OFFICIALS LOYAL

Every governor elected from 1929 to 1969 was a machine-approved nominee selected in the Democratic primary. Those nominated for and elected to the governorship had to have Byrd's approval and be good organization men—usually lawyers who were members of the Democratic Party and men who had worked their way up in the party:

The governor nominated the Circuit Court judges (who generally met the same criteria as machine governors) for the General Assembly's official approval and appointment.

It is evident from this flow chart that local officials—both elected and appointed—generally owed their positions to the Byrd organization. When Sen. Byrd needed votes at the local level to elect his selections for governor, congressman, or U.S. senator, the word went out and these loyal local organization men turned it out:

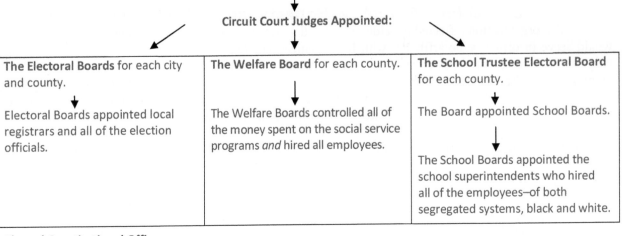

Circuit Court Judges Appointed:

The Electoral Boards for each city and county. Electoral Boards appointed local registrars and all of the election officials.	**The Welfare Board** for each county. The Welfare Boards controlled all of the money spent on the social service programs *and* hired all employees.	**The School Trustee Electoral Board** for each county. The Board appointed School Boards. The School Boards appointed the school superintendents who hired all of the employees—of both segregated systems, black and white.

Elected Constitutional Officers:
- Sheriffs
- Commonwealth Attorneys
- Commissioners of Revenue
- Treasurers
- Clerks of the Court (8-year terms)

- **The state's funding for these offices was controlled by the Compensation Board appointed by the governor.** The Board was chaired by the Clerk of the State Senate and one of Byrd's most trusted lieutenants.
- The Comp Board fixed salaries and levels of expenses for the elected local constitutional officers.
- Studies showed that constitutional officers who won election as Republicans frequently received less compensation from the state than a similar officer in a like-sized county where the constitutional officer was a Democrat.
- *Other factors*: Contracts for legal work for the Highway Department were awarded to contractors known to be loyal to the Democratic Party. Deposits of state funds were placed in friendly banks.
- Incorporated cities were organized under charters granted by the state and were a little more insulated from the organization's control. However, the Comp Board still maintained some control over the salaries and office expenses of the constitutional officers. There were no statutory guidelines for salaries and expenses except as stated in the Appropriations Act, enacted by the General Assembly and proposed by the governor. Both of these state government branches were controlled by loyal organization men from the 1930s until the mid-1960s.

The applications of known Republicans, liberal non-organization Democrats, and citizens of color, particularly African-Americans, were often found lacking. An illustration of this is related by Republican Glen Williams, later a U.S. district judge, who recalled that a college graduate was notified of his rejection to register by a postcard which read, "Yo hav fald to rechister."[8] While this was the situation for those outside the organization, Virginians known as loyal Byrd Democrats had little trouble passing all of the registration requirements during the mid-1900s.

During this part of Virginia's history the Commonwealth's Democratic Party was not a monolithic entity. There were those who called themselves Democrats who disagreed with Byrd's strategy. They felt that the state should pay more attention to public education, improving public health, and maintaining better mental hospitals—areas in which Virginia generally ranked last or close to last among the states on per capita expenditures and quality of services. This liberal faction within the Democratic Party did field some candidates in the party primaries but with very little success.

State Republicans fared no better in winning elections. While there were pockets of GOP strength in Southwest Virginia and some in the Shenandoah Valley, they were few and far between. Some local office-seekers cautiously took the label of Republican and a few were even elected. The extent of these successes, however, is illustrated by the fact that from the 1930s until 1964 the number of Republicans in the General Assembly averaged between 6 to 8 members of the total of 140 legislators— and never exceeded a total of 10 elected members.

Winning a Democratic primary for statewide and most local offices was truly tantamount to election. Many Democratic officeholders did not have any challengers for re-election in primaries nor the general elections. Those who did have intraparty contests rarely had an opponent in the general elections. So the Byrd Machine kept a tight rein on the electorate and the finances of the state, and Virginia became "a political museum piece."

The Commonwealth Changes

The major power of the Byrd Machine rested in the rural areas of the Commonwealth. Virginia's unique local government structure with every city having its own independent government with no overlapping with the adjacent counties gave the organization's hierarchy more sway within the county governments. The cities were a little less bound to the Byrd Machine, but still highly influenced by it into the early 1950s. The make-up of the Old Dominion, however, began to change after December 7, 1941.

World War II had a double impact on the population of Virginia. Hundreds of thousands of young Virginia men eventually joined the military, while women also began serving in various capacities in the services and civilian support positions. Many had never been outside of Virginia and some had lived their lives within 150 miles of their birthplace.

The population of the state was exploding as the intensified mobility of the state's population was taking place. Military installations were established or grew, and federal agencies expanded rapidly, with a population that quickly spilled over into the Virginia suburbs.

People from every sector of the United States found themselves living on Virginia soil. Many remained and began to make a life for themselves and their families in the Old Dominion. With this influx of new citizens in the urban parts of the state, an energized political dynamic began to develop. The Byrd Machine, with its main base in rural Virginia, did not react to these new conditions and found itself in retreat.

One of the cornerstones of the Byrd Machine—its frugality in state expenditures based on its low tax and pay-as-you-go policies—began to be challenged by many citizens. It would take two decades for those who saw the need and wanted more state services—better schools, better roads, improved mental health facilities, greater participation in the elective process—to gain success at the polls.

Numerous Democratic political contenders emerged who wanted to set Virginia free from the yoke of the Byrd Machine. In the meantime, the weak Republican Party of Virginia had gained confidence by recent elections, such as the election of Republican councilmen in Radford in the late 1940s and the election of three congressmen in 1952. There was also a rising tide of resentment against the national Democratic Party and the presidency of Harry Truman. The GOP began to field increasingly stronger candidates, including St. Sen. Ted Dalton, who called for a repeal of many of the oppressive Byrd-era policies and a greater investment in public services. Most of these proposals were later enacted by subsequent governors.

1954: "Separate But Equal—Inherently Unconstitutional"

During the 1954 session of the General Assembly, moderate and liberal Democrats became more aggressive in pushing for more state services for their constituents. Their efforts disturbed some of Byrd's lieutenants, who feared the machine was weakening.

Their fears were justified. However, by late spring the U.S. Supreme Court gave the machine a reprieve. Under the guidance of Chief Justice Earl Warren, appointed by the Republican President, Dwight Eisenhower, the Court handed down its unanimous decision in the case of *Brown vs. the Board of Education*. This ruling declared the doctrine of "separate but equal" for schools for "Blacks and Whites" was "inherently unconstitutional."[9] The leader of the machine, Sen. Harry F. Byrd, Sr., immediately condemned the decision as stomping on the rights of states to control their own schools. The machine had for years vigorously fought for state-forced segregation in state and federal courts. They now found new life in this decision. The majority of the restricted Virginia electorate agreed.

The machine leaders developed legislation and a constitutional amendment to allow the state to provide tuition grants to students going to private schools. The legislature also decreed that state funding for localities would be cut off to any locality which integrated its schools, even if that integration was carried out under court orders. This stance by the Byrd Machine became known as "Massive Resistance." In the meantime, St. Sen. Ted Dalton vocally opposed the strident segregation measures being proposed. Republicans, however, were divided and the Democratic organization was taking a stance supported by the majority of Virginia voters.

Following the 1956 victory of Eisenhower as President, Virginia Republicans tried desperately to unite and revive their fortunes for the 1957 gubernatorial campaign with Ted Dalton as their candidate. But the integration of the school systems continued to dominate the political scene. Dalton's moderate stance on Massive Resistance and his vocal insistence that the law passed by the General Assembly would be declared unconstitutional made his campaign a steep uphill fight. Finally, Eisenhower doomed the Republican's efforts by sending federal troops into Little Rock, Arkansas, to compel the admittance of black students to the city's high school.

In 1959 the courts, both a three-judge federal court and the Virginia Supreme Court, ruled that the anti-desegregation, Massive Resistance law passed in 1956 was unconstitutional. Gov. Lindsay Almond, elected over Dalton by supporting this legislation, recognized the legal realities and declared before a special Joint Session of the General Assembly that the time for Massive Resistance was at an end. After a very tough legislative fight, the moderate forces in the General Assembly prevailed and also approved an Almond budget with sufficient funds to reopen the local school systems that were closed under the "no state funds for local integrated schools" Massive Resistance law.

Racial tension continued in the Commonwealth for another score of years, but the foundation which had been laid by Dalton during the 1950s began to bear fruit in the 1960s. Recent emigrants to Virginia with Republican leanings began to emerge and take an active part in the local GOP. College Republicans—such as Dick Obenshain, Linwood Holton, Caldwell Butler, and John Dalton—began to take leadership roles at various levels of local, congressional, and state GOP activities.

Though they were essentially boxed out of any meaningful participation in legislating, Republicans began to be elected in greater numbers to the General Assembly. The progress in securing Republican votes encouraged some of the young party activists to begin prepping for future elections. One of these was A. Linwood Holton. While the national results of the 1960 Presidential election saw the youthful, telegenic Jack F. Kennedy narrowly win the White House over the sitting Republican Vice President, Richard Nixon, Virginians continued to vote for the GOP presidential candidate. Nixon's 52 percent margin in the Commonwealth was probably the result of conservative Democrats and Byrd's continuing posture of "silence is golden" in national presidential elections (to shun liberal Democrats) rather than an upsurge in Republican activities. This did not deter the young Republicans. The GOP was still a lowly but growing minority in the General Assembly.

The Speaker of the House of Delegates and Byrd stalwart, E. Blackburn Moore, continued the practice of ignoring the Republicans, sitting them in the remote right-hand corner of the House Chamber (anti-machine, moderate Democrats were seated in the left-hand corner and the majority organization Democrats occupied the center seats), assigning them to committees which never met, and making certain no bill sponsored by a GOP member was ever reported from committee.

Some of the machine members, however, realized the political culture of the state was changing. Democratic Lt. Gov. Mills Godwin actively traveled around the state prior to the 1965 gubernatorial election and heard what citizens were saying, in essence: "Yes, we appreciate the conservative bent of the state's Democratic leadership, but we also feel the state needs to meet its responsibilities to the citizens of the state—better schools, better treatment of the mentally ill in state hospitals, a more inclusive electorate, to name a few."[10] Godwin succeeded in winning the election for governor.

The Republican members of the General Assembly, emboldened by their recent gains, refused to be quiet about the manner in which the affairs of state were conducted in the Capitol—votes taken in closed meetings, Republicans and moderate/liberal Democrats barred from full participation in the process, few public hearings, most of the shots called from the third floor (the governor's office), and the legislature working only on information supplied by the executive branch.

Godwin's proposals during his campaign included advancing state services. In his inaugural address Godwin made it clear that during his administration he intended to move the state forward everywhere. While he indicated his intentions to make improvements in schools, colleges, roads, hospitals, parks and prisons, his main thrust was to improve education. To enact this ambitious agenda he needed resources.

Godwin received the infusion of revenue he needed by convincing the 1966 General Assembly to pass a statewide sales tax. Enacting the sales tax was a move he had, as a state senator, opposed just six years earlier. Godwin now heard the voice of the citizens of Virginia, and acted accordingly. Harry F. Byrd, Sr., did not live to see another vaulted fiscal cornerstone of the Byrd Machine go by the boards. He died in 1966.

In 1968 Godwin won legislative and voter approval for an $80 million general obligation bond issue. Then in 1969, the General Assembly adopted a new Constitution for Virginia essentially as recommended by a Constitutional Revision Commission appointed by Godwin. The stage was set to totally abandon "pay as you go" as the newly approved 1971 Constitution eased the limitations on state borrowing earlier imposed under Byrd's guidance.

The Equestrian Monument of George Washington towers over Capitol Square, where the Virginia General Assembly holds its legislative sessions. Photo by Anne Marie Morgan.

With Godwin's progressive program adopted almost intact, it was evident the 1965 election had brought a new, changed political environment to Virginia. Republican legislative leaders firmly believed they deserved significant credit for the administration's progressive achievements. The Republican minority in the General Assembly, led by the sharp-tongued, articulate Minority Floor Leader, M. Caldwell Butler, actively supported the vast majority of Godwin's legislative package, including the sales tax.

Butler maintained to his caucus and to Republican stalwarts across the state that the two-party system came of age in Virginia with the 1966 General Assembly.[11] While the full impact of the two-party system would not be fully established for several decades, Butler was essentially correct.

In the meantime, the electorate itself grew because federal courts had ruled that the poll tax was unconstitutional for national elections, and Virginia's Supreme Court followed suit for state elections.

St. Sen. Harry F. Byrd, Jr., had succeeded his father to the U.S. Senate. But a Republican was elected to fill his vacated State Senate seat from the former stronghold of the Byrd Machine. This special election was another indication that the Virginia Republican Party was coming of age and there really would be a two-party system in Virginia.

From this threshold there proceeded a series of Republican victories in Virginia's gubernatorial elections. The election of Virginia's first Republican governor in the 20th century, Linwood Holton, took place in 1969. Helped by an ambitious, verbose, unabashed liberal Democrat, Henry Howell, whose campaigns tended to split the state Democrats, Republicans also won the governor's chair in 1973 and 1977. The GOP soon won half of Virginia's 10 Congressional seats for the first time in a hundred years.

Remarkably, former Democratic Gov. Mills Godwin became the focus of state Republican leaders to carry the GOP flag in the 1973 election, and Godwin accepted the nomination of the 1973 Republican convention. While the beginning shadows of the Watergate scandal of GOP Pres. Richard Nixon were beginning to creep across the political landscape of Virginia, Godwin was able to win a narrow victory over his liberal opponent. Republican John Dalton, who earlier had been elected state senator and then lieutenant governor, was elected governor four years later.

In providing three successive Republican victories in the gubernatorial elections, Virginia voters also showed their willingness to split their tickets, frequently electing Democrats as lieutenant governors and attorneys general. When, in 1977, Lt. Gov. Dalton was elected governor, he helped carry his Republican running mate, Marshall Coleman, into the state's top attorney's office, while the expanded electorate put a centrist Democrat, Charles "Chuck" Robb, into the lieutenant governor's chair.

The 1980s Belong to the Democrats

Robb, the son-in-law of former Pres. Lyndon B. Johnson, worked diligently to convince Virginia Democrats that he had a middle-of-the-road political philosophy which could help them to again capture the Governor's Mansion. His approach worked and he led a sweep of the statewide elections in 1981.

The administration of Chuck Robb proved to be in line with the thinking of many Virginia voters. Good economic times helped Robb keep the ship of state in the middle of the road and satisfy the electorate's newfound appreciation of increased state services. Despite occasional bad publicity, Robb left the governor's office with a high positive public rating.[12]

The 1985 statewide elections were considered a referendum on Robb's administration. Attorney General Gerald Baliles and the Democratic Party, after considerable intraparty maneuvering, assembled a rather remarkable and very attractive team to run. Labeled "the rainbow ticket," it featured Baliles for governor, a veteran African-American state senator from Richmond, L. Douglas Wilder, for lieutenant governor, and a white female delegate from rural Virginia, Mary Sue Terry, for attorney general. The state was prospering, and Baliles's message of strengthening education and transportation hit a responsive chord with the growing number of urban and suburban voters, who elected all three to office.

The politically savvy Democratic lieutenant governor used his political foresight throughout his term as the second-ranked Democrat, only a heart-beat away from the Governor's Mansion, to travel and build a base for securing the party's nomination for the 1989 governor's campaign. The attorney general, as a good Democratic loyalist, agreed to run for reelection and let Wilder be the Democrat standard-bearer. To complete the ticket, the Democrats selected an attractive Northern Virginian and generous contributor to the Democratic Party, Donald S. "Don" Beyer, Jr., to run for lieutenant governor. The Democratic ticket prevailed again.

During the 1980s the Republican candidates took their lumps, but all of the elections were strongly contested. C. Richard Cranwell, the House of Delegates Democratic Majority Leader during this period, commented to my university class: "The Virginia Republicans' problem was their Republican President Ronald Reagan's economic policies were too successful. Virginians were prosperous and happy with the direction their state was taking."[13] This all changed in the 1990s. Wilder had to deal with an economic downturn almost as soon as he took the oath of office for governor and enacted austere budgets.

Two-Party Competition Solidifies

The 1993 election for governor also bore out the axiom that frequently the electorate votes its pocketbooks. This situation, however, was enforced by the astute, anti-crime, anti-parole campaign of the Republican gubernatorial nominee, former Delegate and Congressman George Allen. The Democrats had outsmarted themselves in the 1991 redistricting. They placed Allen in a district with a fellow and more senior Republican Congressman. So this moderate, attractive candidate, frequently compared to Ronald Reagan in his campaign style, decided to run for governor and won the nomination.

In the general election, Allen overcame a 27-point early lead in the polls by his opponent, Attorney General Mary Sue Terry (who was in her second term). The electorate proceeded to split tickets again in 1993. Democrat Don Beyer easily won re-election for another term as lieutenant governor. Republican Henrico County Commonwealth's Attorney James S. "Jim" Gilmore, III, was elected attorney general.

Gilmore's substantial win set up the scenario for the 1997 election where he represented the Republican Party at the top of the ticket and Don Beyer headed the Democratic ticket. Running on his "No Car Tax" slogan, Gilmore prevailed over the two-term Democratic lieutenant governor, winning 55.8 percent of the vote and leading a Republican sweep in 1997. Polio victim and business executive John Hager won the lieutenant governor's race and St. Sen. Mark Early was elected attorney general. This was the first time in modern Virginia history that Republicans swept all three statewide offices.

Gilmore pushed through the General Assembly a version of his campaign's popular theme—"No Car Tax"—which provided tax relief on the local personal property tax on cars. However, a number of local elected officials touted this legislation as good politics, but very bad public policy.[14]

For the next two gubernatorial election cycles, the critics' charges prevailed. The Democrats returned to a centrist for the first statewide race of the new century. Northern Virginia millionaire and former state Democratic Party Chairman Mark R. Warner had run unsuccessfully against Republican incumbent U.S. Sen. John Warner in 1996 but had established a statewide base, and he received his party's nomination to run for governor in 2001. While Mark Warner won the election for governor, for the down-ticket races the citizens of Virginia again split their ballots. Former Richmond Mayor,

Democrat Timothy M. "Tim" Kaine, received the nod for lieutenant governor, while Republican Jerry Kilgore won the race for attorney general.

In the second governor's race of the 21st century, Lt. Gov. Tim Kaine succeeded the popular Mark Warner to the governor's chair by beating Kilgore. But Kilgore's Republican running mates, however, gained success as the voters again split their votes. St. Sen. William T. "Bill" Bolling narrowly bested his liberal opponent, and Del. Robert "Bob" McDonnell was elected Attorney General.

The Attorney General's race between McDonnell and St. Sen. Creigh Deeds produced the closest statewide race in history. At the end of the official count, McDonnell had a 323-vote margin out of the 1.9 million votes cast.

Four years later the same two candidates vied for the governorship. The results, however, were much different in 2009 than they were in 2005. The Democratic presidency of Barack Obama was then very unpopular in Virginia among a number of voters, many of whom had supported him a year earlier.[15] Gov. Tim Kaine had been forced to cut more than $4 billion from the state budgets, and while he was presiding over this shortage of revenue as the national and state economies faltered, he accepted Obama's invitation to take over the chairmanship of the National Democratic Committee. This performance of two

Spring at the State Capitol. Photo by Bob Brown, *Richmond Times-Dispatch.*

jobs by the sitting Democratic Governor did not seem to sit well with some in the electorate and lessened the assistance he could give Deeds' campaign.[16]

McDonnell's campaign successfully energized the Republican base in the state and pulled a majority of the Independents and some disenchanted Democrats into his camp during the summer and fall of 2009.[17] He swamped Deeds by 17 points and helped carry his running mates—Lt. Gov. Bill Bolling for re-election and St. Sen. Ken Cuccinelli for Attorney General—into a historic Republican sweep.

This quick review of the statewide races since the end of Byrd Machine control of the state is clear evidence that Virginia is now a competitive two-party state, particularly when it comes to statewide elections. The quality of the candidates frequently dictates how the citizens will react, and party labels may not be as meaningful in state elections. The Virginia voter will readily split the ballot when one candidate is perceived to be better than another or when one campaign catches his attention.

More Proof: The Movement to a Two-Party Legislature

A brief look at the history of General Assembly elections provides another example of how Virginia has developed into a two-party state. The legislature was a bastion of support for the Byrd Machine in the 1920s thru the 1960s. From 1920 until 1962 there were never less than 37 Democrats in the 40-member State Senate nor 91 Democrats in the 100-member House of Delegates. This means that the Republican membership in the General Assembly for more than 40 years was always less than 9 percent.

In the late 1950s and 1960s, as the state's population began to grow, people began to seek more services, and the party developed popular spokespersons who more accurately espoused the wishes of the people. It was then that the Republican members in the legislature began to increase in number. Riding Linwood Holton's coattails in 1969, the GOP representation in the House jumped from 17 to 24 and in the Senate to seven. Pres. Nixon's Watergate scandal caused a slippage in the Republicans' steady growth during the late 1960s and early 1970s. GOP numbers in the House and Senate dropped before beginning a steady upward climb.

Regardless of the outcomes in gubernatorial races, GOP representation in the legislative houses continued to grow. Despite the 1981 and 1991 gerrymandering efforts of the Democratic majorities in both houses (or maybe because of it) they continued to lose strength. By 1992 the Republicans had 41 Delegate and 18 Senate seats. The Democrats' 1991 redistricting efforts had placed eight Republican delegates into four districts—feeling certain that the four junior Republicans would bow out and let their senior colleagues run in the newly drawn districts. The four junior delegates did just as the Democrats expected, except with one twist. In 1992, all four ran for State Senate seats and all four were successful in ousting veteran Democrats in the upper house!

In 1996, GOP candidates won two more State Senate seats to begin a power-sharing period within this body. So until there was a special election in 1998, this unique situation existed in the Senate, with bipartisan co-chairmen of committees and alternate party majorities in the various committees. People didn't think it would work, but it did. Because of this cooperation, the redistricting of the State Senate in 2001 was handled much more gentlemanly than in the past or than it was in the House.

In 2000, the Republicans gained the majority in the House with 52 members. The former minority party did the 2001 redistricting and in the first post-redistricting election moved to a 64 to 34 seat advantage, with two Independents who caucused with the Republicans. This Republican advantage has gone up and down since 2002, but as of 2011 the GOP held a 59 to 39 advantage as those two Independents (both former Democrats) continued to hold their I-status while still voting with the majority.

On the other end of the Capitol, the Democrats regained control of the Senate with a 22 to 18 margin. Then, in the Nov. 8, 2011, election after the decennial redistricting, the GOP won 67 seats in the House of Delegates, while an Independent who caucuses with the Republicans was re-elected. This election outcome gave them the largest Republican majority in the House in history. The GOP picked up two seats in the Senate for a 20-20 tie with the Democrats.

It is evident that the Commonwealth's political climate has undergone a significant transformation since the era of the Byrd machine. All of this history indicates that Virginians are now independent thinkers in their voting habits. Political writers may try to label Virginia, but it is accurate only to say that it is a two-party state. Since 1964, Virginia voted for the Republican candidate for President—until 2008. Because of this, the media called Virginia a "Red" (or Republican) state. But since 1964, the voters have elected an equal number of Republican and Democratic candidates for governor—six of each. Could it be that many Virginia voters really do look at the candidate more than the party when casting their ballots?

Arthur R. "Pete" Giesen, Jr., represented the 10th, 15th, and 25th Districts in the House of Delegates from 1964-1996. He is the Vice President of Academic Affairs and an adjunct Professor of Political Science at James Madison University.

CHAPTER 5
Commemorating the Anniversary of Public School Closings in Virginia

By Henry L. Marsh, III
Member, Virginia Senate

More than 50 years ago, in an act of defiance to the 1954 landmark U.S. Supreme Court decision in *Brown v. Board of Education* that desegregated the public schools throughout the land, Virginia, followed by other Southern states, enacted numerous laws designed to deliberately nullify, obfuscate, and delay the ruling and to minimize desegregation wherever it occurred. Virginia embarked upon a course of Massive Resistance to public school desegregation and had the dubious distinction of establishing a public policy that deprived thousands of African-Americans and white students of an education.

Before that momentous High Court ruling, in Virginia and across the South African-American students were educated in a dual school system by law, one Black and one white, in abysmal school conditions. The curricula, textbooks, equipment, and school buildings were substandard. African-American schools were without gymnasiums, restrooms, cafeterias, lockers, or auditoriums with fixed seating, and students were issued textbooks that were in utter disrepair and discarded by white schools.

Students of Robert Russa Moton High School in Farmville, in April 1951, were led by 16 year-old Barbara Johns to protest the longstanding unequal conditions at the school. The students, mentored by Reverend L. Francis Griffin, called upon Oliver W. Hill, Sr., and Samuel F. Tucker, members of the Hill, Tucker, and Marsh law firm in Richmond, to represent them in the lawsuit against the Prince Edward County School Board. The protest undertaken by these students led to the 1952 federal court case, *Davis v. County School Board of Prince Edward County,*[1] which was eventually consolidated with four other cases from Delaware (*Belton v. Gebhart*), South Carolina (*Briggs v. Elliott*), Kansas (*Brown v. Board of Education*), and the District of Columbia (*Bolling v. Sharpe*). The merits of the Virginia case constituted the basis of the argument before the Court, and the five consolidated class action lawsuits culminated in one of the most pivotal decisions ever rendered by the U.S. Supreme Court, as *Brown v. Board of Education of Topeka, Kansas.*[2] This landmark decision was the catalyst for the Civil Rights Movement and subsequent events in Virginia that influenced the evolution of civil rights in both the Commonwealth and the nation.

Response to the *Brown* decision came quickly in the General Assembly of Virginia. On August 30, 1954, Gov. Thomas B. Stanley appointed 32 legislators to the Commission on Public Education, which was charged with examining the effect of the decision on the Commonwealth and making recommendations. The Commission issued a report on November 11, 1955, stating emphatically that "separate facilities in our public schools are in the best interest of both races, educationally and otherwise, and that compulsory integration should be resisted by all proper means in our power."[3] The

Barbara Johns and Moton High School students are depicted in the Civil Rights Memorial on Capitol Square. The students walked out in 1951 to protest the deplorable conditions of their segregated school. Photo by Anne Marie Morgan.

recommendations of the Commission on Public Education became law and the Pupil Placement Board was created for the purpose of assigning students to particular public schools. Tuition grants were to be provided to students who opposed integrated schools.

Massive Resistance was a clarion call across the South to resist and prevent the integration of the races at any cost. In fact, all levels of Virginia government demonstrated intense resistance to compliance with the *Brown* decision as the state exhausted every possible means to avoid desegregation. The system of laws put into place formed the legal infrastructure for the resistance movement, which included the diversion of public education funds to support private segregated academies, denial of state funds for any public school that agreed to integrate, and the closing of public schools. In 1959, Virginia abandoned the "Massive Resistance" approach for "Freedom of Choice," a new tuition grant/scholarship program enacted for white children attending non-sectarian private schools or public schools outside of the locality in which they resided. Legislation was also passed giving tax credits for donations to private schools and repealing compulsory attendance laws, making the operating of public schools a matter of local choice.

The resistance lasted 10 years, during which time schools were closed in several localities including Warren County, Charlottesville, and Norfolk for various periods of time, and military enforcement of the law to integrate schools that did stay open was necessary. Prince Edward County closed its public schools for five years, from 1959 to 1964.

Thousands of African-American students and hundreds of white students could not graduate and were denied education. In other parts of the Commonwealth, African-American students, and there were very few, attending white schools were harassed, threatened, isolated, humiliated, and treated with contempt. In 1964, almost 10 years to the date after Brown, the United States Supreme Court ruled in *Griffin v. School Board of Prince Edward County*,[4] requiring the reopening of Prince Edward County schools. The General Assembly responded by repealing the laws it had enacted to protect segregated schools. Piece by piece, the legislative architecture of Massive Resistance was dismantled.

I joined the legal battle to destroy Massive Resistance in May, 1961, during my first month as an attorney with the law firm. During the next 20 years, a significant portion of my time was devoted to the fight to end Massive Resistance. I argued numerous cases in state and federal courts to enjoin school boards from operating segregated schools, to enjoin the payment of tuition payments for students attending racially segregated schools, to protect the membership list of the NAACP, to represent citizens subpoenaed to appear before a legislative committee of the Virginia General Assembly, and to represent citizens seeking to protect their constitutional rights.

Notwithstanding the formal end of Virginia's Massive Resistance, desegregation cases continued to be heard in federal courts until 1984, and the last case was finally dismissed in 2001.

In 2003, the General Assembly of Virginia passed a resolution expressing profound regret over the closing of Prince Edward schools, and in 2004, in addition to several other related measures designed to seize and maximize

TABLE V

Differences in Course Offerings in the High Schools of Prince Edward County, Virginia For the School Year 1951-1952

Courses Which Are Offered to White High School Students but not to Negro High School Students:

Subject	Unit Value	Grade in which Offered
Trigonometry	½	12
Physics	1	12
World History	1	10
Geography	1	9
Latin I and II	2	9 and 10
Spanish I and II	2	11 and 12
Band	1	all
Typing, second course	1	11
Shorthand, second course	1	12
General Shop	½	8
Woodwork	½	9
General Metal Work	½	10
Machine Shop	½	10
Electricity	½	10
Mechanical Drawing	½	9
Pre-trade	1	11-12
Total Unit Value	13½	
Total Courses	18	

Courses Which Are Offered to Negro High School Students but not to White High School Students:

Subject	Unit Value	Grade in which Offered
Dramatic Arts	1	11-12
French I and II	2	10 and 11
Free-hand Drawing	½	10-11
Chorus	½	9
General Music	1	9-10
Business Mathematics	1	12
Clerical Practice	1	12
Consumer Buying	½	
Total Unit Value	8	
Total Courses	9	

Differences in Course Offerings, Davis v. Prince Edward County, U.S. District Court, Eastern District of Va.[5]

Virginia's Redemptive Moment, established the Brown v. Board of Education Scholarship Program to provide educational opportunities to persons throughout the Commonwealth who were affected by the school closings.

In 2004, the Dr. Martin Luther King, Jr. Memorial Commission, of which I am Chairman, was directed by the General Assembly to lead and coordinate the two-year commemoration of the 50th anniversary of the Brown decision and to follow through on subsequent initiatives and outcomes of the observance. 2009 marked the convergence of the anniversary of several historic events and milestones in Virginia and United States history, including the 50th anniversary of the closing of public schools in Virginia and the 55th anniversary of the 1954 Supreme Court decision in *Brown v. Board of Education*. The public school closings in Virginia and the national commemoration of the landmark decision in *Brown* were recognized statewide and nationally. Therefore, in adherence to its duties and mission, the Commission, together with the Brown v. Board of Education Scholarship Committee, appointed the Special Subcommittee on the Fiftieth Anniversary of Public School Closings in Virginia to assist the Commission in planning and leading the Commonwealth to commemorate these historic events. The Special Subcommittee was composed of members of the Commission, the Brown v. Board of Education Scholarship Committee, and representatives of the legal, business, and corporate communities, the state and federal court systems, professional education organizations, public and higher education officials, teachers, historians, relevant state agencies and local governing bodies, community organizations, recent *Brown* scholars, and localities in which public schools were closed to avoid desegregation.

The significance of *Brown* is best understood by examining the past, the present, and the implications of the decision for the future. The Brown decision was the first step in striking down long-standing laws that denied equal rights to African-American citizens and was the advent of the modern Civil Rights Movement. The road to *Brown* and the Civil Rights Movement is a story of a people—individuals who tapped into an inner courage and strength that has sustained them for centuries of injustice, indignities, and discrimination to right social inequities and injustice, claim their inalienable rights, and make the future better for generations to come.

––––––––––––––––––––

Henry L. Marsh, III, is a member of the Virginia Senate, representing the 16th District since 1992. He is Chairman of the Senate Courts of Justice Committee and Member of the Virginia State Crime Commission. He previously served on the Richmond City Council. Article adapted from Virginia Capitol Connections (Richmond, Fall, 2009).

PART II: THE LEGISLATIVE BRANCH

The Virginia General Assembly is another example of how the Commonwealth led the American colonies in implementing representative government. The legislature was first established at the Jamestown settlement in 1619—before the Pilgrims had even landed in the New World—and is the oldest continuous lawmaking body in the United States. But since that time it has undergone numerous permutations, including its permanent transformation into a bicameral legislature.

When Virginia's revolutionary leaders hammered out their first state Constitution in 1776, they applied their political theories, including the need for a separation of powers, to the institutions they established. James Madison's well-known views on the subject were immortalized after the American Revolution in *The Federalist Papers*: "The accumulation of all powers, legislative, executive, and judiciary, in the same hands, whether of one, a few, or many ... may justly be pronounced the very definition of tyranny."[1] But Madison did not believe that any of the states had struck the proper balance by 1788, including Virginia: "If we look into the constitutions of the several States, we find that ... there is not a single instance in which the several departments of power have been kept absolutely separate and distinct."[2] The General Assembly possessed the lion's share of authority during this era but that would change.

In Chapter 6 of Part II, *The Legislative Branch,* some of Virginia's most knowledgeable experts on the General Assembly, three deputy clerks of the House of Delegates and state Senate, relate the story of the General Assembly and how it evolved into the lawmaking body that it is today. One of the most significant features is that it is comprised of part-time *citizen*-legislators who make laws during brief Assembly sessions, instead of full-time, professional politicians. This fact also makes it more difficult for them to thoroughly examine legislation in such a short period of time when thousands of bills are introduced, which has been a common occurrence.

It is essential to know all of the terms used by lawmakers and the stages that legislation must pass through in order to fully understand and follow a bill's progress. The authors go into great detail about today's procedures for making the Commonwealth's laws, including the extensive vocabulary of legislating, and they provide some of the most comprehensive descriptions that have ever appeared in a modern text on Virginia government. As deputy clerks, the authors engage in these legislative processes throughout the year and help ensure that the proper rules are followed. In Virginia, lawmaking is a complicated process and bills must undergo three "readings" in each chamber, which provides more time for deliberation. Bills can be defeated or amended during most of these stages, and the authors explain how these opportunities for decision-making are built into the legislative schedule. Readers should note that the Senate and the House employ similar procedures, but some differences do exist, including the use of proxy voting in the upper chamber. The authors also describe the options that governors may choose to modify or defeat bills. At every step, including the reconvened session held six weeks after the General Assembly's regular session has adjourned, legislation can succeed or fail. In the Commonwealth, bills also can be altered in very minor ways or almost beyond recognition as substitute measures. During modern General Assembly sessions, Virginians can track legislation from a distance through the on-line Legislative Information System when they cannot attend meetings on Capitol Square. This virtual approach enables a greater number of citizens to observe and participate, but the details in this narrative will enhance understanding and help clear up any confusion about terminology and procedures.

This chapter also emphasizes the enormous power of Virginia's Speaker of the House, which should be compared to the authority of the lieutenant governor as described in Chapter 10. The lieutenant governor is one of the Commonwealth's three statewide officeholders elected by the voters, and although the Speaker is not, he wields more power than the lieutenant governor. Both preside over their respective chambers and can rule on whether amendments are "germane" to bills and can be attached (or not) to legislation. But the Speaker votes on every bill that comes to the floor, while the lieutenant governor can only break tie votes. Chapter 10, written by a lieutenant governor who was elected twice, explains that the latter does occur, but infrequently—thus, individuals who hold that office often work on a plethora of initiatives to increase their effectiveness. Unlike the lieutenant governor, Virginia's Speaker also assigns delegates to committees and determines which committees will consider the bills that are introduced. Because the Speaker lawfully exercises these extraordinary powers, it would not be difficult for him to assign members and steer bills in ways that could be helpful or fatal to legislation.

Surrounding trees and buildings cast shadows on the State Capitol as the sun begins to set. Photo by Anne Marie Morgan.

During a legislative session, it is common to hear the members say that "the governor proposes, but the General Assembly disposes." They are usually referring to the state budget, which is introduced or amended annually by Virginia's governor but altered substantially by lawmakers, who like to assert their independence from the chief executive. The budget is actually a policy-oriented document since it provides appropriations for programs and causes that both the executive and legislative branches have agreed to fund. Thus, it is a source of power over the allocation of scarce resources (perhaps winning the gratitude of voters), as well as a bone of contention among all parties as they vie to fund their favorite programs. The latter is made more difficult during economic downturns because by law, Virginia's budget must be balanced and cannot accrue deficits. Much like other aspects of the General Assembly, the process of crafting a budget has changed, as Chapter 7 describes. This narrative is written by an experienced veteran of these legislative battles who is also the former chairman of the Appropriations Committee, the powerful budget-writing panel in the House of Delegates. As the author explains, the House and Senate always craft their own spending plans and kill the measures introduced by the opposite chambers, so the tough decisions are made in negotiations between the budget conferees. Sometimes these talks have been arguments instead of discussions and the Assembly has not adjourned on time. Occasionally, the worst disagreements are with a governor, who has a line-item veto that can eliminate specific items with a stroke of a pen. And unless both houses overturn the veto with a super-majority, the individual measure will not receive the funding that was intended by the legislature. The author adds that overall, Virginia's budget-making process *works* and contributes to the Commonwealth's reputation for sound fiscal discipline.

Chapter 8 tells the history of women members of the General Assembly, which is a subject rarely found in Virginia textbooks. The author is the Librarian of Virginia, and her scholarly research indicates that these women had to overcome many obstacles to win election to the state legislature. The political machine that ruled Virginia in the early to mid-20th century, the Byrd Organization, was not very welcoming to women as participants in governance. And although most state legislatures had ratified the U.S. constitutional amendment granting women the right to vote by 1920, the General Assembly did not get around to approving the measure until 1952. But as the author notes, women initially succeeded in winning elections by *not* campaigning on "women's issues," and they deliberately chose to eschew attention to their gender. But the women of the House and Senate believe that they have made a significant difference in the focus of legislative concerns and the content of bills that have become law— especially as their numbers increased.

The longest-serving delegate in the Virginia General Assembly shares his perspective on the legislature past and present in Chapter 9. He recounts the enormous changes that have taken place that he witnessed first-hand during the last half-century, with perhaps the most significant being the establishment of annual sessions, the General Assembly's transformation into a competitive, two-party legislature, and greater transparency throughout the lawmaking process.

This section concludes with a chapter on lobbying, a profession that is sometimes derided in political ads as a "special interest" but which is an important and legitimate avenue for citizens and organizations to influence public policies. Three Virginia lobbyists share their views about the art of influencing public officials and how these advocates work to win passage of legislation, modify bills, or defeat them. As the first author relates, a great deal of knowledge, skill, patience, and tactical prowess are needed to achieve legislative and policy goals, and in light of Virginia's brief General Assembly sessions, lobbyists often need to begin their work before lawmakers even convene. Additionally, he notes that professionals must be vigilant and look for bills that may be beneficial *or* detrimental to their causes. These measures can appear with lightning speed during the fast-paced sessions. Lobbyists often must be effective motivators, too, in order to rally like-minded citizens to contact their elected officials and create momentum for their viewpoint through grassroots mobilization campaigns. The author also explains that it is essential for lobbyists to be honest and forthright with public officials. The two final authors build on this idea, focusing on the role and ethics of lobbying. As they make clear, Virginia does not have many laws to restrict lobbying activities and prefers transparency through reporting attendant expenditures. The authors' ultimate goal is to ensure that professionals are above reproach in their conduct, and they offer practical suggestions compiled by a Virginia association of lobbyists. This focus is indispensable if lobbying is to remain an effective component of state lawmaking and a means of representing Virginians who do not regularly walk in the halls of power.

"George Washington," a.k.a., James Renwick Manchester, walks past the Houdon statue of George Washington in the State Capitol Building. Photo by Bob Brown, *Richmond Times-Dispatch.*

CHAPTER 6
The Virginia General Assembly and the Process of Making State Laws

By Jeffrey A. Finch, B. Scott Maddrea, and John McE. Garrett
Offices of the Clerks, House of Delegates and Virginia Senate

Virginians are proud to claim the General Assembly as the oldest continuously meeting legislative body in the Western hemisphere. In fact, it is among the oldest such bodies in the world.

However, the Virginia General Assembly has not always existed as it appears today. In its earliest form, the General Assembly did not resemble what we would recognize as a legislative body. To trace the roots of legislative processes in Virginia, it is necessary to return to the earliest days of the colony—some 400 years ago—since many of the elements of the modern legislature have their beginnings in that first Assembly. And to truly understand the origins of the modern legislature, it is necessary to go back to a time before the first colonists set foot on the shores of the North American continent.

The concept of separation of powers and the division of government into the legislative, executive, and judicial branches—each separate and distinct at both the state and federal levels—has been engrained in most Americans' sense of how democratic governments are organized. But within the legislative branch, the federal government and 49 of the 50 states have well-

Picture taken outside the House Chamber: "The First Legislature in the New World." Photo courtesy of the House Clerk's Office and the Library of Virginia.

established "bicameral" systems, based on two legislative chambers (usually a Senate and a House), which operate both independently of—and in coordination with—one another. This bicameral model is described in a historical look at the composition of state legislatures:

> Of these two branches in the legislatures of this country, though they are in fact equal in power and dignity, the one, being a smaller and more select body, is usually regarded as the upper house, and the other, consisting of a larger and less select body of members, as the lower. The members of the former, commonly called the senate, are usually required to possess certain peculiar qualifications, as to age and residence; are chosen by more numerous constituencies, and sometimes by a comparatively select, that is, a more highly qualified body of electors; and are not unfrequently elected for longer terms of office. The

members of the latter, variously known as representatives, burgesses, commons, or delegates, are chosen by smaller constituencies; sometimes, by a more popular suffrage, that is, by electors of less qualifications; and often, for shorter periods of official duty. There are States, however, in which the qualifications of the electors, the term of office, and the conditions of eligibility, are precisely the same, in reference to both branches.[1]

The most common perception is that the bicameral structure was brought to this continent by the early settlers, who structured their government after the English parliamentary system. Certainly there is some validity to this assessment. The English system was the one with which the colonists were most familiar and it is understandable that, in the absence of alternatives, they would fall back on this model. But to say that the parliamentary system was purposely imported from England would be an oversimplification.

Although the colonists first landed on these shores and established an English-speaking colony in Jamestown in 1607, the roots of governance actually pre-date the settlement. In fact, the foundations for the governance of Virginia were laid well before the first ships departed England.

Change is almost never easy and to suggest the transformation occurred smoothly or followed some grand design would be not only misleading, but historically inaccurate. In fact, the directors of the Virginia Company originally set up the General Assembly to guard the fiscal affairs of the colony and help avoid bankruptcy until the colony could flourish. "Under the royal charters of 1606, 1609, and 1612, the Virginia Company of London had been established and confirmed as a joint-stock company capable of supplying capital and management for the expensive adventure of English colonization in North America."[2] The establishment of the colony was at its core a business decision and as such, the structure of the governance was not modeled after the English parliamentary system or any known political model, but developed as a business.

But there would soon be a profound change, and "[t]he General Assembly's metamorphosis from corporate appendage to representative legislature is a remarkable story made all the more amazing when one considers the tremendous hardships that beset the early settlers."[3]

Transformation from the Virginia Company to the Virginia General Assembly

The colony was originally governed by a series of charters from the Virginia Company of London. "The charter of 1606 envisioned a resident council and a president to manage local affairs. That arrangement proved unsatisfactory, and in 1609 the company scrapped it in favor of a governor-general and a council of advisers."[4]

The new model proved no more economically viable than the original. Still unable to show a profit or give investors a return on their investment, Sir Edwin Sandys, the newly appointed treasurer of the Virginia Company, directed the pursuit of an entirely new, and quite ambitious, course of action. Whereas the Virginia Company had originally retained ownership of land in the New World, under Sandys' plan much of the land would be placed in private hands. Each colonist with seven years' residence in Virginia received 100 acres. And every investor in the Company received 100 acres per share of company stock. In addition, 50 acres were given to individuals who paid their own passage to Virginia or paid the passage for another person. Known as the "headright" system, and embodied in the Great Charter of 1618, these reforms represented the foundation of the colony's land policy for the rest of the century.[5]

In addition to overhauling the colony's economic foundation, the Great Charter of 1618 laid the foundation for the creation of a legislative assembly. "By the Great Charter of 1618 the Virginia Company also authorized the popular election of representatives from eleven areas of the settlement to meet with Governor George Yeardley and the Council and suggested solutions for the problems of Virginia's rapidly growing society."[6] Known as the General Assembly, this body "would meet annually except in cases of emergency, when it could be convened on short notice. It would serve as a courts of justice, and the company gave it authority to enact such general rules and ordinances as should seem necessary to effect directives from London or to address local needs. Any of its enactments were subject to a gubernatorial veto and review by the company."[7]

On July 30, 1619, the first General Assembly was convened and lasted five days, until August 4th.

The First Assembly (1619)

In many respects, that first General Assembly comprised of 22 Burgesses was quite different from the General Assembly of today. One of the most obvious differences was that there initially was no concept of the separation of powers, so the Governor, Council, and House all sat as one body while in session. Since there was no capitol building to speak of, the first Assembly met in the choir box of the Jamestown church, as "[t]he most convenient place we could finde to sitt in":[8]

> After taking the oaths of allegiance and supremacy, the members proceeded to their business. The assembly first considered its members' qualifications and ejected two, pending clarification of their patents from London. That done, it proceeded to its legislative business. The assembly's legislative work is divisible into four parts: examining the 1618 instructions to see what changes, if any, were desirable, enacting certain instructions into law, proposing new ordinances, and drafting petitions to the company. Six revisions to the Great Charter were adopted, and the assembly enacted regulations touching on such matters as Indian relations and the price of tobacco. After some criminal cases were resolved, "the intemperance of the weather and the falling sick of divers of the Burgesses" forced Yeardley on August 4 to prorogue the assembly to the following March.
>
> In spite of the session's brevity, only five days, this first general assembly had achieved an important beginning. These twenty-seven men (the governor, six councillors, and twenty burgesses) ushered in a new era in colonial government. Although the assembly would undergo modifications and its right to exist would be in jeopardy after the company lost its charter, that first meeting established a singular precedent for the evolution of representative political institutions and self-government in English North America.[9]

The First Speaker

Sir John Pory was the first Speaker of the House. He was appointed to this position by Gov. Yeardley and not elected by the membership as is today's Speaker. In all likelihood Pory was selected for this role because he was the only member of the Assembly to have served in Parliament or otherwise held elective office in England, having served in the House of Commons from 1605 to 1611. However, Pory's service in Parliament was hardly marked with distinction. History records that Pory displayed "questionable" legislative ability and was "too often whittled" and "too much in love with the pot"[10] — serving on just five committees during his tenure.

Nonetheless, Pory possessed "a practical understanding of legislative organization and procedures that he could teach others to use in the fledgling assembly."[11] In fact, some aspects of today's Assembly trace their roots back to Pory's tenure. For example, Pory maintained the first Journal of the Assembly's deliberations, and while the formal requirement for maintaining a Journal was not added to the state Constitution until 1852, Pory nonetheless established the precedent during the first Assembly. Pory also introduced the first set of rules, standardizing the movement of bills and the courtesies for controlling debate and maintaining decorum. Over time the need for more elaborate rules expanded and between 1652 and 1659, the Assembly began standardizing rules for proceeding. Finally, it was the Speaker who delivered the first opening address, something akin to the modern State of the Commonwealth, traditionally delivered by governors on the opening day of the session. Why Pory gave the first address in Virginia rather than Gov. Yeardley is not known exactly, although at least one writer has opined that Yeardley deferred to Pory simply because the Speaker was the better orator. While the tradition of an opening address by the governor actually dates back to the 14th century, Pory and his successors continued to give the opening address in Virginia until approximately 1651, when the tradition returned to the executive.

From Unicameral to Bicameral

In 1639, King Charles authorized annual meetings of the General Assembly and further agreed that no taxes could be levied on the colony without the consent of the legislature. In addition, the Burgesses were given not only the power to tax, but to form parishes, draw county lines, regulate church and military affairs, and revise, as needed, existing laws.[12]

However, it was not until 1643 that the concept of the separation of powers began to surface, when in March of that year, the General Assembly changed from a unicameral into a bicameral structure. The move was precipitated by Gov. William Berkeley, who divided the General Assembly into a House of Burgesses and Council of State in an effort to wrest influence away from the councilors. "Although the house began to resemble a 'little parliament,' the burgesses, unlike their English contemporaries, chose their presiding officer and clerk. Demonstrating the significance of this bicameral division, Thomas Stegge stepped down from the Council of State to take the Speaker's position."[13]

1699: The Move to Williamsburg

Eight decades of development turned the General Assembly into something quite different from the visions of its creators. Through accident, default, and necessity, it had garnered an important share in regulating colonial life and, to that end, the whole growth process had afforded valuable instruction in the practical skills required of legislators and much learning about the nature of power. For good and ill, those lessons endure in the traditions of self-government that are the fabric of the American political culture.[14]

On October 21, 1698, the state house in Jamestown burned to the ground, and while the loss of the state house was unfortunate, it led to the move of the seat of government to Williamsburg, "a much more advantageous location in every way than Jamestown."[15] The Assembly met in Williamsburg from 1699 to 1780.

During the 161 years from 1619 to 1780 that the Assembly met in Jamestown and Williamsburg, the size of the House was in a state of constant change, in large measure due to the growth of the colony and the requirement that each locality have two representatives.

Over time the composition of the House of Delegates also shifted as representation was apportioned by locality. As the number of cities and counties increased, so, too, did the size of the legislature. In 1695, the House consisted of 47 members and by 1712, the House had grown to 51. By

1756, the House was comprised of 104 members (12 more than when the House convened in 1752, due to the creation of six new counties that session alone). By 1830, the size of the House had grown to 134 members, which was short of the constitutional provision at that time allowing the General Assembly to increase that number to 150 by a two-thirds vote. The House peaked in size in 1851 at 152 and by 1879 had decreased to 138 members. Finally, the Constitution of 1902 established the number for the size of the House as between 90 and 100, a constitutional provision that still stands today.

Constitution of 1776: From Colony to State

The Revolutionary War and America's bid for independence had an enormous impact on the Commonwealth's government as Virginia evolved from a British colony to one of the original 13 states. With this transition came the transformation of the House of Burgesses into the House of Delegates.

The organizational and name change to the House of Delegates was formalized in the Constitution of 1776, which was adopted on June 29th of that year. This document also established annual legislative sessions and created a true bicameral legislature:

> The framers provided for a legislative department that 'shall be formed of two distinct branches, who, together, shall be a complete Legislature.' The two houses were named the House of Delegates and the Senate. The framers also established that 'each House shall choose its own Speaker, appoint its own Officers [and] settle its own rules of proceeding...'
> The office of Speaker of the Senate remained in existence from 1776 to 1851."[16]

The membership of the House continued to be determined by annual elections, with each county electing two members and each city one member while the senators were elected for four-year terms. Perhaps more interesting, *all* legislation had to originate in the House of Delegates. The Senate could only approve, reject, or amend—and in the case of "money" bills, could only approve or reject. In addition, the House and Senate jointly elected the governor, who served a three-year term.

It is interesting to note that Thomas Jefferson complained that the Constitution vested too much power in the General Assembly. However, through the years there has been a gradual erosion of legislative power as the office of the governor grew to be substantially more powerful than the executive of that era.

Today's Virginia Legislature

Responsibilities of the General Assembly

Today the chief responsibilities of members of the General Assembly are not significantly different than those of early legislators. Members still represent citizens in the formulation of public policy, enact laws of the Commonwealth, approve the budget, levy taxes, elect judges, and confirm appointments by the governor.

Legislative Districts

Every ten years, following the U.S. Census, the General Assembly redraws legislative districts. These districts are no longer drawn to coincide with city and county boundaries, but instead, to insure that each member of the House and the Senate represents an equal number of citizens in their respective bodies. Thus, the 140 legislative districts of the General Assembly are drawn from the total population of the Commonwealth.[17]

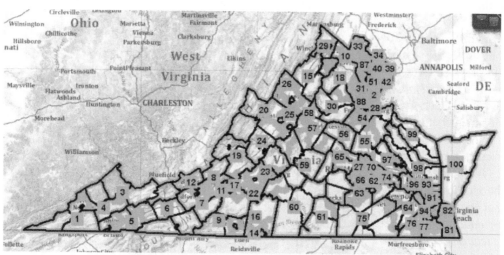

2011 House of Delegates Districts

This process called "redistricting" is based on the constitutional principle of "one man, one vote." Using data from the 2010 census, the 100 House members represent approximately 79,000 citizens and the 40 state senators represent approximately 197,000 citizens.

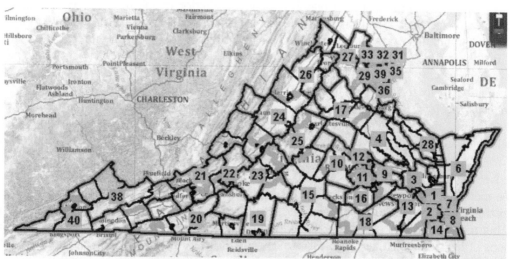

2011 Virginia Senate Districts

General Assembly Members

Members of the House of Delegates are elected for two-year terms and members of the Senate for four-year terms. The general elections for the legislature occur in odd years (in contrast to federal elections, which are held in even years), when voters choose the entire membership of each body. This means that the entire House of Delegates is elected every two years and the entire Senate every four years (unlike Congress, which staggers the terms of senators so that all U.S. Senate seats are never up for election in the same year). The annual salary for state senators is $18,000 and for delegates is $17,640. To qualify for office, the Constitution requires legislators to be at least 21 years of age at the time of the election, residents of the district they represent, and qualified to vote for General Assembly members.[18]

The House of Delegates is presided over by the *Speaker of the House*, whom delegates elect from among their membership for a term that coincides with his term of office as a member of the House. In addition to the Speaker, the House leadership consists of a *majority leader*, *majority caucus chair*, *minority leader*, *minority caucus chair*, and the chairs of the standing committees.

A statewide elected official, the *lieutenant governor*, presides over the Senate as a constitutional

The renovated State Capitol showing the Bank Street Visitor Entrance and underground extension. Photo courtesy of the House Clerk's Office.

responsibility. Unlike the Speaker of the House, the state Constitution establishes that the lieutenant governor is not a member of the Senate and only has the power to vote on legislation in the case of a tie. The Constitution of Virginia also provides that the lieutenant governor is first in the line of succession to the governor. In the absence of the lieutenant governor, a president *pro tempore* who is elected by senators presides over the Senate.

In addition to these two officials, the Senate leadership consists of the *majority leader*, *majority caucus chair, minority leader, minority caucus chair,* and the chairs of the standing committees of the Senate.

The House and Senate each elect a clerk and a sergeant-at-arms and employ a full-time, professional, non-partisan staff to oversee the day-to-day administrative operations of the respective bodies.

Citizen Legislature

The members of the Virginia General Assembly are part-time "citizen legislators"—that is, they have occupations besides being a legislator. The legal profession once dominated the membership of the Assembly, but today educators or professions within the educational environment account for one of the largest groups of legislative "citizen" professions. While there are still many lawyers, the members come from a varied list of professions and occupations, including business executives, small business owners, consultants, engineers, farmers, funeral directors, grocers, landscape architects, pharmacists, physical therapists, realtors, public information officers, veterinarians, writers, computer technology and software developers, and retirees.

Although the General Assembly meets only a few months out of the year (typically seven to nine weeks) and Virginia lawmakers are not considered to be "full-time," that does not mean legislators do not have full-time responsibilities serving the needs of their constituents. When the members are not in session, they often serve as members of study committees, boards, and commissions, are invited to speak at government-related functions, attend local government meetings, and respond to the demands, requests, and needs of their constituents. These duties are directly related to service as a legislator and often require weekly travel within the district and across the Commonwealth.

How a Bill Becomes a Law: The Legislative Process

Article IV of the Constitution

Article IV of the Constitution of Virginia is the basis for the legislative process. Within this article, various items are defined relative to the makeup and procedures of the General Assembly. Specifically, the first five sections establish our bicameral system of legislative structure with the House of Delegates and Senate and set the size of each body, the qualifications of members, and when they are elected. Another provision provides for the members to be paid. (The legislators' salary is set by the Appropriations Act as passed by the General Assembly, with the provision that no member may ever increase his salary during the term for which he is presently serving.) Article IV further provides that the Regular Session of the General Assembly is 60 days long during even-numbered years and 30 days long during odd-numbered years, unless extended by a two-thirds vote of both houses. Normally, the odd-year Session is extended 16 days for a total of 46 days. In addition, the governor may call the General Assembly into Special Session on any matter about which he desires the legislature to meet and if petitioned by two-thirds of the members of each house.

Gov. Robert F. McDonnell addresses the Joint Assembly of the House of Delegates and Virginia Senate during the 2010 Session. Photo courtesy of Michaele White, Office of the Governor.

After each Regular or Special Session adjourns *sine die* (the day the legislature completes its work), it is followed by a Reconvened Session held on the sixth Wednesday after the adjournment. The purpose of the Reconvened Session is limited to the consideration of legislation returned by the governor with recommendations (amendments) or with his objections (vetoed). The Reconvened Session usually meets for one day, but the Constitution allows for the Session to meet for no more than three days. However, the legislature may, by a majority vote of the elected members of each house, extend the Reconvened Session for up to an additional seven days.

At the beginning of each Regular Session, the governor addresses the General Assembly in a Joint Session (a meeting of both the House of Delegates and the Senate together held in the House chamber) to deliver his annual State of the Commonwealth Address. In addition, if a Special Session is called, often the governor will be invited by the legislature to address the members in Joint Session to outline his proposals relative to the Special Session.

Section 11 of Article IV addresses basic principles of passing a bill into law:

- Only a bill (as opposed to a joint resolution) can become law.
- Each bill must be printed.
- Each bill must be referred to a committee in each body.
- Each bill must be read or printed in the daily calendar, by title, on three different calendar days, unless such reading is dispensed by a four-fifths vote of that body.
- Each bill must pass each body in the exact same form.
- There must be a recorded vote on passage in each body.

The chart on the following page depicts the legislative process and how a bill becomes a law.

Where Does Legislation Originate?

Although the Rules of the House of Delegates and Senate provide that only a member may introduce legislation, the ideas that inspire bills can come from a multitude of sources, such as:

- ✓ Individual legislators
- ✓ State agencies (the executive, judicial, legislative, and independent agencies)
- ✓ Study committees
- ✓ Local governments (county, city, or town)
- ✓ Businesses
- ✓ Lobbyists
- ✓ Citizens
- ✓ Neighborhood associations and other civic groups
- ✓ School administrators, teachers, or parents.

In some cases, it is as simple as an individual approaching a legislator with an idea for a new law. In other cases, the impetus for legislation comes from judicial decisions or from individuals or groups who have identified problems with existing laws.

These ideas are given to a General Assembly agency called the Division of Legislative Services, which is charged with crafting these ideas into specific language to create legislation (a bill) and incorporating this into the entire body of existing laws, the Code of Virginia. Bills are usually created by deleting and/or adding new language to the existing laws, but sometimes it is necessary to create a new law.

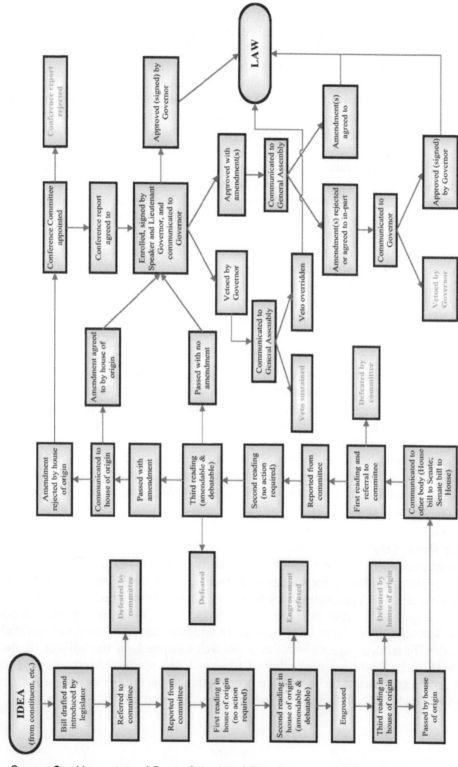

Source: Graphic courtesy of Penny Cabaniss, Office of the Vice President for Management and Budget, Office of State Governmental Relations, University of Virginia.

Once the staff at the Division of Legislative Services has drafted the legislation to the satisfaction of the General Assembly member, the bill is signed by the legislator, who becomes the chief patron. The chief patron then delivers the legislation to the respective Clerk's Office for introduction, and the bill is numbered in the order received, referred to committee, and printed.

Bills can be introduced in either body. A bill introduced in the House is known as a House Bill (HB) throughout the process and its number is assigned by the staff of the House Clerk's Office. Senators' bills are introduced in the Senate, numbered by the Senate Clerk's staff, and known as Senate Bills (SB).

Legislators may also introduce Resolutions and Joint Resolutions, which do not make or change the laws of the Commonwealth. Resolutions may create a study on a certain subject matter, commemorate an individual or a group for an outstanding achievement or in recognition of an event, memorialize the death of a prominent individual in the member's district or someone of statewide significance, or propose amendments to the Constitution of Virginia. Because resolutions do not have the force of law, they are not presented to the governor for his review and action.

It is important to note that companion bills or resolutions are often introduced in both the House and Senate. These measures are the same or nearly the same as bills or joint resolutions which were introduced in the other house. This allows members of each body to be the chief patron of a piece of legislation, and there is a perception that it can increase the likelihood of the bill's passage.

Referral of Legislation to Committee

In the House, the Speaker refers all legislation to committee and has absolute discretion in this regard. Although the Constitution requires that bills be referred to committee in order to become law, the Speaker is not bound by any rule to refer legislation to a specific panel and can refer any measure to any committee regardless of subject matter. However, typically he refers bills to the committee having jurisdiction over the issue addressed by the bill.

In the Senate, the Rules of the Senate provide that the Clerk refer bills based on the jurisdiction of each committee, which is defined by the subject matter stated in the Senate Rules. For example, bills relating to taxation are referred to the Finance Committee and bills concerning highways are referred to the Committee on Transportation.

Committee Process

The committee process is the heart of the legislative process. Legislative committees afford the General Assembly the opportunity for closer study and more detailed analysis of legislation than is possible during floor debate. This preliminary screening allows the committee (usually composed of 22 members in the House and 15 members in the Senate) to hear from the legislator who introduced the bill and other lawmakers who either favor or oppose it. In addition, the committee will normally hear from lobbyists and other interested persons who may be well-informed on the subject of the legislation. Citizens who wish to be heard are also allowed to attend and speak at committee meetings. Thus, committees are an integral part of the legislative process that allow the General Assembly to work more efficiently and thoroughly through these small groups formed around specific subjects.

House of Delegates Committees

The membership of the standing committees and any special committees of the House (such as Joint Rules, legislative study panels, etc.), is determined by the House Speaker. As with bill referrals, the Speaker has almost absolute discretion in appointing committee members. The Rules of the House only require that the committees be proportional to the makeup of the body as a whole with regard to political affiliation. This ensures that whichever party is in the majority in the House receives a majority of seats on each committee and that "to the extent possible" the Speaker appoints at least one member to each panel from each of the state's 11 congressional districts. The Speaker may be further constrained by caucus or internal guidelines that limit the number of committees on which members may serve but, generally, the Speaker's appointment authority is unrestrained. In addition to party affiliation and geography, the Speaker will consider various factors, such as race, gender, expertise through education or professional experience, seniority, philosophy, assignment to other committees, and potential meeting conflicts. The Speaker also names a chairman and vice-chairman of each committee. Typically, the chairman is from the majority party caucus and is the longest-serving member of the panel, with the caveat that no member can chair more than one committee.

The House of Delegates has 14 standing committees:

- Privileges and Elections
- Courts of Justice
- Education
- General Laws
- Transportation
- Finance
- Appropriations
- Counties, Cities and Towns
- Commerce and Labor
- Health, Welfare and Institutions
- Agriculture, Chesapeake and Natural Resources
- Militia, Police and Public Safety
- Science and Technology
- Rules

These committees, for the most part, handle legislation that falls under the purview of their broad subject heading; although, as previously noted, they may receive other legislation if referred by the Speaker. The committee chairman is responsible for the panel's agenda and guiding it through its work.

Most of the standing committees in the House utilize subcommittees to further review and discuss legislation. The committee chairman may assign a bill to a subcommittee, made up of a portion of the panel's membership. Given the large volume of legislation and the short session length, committees and subcommittees are essential to prioritizing the work of the body. Any citizen can appear before a subcommittee or standing committee to speak as a proponent or opponent of legislation, which makes them an integral part of the legislative process.

Subcommittees cannot pass or defeat a bill. Their function is to recommend action to the full committee. The subcommittee has the option to amend the bill, recommend that it be reported, or recommend that the bill not receive further consideration. Recommendations of the subcommittee are

Members of the House of Delegates listen during a committee meeting. Photo courtesy of Michaele White, Office of the Governor.

reported back to the full committee for final action. Typically, the standing committees will not take action on bills without a subcommittee recommendation. But even if a subcommittee votes favorably or unfavorably on a piece of legislation, the power to report the bill to the floor or to defeat the measure rests with the membership of the full committee.

After receiving the report of the subcommittee, the committee acts on those recommendations, including consideration of any proposed amendments. Before taking final action, the full committee has the option to further amend the bill and vote on the action to be taken. Once the committee receives the subcommittee's report (its recommendation and any amendments), the committee may receive further testimony on the legislation from the patron and any other interested parties.

Pursuant to the Rules of the House, committees can act on legislation in any of the following ways:

- ➢ **Report**: The majority of the committee approves of the bill and it is reported to the floor for consideration by all the members of the House. The bill may be reported with or without amendment.
- ➢ **Refer**: The committee approves a motion to refer the bill to another committee for review; the second committee would then decide the fate of the legislation in the same manner (hearing the bill presented at a committee or subcommittee meeting and taking the recommended action) as the first panel.

➢ **Pass by Indefinitely (PBI)**: This is the most adverse of all the actions that a committee can take. The bill is passed by for an indefinite period of time—which essentially kills the bill.

➢ **Lay on the Table**:[19] The effect of this motion is similar to PBI; however, unlike a motion to PBI, there is no debate allowed and a vote is taken immediately. Whereas a vote to pass a bill by indefinitely is a definitive statement by the members that the legislation will receive no further consideration, a motion to lay a bill on the table means the bill remains with the clerk until brought back for further consideration. Even though the committee will typically have no intention of taking up the bill at a later date, a motion to lay on the table is considered a kinder and gentler way to defeat legislation.

➢ **Continue/Carry Over**: A bill introduced in an even-numbered year session may be continued or carried over to an odd-numbered year session for further action or study during the interim.

➢ **Pass by for the Day**: The committee is not ready to act on the bill and thus decides to delay action by passing the bill by until its next meeting. If the bill is not taken up before the deadline, then it is considered Left in Committee or No Action Taken.

➢ **Left in Committee or No Action Taken**: No motion is made on the bill and, as a result, it dies at the time of the deadline for committee action.

➢ **Incorporate into other Legislation**: The bill is incorporated or included in another measure through a substitute. The bill may have similar or duplicate language with the same intent. This is designed to reduce the number of bills addressing the same issue or perceived problem.

Senate Committees

There are 11 standing committees in the Senate:

- Agriculture, Conservation and Natural Resources
- Commerce and Labor
- Courts of Justice
- Education and Health
- Finance
- General Laws and Technology
- Local Government
- Privileges and Elections
- Rehabilitation and Social Services
- Transportation
- Rules

Every four years, at the beginning of a new term, the Senate elects committee members. At least 15 members are elected to each committee, which constitutes at least 40 percent of the Senate membership on each panel. The election is in the form of adopting a report presented by the majority party, which lists each committee and its members. The first senator listed is the chair of the respective committee. The Rules of the Senate state that each senator must serve on at least three and no more than four committees. In electing committee members, party, congressional district, geographic representation, and political philosophies are considered, as well as all applicable Senate Rules.

The Senate Committee on Rules is comprised of all committee chairs and establishes the committees' meeting schedules. The panels generally meet once or twice a week in the morning or afternoon, and their actions are an integral part of the legislative process. Committees make the decisions as to which legislation will be reported (or passed)—with or without amendments—and which will require no further action. Usually, committees only report about two-thirds of the legislation referred. This has the effect of reducing the number of bills considered on the Senate floor. The committee stage is also the only time in the legislative process when a citizen can directly address legislators who are deciding the fate of legislation. As in the House, committees have various options available to them for action when considering legislation.

The Senate Rules specify that each committee must take a recorded vote when it reports a bill to the floor of the Senate. A senator may vote Yea, Nay, or abstain from voting. Senators may abstain if they have a conflict of interest—that is, a financial gain or loss as a result of the legislative action.

It is sometimes unavoidable for senators to be absent from a committee meeting when a vote is taken. However, the Rules of the Senate establish that if a senator has answered to the roll call at the beginning of the meeting but has to depart prior to a vote, he may leave his voting proxy with another committee member. The senator is required to advise the committee chair of his intent to use a proxy. He also must complete a form designating the senator who will vote in his place and how the vote should be cast. The senator holding the proxy may then vote Yea, Nay, or abstain for the senator who left. The proxy vote would not be invalid should the senator return prior to the adjournment of the committee.

Virginia Senate Chamber. Photo by Bob Brown, *Richmond Times-Dispatch*.

Required Constitutional Readings of Bills

Article IV, Section 11 of the state Constitution establishes that bills must receive three readings in both the House and the Senate. These do not have to be literal readings; the Constitution has been amended so that having the bill's title read by the Clerk or printed in the daily calendar[20] suffices as a reading.

First Reading

In the house of origin, once a bill is reported from committee, it is placed on the daily calendar on First Reading. The First Reading of legislation is a procedural step that allows members who were not on the committee to know which legislation was reported and to prepare themselves for its consideration.

Uncontested and Regular Calendars

Both the House and Senate utilize Uncontested and Regular Calendars to handle legislation reported from committee more efficiently.

If the bill is reported from committee *without* a negative vote or abstention, it is placed on the Uncontested Calendar First Reading. If the bill is reported *with* a negative vote or abstention, then it is placed on the Regular Calendar First Reading. In the House, any member may object to the placement of a bill on the Uncontested Calendar and request that it be moved to the Regular Calendar for consideration. Once that bill is moved, it stays on the Regular Calendar.

In the Senate, a member may request that a bill be pulled from the uncontested block for individual consideration, but it is not physically moved from the Uncontested to the Regular Calendar.

The bills on the Uncontested Calendar are voted on *en bloc* (in a block) so that one vote records the action on all the bills in that category, whereas the bills on the Regular Calendar are voted on one at a time.

Second Reading

The second reading of a bill occurs the following session day and the bill is printed in the Calendar under the Second Reading heading.

In the House, the chief patron of the bill (the member who introduced the measure) will explain the bill to the membership of the House. Delegates may ask questions of the chief patron or speak for or against the measure at this time. In addition, the committee amendments, if any, will be explained and a motion made to adopt these amendments by voice vote. Once adopted, they then become part of the bill. Members may also wish to offer additional amendments from the floor, which must also be explained and voted on to be adopted. Like committee amendments, the adoption of floor amendments is by voice vote.

Once an explanation of the bill, consideration of amendments, and exhaustive debate have taken place, a motion to engross the bill

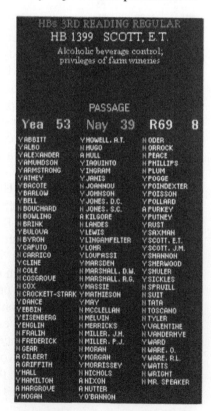

Image of the electronic voting board of a vote on the passage of a bill. Photo courtesy of the House Clerk's Office.

and pass it on to its Third Reading will be in order. This motion is acted on by voice vote and, if it fails, the bill is defeated.

A bill is "engrossed"—that is, prepared for final passage—when the amendments that were agreed to are incorporated into the original bill and the bill is reprinted in an engrossed form. This shows the amendments that have been adopted, which may include additional language or reflect stricken language. If there are no amendments, the bill as originally introduced is the engrossed bill version.

It is important to remember that under the state Constitution, one-fifth of the body may demand a recorded vote on any motion normally decided by a voice vote. This will sometimes occur on controversial amendments and on the motion to engross certain bills. A majority vote is all that is required to adopt or agree at this stage. A "division vote," or hand-count vote, may be requested by a single member on any motion or decision of the body.

In the Senate, Second Reading is when the Senate considers committee and floor amendments to legislation. On the Uncontested Calendar, bills are read by number, amendments are taken up and adopted or rejected, and then all of the legislation is advanced to Third Reading *en bloc*, just like in the House. On the Regular Calendar, each bill is read by its title, amendments are considered, and then each bill is advanced individually to the Third Reading. In both houses, when an amendment to a bill is not yet ready, that bill may be "passed by for the day" and taken up on a subsequent day.

Third Reading

Third Reading is the stage in which a bill's final version is presented and final passage is considered by the legislative body. In the House, the bills on the Uncontested Calendar of Third Reading are given their final reading by bill number, a single vote is taken for the bills *en bloc*, and the Speaker asks, "Shall the bills pass?" A recorded vote is taken and announced and a pronouncement made that the bills are passed. Each bill appearing on the Regular Calendar of Third Reading bills is read by its number, and unless any member desires to speak one more time either for or against (which is rarely done on Third Reading), the Speaker calls for the vote ("Shall the bill pass?"), and a pronouncement is made as to whether the bill passed or was defeated. Most—but not all—bills pass once they are considered on Third Reading.

In the Senate, bills on Uncontested Calendar Third Reading are also read by number and then passed in a group with one vote; however, a senator may ask that a bill be removed from the "bloc" so that it can be debated. Bills on Regular Calendar Third Reading are considered individually and debated before the Senate takes a recorded vote on the passage of the legislation.

When senators vote on a bill's passage, they may vote Yea, Nay, or may abstain—the same options as in committee. But on the Senate floor, a senator has another option. He may "pair" his vote with another senator who is not present. The Rules of the Senate provide for pairing and allow an absent senator to indicate his position on a bill. When the vote is taken, the "paired" senator attending the daily session will not cast a vote; however, prior to the closing of the vote, the senator will rise, and after being recognized by the presiding officer, will announce that he is pairing with the senator who is absent. He will state how each of them would have voted. Neither vote is counted in the vote totals, but the members' positions do appear in the record.

All legislation that passes must then "cross over" to the other chamber for deliberation there.

Consideration by the Second Body

In the second chamber, the bill goes through essentially the same procedure as it did in the house of origin, but the process is accelerated. The First Reading occurs when the bill is referred to committee. In committee, the bill is considered and reported by the members. (The committee may also choose not to report the bill.) The Second Reading occurs when the bill is reported from committee. On Third Reading, the second house hears the bill explained, considers any amendments from the committee or from the floor, and votes on the bill as communicated by the house of origin or as amended by the second house.

Capitol Police Officer Henry Gary lowers the state flag, indicating that lawmakers have finished their session for the day. Photo by Bob Brown, *Richmond Times-Dispatch.*

If lawmakers approve the bill without any changes by the second house, then the bill is prepared as enrolled legislation and is presented to the governor. If the second house agrees to amendments, then the bill is communicated back to the house of origin for its concurrence. If the house of origin agrees to the amendments, the bill is prepared as "enrolled" legislation—that is, printed as an enrolled bill, examined and signed by the presiding officer of each chamber, and presented to the governor.

If the house of origin rejects the second house's amendments, the rejection is communicated and the second house generally makes a motion to insist on its amendments and request a committee of conference. The two chambers' positions on the legislation have now reached the point of disagreement, thus initiating the conference committee process.

Conference Committee

The conference committee process is how lawmakers attempt to resolve the matters on which they disagree. If the House amends a Senate Bill, or the Senate amends a House Bill, and the house of origin disagrees with the amendment, a conference committee, comprised of usually three members from each house (with the exception of the budget bill, which often has five or six members appointed from each house), may be formed to resolve any differences.

The Speaker appoints all House conferees and is not bound by any rules regarding the makeup of the committee. In the Senate, however, the chairman of the committee of original jurisdiction (the first panel that heard the bill) appoints the Senate members to the conference committee. In addition, Senate Rules state that, if the bill going to conference is a Senate Bill, the chief patron of that bill must be appointed as a conferee. The Speaker will typically appoint the chief patron of a House Bill as a conferee, but is not compelled to do so.

If a majority of the members representing each house agrees to a conference report, each member signs the report, which also notes dissents (by conferees who do not support or agree to the conference report). The report is presented back to each house for consideration and a final recorded vote taken to adopt the conference report. If the report is adopted by both houses, the bill is passed and subsequently enrolled. If the report fails to be adopted in either house, the bill is defeated for that Session.

Executive Review and Governor's Options

Once a bill has passed both the House and the Senate in the same form, it is enrolled and signed by the presiding officers of each house. It is then ready to be presented to the governor for his review and action. Article V, Section 6 of the Constitution of Virginia provides that the governor must act within seven days of being presented the legislation if there are at least seven days remaining in the Session. If there are fewer than seven days left, the governor has 30 days to review the legislation. Most legislation falls under the 30-day executive legislative review period.

The governor has various options available to act on the legislation:

➢ The governor may sign the legislation into law.
➢ The governor may veto the legislation and, unless two-thirds of each body votes to override the governor's veto, the bill will fail.
➢ If the governor sends the bill back to the General Assembly with amendments, both the House and Senate must approve the amendments in order for them to be adopted. If either body does not approve the amendments, the bill then goes back to the governor in its original form for his final consideration. He can either sign the bill into law or veto it.
➢ If the first house agrees to only part of the recommendations and the second house agrees to the same, then only those recommendations agreed to by both bodies are incorporated into the bill. The bill is reenrolled and again presented to the governor for his action to either sign or veto.
➢ If both the House and Senate reject the amendments and support the bill as originally presented to the governor with a two-thirds majority vote in each house, the bill does not have to be returned to the governor and it becomes law in its originally passed form.

> The governor must submit amendments in a form that allows the General Assembly to consider each amendment individually, meaning that they are specific and "severable." If either house of the General Assembly determines that the governor's amendments are not specific and severable, the bill returns to the legislature in the form presented to the governor and may be considered as originally introduced.

> The governor may choose not to take any action on the legislation and the bill becomes law without his signature.

Bills that become law at a Regular Session are enacted on July 1 of that year, unless another date is specified in the bill. Bills passed during a Special Session become effective on the first day of the fourth month following adjournment *sine die* of that session. All bills enacted into law are assigned a chapter number. All chapters of a session are compiled and bound as the *Acts of Assembly,* and later the *Acts of Assembly* are incorporated into the Code of Virginia.

Conclusion

The modern General Assembly does not much resemble the Assembly that convened on Jamestown Island on July 30, 1619. The membership is larger, more diverse, and as a whole, better educated, but at its core the General Assembly remains a legislative body comprised of more or less average Virginians dedicated to bettering the lives of their fellow citizens.

In the nearly 400 years since that first session on Jamestown Island, the General Assembly has moved from Jamestown to Williamsburg, and during the American Revolution, from Williamsburg to Richmond. Since the General Assembly's move to Richmond, the legislature still occupies the State Capitol Building originally designed more than 200 years ago by our nation's third president, Thomas Jefferson, making it the second oldest working capitol in America. (The Annapolis, Maryland, statehouse is older, having been occupied since 1780.)

While the Commonwealth as a whole, and the General Assembly in particular, may bear little resemblance to the first Assembly that gathered in the choir box at Jamestown, many of the processes and procedures which guide the operations of the legislature still trace their origins back to that first session. The introduction of legislation, the readings of bills, the referral of bills to committee, and the keeping of a Journal are not dissimilar to what occurred more than 300 years ago. Today, the members of the House still elect one of their own to serve as Speaker and each legislative session still opens with a State of the Commonwealth address. The separation of powers between the legislative and executive branches of government has expanded and the Assembly has divided into a distinct House and Senate, but the basic process by which laws are made today is an enduring legacy of the one developed on Jamestown Island centuries ago.

Jeffrey A. Finch is the Deputy Clerk for Legislative Operations with the Virginia House of Delegates and has worked for the Virginia General Assembly since 1981. John McE. Garrett is the Chief Deputy Clerk of the Senate of Virginia and has worked in various capacities for the Commonwealth of Virginia since 1973. B. Scott Maddrea serves as Deputy Clerk of Committee Operations for the Virginia House of Delegates and has worked for the Virginia General Assembly since 1986.

CHAPTER 7
Virginia's Budget Process: Following the Money

By Vincent F. Callahan, Jr.
Former Delegate and Chairman, House of Delegates Appropriations Committee

Two of government's most essential functions are taxing and spending. Hence, Virginia governs on its pocketbook, a pocketbook fueled by revenues and expended by appropriations. This treatise will deal with the spending side.

Virginia's government has a long and colorful history, always funded by some type of financial process; therefore, the historical context should be addressed.

Founded in 1607 as a money-making scheme by capitalist investors, the first permanent English settlement in the "New World" at Jamestown in that vast British territory known as Virginia has evolved through a panorama of colonial government, insurrection, revolution, civil war, reconstruction, massive resistance, and—despite periodic economic crises—unprecedented prosperity in the latter part of the 20th century and into the 21st century.

The General Assembly of Virginia is the oldest legislative body in the Western Hemisphere, dating back to 1619. During this history, governors (colonial, confederate, and commonwealth) have come and gone, but the General Assembly has remained as an evolving institution that, in the final analysis, controls the purse strings of the state and hence the financial well-being of the Commonwealth.

The Virginia General Assembly traces its origins to the "Great Charter," fashioned in 1619 by the Virginia Company of London, the original entrepreneurs in the founding of Jamestown. The Charter led to the establishment in 1619 of what was to become the General Assembly.

The detailed disposition of public revenues, what we now label appropriations, were inaugurated in 1629 and, finally, in 1632, the right of taxation was assumed by the colonial assembly.[1] This taxing and spending apparatus, known in colonial Jamestown as the Committee on the Public Levy, became law, and has continued ever since, although in modern times the appropriations mechanism is separate from the taxation powers of the state.

The Business of Government

Virginia's government is now a very big business, with annual appropriations approaching $40 billion. All of these dollars are allocated by an elaborate process that has its roots in the Commonwealth's Constitution, which states in Article X, Section 7 that "[n]o money shall be paid out of the State treasury except in pursuance of appropriations made by law,"[2] and goes on to require that expenses shall not exceed revenues.

Unlike the federal government, Virginia's budget has to be balanced. As will be discussed later, the requirement of a balanced budget has had a profound effect on the appropriations process in Virginia, and on the health of the state as whole.

My personal experience with the General Assembly goes back more than 40 years, as I first took office in 1968. The General Assembly at that time was a mere shadow of its current organization. Two-party government was almost nonexistent. Republicans consisted of a mere corporal's guard of 14 members (out of 100). The overwhelming Democratic majority tolerated the members of the minority party, even socialized with them. But when it came to legislative matters the Republicans were effectively shut out. In my first year I was assigned to the grandly named Federal Relations Committee. It never met.

Prior to the adoption of the revised Constitution in 1971, with the exception of occasional special sessions, the General Assembly met only on even-numbered years. Support staff was extremely limited. Members had no offices and no aides. They operated out of hotel rooms and the only desks available were the ones assigned on the floor of the House and Senate. The entire General Assembly exuded a certain bygone-days allure; in fact, the Speaker of the House in 1968 was, believe it or not, the son of a Confederate officer who had served on the staff of Robert E. Lee. As a freshman Republican, I was designated to inform the Speaker that the following day, Abraham Lincoln's birthday, I was going to introduce a resolution that we adjourn in honor of the sixteenth president. The Speaker was somewhat chagrined, but being the Southern gentleman that he was, voiced no objection. The House ever since has adjourned in honor of President Lincoln on his birthday, noting, among other facts, that he preserved the Union—all done in the former capital of the Confederacy.

Prior to my taking office, Virginia operated on a "pay as you go" policy, meaning that there was no borrowing by the state and, therefore, no state debt. That changed in 1968 with the approval of the first state bond issue in modern history, designated for mental health and higher educational facilities.

With the constitutional revision in 1971, the ability of the commonwealth to borrow money was significantly expanded, although there are still constitutional limits to the debt that can be incurred in any budget cycle. The General Assembly has the authority to contract debt utilizing several mechanisms, including general obligation bonds requiring voter approval.

A sinking fund is required in the budget to amortize the payment of all debt incurred by the state. The General Assembly has consistently limited its borrowing to a level significantly below the permitted debt ceiling. All of these measures add to Virginia's maintenance of a healthy and responsible financial entity.

From Closed Doors to Openness

When I first arrived in Richmond, the two-year budget was $3 billion or $1.5 billion each year. (As previously noted, current annual spending is now in the neighborhood of $40 billion.) Until the 1980s, when the governor introduced the budget bill, it was referred only to the House Appropriations Committee. Nothing was introduced at that time in the Senate, and that body did not consider any budgetary items until the House had passed its version of the budget bill and sent it to the Senate.

I was appointed to the Appropriations Committee in 1972 and thus gained admission to this inner sanctum of the House of Delegates. It met behind closed doors in a windowless, smoke-filled top floor room in the Capitol building. Armed guards restricted access to committee members only. Other legislators and the general public were barred. Transparency was nonexistent. While there was an Appropriations Committee Chairman, the whole operation was run by the governor's budget director. Separation of powers was, in essence, ignored.

House "consideration" of the budget bill at that time consisted of rubber-stamping whatever the governor wanted, and very few substantive alterations were made by the committee. Amendments on the floor of the General Assembly were not even considered. The bill always passed with an overwhelming "aye" vote, with very little debate. The bill then went to the Senate, which followed suit.

Beginning in the 1970s, things began to change. Those changes resulted from the growth of a meaningful two-party system in Virginia, including the election of the first Republican governor since Reconstruction. There was a general movement towards more open government, and increased realization, fueled by pragmatic political considerations, that the legislative and executive branches were indeed distinct and should function as such.

New quarters and increased staffing for the General Assembly played a leading role in the emerging independence of the legislative branch. The Appropriations Committee structure was expanded and solidified, with both the House Appropriations Committee and, later, its Senate Finance Committee counterpart, employing highly professional permanent staffs, completely independent of executive interference—or "meddling," as we liked to call it.

An important segment of the growing strength of the legislative branch of state government is General Assembly oversight of the expenditure of legislatively appropriated funds by the executive branch. This is the watchdog function of the Joint Legislative Audit and Review Commission (JLARC), a House-Senate body that is similar to the U.S. General Accounting Office, a congressional oversight body of the federal executive branch. I was a charter member of JLARC when it was established in 1973 and thereby involved in more than 350 studies, directed at insuring that legislative mandates are properly implemented by the executive branch. An example of JLARC'S significance was a study that led to a landmark revision of the manner in which state funds are allocated to Virginia's 132 local public school districts. JLARC has been nationally recognized for its major accomplishments in the husbanding of public monies.

FIGURE 1: Where the money comes from—General Fund:[3]

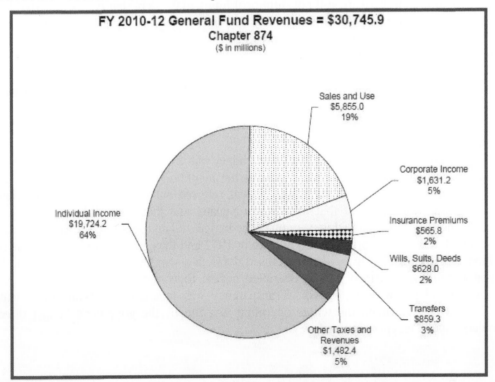

The Budget's Route

The Commonwealth of Virginia has an executive budget; that is, it originates in the office of the governor. That budget is divided into two parts: the general fund and the nongeneral fund. The former is derived primarily from state taxes.

The nongeneral fund, which is slightly larger than the general fund, is composed of dedicated revenues such as state and federal highway funds and Medicaid. As the term implies, dedicated revenues received by the state must be spent in accordance with federal and state program-specific statutory requirements.

FIGURE 2: Where the money comes from—Nongeneral Fund:[4]

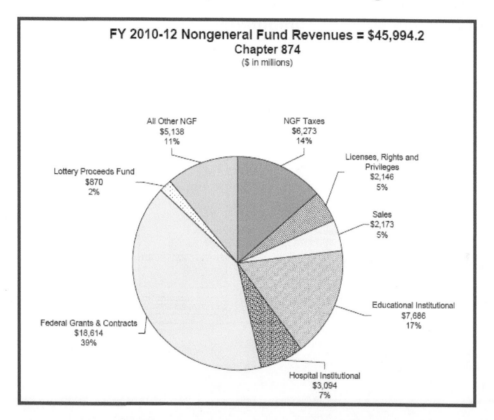

Another factor affecting the budgetary process is the proliferation of federal mandates—spending that the state must match due to legislation by the U.S. Congress. The classic example is Medicaid, a budget item that includes federal nongeneral fund money that must be matched by state general funds. When I first took office, Medicaid was virtually nonexistent as a budget item. It is now more than $5 billion per year, of which approximately one-half is an obligation of the state, required by the federal government but not reimbursed by any funding.

The biennial budget process begins when the governor proposes the budget, utilizing revenue forecasts developed by the executive office. It is introduced in the General Assembly, which has the authority to revise it, provided always that proposed expenditures do not exceed anticipated revenues.

It is important to bear in mind that budget proposals, as well as revenue forecasts, are initially long-term forecasts and always an uncertain process. For instance, work on the two-year budget proposed for the fiscal years beginning on July 1, 2010, was accompanied by revenue forecasting, initiated as early as the summer of 2009. As a result, the budget process involves a certain amount of guesswork and resulting uncertainty as to the amount of revenue the state will take in, together with the needs of the state government itself—a very complicated task for budget forecasters.

Both the executive and legislative budget-makers in Virginia have traditionally adhered to a conservative and cautionary approach to spending the state's revenues. Nevertheless, on occasions when revenue forecasting is inaccurately predicted due to unexpected adverse economic circumstances, draconian cuts to the state budget become necessary.

FIGURE 3: All revenue sources combined:[5]

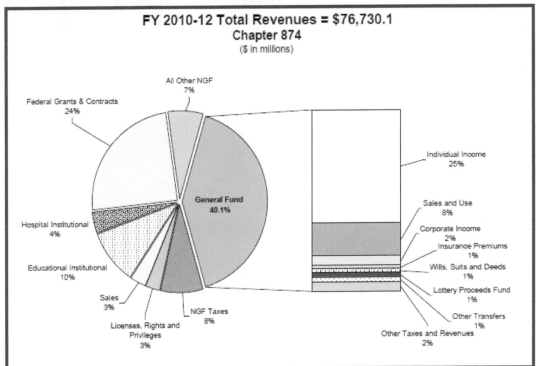

Unlike the U.S. Congress, the Virginia General Assembly does not have a revenue forecasting agency such as the Congressional Budget Office. Virginia legislators must rely on figures emanating from the office of the governor. In times of economic upheaval, they are often inaccurate, sometimes on the positive side but in the recent past on the negative side of the ledger, resulting in reductions of previously appropriated revenues. If anticipated revenues do not materialize to appropriated levels, cuts have to be made by the governor when the legislature is not in session and by the General Assembly when it is. These cuts are controversial and painful. Citizens expect a certain level of state services, and when they are reduced, those who hold elective office are held accountable.

Following a severe recession in the early 1990s, the ever-cautious General Assembly decided that the Commonwealth needed a savings account. Virginia's Constitution was amended in 1992 to require that funds must be set aside in the Revenue Stabilization Fund, commonly known as the "Rainy Day Fund." The Rainy Day Fund, as specified in Section X, Article 8, was funded by an amount of state revenues not to exceed 10 percent of the commonwealth's average annual tax revenues derived from taxes on income and retail sales. In 2010, the amount was raised to 15 percent of those annual revenues through voter approval of a state constitutional amendment. During good economic times, this Rainy Day Fund has exceeded $1 billion, but in adverse times it is drawn down, within constitutional limits, to help alleviate cuts in expenditures.

Virginia's budget is a biennial document, embracing the period beginning on July 1st of even-numbered years, and expiring two years later. It is revised and updated in odd-numbered years during the General Assembly's short 46-day session.

The budget is introduced by the governor in mid-December prior to the convening of the 60-day legislative session in January. This December introduction is a relatively recent innovation and is designed to give the General Assembly and the public more time to scrutinize its contents. Accompanying the new biennial budget is the so-called "caboose" bill, to tie up loose ends for the remaining six months of the existing budget.

In the early 1980s, in a highly controversial move, the Virginia Senate successfully sought to be involved earlier in the budgetary process previously initiated by the House. Now, identical budgets are introduced by the governor in both the House and Senate, although when final passage is considered, the Senate bill is shelved and the House bill becomes the only vehicle.

In the House, the Finance Committee considers legislation that involves taxes and the Appropriations Committee deliberates the spending side of the equation. But in the Senate, the Finance Committee addresses both taxing and spending measures.

During the deliberations on the budget, the House and Senate operate independently of each other, and the governor has minimal involvement.

Both bodies of the General Assembly consider the bill, traditionally initiating substantial revisions, passing their respective versions in time for those provisions to take effect at the beginning of the new fiscal year.

FIGURE 4: How the money is *spent*:[6]

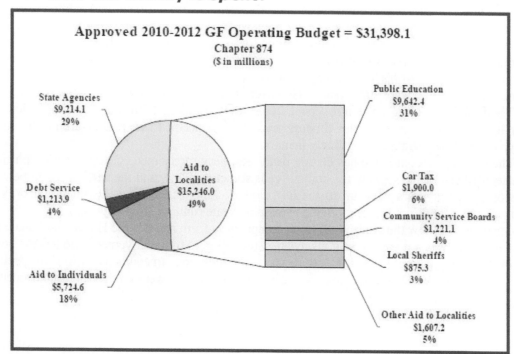

The money committees operate within narrow self-imposed deadlines, with subcommittees addressing individual areas of state expenditures, such as health and human resources, commerce and trade, the judiciary, agriculture, education, and public safety, among others. Public hearings are held before and at the beginning of each session. Critics have called the public hearings mere window dressing—an allegation that has some substance.

Amendments to the budget can be introduced by both the governor and members of the General Assembly, including those who are not members of either the House Appropriations or Senate Finance Committees. By current rules, such amendments may be pre-filed prior to the opening of the legislative session, but must be submitted by the end of the first week of the session.

All amendments are considered in the pertinent subcommittees. The proliferation of appropriations subcommittees are of relatively recent origin, and when first created were initially notorious for sometimes meeting without notice to the public. The subcommittees may consider and approve, defeat, or table budget items, including proposed amendments. At present, however, committee rules require posting times and dates of all subcommittee meetings, and all meetings are held in public.

About midway through the session, the two chambers complete work on bills originating in their respective bodies, and bills that pass are sent to the other chamber—the appropriations bill among them. This is known as "crossover."

The budget bills are the last measures taken up prior to crossover. Heavily amended, the House and Senate bills are subject to further floor amendments on their respective plans. Floor amendments of any substance invariably fail, and the budget bill has always passed, usually with lopsided votes in favor. In recent years, however, increased partisanship has resulted in closer vote margins.

When the competing budget bills reach the opposite chamber, they are referred to committee—the House bill to the Senate Finance Committee and the Senate bill to the House Appropriations Committees. The two committees summarily reject the other body's bill, resulting in both bills being referred to a joint House-Senate conference committee.

The conference committee is made up of senior members of both "money committees," with representation of both political parties, charged with producing a compromise budget before the session adjourns. This it eventually accomplishes, usually after confrontational and contentious meetings, characterized with posturing and maneuvering somewhat akin to a poker game. The Senate and the House both hold firmly to their respective positions for as long as possible. In one memorable meeting, the chairmen of the respective House and Senate committees almost came to fisticuffs, pitting a tough-as-nails former Marine against his Tidewater aristocratic counterpart. Cooler heads prevailed, although not before the Capitol Police were summoned. However, something has to give, and the final product is a result of both sides yielding on controversial items, thus enabling both sides to claim victory. The governor has little involvement in this process, except on occasion to exert pressure on the conference committee to finish deliberations in a timely manner.

The conference committee has certain deadlines, very rarely met. Charged with reporting a bill by the scheduled end of the session, the committee is sometimes late, and the session has to be extended. One session in recent years went up to the last days of June, threatening the shutdown of Virginia's government should funds not be appropriated to keep the state running after July 1st.

Once the bill (now the House bill) in its compromise form reaches the House and Senate floors, a final vote is taken. When it passes, as it always has, the bill goes to the governor, who has the power of a line-item veto. The governor has the opportunity to offer additional amendments or to veto specific items at a Reconvened or "Veto" Session that convenes six and a half weeks after the adjournment of the regular session.   Only after this process is concluded and the bill is signed by the governor, usually in April of each year, is the budget then in place for the next fiscal year.

Both houses have the option to accept or reject the amendments. These final amendments, usually minor in nature (with some notable exceptions), do not jeopardize the final passage, and the bill, with or without gubernatorial amendments, goes back to the governor's desk for approval.

The budget conferees negotiate, from left, Sen. R. Edward Houck (D-Spotsylvania), Senate Finance Committee Chairman Sen. Charles J. Colgan (D-Prince William), House Appropriations Chairman Del. Lacey Putney (I-Bedford), and Del. Phil Hamilton (R-Newport News) in February, 2009. Photo by Bob Brown, *Richmond Times-Dispatch.*

This has been a brief account of how the Virginia appropriations process works. But there is more to it than the broad outline of introduction, public hearings, amendments, floor action, House/Senate conferences, and the final goal of a gubernatorial signature.

The process works. Virginia's financial administration has been nationally recognized as the best in the United States, with accolades for fiscal integrity that are without peer among the 50 states. Virginia annually receives the coveted AAA bond rating, awarded by Wall Street rating agencies, which has a dramatic effect on low-cost borrowing capacity. Virginia is one of only a handful of states to consistently achieve this rating, dating back to the 1930s. In addition to being cited as the best fiscally-managed state in the U.S., Virginia has also been recognized by national publications as the best place to educate children and the most business-friendly state in the U.S.

All of these accomplishments are attributable to the solid foundation of responsible legislative budgeting, a tradition that the United States Congress, both House and Senate, could well emulate.

Vincent F. Callahan, Jr., represented Fairfax County in the House of Delegates from 1968 to 2008, and was a member of the Appropriations Committee from 1972 to 2008, Co-Chairman from 1998 to 2002, and Chairman from 2002-2008. He was also a member of JLARC from 1973 to 2008 and Chairman from 2000-2002.

CHAPTER 8

A Lady's Place is in the House (of Delegates): Virginia Women and Politics, 1909-2009

By Sandra G. Treadway
Librarian of Virginia

Virginia women were rather late in the game in creating an organized movement on behalf of woman suffrage—at least, compared to their counterparts in many other states. The woman suffrage movement in the United States traces its roots back to a women's rights convention held in Seneca Falls, New York, in 1848, although it was not until 1869 that national organizations dedicated to publicly promoting women's right to vote were established. Richmonder Anna Whitehead Bodeker tried to get others in the city interested in the cause in the early 1870s and sponsored appearances by prominent suffrage speakers such as Susan B. Anthony and Paulina Wright Davis. Only a few brave souls supported her efforts, though, as in the aftermath of the Civil War woman suffrage was seen by most in the South as part of the Reconstruction agenda being forced on the southern states by Radical Republicans in the North.[1]

The tide of opinion was slowly turning in Virginia, however, and by 1909 when the Equal Suffrage League was founded by a group of well-connected women in Richmond—many of whom had been born or come of age in the New South, not the Old—the movement finally gained traction and spread to cities and even rural communities across the Commonwealth. The Equal Suffrage League launched a full-court-press on Virginia's political establishment, intensifying the campaign with members of the General Assembly in 1919—the year Congress passed the Nineteenth Amendment to the U.S. Constitution and sent it to the states for ratification. Virginia women won the right to vote a year later in 1920 when all American women did, when the Nineteenth Amendment received the required approval of 36 states and became the law of the land. Virginia's General Assembly did not go on the record supporting the Nineteenth Amendment until 1952.[2]

Running for public office was *not* the first priority for Virginia women following passage of the Nineteenth Amendment, even though logically one might think it would be. With lightning speed, the Equal Suffrage League changed its name and transformed itself into the League of Women Voters and immediately set about encouraging women across Virginia to register to vote. The League also launched a campaign to educate women on the workings of government and the responsibilities of citizenship. The League was highly successful as Virginia women, even those who had been opposed to woman suffrage, did turn out and register to vote in large numbers. And as members of clubs and organizations that had long sought societal improvements and government reform, Virginia women were energized not only to vote but to lobby local and state governments on behalf of reform issues. These were issues that they were proud to argue for and support from a woman's perspective. Groups such as the Virginia Federation of Woman's Clubs and numerous others quickly developed new advocacy techniques that proved extremely effective in capturing the attention of elected officials. Virginia women discovered, as suffragists had argued all along would be the case, that the ability to vote did make a difference.[3]

To a remarkable degree, organized women now armed with the vote followed through on the promises that the suffragists had made—among them promises to expand the electorate, work for peace, make government more accountable, and protect the most vulnerable and needy in society. In the 1920s and 30s, Virginia women saw tangible results in terms of new legislation on issues that mattered to them: public welfare, the regulation of child labor, education, and equalization of property rights, to name only a few key concerns. Thus, it is no surprise that this is where women's organizations decided to concentrate their efforts. They perfected the art of lobbying the legislature for change, and slowly but surely reform happened. For many that was enough. That was what they wanted most from the franchise.[4]

The Trailblazers

Still, while this was the approach the majority of politically active Virginia women opted to follow after passage of the Nineteenth Amendment, there were those who wanted more—and it is these women whom this chapter will highlight. There were women who wanted to get inside the decision-making process, to have a seat not just in the gallery but on the floor of the General Assembly. They wanted this badly enough that they were willing to put themselves forward as candidates. While they were very few in number, they are worth knowing about and worth remembering for their legacy that continues to echo in the halls of the State Capitol Building designed by Thomas Jefferson even today.

The women who first entered the political fray in Virginia were not the individuals that anyone familiar with Virginia women of this period might expect to have done so. They were not the most prominent civic or club women nor were they among the leadership of the suffrage movement, many of whom had the connections and experience that might have prompted them to consider running for office.

Voters in two Virginia localities were willing to take a chance on women who downplayed gender associations. Following the general election in November, 1923, Sarah Lee Fain, from the Tidewater city of Norfolk, and Helen Timmons Henderson, from the opposite corner of the state in far southwestern Virginia, found that they had earned the distinction of being the first women elected to the Virginia General Assembly.

As one would expect, Fain and Henderson found themselves in the spotlight from the moment they arrived in the state capital in January, 1924. The newspapers covered their presence both as news and on the society page, and both women handled the publicity well. When

Dels. Sarah Lee Fain and Helen Timmons Henderson. Photos courtesy of the Library of Virginia.

interviewed, they stressed how seriously they took their legislative responsibilities. They downplayed the historic aspects of their election and emphasized their commitment to representing the needs and interests of their constituents. Never once did they identify themselves with what might be perceived as "women's issues" or suggest that they brought a woman's agenda to the legislative process.[5]

Fain easily won reelection in 1925, becoming the first woman legislator in the South elected to a second term, and served in the House of Delegates through 1929. She decided not to run that year in order to prepare herself for a bigger challenge. She ran for the House of Representatives in Congress in 1930, and although her campaign received a good deal of attention, she was handily defeated.[6]

Fain's legislative colleague, Helen Timmons Henderson, had died in the summer of 1925, but Fain was joined in the House in the 1926-27 session by Sallie Cook Booker, of Henry County. Booker served two terms in the House of Delegates, winning handily in 1925 but only narrowly defeating a challenger for her second term who made gender an issue and asserted repeatedly that service in the Assembly was properly a man's job. In her early seventies by 1929, Booker opted not to run again.[7]

Still, for a short while, it appeared that women's presence might be on the rise in the Assembly. In the 1928-1929 session, the number of women doubled to four. Joining Fain and Booker were Nancy Melvina Caldwell, of Galax, in southwestern Carroll County, and Helen Ruth Henderson, whose mother had served in the Assembly in 1924.[8]

When asked about their history-making role, these women exhibited pride in being among the first to open the legislature's doors for other women, but they were uncomfortable talking about or identifying themselves in any way with what might be perceived as a women's agenda. They listened to but gave no special attention to representatives of the women's organizations that lobbied them and their male colleagues heavily throughout the 1920s and 1930s—and endorsement or support from women's groups was not a critical factor in any of their elections. And other than Sarah Fain, none of these women saw their involvement in politics as anything more than a short-term commitment.

But any hopes that women's presence in the Virginia legislature would continue to rise were quickly dashed. Thirty-six more years would pass before four women would sit in the Virginia House of Delegates again at the same time.[9]

A New Generation

Virginia women continued to serve on local and state Democratic committees and to represent the Commonwealth on the party's national committee in the 1930s and 40s. Between 1933 and 1954, however, they were completely absent from the state Assembly's rolls. By the 1950s, though, a new generation—women who had been born in the twentieth century and come of age after 1920—emerged on Virginia's political scene. Well-educated and hailing by and large from the state's rapidly growing urban areas—particularly in northern Virginia, a short distance from the nation's capital—these women differed markedly from the earlier generation of women legislators. Most were not native Virginians, and they brought to Virginia politics perspectives nurtured in other parts of the country. They were also comfortable acknowledging that as women they had a point of view that had often been ignored by the state's male leaders and that needed to be heard. And these ladies most definitely had an activist agenda.

The first of this second wave of women legislators was Kathryn H. Stone of Arlington. She won her bid and took her seat in January, 1954. When Virginia formulated its Massive Resistance strategy in response to the landmark *Brown vs. Board of Education* U.S. Supreme Court decision, Stone staunchly opposed this course and fought to keep as many of the state's public schools open as possible by advocating local option rather than blanket disregard of the Constitution.[10]

Women legislative candidates in other parts of the state also achieved noteworthy success. Kathryn Stone served her first two terms in the House alone, but in 1958, Inez Baker from Portsmouth joined Stone in Richmond. Also elected that same year was Charlotte Giesen, who worked for the Radford newspaper and had served for several years on the Radford City Council. The first Republican woman elected to the Assembly, Giesen held views that were very similar to Stone's. She supported integration of the state's public schools, abolition of the poll tax, more open elections, stronger compulsory education laws, and better funding for public education. Giesen stood successfully for election twice, then was defeated in her bid for a third term by a slim 125 votes.[11]

Del. Charlotte Giesen. Photo courtesy of the Library of Virginia.

The times were a-changing, though, and in the 1960s, two women who would have a profound impact on modern Virginia—both sent from districts in the northeastern part of the state and both passionately committed to women's rights—arrived at the State Capitol.

Dorothy S. McDiarmid represented Fairfax County. Among her early accomplishments was the championing and securing of funding for statewide kindergarten programs. Her legislative agenda widened over time as she gained her legislative footing. To advance that agenda, McDiarmid knew that organization and strategy would be the keys, and as the number of women in the Assembly increased in the 1970s and 80s she reached out to her female colleagues, asking them to join together to support bills that mattered to women, ranging from the equitable distribution of property in divorces to the controversial Equal Rights Amendment. She was the first woman named to the powerful Rules Committee, and before her career concluded, she came to chair the most prized committee of all: House Appropriations.[12]

Mary Marshall of Arlington joined McDiarmid in the House in 1966. A strong proponent of civil and women's rights, Marshall joined with McDiarmid to make a formidable team that their male colleagues in the Assembly simply could not ignore.[13]

Given the gains that women had made in the lower house of the Assembly, it was only a matter of time before a woman would run successfully for a seat in the State Senate. And in 1979, Republican Eva Scott did just that. Scott had begun her political career eight years earlier, running for the House as an Independent in her home county of Amelia. A pharmacist with strong conservative leanings, she served in the House through 1979, joining the Republican Party prior to her Senate bid. Scott's positions were distinctly different from those of the other women then serving in the Assembly. She was a strong proponent of local autonomy and an adamant opponent both of regional government and of the increased control over education given to the state under the Constitution of 1971. She was also the only woman in the General Assembly to vote against the Equal Rights Amendment in the ten years that it was under consideration.[14]

Strength in Numbers

The number of women in the General Assembly continued to rise in the 1990s. Depending on the year, there were regularly 14 to 15 women sitting in the House, and although there were no women in the Senate between 1983 and 1988, there were two to three in the Senate at the same time throughout the 1990s.

Attorney General Mary Sue Terry. Photo courtesy of the Library of Virginia.

Service in the Assembly became an important stepping stone to higher office for several of these women. Mary Sue Terry of Patrick County, for example, who served in the House from 1978 through 1985, later became the first woman to run successfully for attorney general. She served as attorney general for two consecutive terms. (In 1993, she also became the first woman to run for governor—although unsuccessfully.) Leslie Byrne, who represented Fairfax from 1986 through 1992, left the House to run for Congress, and has the distinction of being the first woman member of Virginia's congressional delegation.[15]

The color barrier for women would not be broken until 1984 with the election of Norfolk's Yvonne Miller. Miller had grown up in North Carolina and came to Virginia to attend Virginia State College (now University) in Petersburg. Miller served two terms in the House then, in 1987, ran for the 5th district State Senate seat that she still holds today. She is currently one of the most influential members of the General Assembly, fourth in seniority in the State Senate. Since her election, two other African-American women have joined her in the Senate, representing the nearby Tidewater cities of Hampton and Portsmouth.

Twenty-five women served in the 2010 session of the General Assembly, eight in the Senate, and 17 in the House of Delegates, an increase of two from the 2009 session. Until 2008, the House numbers had remained fairly static, but slowly the number of women delegates has been growing. The increase in the number of women senators has been more dramatic and the leadership of the Democratically-controlled body has taken note. Seven of the Senate's eight women were selected in 2008 to chair some of the Senate's most important committees, among them the Committees on Rules, Privileges and Elections, Transportation, and Local Government. The Senate's Democratic Caucus was also chaired by a woman, and for the first time a woman was appointed to the select group of senators who serve on the powerful conference committee that negotiates frantically into the final hours of the Assembly session to resolve the differences between the House and Senate versions of the state budget.[16]

Sen. Yvonne Miller. Photo courtesy of the Library of Virginia.

Despite the impressive progress that women have made in the Assembly since Sarah Lee Fain and Helen Timmons Henderson first took their seats on the floor, the sobering reality is that Virginia does not stack up well against most of her sister states. While women now comprise 19 percent of the Assembly's membership (up from 10 percent in 1988), Virginia ranks 38th in the nation in terms of women's representation in the statehouse.[17] Virginians do not like being in the lowest tier on anything, but this statistic is often overlooked. Recent governors have tried to enhance women's presence in government by naming women to key positions within their Cabinets.

If you ask some of the longtime Assembly members, they will tell you that they have made a difference in several key areas as women. Sen. Janet Howell believes that the Assembly's willingness to look closely at issues relating to domestic violence and women's health stems directly from pressure brought to bear by women legislators. She also recently commented that she regularly receives calls from women who live outside her district who feel that their own representative will not take them seriously. Yvonne Miller shares this view and has publicly said that the women she has worked with in the Assembly have been much more willing to listen, to find solutions to problems, and to identify resources to meet needs without resorting to grandstanding or to polemics.[18]

The story is still unfolding. The point at which women's presence in government is no longer regarded as news is not yet known. The story that began with the founding of the Equal Suffrage League in 1909 can indeed tell us something important about women and political power in the twenty-first century. Although women may not be where they would like to be in Virginia's political life quite yet, one suspects that the ladies who met in Mrs. Crenshaw's parlor more than one hundred years ago to launch the League would still be very pleased.

Sandra Gioia Treadway has served as director of the Library of Virginia since 2007. She is co-editor of several volumes on Virginia and women's history topics and the author of "Women of Mark: A History of the Woman's Club of Richmond, Virginia, 1894-1994." She serves on several state boards, commissions, and advisory groups and is past president of the Southern Association of Women Historians.

CHAPTER 9
From the Front Lines:
Virginia's Longest-Serving Delegate

By Anne Marie Morgan
State Capitol Correspondent and Bureau Chief

Delegate Lacey E. Putney is living history. Not only has the quintessential Southern gentleman experienced the General Assembly's modernization firsthand during the last half-century, but he can recount those changes in colorful detail, providing insight into the ways Virginia has been governed in both the past and the present.

Putney has served in the House of Delegates representing Bedford County and nearby areas for 50 years. He may, in fact, hold the record as the longest-serving delegate in Virginia's history. At the time of his first election, the General Assembly was a staid, tradition-bound body of politically disciplined Southern Democrats—many of whom were members of the political organization headed by Sen. Harry F. Byrd, Sr. "When I arrived here in 1962, there were 95 of us in the Democrat caucus, and five in the Republican caucus," said Putney.

But in 1967, after a probing conversation with a local party leader about which Democratic candidates he would endorse, Putney came face-to-face with party discipline: He was told he would not receive the Democratic imprimatur to run for re-election. The delegate, however, was undeterred. "You can take these papers, and do whatever you wish. I am going to run," Putney retorted. "I ran as an Independent and have done so ever since." In retrospect, his declaration of independence was emblematic of the General Assembly's gradual shift away from one-party dominance. Other significant changes were also on the horizon.

Photo courtesy of Lacey Putney.

Putney explained that until the latest revision of Virginia's Constitution was implemented in 1971, the General Assembly was even more part-time than the citizen legislature it is today. "We used to meet every two years, and our salary was 1800 dollars for the two-year term. There were no offices, there was no such thing as a computer, and the term legislative aide had not been invented. There was one secretary for each Congressional district, and if you could find the secretary, you may get a letter done once every week or two," he laughed. Today, state lawmakers have their own private offices, allowances, legislative assistants, and receptionists. Communications between lawmakers and others are prolific and virtually instantaneous through e-mails, iPads, and Blackberries. Constituents can call a designated hotline to express their positions on any matter to any delegate or senator. The clerk's offices and legislative agencies employ full-time professional staffs who work on Capitol Square year-round.

During his early years in the General Assembly, fewer bills were introduced and there was less transparency throughout the lawmaking process. Putney noted that unlike today, when a bill can be postponed for consideration until the next session, "there was no such thing as carryover legislation, which was made possible by the sweeping constitutional amendments that took place in 1971. A bill that was not favorably approved was dead. There were very limited records of what took place in committees and subcommittees compared to today when there is a track record," he said. Not only do the records exist today, but the schedules, calendars, actual legislation, and legislative histories are all accessible to state officials and the public through the on-line Legislative Information System, and the votes of delegates and senators on bills can be retrieved almost as soon as they are cast. In recent years, the General Assembly's daily sessions have been streamed live on the Internet.

As the legislature—and state government in general—began to assume more responsibilities in the 1960s, many Virginia officials started to wonder whether the business of the Commonwealth could be done without yearly General Assembly sessions. "To me, annual sessions are number one on the list of the greatest, significant changes that took place in those years," Putney declared. The yearly sessions were authorized by the revised Constitution and instituted when the latter took effect. The volume of legislation introduced by lawmakers increased substantially, and the leisurely pace grew more frenetic. In fact, delegates and senators collectively began to introduce thousands of bills each year that addressed a large array of causes. Many were serious, substantive measures, while others were not. But lawmakers also found that even if some had no chance of passing, these "brochure bills" could nevertheless be prominently featured in political campaign literature. Because of the towering stacks of legislation on many committee dockets, "we definitely have more subcommittees today and many of them start much earlier," said Putney. The General Assembly sessions in odd years that were 30 days long were eventually extended to 46 days, and that has been the annual practice ever since.

For many years, it was the norm for Speakers of the House and committee chairmen to run tight ships. Speakers would assign bills they did not like to unfriendly committees, while chairmen would exercise a prerogative to ignore bills or send measures they eschewed to subcommittees that never met. "I'm not sure that we thought of it as chairmen having a lot of power, but obviously they did," Putney observed. Initially, the handful of Republicans in the General Assembly had little to do because they were not assigned to any meaningful committees. "A number of them walked the halls while the rest of us were working and bogged down with work we had to do in the committees," he said. When the GOP's numbers grew, Democratic leaders of that era made sure that Republicans did not receive much credit. Putney recounted one former Speaker's admission to the press that "of course, they were not going to let a Republican get a good bill through. Instead, they would take the idea and put a Democrat on as the chief patron."

Del. Lacey Putney gives a speech on the state budget during a floor session of the House of Delegates. Photo courtesy of Lacey Putney.

Several Senate Finance Committee chairmen, in particular, were legendary in wielding power. Sen. Edward E. Willey, who served through the early 1980s, and Sen. Hunter B. Andrews, who succeeded him until the mid-1990s, "ran their committees with an iron hand," said Putney. "There was never going to be a subcommittee structure under those chairmen that would weaken their control on the committee."

But creative legislators could occasionally circumvent the restrictive rule of the chairmen. Putney recounts how Del. Leslie Byrne's proposal to require trucks to cover their loads on highways continually met a roadblock in committee. However, an opportunity arose on the floor of the full House of Delegates to attach her provision to a highway bill that addressed a different subject. As a general rule, members of the General Assembly did not—and still do not—like to attach assorted amendments to legislation because the bill could become so laden with provisions that it strays from its initial purpose or "clutters" the Code of Virginia. Even today, lawmakers call that "a Christmas tree" (adorned with amendments), deriding it as a practice used by the U.S. Congress—and *not* by Virginians. But Byrne made a motion to attach her amendment on covered trucks to the legislation. Speaker A.L. Philpott subsequently ruled that it was "germane"—that is, was sufficiently relevant and could be attached. As Putney and his seatmate lamented that "germaneness as we knew it was dead," the full House agreed to the amendment and the bill eventually became law.

The absence of open government in the 1960s and 1970s was especially evident during budget-related meetings, when an armed Capitol Police Officer was posted at the door of the Appropriations Committee. "Members of the Committee, including myself, were not permitted in the room because the decision-making was done by a five-member executive subcommittee," Putney explained. "And when they decided that we lesser lights might want to come in and learn a little bit, they would open the door. There were times when we were all there, but when many of the key decisions were being made, they were made by the five-member executive subcommittee, and others of us were told about it later." The budget conferees sometimes could not be located on Capitol Square. It was not unusual for them to travel to a remote cabin owned by one of them in order to discuss money matters away from the prying eyes of the public, reporters, and other legislators. "Today, as far as I know, everything is done in the sunshine and everybody is permitted to be in on every subcommittee," Putney added. That includes the negotiations of the budget conferees. But sometimes, when a matter is particularly sensitive, the staffs of the Senate Finance and House Appropriations Committees carry notes with offers and counteroffers from one chamber's conferees to their counterparts that will not be read by reporters or other observers.

The lack of transparency in the earlier years of Putney's service as a delegate was also on display during interviews of prospective judges that were conducted by members of the House and Senate Courts of Justice Committees. Once the interviews or votes began, a Capitol Police Officer often would stand guard at the doors of the committee room to prevent anyone from entering. Judges of that era had broad appointive powers such as selecting school board members. "Because of the political power and influence of a judge, choosing between competing candidates for a judgeship could bring a lot of emotional debate to the forefront and put more pressure on members of the General Assembly than we see today," said Putney. "That's because today, the judge is limited primarily to the judicial branch of government—which is the way I think it ought to be."

For years, the House Courts of Justice Committee employed a unique strategy to dispatch legislation that had piled up. The panel held marathon, late meetings on Sunday nights when the members would delay considering dozens of measures and unpopular bills until the early morning hours. Frequently, the tedium would wear out the bills' supporters and journalists, who would yawn, grow increasingly tired, and go home. Because the panel had to meet deadlines to finish its deliberations, many bills were not mentioned at all or were killed outright with few eyewitnesses present. "That was a routine practice then," Putney observed. The yearly ritual was given the well-deserved sobriquet of "Night of the Long Knives."

A prominent stereotype of politicians of the previous era was that they huddled together to conduct their business in smoke-filled rooms. But that was literally true. Cigarette and pipe smoke were ubiquitous, turning the air in the House and Senate chambers into a light gray fog. That changed after passage of the Virginia Clean Indoor Air Act in 1990.

Putney is wistful when he speaks about the camaraderie that was the norm during his early time in the legislature. The current 9th Street Office Building was the Hotel Richmond, and most of those who lived some distance from the city of Richmond stayed there. "Our families came to know each other. We would chat in the lobby of the hotel at the end of the day and had a pretty good account of what each chamber did that day. It was not unusual for four or five couples or more to walk, and there were a lot of good restaurants around the corner," said Putney. "It was more of a family-type gathering, and when the vast majority of members were in the same party, I guess you could expect more of that."

Not everyone agreed on all legislation, but Putney said "we got along beautifully." He recounted how the head of the AFL-CIO knew which lawmakers would never vote to weaken the right-to-work law: "But we went to dinner together, we enjoyed the relationship from both sides of the aisle and both sides of the philosophical spectrum. Things were not nearly as partisan as they came to be some years later." Putney said he wished he could explain when and how that atmosphere began to ebb and became more of an intramural competition between the two parties. "I think it was cotemporaneous with the growing close-to-equal numbers on both sides of the aisle," Putney said. "I suppose it's natural when your numbers are closer, vying for control of whichever house. One or two elections become far more vital to one party or the other—that coupled with annual sessions and carryover legislation constantly changing things." He added that some legislators became disillusioned with the annual sessions, claiming that "the stability of the law was not nearly as good as it was when we met every two years and would permit time for legislation to be implemented and a body of opinion to be developed around the legislation."

Governors, with their line-item vetoes and other prerogatives, could wield enormous power and strike a hard bargain. Putney said there were occasions when "the governor had the elevator shaft steaming hot from bringing members up from the Finance Committee to twist their arms." He recalled one time when a colleague decided to change his position on a bill after one such visit. Putney said to him, "What you're going to tell me is you've been promised a bypass or whatever you want in your district." The delegate started grinning before he could finish. Putney added that he, too, had received a call and was asked if he wanted a bypass around Bedford. "And I said, look, if they never dump another wheelbarrow load of asphalt in my district, I'm not going to vote for something that I think is wrong in principle."

During those years, the General Assembly was replete with raconteurs who told colorful stories. Putney recounted an evening when Del. Ray Garland—the erudite William F. Buckley of the General Assembly—was speaking on the floor during a night session, "and I never heard as many long words in my life." At the conclusion of Garland's stem-winder, the floor leader, Del. Jim Thompson, stood up, and asked the Speaker if the distinguished minority leader, Del. Jerry Geisler, could take the floor and interpret what the "gentleman from Roanoke" just said. No one expected Geisler to stand up, but he "gets up, puts his cigarette out, and goes out to the aisle microphone—in those days we didn't have microphones on the desks—and he said, 'Mr. Speaker, it's abundantly obvious to me that the gentleman from Roanoke is grossly inebriated by the exuberance of his own verbosity,' and sat down. The gallery went crazy." A few storytellers sometimes imbibed what Putney called "liquid courage" during the breaks. But he said the legislators had great moments of levity.

Their ranks were slowly changing and a new breed of Virginia lawmakers emerged. During the 1990s a group of Democratic delegates who sat near one another on the House floor formed the "Coffin Corner," and all of the members would wear camel jackets at the same time one day a week. Their hi-jinks included sauntering into the storied House chamber wearing helmets with flashing lights. Their wit and repartee were renowned, and one year a number of them decided to quote pedantic Latin phrases during floor sessions. Eventually, the growing contingent of Republicans formed the "Amen Corner" and wore crisp blue jackets with ties that resembled American flags. They were equally adept at skillful sparring during debates.

By 1998, Virginia voters had elected an almost evenly matched number of Democratic and Republican delegates to the House, and the members decided to implement a power-sharing agreement. That's when Putney made the decision to join the Republican caucus, although he remained an elected Independent. Putney then became the chairman of the Privileges and Elections Committee. "And I can tell you not only did I feel like a fish on land, but all of the members of the Republican caucus had to because they had never presided over committees," Putney said. Today, the GOP delegates and senators have not only presided over committees, but over the full House and Senate when they have subsequently held majorities. Both Republicans and Democrats have transformed the General Assembly into a model of modern efficiency.

Putney said he never had the ambition nor intended to serve in the General Assembly for 50 years. The part-time job "is certainly not a money-maker," he said. "Trial lawyers can never calculate the money they lost in doing this." There have been unexpected moments, such as when he was elected Acting Speaker of the House in June, 2002, when the previous Speaker, S. Vance Wilkins, Jr., resigned unexpectedly. He remained in the office until the new Speaker, William J. Howell, was elected the following January.

Putney is chairman of the House Appropriations Committee and a member of the Joint Legislative Audit and Review Commission, and the energetic octogenarian does not seem to have slowed down. He was persuaded by his wife, Carmela, and others to run for re-election in 2011. "Unless a person feels that he is contributing in a way that makes Virginia different and unique, there is no way you can justify the campaigning, the fundraising—and no one despises fundraising more than I," Putney observed. But he recounted one example that illustrated how he felt about the job and Virginia itself.

In late 2010, Gov. Robert F. McDonnell called and asked him to go to New York with some other General Assembly leaders to meet with the bond-rating agencies. "The day that we met with all three of them was one of the more informative, educational, broadening experiences of my lifetime," said Putney, "sitting there discussing Virginia's fiscal health with people who do the bond rating and fiscal advising to countries, counties, cities, private industries. And to the hear the report that we heard—with only Virginia and a small number of states with a Triple-A rating—to hear these people sing the praises of the Commonwealth in managing our fiscal affairs, makes you feel good, and makes you feel that there's something right and unique about Virginia."

He continued with a smile. "These things don't happen overnight. It's the result of a lot of good people with good fiscal policies. This is something that all of us should take great pride in." Such observations have prompted Lacey E. Putney to keep on running—turning a legislative sprint of a two-year term into a half-century marathon on behalf of the Commonwealth.

_____

Anne Marie Morgan has worked as a broadcast journalist for many years and is the State Capitol Bureau Chief for Virginia Public Radio. She teaches an array of courses as an adjunct Professor of Political Science at the University of Richmond School of Professional and Continuing Studies. She also served as a Member and Chair of the State Board for Community Colleges, governing 23 Virginia colleges on 40 campuses.

CHAPTER 10
The Lieutenant Governor:
Presiding Over the Virginia Senate

By Lieutenant Governor Bill Bolling

In Virginia, the governor serves as the state's Chief Executive Officer. Virginia's system of placing executive authority in the governor is the same as every other state in the nation.

However, when it comes to deciding who serves as the state's "second in command," the system used varies greatly from state to state. In Virginia, the "second in command" is the lieutenant governor, but this is not the approach used by all states.

According to the National Lieutenant Governor's Association, 45 states and four territories have a lieutenant governor.[1] In three states and one territory the "second in command" is the Secretary of State. In five states the President of the State Senate is the first line of succession to the governor.

The official responsibilities of Virginia's lieutenant governor are set forth in Article V of the Constitution of Virginia.[2] His official duties are twofold: First, the lieutenant governor serves as president of the State Senate and presides over the Senate when the General Assembly is in session. He is authorized to vote on legislation to break a tie vote among the senators. Between 2006 and 2011, I had the opportunity to cast 18 tie-breaking votes on a vast array of policy issues, including taxation, health care, and energy legislation. Second, the Constitution of Virginia provides that the lieutenant governor is first in the line of succession to the governor.[3] Should the governor be unable to serve due to death, disqualification, or resignation, the lieutenant governor becomes governor.

In addition to these constitutional responsibilities, the Code of Virginia provides that the lieutenant governor shall serve as a member of several state boards, commissions and councils, including the Board of Trustees of the Jamestown–Yorktown Foundation and the Center for Rural Virginia; the Board of Directors of the Virginia Economic Development Partnership and the Virginia Tourism Authority; the Virginia Military Advisory Council, the Commonwealth Preparedness Council, and the Council on Virginia's Future.[4]

While the lieutenant governor's position is considered to be a part-time position, much like that of a member of the General Assembly, fulfilling the duties and responsibilities of the office can require a great deal of time. Because of this, many have advocated making the lieutenant governor's position a full-time job.

Photo courtesy of Bill Bolling.

Virginia's current governor, Bob McDonnell, has made his lieutenant governor a member of the governor's cabinet and asked me to serve as the state's Chief Jobs Creation Officer.[5] In this role, I am responsible for overseeing Virginia's economic development efforts.

I have met with company CEOs to discuss how the state can help their businesses grow and expand, negotiated economic development deals to bring new business and industry to Virginia, and visited with countless business groups to promote the Commonwealth's economic development efforts.

This is the first time a lieutenant governor has served as a member of the governor's cabinet and the first time that a lieutenant governor has been assigned specific and significant responsibilities within a gubernatorial administration.

From left, Sen. John Chichester, House Speaker William J. Howell, Lt. Gov. William T. Bolling, and Gov. Timothy M. Kaine join the applause for Queen Elizabeth II during her visit to the State Capitol in 2007. Photo by Bob Brown, *Richmond Times-Dispatch*.

The lieutenant governor is elected at the same time as the governor, but the governor and lieutenant governor are elected separately, i.e., they do not run as a ticket. Therefore, it is possible to have a governor and lieutenant governor of different political parties.

This process also varies from state to state. In many states the governor and lieutenant governor run together as a ticket, much like the president and vice president. However, in other states, like Virginia, the governor and lieutenant governor are elected independently.

Interesting Facts about the Office of Lieutenant Governor[6]

- The Lieutenant Governor, unlike the Governor, can stand for reelection in succeeding terms.
- While serving in the chair as presiding officer of the Senate, the Lieutenant Governor is addressed as Mr. President.
- The Virginia Constitution of 1851 first provided popular election of the Lieutenant Governor. During the period of Reconstruction (1865-1870) the commanding general of the military district of Virginia named the Lieutenant Governor.
- Upon the end of Reconstruction (1870), the Lieutenant Governor was again popularly elected.
- In forty-two states the Lieutenant Governor is the first in the line of succession to the Governor. In three states and one territory the Secretary of State is first in line, and in five states the President of the State Senate fills this capacity.
- Of the 13 colonies, only Massachusetts and Connecticut made the office a permanent part of the government. The office existed in the other colonies on an as needed basis.
- Under the Constitution of 1869, known as the Underwood Constitution, the Lieutenant Governor was granted a vote in the case of a tie while sitting as President of the Senate.
- During the Constitutional Convention of 1901-1902 Joseph Edward Willard was administered the oath of office of Lieutenant Governor. This is only time an inauguration took place during a Constitutional Convention.
- Since Virginia initiated the popular election of its Lieutenant Governor in 1851, no Governor has died in office.
- Three Lieutenant Governors died in office: Saxon Winston Holt, Lewis Preston Collins II, and Julian Sargeant Reynolds.
- Eight Lieutenant Governors went on to become Governor: James Hoge Tyler; James Price; William Munford Tuck; Mills Edwin Godwin, Jr.; John Nichols Dalton; Charles Robb; Lawrence Douglas Wilder; and Timothy M. Kaine.
- One Lieutenant Governor resigned from office: Elisha W. McComas.
- Lieutenant Governors who become Governor have their portraits hung on the third floor of the State Capitol in Richmond.
- Lieutenant Governors who do not become Governor have their portraits hung in the Senate Chamber.

The benefit of electing a governor and lieutenant governor separately is primarily one of independence, balance, and oversight. However, advocates of electing the governor and lieutenant governor as a ticket feel that it would strengthen the Office of Lieutenant Governor and promote consistency in policy should the lieutenant governor need to succeed the governor.

While the governor is limited by the Constitution of Virginia to serving only one four-year term, there is no limit on the number of terms that can be served by the lieutenant governor.

The position of lieutenant governor is often seen as a stepping stone to the Office of Governor. In fact, five of Virginia's past ten governors served as lieutenant governor before being elected to the state's highest office.

History of the Office of Lieutenant Governor[7]

The Office of Lieutenant Governor can be traced back to the Virginia Council of London. The King appointed the Council, which in turn appointed the lieutenant governor or deputy.

In 1680 the English crown forbid colonial governors to be absent from the colonies without leave. Consequently, careful arrangements were made so that the lieutenant governor could exercise all the governor's powers subject to instructions and orders from both the crown and the governor.

After the Virginia Council of London dissolved, the King appointed the governor. The governor would then form a governor's Council from which a member would be designated to serve as lieutenant governor.

These titular governors were frequently absent for prolonged periods and in some instances the titular governor never came to Virginia. Consequently, the conduct of the governor was left in the hands of the lieutenant governor. Virginia's first Constitution, adopted on July 29, 1776, provided a Council of State from which a president was annually selected from its members. The president acted as lieutenant governor in the case of the death, inability, or necessary absence of the governor from the government.

Under the Constitution of 1830, the size of the Council of State was reduced from eight to three members who were elected by the joint vote of both houses of the General Assembly for three years. The senior member of the Council was the lieutenant governor.

The members of the Constitutional Convention of 1851 voted to abolish the Council of State and provided for the popular election of the lieutenant governor. The individual had to be 30 years of age, a native citizen of the United States and a resident of Virginia for five years prior to his election. Unlike the governor, a lieutenant governor could stand for reelection in succeeding terms.

The Constitution of 1869, also known as the Underwood Constitution, granted the lieutenant governor a vote in the event of a tie while sitting as president of the Senate. The Underwood Constitution also changed residency requirements for the lieutenant governor from a native citizen of the United States to a citizen for ten years and from a Virginia resident for five years to a resident for three years.

The Constitutional Convention of 1902 changed state residency for the lieutenant governor back from three to five years.

In all, 38 individuals have served as Virginia's lieutenant governor.

William T. Bolling served his first term as Lieutenant Governor from 2006-2010 and was re-elected to a second term, which will expire in 2014. He serves as Virginia's Chief Jobs Creation Officer and as a member of the Governor's Cabinet. He previously served as a State Senator from 1996-2005 and Member of the Hanover County Board of Supervisors from 1992-1995.

CHAPTER 11
Lobbying in Virginia:
Making a Case for Policies

By Eldon James
President, Eldon James & Associates, Inc

What do you think of when the word "lobbyist" is heard in a news report or a political conversation? More often than not the word brings to mind negative images of influence and worse. Media accounts of the derailing of what might be a beneficial policy change or the indictment or conviction of someone for corruption associated with lobbying activities are the first images for most. Unfavorable impressions formed by political ads that accuse politicians of being "bought by special interests" are also very common. This is unfortunate because lobbying, like any other human endeavor, has good and bad participants. We remember the negative examples because of the sensational scale and profile of the scandals that hit the headlines.

So, what is the real world of lobbying, and when did it begin in the United States? The approach has certainly existed since the colonial era, when the early Americans would petition the Parliament to change its policies[1]—although there seems to be no record that they called it "lobbying." The First Amendment's rights to free speech, to "peaceably ... assemble, and to petition the Government for a redress of grievances"[2] were enacted in 1791 and are closely associated with the activities of lobbyists.

A report by National Public Radio tells of a legend about the Willard Hotel in Washington, D.C., during the post-Civil War era: "that the word lobbyist was coined there during the Ulysses S. Grant administration. It was said that President Grant used to come to the hotel's lobby to have a brandy and a cigar and was often surrounded by petitioners who eventually became known as lobbyists."[3] But the term "lobby" had been used before that time. One of the first recorded references appeared as early as 1808 in a Congressional debate over moving the nation's capital away from Washington, D.C.: "We have heard it said that if we move to Philadelphia we shall have a commanding lobby; we shall learn the sentiments of the population!"[4]

If you look up the categories of lobbying and lobbyists in an array of reference books, the themes are generally the same, describing a lobbyist as someone who tries to influence the decision-making of legislators and other government officials on behalf of a business, an organization, or a cause. It is interesting to this writer that a key word is often absent or is far down the list in those definitions: *education*. In the effort to have an impact on decision-making the lobbyist, in reality, must be an educator. He must use his resources (time and words) to effectively educate decision-makers on the good and bad aspects and the tradeoffs of the choices they must make.

Virginia law provides broad, general definitions and establishes basic parameters of how lobbying can be done. A lobbyist is:

1. An individual who is employed and receives payments, or who contracts for economic consideration, including reimbursement for reasonable travel and living expenses, for the purpose of lobbying; 2. An individual who represents an organization, association, or other group for the purpose of lobbying; or 3. A local government employee who lobbies.[5]

A Virginia lobbyist must register annually and provide yearly activity reports. These rules provide transparency about clients for whom the lobbyist works, any gifts to officials being lobbied, and any entertainment or events sponsored by the lobbyist that were attended by a government official.

The Job of the Lobbyist

So how does it really work in Virginia?

As with most states, in Virginia the majority of lobbyists can be placed into one of three groups: those representing businesses and private sector trade associations such as the Bankers Association or the Chamber of Commerce; those representing nonprofits, such as the Community Health Centers or the Association of Area Agencies on Aging; and those representing local governments (which are specifically mentioned in the Code of Virginia definition). Each operates a little differently because of their dissimilar natures.

Businesses—primarily corporations—and trade associations noticeably outspend the others. In 2010, according to the Virginia Public Access Project (VPAP), 74 of the top 100 spenders were private

Lobbyists work while observing a Virginia Senate Committee meeting at the General Assembly Building. Photo by Bob Brown, *Richmond Times-Dispatch*.

businesses or trade associations.[6] Their focus is on laws and regulations that they perceive as unfriendly to business or on the items in the state budget that are critical to a particular business sector. For example, legislation considered unfriendly to the payday lending industry motivated significant lobbying expenditures in 2008. That year the two top spenders on lobbying were proponents for payday lending, and together they spent more than $3.3 million.[7] By comparison, according to VPAP, the top 20 spenders in 2010 together spent less than $3.2 million.[8]

An example of a private-sector business interest in the budget process is the health care lobby. The groups of lobbyists who represent hospitals, long-term care nursing homes, and home care services for the aging are engaged in monitoring state Medicaid spending proposals. They fear that reductions in the Medicaid budget will lead to losses for healthcare providers and force them to pass those costs onto other payers or lose money.

Nonprofits generally spend considerably less but often have the "It's the right thing to do" argument on their side. Access to services for the disadvantaged and vulnerable is a cause that tugs at the heartstrings of public officials, and these lobbyists know it.

To those outside of the inner workings of government the first reaction to the idea of a local government lobbyist is: "Why would that be necessary?" When you understand the relationship between Virginia state government and its cities, towns, and counties (political subdivisions of the state) you realize that local budgets and operations are tied tightly to the decisions made in Richmond. Approximately 50 percent of Virginia's General Funds are directed to localities to support a variety of programs, from the shared responsibilities of K-12 education and public safety to grants that support state priorities such as the Water Quality Improvement Fund. With Virginia operating as a Dillon Rule state, localities can only engage in activities authorized by the Commonwealth. (See Chapters 23 & 24 for an explanation of the Dillon Rule.) This means daily activities at the local level are strictly controlled by the General Assembly, whether it is how to advertise for a public hearing for a rezoning decision or how neighboring localities enter into agreements to support each other in an emergency. Local governments, therefore, have registered lobbyists actively engaged in an array of issues that impact daily operations and local tax rates.

How do lobbyists do their job?

Lobbying Virginia government is a long-term enterprise. The most effective lobbyists and those they represent develop long-range goals. These objectives are implemented incrementally through annual strategies that are achieved through developing personal relationships with decision-makers. Fostering these relationships can consist of having meetings with the policymakers, taking them to lunch, briefing them on the salient issue, giving them educational literature, and arranging for constituents with an interest in the same issue to contact elected officials and encourage them to make the appropriate decision.

One of the essential factors in effective lobbying is establishing trust with the policymakers with whom one comes into contact. The word of a lobbyist is his bond. If a policymaker finds that a lobbyist has not been truthful—or has even just stretched the truth—in the presentation of his case, then that lobbyist will quickly lose the trust of the decision-maker and his own effectiveness as an advocate for his issue is greatly reduced. For instance, an advocate of seat belt usage could lose credibility if he erroneously claims that a mandatory seat belt law in Virginia would save thousands of lives annually, but the state official realizes that the highway death rate in the Commonwealth the year before was only 900 fatalities.

If a lobbyist inadvertently misstates a fact, to keep the trust of the government official he is trying to influence, he must communicate his mistake to that individual as quickly as possible and set the record straight.

The Annual Cycle

The lobbyist's legislative year begins in May. The annual registration filed by a lobbyist with the Secretary of the Commonwealth covers a year that begins on May 1 and ends April 30. This is because in most "normal" years the final General Assembly session of the legislative year is held in April. The Reconvened Session, commonly referred to as the Veto Session, is held on the sixth Wednesday after the adjournment of the Assembly's Regular Session. Unless a Regular Session must be extended, this means that the Reconvened Session is held in early April in odd-numbered years and in mid-April in even-numbered years.

Lobbyists will often spend May and June each year working with those they represent to begin framing their specific plans for the legislative session that begins the following January. This is done primarily for reasons of timing, availability, and accessibility. It can take time to develop the annual program for some, especially when it is a trade association or membership organization with diverse interests, and time is needed to develop a consensus. Those with more sophisticated public policy programs have multi-year plans; therefore, developing consensus is an ongoing process, saving time in the spring. Even so, unexpected events or opportunities can require reevaluating priorities.

Availability and access to legislators is generally easier in the spring and summer. This "off-season" time is when constituents and interest groups can participate in longer meetings with lawmakers, legislative staff, and administration officials because they are not under the pressure of the General Assembly session. Meetings in the legislator's district office can be more relaxed with time to explore the details of an issue, in contrast with meetings in the General Assembly Building or the Capitol during the session when a few minutes can be considered a long meeting. Those meetings during the session are focused on bullet-points that can be delivered as an "elevator speech"—or the span of time it takes to ride an elevator. During those times, lobbyists actually do wait in lobbies in order to catch a legislator coming out of his office or a meeting.

In every odd-numbered year in Virginia someone in the Assembly must run for election. In those years it becomes increasingly difficult to get quality time with those being lobbied as the calendar advances past Labor Day and approaches Election Day. After the voters have spoken there is a scramble to congratulate winners and become acquainted with new members. In those election years, taking advantage of spring and summer is essential. This is somewhat more critical for the nonprofit and local government lobbyists than for the business and trade association lobbyists. The latter have the advantage of being able to make campaign contributions. For nonprofits and local governments the contributions to campaigns can only come from individuals acting as private citizens. Thus, businesses and trade associations tend to be much more engaged in campaign fundraising activities. With this advantage in fundraising, business and trade association lobbyists gain more visibility with candidates for elective office during the heart of the fall campaign season.

In the even-numbered years, when there are no regular Virginia state elections to impact the calendar, the opportunity to gain access to legislators for longer discussions stretches into the fall. But as the year advances toward the early winter the frequency of legislative committee meetings increases in preparation for the coming session, and the opportunities for access become compressed. At this stage, lobbyists tend to tie up loose ends and develop the detailed tactics for the coming session.

So, what are the specifics? If a group decides they need a change in state law which requires the passage of a bill, they begin work in the spring to define the specific change that they would like to make. They then must determine which legislator would be willing to be the chief patron of the bill and who is in the best position to be most effective. Several factors can be important, with the two most critical being the knowledge and interest of the potential patron in the details of the issue and his position in the committee structure.

Let's imagine a change being requested in how the Virginia Department of Health manages septic systems and the Department's responsibility for protecting public health. Lobbyists will often look first at the committee which will consider the legislation and approach a "senior" member of the panel—a lawmaker who has held office for a long time. In this case, a member of one of the key committees, the House Health, Welfare, and Institutions Committee or the Senate Education and Health Committee would likely be a very effective patron. Senior members of those committees are in a position of influence and likely have many years of experience with related issues.

The more controversial the issue, the more important it is to have a legislator who sits on the committee which must approve the bill. The legislator also must possess the seniority and respect of other legislators in order to shape opinions. Other factors include the history of the potential patron in working with the various stakeholders on the issue who can help him bring more allies to the effort or convince potential adversaries to "see the light."

Once a legislator has agreed to carry the bill the next step in the process is for the lobbyist to work with the patron to enlist co-patrons and develop understanding and support among other lawmakers. These are key strategies for a successful outcome. Building support within the members of the committees that make up the bill's legislative path and the leaders of the caucuses are integral tactics. As part of this process the lobbyist will work with those he represents to develop a clear and consistent message of why the bill is important. Enlisting those who will be positively impacted by the bill to deliver that message personally to pivotal legislators is most effective. It will impress the legislator even more if the personal messages come from active, voting constituents.

During the planning process for introducing the bill, the lobbyist also focuses attention on anticipating the opposition. The lobbyist identifies key potential allies and adversaries—with the goal of getting the likely allies to weigh in with legislators and lend their support, while attempting to convince adversaries that they should become allies or choose not to work against the effort. This may require refining the potential legislation to remove something that is a source of disagreement. The more the lobbyist can do to remove objections, the greater the opportunity for success. Sometimes that just cannot be achieved with all opponents. In that case the lobbyist must work to make the most compelling case possible and develop a sufficient number of allies to be more persuasive and ultimately successful.

If all of these steps are accomplished then the lobbyist is ready for the legislative session. By the time the session begins the lobbyist will have prepared talking points for supporters and is ready to assist the patron with the information needed to present the bill in subcommittee and full committee. If necessary, the lobbyist will coordinate the bill's supporters to provide testimony in the subcommittee or committee. The House relies more heavily on the work of subcommittees, while in the Senate a bill may only receive a hearing at the full committee level. By the time the bill is heard for the first time in committee or subcommittee the lobbyist should already know who on the committee supports or opposes the bill. Quite often the testimony given is not what leads to the outcome. It is what was done during the months, or sometimes years, in advance.

Generally, the lobbyist is not just working with those he represents on only one issue. Usually, he also must monitor all legislation of interest to be sure that the proposals of others are good for the client. A lobbyist for an environmental organization is naturally interested in bills before the natural resources committees, but he will also watch the local government committees and the budget bills, since they may also address issues of significance. Daily review of all legislation filed is critical to finding opportunities to work in support of the good ideas of others and to identify legislation that may be a threat. When the lobbyist can partner with others to bring those he represents to aid another group it can pay off in the short run with passage of a good bill, and in the long run by helping to build alliances that can be important in the future. As an example, advocates for senior citizens' issues may help advocates for people with disabilities on an affordable housing bill that builds a bond for the two groups to work together in a future session on employment rights for older Virginians.

When a bill is identified that is problematic for the lobbyist's client, the lobbyist must first determine if this is an unintended consequence of what someone is trying to accomplish or is a direct threat to the client. If the problem is unintentional, such as due to unclear wording of the bill, the lobbyist can generally work with the proponents of the measure to amend it and resolve the inadvertent effect.

If the bill is more of a direct assault on those whom the lobbyist represents, the lobbyist must either work to see if a compromise can be reached or mobilize his resources and supporters to oppose the bill. Success in opposing a bill can be its defeat or an amendment that removes or minimizes the negative impact.

Every lobbyist understands that there are three important numbers in the process: 51, 21 and 1. It takes a majority in both chambers, 51 in the House and 21 in the Senate, and it also takes that one signature from the governor's pen for approval. Without the governor's signature on the bill, you are back in the fight in the Veto Session. It is crucial for the lobbyist to know how the governor and his policy advisors view the bill. The more controversial the legislation, the more it will be necessary to engage in another round of lobbying. This second round of lobbying is with the executive branch (primarily the governor's office), utilizing all of the same resources as used with the Assembly.

It is important to remember that for the long-term lobbyist, effectiveness depends on building long-term relationships based on trust and respect. The lobbyist who deceives others to get their support cannot count on building success over time.

Eldon James is the President of Eldon James & Associates, Inc., a consulting firm that specializes in public policy, project, and program management. The firm primarily assists local governments and non-profits. He worked 17 years in state and local government in Virginia before founding Eldon James & Associates, Inc., in 1994.

A Closer Look:
The Role and Ethics of the Lobbyist

By David Bailey
Founder, David Bailey Associates
and Tom Hyland
Former Lobbyist

Whether calling a lawmaker to express a preference for or against legislation or giving testimony in person before a public body, it is not usual for Americans to exercise their First Amendment rights to speak out about public policies and laws. But when those efforts are conducted professionally, that is the role of a *lobbyist,* who is hired by a nonprofit, business, trade, or other type of organization to represent its views before a legislature or executive branch agency.

Lobbyists endeavor "to influence governmental decisions, especially the voting decisions legislators make on proposed legislation."[1] They often monitor government programs and legislation for developments that affect their issues, educate elected or appointed officials about their concerns, testify publicly about policy options, and try to persuade officials to adopt their organization's position.[2] They may work to modify or amend bills, push for passage of legislation, or defeat measures that they oppose. Lobbyists may even advise lawmakers and help write legislation.

Each state establishes by law what it means to lobby and to do so professionally. In Virginia, the state Code defines the act of lobbying as: "1. Influencing or attempting to influence executive or legislative action through oral or written communication with an executive or legislative official; or 2. Solicitation of others to influence an executive or legislative official."[3]

Lobbying in Virginia is both complicated and simplified by several factors that tend to make the Commonwealth unique among the 50 states. Virginia's legislature is a part-time, citizen, non-professional political body that meets in regular sessions only for 60 days in even-numbered years and 46 days in odd-numbered years. Virginia's citizen-legislators are aided by the General Assembly's Division of Legislative Services when drafting legislative proposals, but with the exception of the Senate Finance and House Appropriations Committees, the various legislative committees have not always had the services of a large contingent of professional and expert technical staff available to provide objective testimony and advice. In fact, the legislature's research arm, the Joint Legislative Audit and Review Commission, is generally only called upon to study issues by an act of the General Assembly or by request of one of its members.

The concept of separation of powers limits the ability of the executive branch of the Virginia state government to provide appropriate technical guidance to those legislative committees not served by professional technical staff. As a consequence, Virginia legislators often trust lobbyists as a primary source of professional, subject-specific expertise in developing, considering, and enacting legislation. This fact places a significant ethical and professional obligation upon lobbyists to provide lawmakers with objective, technically sound advice and guidance on the important legislative issues each member of the General Assembly considers.

With a few exceptions, lobbyists in Virginia must register annually with the Secretary of the Commonwealth, and each organization or person who spends more than $500 for lobbying must file a report.[4] Additionally, lobbyists file annual disclosure reports in July of each year which include descriptions of the type of advocacy conducted and the costs of operating as a lobbyist, including any gifts or events valued at more than $50 that were provided to elected or appointed officials in the legislative and executive branches.[5] (Judicial branch officials are highly unlikely to experience any lobbying activity, and matters of gifts to judges are governed by the Canons of Judicial Conduct for the State of Virginia.)[6]

Additional Resources on Lobbying in Virginia

FIGURE A
The Virginia Association of Professional Lobbyists Code of Conduct and Ethics[7]

I pledge to promote excellence in my own ethical behavior and that of other legislative advocates:

BY abiding by both the letter and spirit of ethics and campaign finance laws, regulations, and judicial decrees. I will comply with the registration, filing and disclosure requirements of the Virginia General Assembly and all state agencies. I will not take any action which is known or should be known to violate a law or regulation.

BY notifying my clients when a conflict of interest exists or may arise. I will be responsible for avoiding any act which may result in a conflict of interest.

BY protecting confidences, not only those of my employer or client, but also of elected and appointed officials and professional colleagues. I will never, directly or indirectly, compromise an official or colleague.

BY maintaining relationships with public officials and candidates in such a manner as to avoid any impropriety or appearance of impropriety. I will treat public officials, colleagues, all other individuals, and government itself, with the highest respect.

BY promising to tell the truth when communicating with a public official, legislative tribunal, employer, client, media, or professional colleagues. I will deal in accurate, current and factual information and will not engage in misrepresentation of any nature. I will build a reputation for credibility and dependability.

BY acquiring enough knowledge of public policy issues to be able to fairly present all points of view. I will give legislators both sides of an issue.

BY becoming familiar with the rules, procedures and standards of government agencies with whom I work.

BY conducting business with the sensitivity needed to adhere not just to legal proscriptions, but also to contemporary standards of morality, which can be more restrictive.

BY conducting myself so as not to bring discredit to the profession, government or individual colleagues.

FIGURE B

Virginia Lobbyist Standards of Professional Practice and Competency[8]

Preamble: Above all else are truth and trust: the true coin of the realm for any lobbyist is the value of his/her good name and word.

Where state and local legislatures consist of part-time citizen members—as is the case with those legislative bodies in the Commonwealth of Virginia—the role assumed by the lobbyist is critical to the efficiency, effectiveness and fairness of the legislative process; consequently, lobbyists have a special responsibility for the highest standards of professionalism; legal and ethical conduct; business practices; duties to clients, the Commonwealth, and the general public; professional relationships; confidentiality; and professional competency, as well as the avoidance of conflicts of interest.

Article I—Professionalism:
A. Lobbyists shall conduct all lobbying activities fairly, honestly, and professionally.

B. Lobbyists shall have a basic understanding of the legislative and administrative governmental processes of Virginia, the Code of Virginia and the Virginia Administrative Code, and such specialized knowledge as required to serve his/her client/employer in a competent and professional manner.

Article II—Legal and Ethical Obligations:
A. Lobbyists shall be truthful in communicating with legislators, public officials, other lobbyists, and other contacts and shall seek to provide factually correct, accurate, and up-to-date information.

B. When a lobbyist determines that he/she has provided a legislator, public official, or any other person with factually inaccurate information of a relevant, significant, and material nature, he/she shall promptly provide the requisite factually accurate information to that person or persons.

C. When a lobbyist learns of a material change in information that he/she has provided previously to a legislator, public official, or any other person, and that information has thus become inaccurate, and he/she shall immediately provide to that person the accurate and up-to-date information.

D. Lobbyists shall be familiar with Virginia laws and regulations governing the lobbying profession and shall not engage in any violation of those laws and regulations.

E. Lobbyists shall not knowingly cause a public official or any other person to violate any law or regulation applicable to that person.

Article III—Business Practices:
A. Advertising and Solicitation:
While lobbyists may advertise their services in a respectful and honest manner, no lobbyist shall attempt to solicit the business clients/employers of another lobbyist and may accept clients/employers of another lobbyist only when directly solicited by that client/employer.

B. Compensation, Expenses and Engagement Terms:
An independent lobbyist retained by a client shall have a written agreement with the client specifying the terms and conditions for the lobbyist's services and the basis for and amount of compensation and expenses.

C. Contracts for Lobbying Services:
Pursuant to §2.2-432 of the Code of Virginia, a lobbyist shall not participate in a contract for services under which compensation is contingent upon the achievement of any particular legislative or executive outcome.

D. Political and Electoral Activities:
In conducting any political campaign activities, including political action committee-related work and electoral activities, a lobbyist shall comply fully with all campaign finance and election laws of the Commonwealth of Virginia.

Continued on next page

E. Restrictions on Employment of Lobbyists:
Pursuant to § 2.2-435 of the Code of Virginia, no person shall be employed by a principal as a lobbyist who is a chairman or any full-time paid employee of a Virginia state political party, as defined in § 2.2-101, or a member of his/her immediate family, as defined in § 2.2-3101.

Article IV—Unethical Practices While Conducting Lobbying Activities:

It shall be unethical for lobbyists to engage in any the following practices while lobbying state governmental officials or employees in the Commonwealth of Virginia:

A. Initiating or encouraging the introduction of legislation for the purpose of opposing such legislation.

B. Engaging in, counseling, or knowingly misleading any person to engage in fraudulent or unlawful conduct.

C. Engaging in lobbying without being properly registered as a lobbyist in Virginia.

D. Requesting a Virginia state official or employee to promote to a potential client the lobbying services of the lobbyist or any other lobbyist.

E. Making or facilitating the making of any loan of money, goods, or services to a Virginia state governmental official or employee, except in the ordinary course of business.

F. Knowingly concealing the identity of a lobbying client from a Virginia state governmental official or employee.

G. Making a gift that has been solicited in violation of the Code of Virginia.

H. Knowingly making to a Virginia state governmental official or employee a statement of material fact relating to a specific lobbying activity that the lobbyist knows to be false.

Article V—A Lobbyist's Duties to:

A. Clients:
Lobbyists shall vigorously and diligently advance and advocate their client's/employer's interests by:

1. devoting adequate time, attention, and resources to the client's/employer's interests,

2. exercising loyalty and dedication to the client's/employer's interests, and

3. keeping the client/employer informed regarding the work he/she is undertaking, and, to the extent practicable, give the client the opportunity to choose among various options and strategies.

B. The Commonwealth and Its Elected and Appointed Officials:
Lobbyists shall demonstrate proper respect for the governmental institutions of the Commonwealth before which the lobbyist represents and advocates the client's/employers interests by acting in a manner that shows respect for governmental institutions and that will encourage public confidence and trust in the governmental processes and procedures of the Commonwealth.

Article VI—Relationships with Other Professionals:
Lobbyists shall treat others—both allies and adversaries—with civility and respect.

Article VII—Confidentiality:
Lobbyists shall maintain appropriate confidentiality of client/employer information by not:

1. disclosing confidential information without the client's/employer's informed consent, and

2. using confidential information against the interests of the client/employer or for any purpose not contemplated by the engagement or terms of employment.

Article VIII—Conflicts of Interest:
A. Lobbyists shall disclose all potential conflicts of interest to prospective clients/employers and promptly discuss and resolve all conflict issues.

Continued on next page

B. Lobbyists shall not undertake or continue representations that may create conflicts of interest without the informed consent of clients/employers or potential clients/employers.

C. Lobbyists shall avoid advocating a position on an issue if he/she is also representing another client/employer with a conflicting position on that same issue.

D. When a lobbyist's work on an issue for one client/employer may have a significant adverse impact on another client's/employer's interests, he/she shall notify and obtain consent from the other client/employer whose interest may be affected by this fact even if the lobbyist is not representing the other client/employer on the same issue.

E. Lobbyists shall inform clients/employers if any other person is receiving direct or indirect referral or consulting fees from him/her because of or in connection with the client's/employer's work and the amount of such fee or payment.

Article IX—Competency:
Lobbyists shall maintain their knowledge of governmental process and procedures and specialized knowledge though appropriate methods, such as seminars, continuing study, or other equivalent training so that they are able to represent clients and employers in a competent and professional manner.

Article X—Public Education:
Lobbyists shall seek to ensure better public understanding and appreciation of governmental institutions, processes, and procedures and the importance of the right under the First Amendment to the U.S. Constitution to "petition the government for redress of grievances."

Aside from the few statutory provisions that limit the activities of Virginia lobbyists—such as prohibitions on contingency fees and the employment of legislators and their family members as lobbyists—there are few other limitations placed upon lobbyists in the Commonwealth.

As a means of filling in the ethical and professional gaps that exist in the statutory limitations upon Virginia lobbyists, the Virginia Association of Professional Lobbyists (VAPL)—a professional association of long-time Virginia lobbyists—adopted in 1998 a *Code of Conduct and Ethics for Professional Lobbyists in Virginia.* A separate set of *Standards of Professional Practice and Competency* were also adopted to guide lobbyists in the Commonwealth as they comply with the *Code of Conduct and Ethics.* Both of these documents appear as primary sources above.

Lobbyists in Virginia clearly have the opportunity for unusually significant influence on the legislative process and policies in the Commonwealth. But it should be equally clear that they have great moral and ethical responsibilities to take care that their conduct and practices live up to the minimum guidelines set forth in the *Code of Conduct and Ethics* and *Standards of Professional Practice and Competency.* Although these guidelines at present are voluntary and applicable only to the members of the VAPL, we strongly believe that the General Assembly should consider enacting these principles into the Code of Virginia and develop appropriate remedies for violations.

David Bailey is the publisher of Virginia Capitol Connections news magazine, a lobbyist at the Virginia General Assembly, and the founder of David Bailey Associates. Tom Hyland is a former Virginia lobbyist and career local, state, and federal government official.

PART III: THE EXECUTIVE BRANCH

Virginia's governor is unique among all of the states because the Commonwealth's chief executive is the only one prohibited by its Constitution from running for reelection. The governor can sit out at least four years after leaving office and serve one more term later, but Mills Godwin is the only governor since the Civil War to actually do this—elected first as a Democrat in 1965 and then for a second term as a Republican in 1973[1].

Because Virginia's governors cannot succeed themselves to continue advancing their goals unabated, they hit the ground running the day after they have won the gubernatorial election through the transition period from one administration to the next. Once they take the oath of office in January, the General Assembly session is already underway, so they must work quickly if they want to get any legislative initiatives passed that year. Governors realize that they have only three short years remaining after that, and they need to rely on their close advisors and cabinets to help them achieve their priorities.

Part III, *The Executive Branch*, begins with a discussion of this executive team, the governor and the cabinet, written by a former state official who served 30 years in Virginia government under five administrations. As Chapter 12 explains, the Commonwealth has not always had a cabinet structure, but modern governors find it to be essential. Governors have many constitutional obligations in addition to preparing a state budget, signing or vetoing bills, and advancing their own initiatives. By law, cabinet secretaries are considered to be extensions of the governor and they have delegated authority to carry out functions that the chief executive can legally do.

The author also outlines the modest number of constitutional qualifications for becoming a governor and the extensive powers granted to Virginia's chief executive. The state organizational chart reveals that the Commonwealth's executive branch is considerably larger than the other branches, and the governor's power to appoint a plethora of cabinet secretaries, top officials, agency heads, and members of boards and commissions gives him significant clout. As the author points out, the governor makes more than 4,000 appointments throughout the length of his term.

When studying this section on the executive branch, readers may want to ponder a decades-long dispute about how powerful Virginia's governor really is. Some have asserted that the Commonwealth's governor is more powerful than many other state chief executives because his broad appointive powers enable him to place those who favor his policy preferences in positions of authority, and that can impact decision-making far beyond the end of his term. They also maintain that because General Assembly sessions are so brief and lawmakers are part-time, the governor's full-time presence on the job gives him a powerful advantage. He works all year long executing the laws that they pass, and he can do so with his own spin on regulations that are promulgated by agencies led by his appointees. But others counter that Virginia's governor is not that powerful because he can only serve one term, which is only long enough to accomplish a limited number of goals. They argue that governors should have the constitutional authority to run for reelection and that this would allow voters to hold him accountable.

Resolutions to amend the state Constitution and allow governors to succeed themselves have been introduced in the General Assembly annually, but none has gotten through the entire legislative process in order to be submitted to voters. Most—but not all—former governors believe the length of the gubernatorial term should be extended or that the chief executive should be able to serve two consecutive terms. However, many lawmakers think that the one-term limit preserves the balance of power between the legislative and executive branches. They say governors should be allowed to serve two terms only if they cede some of their appointive powers to the General Assembly, such as some of the positions on the State Board of Education or the Commonwealth Transportation Board.[2]

Although they can only serve one term, Virginia's modern governors tend to promote comprehensive agendas and it is not uncommon for them to achieve much of what they ask the General Assembly to approve. In Chapters 13 through 16, four of Virginia's former governors write about their priorities and accomplishments. Each describes an extensive list of successfully enacted objectives and presents a positive perspective of his administration. They also had their critics, challenges, and controversies, so readers may want to research the news accounts of the day to learn a variety of perspectives about their terms in office. But as the records of these former governors suggest, Virginia's chief executives can and do achieve a great deal during their four brief years on the job. These chapters also illustrate the types of goals that governors tend to pursue and the problems that they endeavor to solve through their policy initiatives.

Gov. Timothy M. Kaine speaks to the members of the news media inside the Patrick Henry Building in 2009. Photo by Bob Brown, *Richmond Times-Dispatch*.

All governors are concerned about their states' prosperity, and Virginia's chief executives are no exception. If businesses are making decisions to locate in the Commonwealth or to expand, the net result is frequently a larger number of jobs, a growing economy, greater tax revenues in the state's coffers, and ample budgets that can achieve additional priorities. Additionally, in today's global marketplace, states must not only compete with international competitors for trading agreements and business deals, but they must also compete with other states which are also courting businesses. The reader will find that as a consequence, all of the former governors made economic development a top priority of their administrations. Thus, Chapter 17, written by one of Virginia's leading experts on economic development, discusses this entrepreneurial role of the governor, the Commonwealth's products and appeal as a business location, and the impact of policies that promote the state's attractiveness.

The attorney general is one of only three statewide elected officials in Virginia. He is often thought of in a law enforcement capacity as a "top cop," and he does play an integral role in the justice system. But as Chapter 18 explains, the attorney general has many more functions to perform as the Commonwealth's chief legal officer and is a member of the executive branch. The primary author, who has served as an attorney general, also describes the office's role as counsel to the governor and state agencies, consumer advocate, defender of Virginia's position in the courts, and fraud investigator, among others. The author also emphasizes the growing role of attorneys general nationwide as policy activists who file lawsuits on behalf of their states' residents and win class-action settlements.

CHAPTER 12
The Governor and His Cabinet

By Bernard L. Henderson, Jr.
Senior Deputy Secretary of the Commonwealth, 2002-2010

It is not difficult to meet the legal qualifications to become governor of Virginia, according to Article V of the state Constitution. To be eligible to serve as governor, one must be a citizen of the United States who is at least 30 years old; one must also have been a Virginia resident and registered voter for the five years prior to election as governor.[1] Once inaugurated, the governor is required to live in the capital city, have a salary that cannot be increased or decreased, and is forbidden from receiving any other "emolument from this or any other government."[2]

Article V also vests the power of the chief executive in the governor.[3] It empowers him to "take care that the laws be faithfully executed."[4] But his authority extends beyond that of carrying out the laws passed by the General Assembly to include his own legislative responsibilities. The governor is required to inform the legislature of the condition of the state, which is done in an annual State of the Commonwealth address, and he may "recommend to its consideration such measures as he may deem

Most of Virginia's living Governors stand under a portrait of Thomas Jefferson while attending the inauguration of Gov. Robert F. McDonnell in January, 2010. From left, Govs. Charles S. Robb, A. Linwood Holton, L. Douglas Wilder, George F. Allen, Robert F. McDonnell, Timothy M. Kaine, Gerald L. Baliles, and James S. Gilmore, III. Photo by Bob Brown, *Richmond Times-Dispatch.*

expedient ...."[5] Modern Virginia governors always take that a step further by initiating their own legislative agendas to accomplish their goals. They ask delegates or senators to sponsor or "carry" their legislation during a General Assembly session, and although the bills do not list the governor's name, lawmakers know which ones are the "governor's bills."

To be enacted into law, legislation that has passed the General Assembly must be signed by the governor, but he also has the option of proposing amendments to bills or vetoing them.[6] However, if any measures are sent to the governor while the General Assembly is still in session, he has seven days to take action on them or they will become law without his signature. The governor's proposed amendments to legislation can take the form of a substantive redrafting of a bill, technical amendments, or other recommended changes. Both houses must agree to his recommendations with simple majority votes before they can officially become part of the bill. Although the governor can veto bills, they also can be overridden by a two-thirds vote of both houses. If a bill is submitted to the governor with less than seven days left in the session or after the General Assembly has adjourned, the governor has 30 days from the date of adjournment in which to act on the legislation.

The governor also may call the General Assembly into a special session that is separate from the regularly convened session in order to deliberate legislative matters.

Additionally, Virginia governors are required to make revenue forecasts and propose state budgets known as "appropriations" bills. They can propose amendments to the state spending plan and, unlike the president of the United States, can veto individual spending items that are listed in the bill.[7] As with other legislation, the General Assembly can agree to or reject his budget amendments and accept or override his line-item vetoes.

The Virginia Constitution also grants other authority to the governor, including serving as the commander-in-chief of the Virginia Guard and exercising vast appointive powers to executive branch agencies, boards, and commissions.[8] The governor also has "judicial" responsibilities, including appointing judges to fill court vacancies when the General Assembly is not in session, and the powers of clemency, restoration of voting rights, and commutation of death sentences.[9]

Virginia's governor serves for one term of four years. It is significant that, unlike all other states, the Commonwealth's governor is forbidden by the state Constitution from succeeding himself.[10] Therefore, he cannot extend his term by running for re-election in order to achieve his goals. That fact tends to drive most of Virginia's modern governors to become activist leaders so that they can accomplish as much as they can during four short years in office.[11]

The Cabinet

The mandate for one term means that governors rely heavily on other members of the executive branch to help them fulfill their extensive constitutional obligations, as well as to advance their numerous initiatives quickly. The individuals whom they select through their broad appointive powers can help boost the rate of gubernatorial success. Virginia's governors tend to appoint state officials who can help them implement their agendas and who are compatible with their governing philosophies.

The Constitution specifically empowers the governor to "appoint each officer serving as the head of an administrative department or division of the executive branch of government" and that they shall "serve at the pleasure of the Governor."[12] In addition to heads of departments and divisions, the Code of Virginia provides for the governor to appoint a chief deputy and a confidential assistant for policy or administration for each executive branch department or division; these two employees also serve at the pleasure of the governor—which means he can keep or fire them whenever he chooses.[13]

State law provides additional specifics about the governor's role as the Commonwealth's chief executive. It declares that unless there is a specific constitutional or statutory exception, the governor is responsible for formulating and administering policies of the executive branch, including resolving conflicts between and among agencies. He is the chief personnel officer of the Commonwealth and its chief planning and budget officer.[14]

Virginia has a strong and effective Personnel Act[15] to protect classified employees of the Commonwealth from having their employment jeopardized for political reasons, but the safeguards accorded to classified employees do not apply to persons appointed by the governor.

The Code specifically authorizes the governor to "designate and empower" cabinet secretaries to perform any duty or function that the governor may legally do himself, but it just as clearly makes any duty or function delegated to and carried out by a cabinet secretary the responsibility of the governor.[16] This is consistent with the maxim in public administration that one may delegate duties and functions but one cannot delegate responsibility.

Composition and Authority of the Cabinet

By Virginia statute, the cabinet consists of the Secretary of Administration, the Secretary of Agriculture and Forestry, the Secretary of Commerce and Trade, the Secretary of Education, the Secretary of Finance, the Secretary of Health and Human Resources, the Secretary of Natural Resources, the Secretary of Public Safety, the Secretary of Technology, and the Secretary of Transportation.[17] In addition to these secretaries, governors have given other positions cabinet rank or status during their administrations.[18]

Each executive branch agency is assigned to a secretary and these assignments are set forth in state law. The governor may change the assignment of an agency when he finds that its function is more compatible with those under a different secretary, and these changes are then incorporated into the statute during the next General Assembly session.

Section 2.2-200 of the Code requires executive branch agencies to: [19]

1. Exercise their respective powers and duties in accordance with the general policy established by the governor or by the secretary acting on behalf of the governor;
2. Provide such assistance to the governor or the secretary as may be required; and
3. Forward all reports to the governor through the secretary.

That same section also empowers each secretary to:

1. Resolve administrative, jurisdictional, operational, program, or policy conflicts between agencies or officials;
2. Direct the formulation of a program budget for each agency;
3. Hold agency heads accountable for their administrative, fiscal and program actions;
4. Direct the development of goals, objectives, policies and plans for the effective and efficient operation of government;
5. Sign documents on behalf of the governor that originate with agencies assigned to them; and
6. Employ personnel and retain consultants to do the work required by statute or executive order.

Additionally, as if those provisions were not clear enough about the authority of each secretary, the subsequent section declares: "Each Secretary shall be considered an extension of the governor in the management coordination and cohesive direction of the executive branch of state government ensuring that the laws are faithfully executed."[20]

Beyond these statutory provisions, governors routinely issue an Executive Order at the beginning of their administration where specific duties of the office are delegated to the chief of staff and to specific cabinet secretaries. This is typically a rather lengthy "nuts-and-bolts" document that even includes such matters as delegating to the Secretary of Administration the authority to close or delay the opening of state government offices due to weather conditions.

Secretaries do not always have an enforceable authority over the agencies in their portfolio that would enable them to control what goes on in those agencies. Many heads of executive branch agencies are not appointed by the governor. Neither are the presidents of Virginia's higher education institutions. These officials are chosen by—and are subordinates of—boards with members who are appointed entirely or in part by the governor; but the members of those boards serve for fixed terms with some terms expiring every year, so it typically takes two or three years into a governor's term before he is able to appoint a majority of the members of these boards.

A highly publicized 2004 case illustrates the lack of control that secretaries sometimes have over their agencies. During the Administration of then-Gov. Mark Warner, the Department of Game and Inland Fisheries got into considerable trouble over expenses charged to the Commonwealth in connection with an African safari trip taken by the agency head and other department personnel.[21] The Secretary of Natural Resources had already disapproved this as travel that is appropriate for the expenditure of state funds. However, the agency head is an employee and a subordinate of the Board of Game and Inland Fisheries, which is appointed by the governor for fixed and staggered terms, so the secretary could not legally prevent these expenditures in spite of his opposition. The trip was taken, state funds were used in connection with it, and neither the Secretary of Natural Resources nor the governor could prevent it.

No secretary has more responsibility and less authority than the Secretary of Education. According to state law, the Secretary of Education "shall be responsible to the governor" for ten executive branch agencies.[22] Of these, only two, the Department of Education and the Commission for the Arts, are headed by persons who are appointed by the governor. Also, while the Code does not make the secretary "responsible" for Virginia's public universities, colleges, and community colleges, the secretary is the link between those institutions and the executive branch of Virginia government.

Few (if any) places except government can there be a situation where a person is legally "responsible" for something that he has no legal authority to control or supervise.

Officials with Cabinet Status

Since the earliest days of the cabinet, governors have given specific members of their personal staff and other officials the status of cabinet secretaries, allowing them to have access to him, attend cabinet meetings, and be regarded as having equal standing with the secretaries in the performance of their responsibilities.

The governor's chief of staff has served as the chair of the cabinet for the past several administrations. In addition to convening and presiding over meetings of the cabinet, except on rare occasions when the governor does so, traditional standing protocol is that access to the governor by members of the cabinet is through the chief of staff. Even though governors and chiefs of staff might insist that members of the cabinet have immediate and direct access to the governor, in the real world, that is simply not typically done. Chiefs of staff also expect members of the cabinet to keep them apprised of any matter that a governor initiates with them in order to keep all parties informed and to make sure that such matters receive proper attention.

The governor's chief counsel and director of policy are also usually considered to be part of the cabinet because the day-to-day nature of their responsibilities cross secretariat lines and their effectiveness depends on having comprehensive information about all matters involving the executive branch. Similarly, especially in recent administrations, due to the increasingly pervasive involvement of the federal government in most state government activities, the Director of the Virginia Liaison Office is considered to be a member of the cabinet.

Many may be surprised to learn that the Secretary of the Commonwealth is not a cabinet secretary by statute. Officially, according to state law, the office of the Secretary of the Commonwealth is subordinate to the Secretary of Administration.[23] Even though the Secretary of the Commonwealth is the oldest government office in the Western Hemisphere, having been continuously occupied since 1607, the position was not given cabinet status until Gov. George F. Allen did so at the beginning of his administration in 1994.

The governor's authority to appoint a large number of individuals to executive branch entities is one reason that gubernatorial power is so extensive. And it is the Secretary of the Commonwealth who is responsible for assisting the governor in making appointments to more than 200 full-time positions and approximately 4,000 seats on boards and commissions during his term. In addition to that responsibility and many others, the Secretary of the Commonwealth is designated by the Code as the governor's confidential assistant in that the secretary is the only official required by statute to take a separate oath promising to keep the secrets of the governor.

Virginia State Organizational Chart[24]

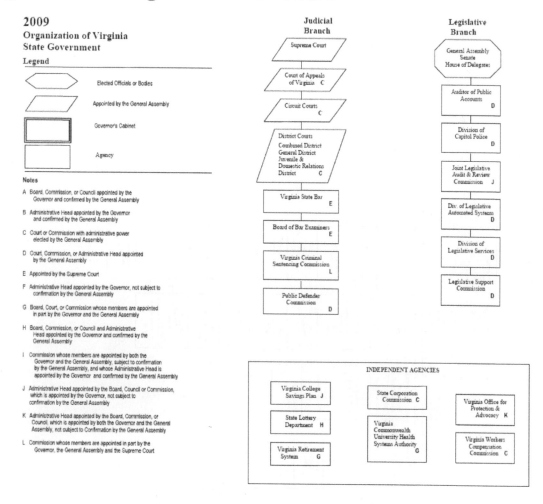

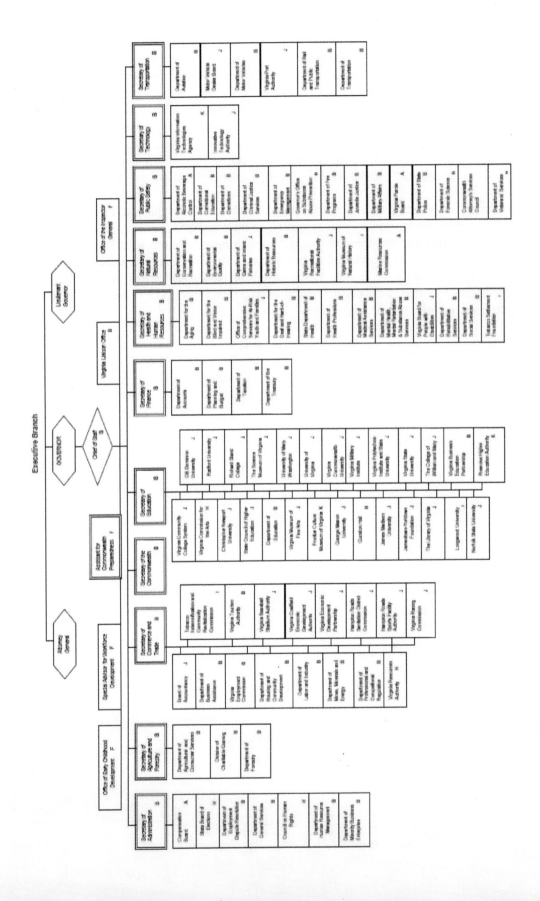

While there may be some differences from administration to administration in the amount of consultation that might typically take place between the governor and the Secretary of the Commonwealth about appointments, it appears that recent governors have all relied on this secretary to provide them with information on who wants to be appointed, who is recommending whom for positions, which appointments need to be made, and to handle the attendant calls and paperwork.

The Secretary of the Commonwealth has responsibilities associated with criminal justice of which many Virginians may not be aware. All requests for executive clemency, including all types of pardons, reprieves, and commutations of sentences, are filed with and processed by the Secretary of the Commonwealth. Information and recommendations pertaining to these requests are compiled by the secretary, who submits them to the governor along with her recommendations. Additionally, the Secretary of the Commonwealth similarly handles all petitions from convicted felons who seek the restoration of their civil rights. The secretary is the officer who processes and executes all requests for persons accused of crimes to be extradited to Virginia or from Virginia to other states.

The Secretary of the Commonwealth is also responsible for maintaining all of the conflict-of-interest disclosure filings of government officials, registering and receiving activity reports of all lobbyists, issuing service of process on all out-of-state defendants in civil lawsuits in Virginia, authenticating the validity of all Virginia government documents and notarized documents to be used by foreign governments, and registering names, emblems, and mottoes of organizations located in the Commonwealth.

When an event during a governor's administration elevates an issue or concern to a high and ongoing level of attention, a governor may ask a particular person to focus on that matter and give him cabinet member status; this will ensure access to the governor and the ability to work with secretaries as co-equals in order to give the matter continued, top-level attention. For example, at the outset of Gov. Warner's administration, one such issue was Virginia's preparedness to deal with terrorism and disasters, so he appointed an Assistant to the Governor for Commonwealth Preparedness and gave that official a staff and cabinet status. Later in the Warner administration, when unemployment and the need for retraining Virginia's workforce became critical, he created a position with a staff to address those issues and gave that person cabinet status. Govs. Timothy M. Kaine and Robert F. McDonnell have continued similar positions within their cabinets.

Interestingly, the lieutenant governor and the attorney general have typically not been included in cabinet activities or invited to attend the meetings. There have been some exceptions to this, especially when those officials have been members of the same political party as the governor. Under the administration of Gov. McDonnell, Lt. Gov. William Bolling has held a cabinet-level status.

Cabinet Members and the General Assembly

While the General Assembly is in session, cabinet meetings take on an elevated level of importance. Meetings are typically held every day the General Assembly is in session and are usually attended by the cabinet secretaries, deputy secretaries, and members of the governor's staff, including policy office staff and support staff from the Department of Planning and Budget. Briefings and updates on legislation of interest to the administration are presented at these meetings and assignments are frequently given to attendees to contact specific legislators or monitor meetings of legislative committees and subcommittees. Sometimes these assignments may have greater relevance to a person's relationship with a particular legislator than to the person's normally assigned duties; for instance, if a particular senator's assistance is needed on a bill of interest to the administration that deals with transportation, and the Deputy Secretary of Natural Resources has a strong positive relationship with that particular senator, then that deputy secretary might be asked to make contact with the senator. It is also important for all members of the administration to know, hear, and

The Executive Mansion on Capitol Square. Photo by Bob Brown, *Richmond Times-Dispatch.*

share information on the entire range of legislative matters of interest to the governor, and these meetings accomplish that purpose. These daily meetings seldom take up anything other than matters related to the legislative session, and information discussed at these meetings is guarded with utmost discretion by attendees.

Secretaries spend a great deal of time working with their agencies to develop and assess legislative proposals, regardless of whether they are significant changes in public policy or mere technical rewrites of sections of the Code that update the way internal functions are performed. Secretaries provide a broader view of the panorama of government than just one agency might have, so they are expected to prevent agencies from proposing legislation that might be advantageous for one agency but inadvertently detrimental or problematic for another agency, function of government, or segment of the public. There are few things more embarrassing to an administration or more enjoyable to its critics than a disagreement played out between government agencies before a legislative panel. Secretaries are responsible for giving general oversight and for monitoring the legislative activities of their agencies to ensure that those efforts are consistent with the overall direction and priorities of the administration, are not in conflict with the operation and function of other agencies, and are considered to be in the best interest of the Commonwealth as a whole.

Even more important than overseeing the legislative activities of agencies is the function of cabinet members to advocate for the governor's legislative initiatives, primarily when they pertain to the members' responsibilities. But this is also done when an initiative has broad application and when the cabinet member has a working relationship with a specific lawmaker whose support might be strategically important.

Cabinet members need to be fully informed about the subject and its legislative history before appearing before a General Assembly committee. Legislators have typically been around much longer than a cabinet member, may have served on the relevant committee, and may have knowledge of the issue. If a question or point arises and the cabinet member does not know how to respond, the only acceptable course of action is to offer to find and provide the information quickly or to yield to someone such as an agency head who does know the answer. Legislators have mastered the art of dodging questions and they have a bloodhound's sensitivity to instances when a person does not know an answer

Gov. Robert F. McDonnell is inaugurated in January, 2010. Photo by Bob Brown, *Richmond Times-Dispatch.*

but is trying to give one anyway; cabinet members should not even try to do this or they will certainly seriously damage their credibility.

Cabinet Members and the Budget

Without question, the single thing that occupies the most time and attention of a secretary is money. Virginia's government will never have enough money to do everything that even reasonable people who generally and conscientiously believe in limited government want it to do. Gov. L. Douglas Wilder often spoke of the challenge of discerning the "necessities rather than the niceties" of government activities.[25]

Virginia's budget is generally structured along agency lines. Appropriations are typically assigned to agencies to fund programs. So agencies have real ownership of, and responsibility for, programs they operate and the funds available to them for that purpose. While it is usually stated as a criticism that an agency always wants more money, it should not be viewed as inappropriate or unacceptable for an agency to want to perform its job better and to recognize that it could do so with more resources. Would it be in the public's best interest if an agency took the position that it was executing its responsibilities in a perfect manner, that everyone should be perfectly satisfied with the way and type of services being provided, and that there simply is no room for improvement? When funds are available, the objective for determining the adequacy of appropriations is to be sure that the agency has a proper purpose, that it is using its resources as economically as possible to meet that purpose, and to see how any allocation of additional resources from a finite source will provide the maximum enhancement of the agency's function. When there are no additional resources available, or when funds must be cut, the objective is to see that the agency will be able to do the very best it can to accomplish its necessary purposes with whatever resources it has. That, in summary, is the job of each secretary. The secretary is to have the knowledge, vision, and perspective of being close enough to the agencies in his secretariat and each program within, but not so close that all other aspects of state government are out of focus. The secretary must have an understanding of the practicalities and priority of each program relative to all other functions of state government, including those outside his secretariat.

The secretaries are involved in the budget process from beginning to end. They are obligated to monitor the financial affairs of their agencies constantly, work with their agency heads to resolve budgetary problems, and carefully review and make adjustments to budget proposals submitted by agencies for the appropriations process. They also work with agencies to make changes before proposed budgets are incorporated into the budget bill and to make the best of bad situations when the desired funds are not forthcoming. Additionally, they advocate for the provisions in the governor's budget bill pertaining to their secretariat and then, after the spending plan is passed, they work with their agencies to do the best they can with the available resources.

Confirmation

Secretaries, the governor's chief of staff, executive branch agency heads appointed by the governor, and appointees to executive branch boards and commissions must be confirmed by the House of Delegates and State Senate. The Virginia confirmation process differs from the federal one in two important ways. First, as soon as a gubernatorial appointee submits the statutorily required paperwork and takes the oath of office, he begins to serve and continues to do so until the General Assembly acts to the contrary. But in the federal government, an appointee does not begin to serve until confirmed or unless the president makes a "recess appointment." Second, in Virginia, confirmation by a majority vote of both the Senate and the House is required for confirmation, while in the federal government, only the Senate confirms and the House has no role (except when the president nominates a person to serve the unexpired term of the vice president and then each chamber must agree).

Confirmation of gubernatorial appointees was as routine and as close to automatic as it could get until the 21st century. Even when the governor was of one political party and the majority in the General Assembly was of a different party, the virtually unanimous position of Democratic and Republican legislators was that the governor had the prerogative to appoint whomever he wanted. This practice continued until recent years, when state lawmakers have applied more scrutiny and even refused to confirm a small number of appointees. It is probably a safe bet that confirmation of secretaries will not be routine for all positions in the future.

The Executive Branch before the Cabinet

Virginia's governors have not always had cabinets. Before authorization to create a cabinet system was approved in 1972, the previous general reorganization of the executive branch of Virginia's government was performed during the administration of Democratic Gov. Harry F. Byrd, Sr., who served from 1926 to 1930.

During Byrd's campaign for governor, he made the occasional general reference to the need for greater economy and efficiency in government, but he did not provide specific details. Once elected though, he unveiled what he called a "Program of Progress" that advocated revolutionary changes in the structure of Virginia government: instituting a "short ballot," substantially increasing the governor's power, and drastically reducing the number of executive branch departments and agencies.[26]

At the time that Byrd ran for governor, other statewide elective offices were the lieutenant governor, attorney general, Treasurer, Superintendent of Public Instruction, Commissioner of Agriculture and Immigration, and the three members of the State Corporation Commission. These officials may have respected the governor as the Commonwealth's chief executive and may have run as his ticket mates, but by virtue of their popular election, they may have considered their primary responsibility to be to the electorate, rather than to the governor. Beyond the governor's popularity with the voters and lawmakers that might imperil the political future or effectiveness of these statewide officials, there was no way for the governor to cause them to do or refrain from doing whatever they wanted.

In addition to the elected officials in the executive branch who headed major functions of government, there were 95 separate executive branch agencies; 27 were established by the Constitution of Virginia and 68 were created by the General Assembly through statute. Several of these executive branch agencies were headed by persons who were not directly accountable to the governor. Some were appointed by boards whose members included gubernatorial appointees, but others were selected by the General Assembly or, in a few instances, by the judiciary. Furthermore, many of the agencies had duplicative or confusingly similar purposes; for instance, there were 16 agencies with responsibilities for the state budget.

Byrd's "Program of Progress" included statutory changes as well as constitutional amendments—all to address the issue of accountability—and they all just happened to increase the power of the governor as chief executive. Specifically, he proposed making the governor, lieutenant governor, and attorney general the only elected statewide officials, abolishing 30 agencies outright, and consolidating the rest into 16 centralized administrative agencies whose directors would be appointed by the governor to serve at his pleasure. The appointments of these directors would need to be confirmed by the General Assembly at its next regular session, but at that time the legislature's regular sessions only convened in January of each even-numbered year, so many agency heads would serve for nearly two years before having to be confirmed.[27]

In advocating these reforms, Byrd said that under the existing structure, "[t]he Governor cannot be as much of an executive as he should be. Public opinion holds him responsible for efficiency in administration, but actually he has very limited power to control and direct administrative functions. If Virginia is to operate with the efficiency approaching a great business corporation, we must concentrate responsibility."[28] Byrd had already developed a powerful political organization, so his proposed legislation was quickly and easily enacted by senators and delegates who were given clear reason to believe that their support would be essential for their political survival. He hit a political rough patch with the proposed constitutional amendments that had to be approved by public referendum; they were rejected by voters in every area except the Shenandoah Valley and Southwest Virginia, but the large margin of votes in favor of the amendments in those areas was more than sufficient to offset the negative votes from the rest of Virginia. However, Byrd's reforms did not include the creation of a cabinet or provide for any structure of management or administration between the agency heads and the governor.

With Byrd's plans enacted and implemented and his political organization in even firmer control of Virginia's government, the structure of government appeared to be like—and functioned as though it was—a family-controlled corporation. The governor was the CEO, the General Assembly was a compliant Board of Directors, and agency heads were experienced bureaucrats who were always dependable in their work and just happened to be loyal to the Byrd organization. Stability in the operation of Virginia's government was a hallmark of the Byrd organization and it was one of the few ruling political organizations in the nation to have an impeccable record of honesty. Even its harshest critics did not try to make a case that the Byrd organization was corrupt or incompetent. It controlled Virginia government for about 40 years and even on the few occasions during that time when a sitting governor dared to exercise a little independence from the organization, the appointed agency heads were never in jeopardy of being removed because there simply was no resource from which to obtain competent replacements.

As time went on, there appeared to be little recognition of the need for a set of managers between the governor and what had grown to be approximately 75 executive branch agencies headed by gubernatorial appointees. Still, Byrd's legacy in establishing a business-like approach to government and limiting the number of statewide elected officials to three continues through the 21st century.

Reorganizing Virginia's Executive Branch

When Gov. A. Linwood Holton, Jr., took office in 1970, he was not only Virginia's first Republican governor, but he was also the state's first modern chief executive who had never held elective or appointive public office. Therefore, he entered office without knowing the heads of Virginia's governmental agencies. Members of the staff within the governor's office were also mostly outsiders to state government. Many longtime gubernatorial appointees who were Byrd stalwarts picked up their pensions and left. Others, who conscientiously believed that they could not work for a Republican or thought they would not be asked to continue, took positions in the private sector or became consultants. Additionally, Holton chose not to reappoint a significant number of sitting agency heads, as was his prerogative. This constituted the most extensive change in the executive branch in anyone's memory and exposed the structural weakness of having no senior management between approximately 75 agency heads and the governor.

Holton realized that Virginia's government was due for a top-to-bottom management analysis,[29] so he created a study commission loaded with many of Virginia's business executives, including loyal supporters of the Byrd organization's candidates, to do the job. In 1971, this group released its recommendations. They included one to establish a management level between the governor and the agency heads that they proposed calling "deputy governors," which was criticized by many legislators.

Legislation to establish the cabinet was introduced in the House of Delegates during the 1972 Session of the General Assembly. The first change from the initial recommendation was to jettison the title "deputy governor" and use "secretary" instead. After an intense struggle in a divided General Assembly, the bill creating the cabinet passed due to a parliamentary tactic by a single junior senator. No one at that time who knew anything about Virginia politics would have predicted that this legislator would one day select his own cabinet, but L. Douglas Wilder did so after his own election as governor in 1989.

View of the State Capitol's South Portico. Photo by Anne Marie Morgan.

Holton proudly signed this legislation and appointed the first cabinet, which took office in July of 1972. His cabinet served quite effectively without disrupting the perception of bureaucratic stability and without significant controversy. Even though legislative proposals were made to abolish or make mischievous changes to it in later General Assembly sessions, such proposals never constituted any serious threat.

Over the years, governors have combined secretariats, split them, created new ones, renamed them and moved agencies from one secretariat to another to address span of control, changing priorities and sometimes, perhaps, for political reasons to satisfy interest groups.

Conclusion

Virginians expect their Governor to lead and be responsible for effectively managing their Commonwealth's government. Despite the generally successful efforts of several governors, especially Byrd and Holton, to better organize and structure Virginia government, there are still significant programs beyond the legal grasp of the governor to manage.

Perhaps it is more than mere coincidence that the two most embarrassing examples of mismanagement in Virginia government in recent years occurred in programs that are beyond the control of the governor. Top officials at the Department of Game and Inland Fisheries went on an African safari and purchased equipment for this junket with government money, and even though the governor's Secretary of Natural Resources was opposed, he could not legally prevent them from doing it. The Tobacco Indemnification and Community Revitalization Commission approved a fraudulent grant to a public official and utterly failed to oversee its use as millions of these dollars were spent by that official,[30] and there continue to be revelations of grants awarded for purposes that are remote to that of the Commission. There are legitimate instances where government programs should be beyond the management of a governor, but those are extraordinary and rare, and there continue to be programs in existence that may not justify that immunity from oversight.

The past several governors have served with at least one chamber of the General Assembly controlled by the opposition political party. Even when that wasn't the case, governors have had at least one chamber controlled by members of his own party who were nevertheless somewhat hostile to them. Legislators who are part of the "loyal opposition" should endeavor to confine their opposition to matters of policy and refrain from trying to limit, circumvent, or undercut the governor's ability to manage our Commonwealth's government. When considering any proposal that impacts the governor's management authority, each legislator may want to ponder the very simple question of whether he would want such a requirement if he were governor. No one, especially in Virginia, serves as governor forever, so tinkering with gubernatorial authority because of one's opinion of the incumbent can be short-sighted, often to the point of being irresponsible. Instead, promoting the good of the Commonwealth and the well-being of its citizens should be the highest priority of the governor, the cabinet, and every state official.

Bernard L. Henderson, Jr., served for 30 years in Virginia government, including as Director of the Department of Commerce under Gov. Charles Robb, Director of the Department of Health Professions during the Administrations of Govs. Gerald Baliles and Douglas Wilder, and the Senior Deputy Secretary of the Commonwealth for Govs. Mark Warner and Timothy Kaine.

The Governors' Priorities

Governor-elect Mark R. Warner and his wife, Lisa Collis, walk toward the inaugural platform on the South Portico of the State Capitol in January, 2002. Photo by Bob Brown, *Richmond Times-Dispatch*.

CHAPTER 13
A Choice for Innovation and Investment

By Gerald L. Baliles
Governor of Virginia, 1986-1990

When I took the oath of office in 1986, the dawn of a new millennium was rapidly approaching. Virginia had transitioned from an "Old Dominion"—in which public access to education and economic opportunity were often limited and exclusive—to a "New Dominion" offering potential and progress for all our people.

Our population was growing, a transformational technological revolution was underway, and a competitive global economy was emerging. Only those states and businesses with the foresight to recognize this unavoidable reality and to embrace a dynamic new direction would thrive. These changes imposed upon Virginia unprecedented challenges. I knew I had only four years to set a course for action and position the Commonwealth as a leader for a new century.

I also knew that too often government simply reacts to problems, drifting from one crisis to another, failing to plan for the future, focusing resources on election-cycle objectives. I resolved to chart a different course.

Former Governor Albertis Harrison once advised that "after the election, the best politics is good government." Through analysis, strategic planning, and

Photo courtesy of Gerald Baliles and the Miller Center.

decisive action, my administration endeavored to follow this sage counsel. We made the connection between investments today and opportunities for tomorrow. We recognized that we live in a competitive world, but we did not resist the tides of change. Instead, we worked to benefit from them by establishing support for the "building blocks" of success in transportation, education, and economic development.

This called for honestly and accurately assessing the problems that created barriers to progress and then effectively communicating both this information and the proposed solutions. There were several key commissions and reports that served the purpose of forging a consensus between legislators, the business community, and the public. They included the Commission for Transportation in the 21st Century; the Commission for Excellence in Education; The Chesapeake Bay Commission; The Future of

Agriculture; The Employer's Initiative for Child Care; Virginia in a World Market; The University in the 21st Century; and the Commission on Prison and Jail Overcrowding.

Legislation and budget priorities followed this consensus. And the results powered positive change in our transportation network, our schools, our farms, our business climate, and our natural and human resources.

For example, our review of the transportation budget showed that there would soon be no funding available for new construction without fundamental changes during my term of office. In addition, there were no coordinated funding sources for our ports, our airports or our public transit systems.

Raising taxes and dedicating revenue to this critical purpose would be difficult. But major investments, especially in infrastructure, both physical and intellectual, require the spending of political capital in order to get financial capital. There are downside risks. It is a choice between the demands of the moment and a foundation for the future.

This is what former Gov. Linwood Holton did to build roads and public buildings, while moving forward on the subject of civil rights. This is what former Gov. Mills Godwin did in creating the community college system with new tax revenues.

It is what needs to be done if we are to use public resources in the public interest.

By confidently sharing the vision of what Virginia could be, we enabled a series of changes that became part of our legacy for the future. A transportation trust fund and new tax revenues infused our infrastructure with billions of dollars for maintenance and construction. Cabinet-level leadership for economic development and natural resources focused attention on managing growth and reducing pollution. We received national recognition for improvements in services for the mentally disabled. A foreign languages program linked academic standards with international trade objectives to give Virginia the edge in global markets. Eight trade missions led to expansion of exports for Virginia products through a new inland port and improved seaport facilities. An unequalled total of nearly 400,000 jobs were created for Virginians in all sectors of the economy. Full funding of state standards for educational quality was achieved. National recognition was given for the state's financial management and for the appointment of women to leadership positions, including the first female member of the Virginia Supreme Court. And the Virginia Tax Reform Act of 1987 returned more than a billion dollars in tax relief to taxpayers through fiscal year 1992.

All of these results were the product of a commitment on the part of many people to investment and innovation, and a sense of obligation, I think, to future generations. To me, they illustrate the necessity to consider the future rather than fear of political failure when the privilege of governing is won.

At least one lesson from that time is clear: that a public sector vision, not hindsight, inspires and promotes results that enable the Commonwealth to rise to its best. By the end of my term in office, Virginia had experienced a decade of growth, and had become one of the top ten state economies in the United States. Where once we followed, we now led.

But leadership is sustained only by continuing to meet the challenges we face. And that is a lesson we can all hope is learned by those who seek to govern.

Gerald L. Baliles served as the 65th Governor of Virginia from 1986-1990, Attorney General from 1982 to 1985, and Member of the House of Delegates from 1976-1982. He is currently the Director of the Miller Center of Public Affairs at the University of Virginia.

CHAPTER 14
On Our Virginia Renaissance:
Expanding Opportunity with Reform

By George F. Allen
Governor of Virginia, 1994-1998

My governor's administration—the Allen or A-Team—was guided by our promises and philosophy of government. We campaigned as "a new generation of honest leadership." Having once held Thomas Jefferson's seat in the House of Delegates from Albemarle County, and as a graduate of his University of Virginia, I found the ideals of Virginian's second governor applicable to present governance.

Gov. George F. Allen signs a law to reform Virginia's welfare system in 1995. Photo courtesy of George Allen.

President Thomas Jefferson defined "the sum of good government" as: "... [a] wise and frugal government, which shall restrain men from injuring one another, shall leave them otherwise free to regulate their own pursuits of industry and improvement, and shall not take from the mouth of labor the bread it has earned."

Throughout the decades, when the leaders of our great nation have abided by these enlightened principles, the cause of liberty has flourished.

In my administration as governor, we were guided by these foundational principles, which I call "common-sense Jeffersonian conservative principles." When government provides for the equal and fair administration of justice— restraining people from injuring one another; ensures an equal, safe playing field for all to compete and succeed to the best of one's ability and diligence—to regulate their own pursuits of industry and improvement; and allows both citizens and businesses of all sizes to reap the benefits of their labor and not redistribute those benefits—not take from the mouth of labor the bread it has earned—then good government creates the environment for liberty, justice, and prosperity.

State government's primary responsibilities—as granted by the owners of the government, the people—are education and law enforcement. Viewing decisions and priorities through these philosophical postulates and understanding that a vibrant, prospering economy is the surest way to fund these responsibilities, allowed my administration to succeed in keeping the promises I made in my campaign for governor in 1993.

Indeed, our campaign for governor sought to inspire, motivate and unite Virginians for audacious change with monumental reforms in Criminal Justice, high academic standards for school children, promotion of pro-family personal responsibility and the work ethic, and making sure the world knows that Virginia is "Open for Business!"

Winning the election meant the owners of the Virginia government supported this ambitious reform agenda. And, it helped persuade the Democrats in the General Assembly—who were in the majority—to join with Republicans to enact these ideas, solutions and initiatives.

Safe Communities

In 1993, Virginia had skyrocketing violent crime rates, and Virginians agreed with our decisive proposal to abolish Virginia's lenient, dishonest parole system that was releasing violent criminals after serving only a quarter of their sentence. We stopped letting criminal apologists control the justice system and started listening to the people, victims, and law enforcement professionals. We said there is an objective difference between right and wrong. We were not persuaded by the psychobabble excuses that a criminal was violent because of "bottle-feeding as a baby" or "his teacher didn't give him enough attention."

We enacted Truth-in-Sentencing, so that when a judge or jury sentences a rapist to 12 years, he serves 12 years, not three. We completely overhauled our juvenile justice system with tougher sentences and programs that instill discipline and respect for law-abiding citizens.

Who was helped the most by these historic reforms that in a few years thereafter reduced violent crime by 16 percent and juvenile crime by 13 percent? The most vulnerable among us: The elderly, women, people in low-income housing projects and in communities stalked by fear—the people who will never be a victim or a statistic because they were assaulted, raped or even murdered by a violent criminal who was released early on parole.

There is still more to do to combat the scourge of drugs and gang violence that endangers our young people. But in Virginia we have shown that common-sense, logical policies that crack down on the criminals and protect the innocent do indeed work. And, the evidence is clear that our approach to violent criminals is much more effective in reducing crime than taking away the Second Amendment rights of law-abiding citizens to protect their families and themselves.

Educational Excellence—Champion Schools

Our Champion Schools initiative was based upon my belief that Virginia's most important asset is our people—their capability, work ethic, and knowledge. Education is truly personal empowerment and the most enduring legacy of our administration is our improvements in the education of our school children.

During the 1980s, the sole education initiative in America was to throw more money at education. But that spending alone did little to increase educational quality because there was too little focus on ensuring students actually benefited from all those tax dollars and learned how to read, write, and speak the English language.

Rather than "give" students self-esteem with social promotion, we believed students should "earn" self-esteem by actually learning and achieving.

In 1994, we embarked on the long and challenging goals of developing new, high academic standards in basic subjects—standards that have since been emulated by other states. Next, we instituted testing to measure student progress against those academic standards. Finally, we brought accountability with School Performance Report Cards, so that parents, taxpayers, educators, business owners, and everyone involved in the educational mission can evaluate schools' and students' academic performance. Virginia's schools are now accredited based not on how many fire drills they run per year, but whether students are learning to read, write, and speak English and learning higher levels of Math and Science, as well as Economics and the History of our country and world civilization.

The School Performance Report Card is similar to an annual shareholder's report. It shows how each and every school performed in each subject at the third, fifth, eighth, and high school levels. And parents, taxpayers, and school administrators can see how their schools are performing compared to others in their county or city and throughout the Commonwealth.

As rigorous academic accountability has taken hold in our schools, Virginia's school children have acquired the educational competence they need to compete and succeed in the internationally competitive marketplace. We made these educational improvements in Virginia on our own, without being told to do so by a swarm of bureaucrats in Washington or because it was mandated by the No Child Left Behind Act or any other federal program.

And in the many years since we passed our Standards of Learning, nothing has made me more proud than the continued accolades Virginia has received as our students and public schools are consistently rated among the very top in the United States of America.

Welfare Reform—Virginia Independence

Ensuring opportunity for our citizens also meant breaking the bonds of dependency on government and we proved that welfare must no longer be a way of life for generations of Virginians.

Despite scare tactics and resistance at every step of the way from the liberal establishment, we passed the strongest, most pro-work ethic, pro-family, comprehensive statewide welfare reform legislation in the nation. It reflected the people's common-sense belief that every able-bodied, able-minded person should be required to work. Welfare is to be a temporary condition, limited to two years. And our changes preceded the federal changes by two years.

Built upon the twin pillars of the work ethic and personal responsibility, our reforms reduced Virginia's welfare rolls by 47 percent by the end of my gubernatorial term, and resulted in a 99 percent paternity establishment rate—the highest in the nation. Furthermore, child support enforcement is way up because we began revoking driver's licenses and professional licenses from people who refused to financially support their children. Welfare rolls are down and we're saving taxpayers hundreds of millions of dollars annually. Best of all, tens of thousands of Virginians and their families have moved from a life of dependency to self-sufficiency and the dignity of holding a job.

We measured welfare success not by how many people were receiving checks from the government, but rather by how many are living independent, self-reliant lives and within a family.

Creating Jobs—Opportunity Virginia

Good government not only provides for its citizens to be well-educated and personally empowered, it also fosters economic opportunities for those citizens with tax and regulatory policies that expand business and job opportunities by attracting businesses to come to Virginia and create jobs for Virginians. "Opportunity Virginia" was our strategic plan to make Virginia more conducive to new investment and jobs.

For all Americans to enjoy prosperity, government must understand that the burden of high taxes—whether in income, energy, investment or purchases—falls heaviest on those who can least afford it. That's why in Virginia we rejuvenated our attractiveness to new and existing businesses, cut the size and cost of government, and lowered taxes. We adopted new tax incentives for major business facilities as well as performance-based grants. We lowered gross receipts and other taxes, especially helping small business owners.

In our administration, we significantly reduced the tax burden on both individual citizens and on businesses of all sizes. We also created low-tax Enterprise Zones to attract jobs for people in struggling urban and rural areas. In our Opportunity Virginia plan, we doubled the number of Enterprise Zones to 50. In Enterprise Zones, lower taxes and prompter permitting resulted in many new jobs and investments, whether in big cities or small towns.

On the subject of jobs, we made sure the entire world knew that Virginia was "Open for Business." With tax cuts and regulatory reform, we set to work aggressively attracting new businesses and new investments to Virginia. Economic development was a top claim on my time as governor. Recruiting businesses from Europe, Asia, and North America were top priorities.

And we produced results, notwithstanding the loss of thousands of military-related jobs. We created the conditions that produced more than 312,000 net new private sector jobs. Though the previous annual record for new business investment in Virginia was a little more than $1 billion at that time, we attracted more than $14 billion in new investment in just four years and transformed Virginia into the "Silicon Dominion." Virginia's economy was transformed from one that relied heavily on tobacco and "low-tech" products to one that predominantly attracted and benefited from high-tech industries.

With unprecedented investment from newly recruited and expanding existing businesses, job growth in 1997 was 7.2 percent—the best in the nation. And to make sure that growth continued, our aggressive regulatory reform effort resulted in the revision or outright repeal of more than 70 percent of all then-existing state regulations. We regulated the regulators. We thought the impact of regulations on people and businesses should not be so burdensome that the piles of red tape essentially block citizens from being able to create wealth and prosper. This determined effort improved Virginia's ability to compete and win in the global economy.

Virginia Renaissance

All these revolutionary changes in Virginia's government occurred in four short years. And although there were some who attempted to block and thwart our reforms at every turn, we kept our promises and produced positive results for the people. We achieved all of this with 10,000 fewer government employees than when we took office, which reduced the size of government and the associated financial burden on the taxpayers. We expanded the transportation pie with private investment through the Public-Private Transportation Act and stopped the "raiding" of the Transportation Trust Fund.

These are great success stories to tell. We have shown that if one builds on the solid rock of principle and not the shifting sand of political expediency, our policies will stand as salutary models that withstand all tests of accountability to the people—whether it is in the realm of taxes, regulations, jobs, education, transportation, or public safety.

America, restart your creative engines!

We were able to spark the 'Virginia Renaissance" in just four years because we ran a campaign for governor on an aggressive agenda, fueled by common-sense ideas and principles, and then kept our promises once in office. Today, many of the challenges we face as a nation—the economy, jobs, energy, education, and mounting national debt—can be met if our leaders in Richmond and Washington embrace our foundational principles of governance and recommit to serving and trusting the people of our country.

George F. Allen served as U.S. Senator from 2001-2007, the 67th Governor of Virginia from 1994-1998, Member of Congress from 1991-1993, and Member of the House of Delegates from 1982 to 1991. He is currently the founder and Chairman of the American Energy Freedom Center and President of George Allen Strategies.

CHAPTER 15
A Time for All Virginians

By James S. Gilmore, III
Governor of Virginia, 1998-2002

Being elected governor in 1997 was a great opportunity to set a new program and agenda for the Commonwealth. I was elected on the eve of a new century. When I took office in January, 1998, the Internet and cell phones were just beginning to become a huge part of our lives. Innovative technology was changing by the hour and jobs were abundant. During my four years in office, Virginians, not the government, created nearly 250,000 new jobs. And during those years, government was supportive and fostered an environment for growth.

Gov. James S. Gilmore thanks Virginia's first responders outside the Pentagon following the Sept. 11th, 2001, terrorist attack. Photo courtesy of James Gilmore.

During my first year in office there was a budget surplus of nearly $900 million. But by the end of the Gilmore administration in 2002, much had changed. The national economy declined, the September 11th terrorist attack had struck Virginia at the Pentagon, and America was at war.

Virginia is the only state in America that limits its governor to one four-year term. The challenge was, in one term, to set new directions, to defy conventional wisdom, and to prepare Virginia to enter the

21st century unburdened by old thinking and approaches. True change is difficult to achieve in one four-year term. The motto of my inauguration as governor was "A time for all Virginians." This summary shows how my administration sought to achieve that ideal and to prepare Virginia for the new century ahead.

First Secretary of Technology

While serving as Attorney General and during my campaign for governor, I grew to fully understand how the new information technology age provided a great opportunity for the future of Virginia. My goal was to see the Commonwealth recognized across the nation as a leading information technology state. To help achieve this objective, I established the new office of Secretary of Technology in my cabinet. This was the first such cabinet position in the United States and was later emulated by other states. My goal was to make the government of Virginia the most innovative in the U.S. in the use of computers and software.

Our administration ensured that Virginia would be a national hub of on-line technology for years to come. On Jan. 13, 1999, I delivered the annual State-of-the- Commonwealth address with a live Web stream over the Internet for the first time ever and welcomed on-line guests from across Virginia and the world. During my four years in office, we did all that we could to promote this new high-tech industry, and today we are one of the leading states for Internet traffic. We also created an Information Technology Commission to formulate the first statewide Internet policy. The Commission's recommendations stayed true to market-driven principles and also embraced our Virginia ideals of freedom and democracy. Web-enabled government, privacy, security, and the protection of children were cutting-edge Internet challenges addressed by sound, comprehensive legislation that continues today to build on our progress.

Balancing Government Spending With Tax Reform

A guiding principle of my administration was a healthy respect for the wallet of the taxpayer. The more money that a citizen can keep, the more independent and empowered that individual becomes. Too often government has treated working men and women as if they are servants—and seems to behave as though its citizens exist primarily to give more tax money to finance ever-expanding government programs and functions.

I governed with a different vision: one of a government that treats the property of its citizens as the hard-earned fruits of a long day's work. My vision was to keep a promise made to the public to give tax relief to working Virginians.

The "No Car Tax" pledge made during my gubernatorial campaign was a commitment to empower the vast majority of Virginians who depend upon their cars to make a living and raise their families. Regular working citizens were heavily burdened by a tax on the very means that enabled them to get to work and to care for their children.

I'm proud that in the first year of my administration, the General Assembly unanimously passed the phase-out of the car tax. This was a promise kept—by Republicans and Democrats alike who were elected by our constituents. We phased out 70 percent of this car tax in my four years as governor. The benefit of that tax cut continues to this day, providing working men and women with nearly $1 billion in annual tax relief, the largest and most empowering such measure in Virginia's history. Since my term ended, the car tax phase-out has stalled. Now we need to finish the job and eliminate the last 30 percent of the personal property tax on cars, reimbursing our localities in good faith for every dollar they forego.

My administration governed on the basis that government must exercise some restraint in spending. I understand that we need to pay taxes to carry out essential efforts in education, transportation, and other public initiatives, but keeping more money in the hands of those citizens who earned it should always be our goal.

Virginia is enriched by a large presence of members of the military and their families. Our men and women in uniform protect our freedom both at home and abroad. Our goal was to encourage them to choose the Commonwealth as their home, and I'm happy to report that many have decided to live here to raise families, start new businesses, and grow our ever-expanding economy. For this reason my administration eliminated the income tax on the first $15,000 of pay for military personnel living in Virginia.

Other taxes were cut, too, but at the same time we also undertook major new initiatives. During my administration, our policy focused on balancing our budget, providing for forward-looking programs, and remembering the taxpayer. This was the right balance to help our state advance into the 21st Century.

Those who suffered the impact of the national recession after September 11th were not overlooked. We extended unemployment benefits statewide and started new training and job placement services. A new "tobacco commission" was established to provide major redevelopment initiatives to assist the Southside counties harmed by the loss of jobs in the textile, furniture, and tobacco industries. We undertook trade missions on three continents to secure new jobs and new business for the Ports of Hampton Roads.

Transportation

At the time of my election as governor, traffic congestion was identified as a major challenge. We needed new roads for economic development that required major projects. The question was how to advance transportation in one four-year term when the largest portion of revenues for transportation resided with the federal government.

Thanks to the hard work of my Secretary of Transportation, the Virginia Department of Transportation, and our federal elected officials, the Commonwealth added $670 million in federal funds in 1999 to address our traffic congestion, especially in Northern Virginia. That figure represented a 62 percent increase—or an additional $250 million per year—over the previous year's funding. My administration nearly doubled road construction in Virginia, spending $2.1 billion without raising taxes. We can see the progress by looking at the new Woodrow Wilson Bridge and the Springfield Interchange, projects that are utilized each day by nearly 400,000 drivers.

In addition to those two major projects, we advanced the Fairfax County Parkway and approved studies for the Coalfields Expressway in Southwest Virginia. We initiated and completed thousands of additional projects statewide. VDOT implemented significant reforms to accelerate the process of securing environmental impact studies so as not to delay road projects. We utilized public-private projects to provide Virginia with up-to-date ways to leverage private capital for road construction. And a ground-breaking private contract was initiated to provide for maintenance on the Interstate highways, giving the public better service with more efficient use of taxpayer dollars.

Major mass transportation initiatives were begun, including placing more trains on the Virginia Railway Express and planning for Metrorail to Dulles Airport. Due to the 9-11 attack, Ronald Reagan National Airport in Northern Virginia was initially shut down. But through aggressive efforts, the airport was reopened with minimum delay, saving thousands of transportation jobs and preserving the economy of our state.

Affordable and Quality Education

Virginia has always had a long-standing promise to provide affordable public higher education opportunities for our residents. I am a proud product of that educational system, and I recall how difficult it is for working families to send a child to college. During my time in office, I successfully enacted a 20 percent across-the-board tuition cut to keep that promise to the families of Virginia. At the same time, my budgets provided an additional $75 million to our state-supported colleges so that this program to reduce tuition and fees for in-state, undergraduate students would not be a hardship for these institutions.

The governor appoints the boards of visitors of all of Virginia's public universities and colleges. I personally spoke with every appointee to impress upon them that not only did they serve as members of a board of directors to support the schools, but also to provide oversight on behalf of the taxpayers. This new philosophy anticipated the changes that followed years later when the corporate world initiated greater accountability.

One of the greatest gifts that parents can give to their children is a college education. I was convinced that parents should be empowered to give that gift without being saddled with life-long debt. Education should never have to be interrupted or deferred because of high tuition.

During my time as governor, I believed that the future of the Commonwealth would be advanced by giving special attention to several Virginia universities. For that reason, I budgeted millions of dollars to enhance the quality of education at Virginia's two historically black public universities. This action made Virginia the only state to voluntarily match 100 percent of federal land grant program funds. I aspired for historically black universities to receive the same amount of attention as our other colleges. My administration also made concerted efforts to reach out to our minority communities, including recognizing Martin Luther King, Jr., with his own state holiday and welcoming Coretta Scott King to the governor's mansion.

Likewise, I believed that our state would benefit from continuing efforts to provide a major university in Northern Virginia. For that reason, George Mason University in Fairfax County was given additional appropriations.

Higher education was only one of my interests. I also shared the concerns of parents and educators alike about the quality of kindergarten through 12th grade education in Virginia. I sent a message directly to parents and educators during my four years in office that "Virginia's schoolchildren are my administration's key priority." My predecessor made a commitment to raise student achievement by establishing the Standards of Learning. But the entire program could not be implemented in his four-year term. I chose to continue this effort to enhance the quality of K-12 learning in Virginia by bringing together teachers, parents, principals, and superintendents to implement the Standards of Learning and to give them definition.

Virginia continues to use the Standards of Learning as a tool to identify the system's strengths and weaknesses, establish goals, and ensure that no child is left behind. This program has allowed both Democratic and Republican governors to target our efforts and resources to raise the achievement of our students and the quality of our schools. Virginia's School Performance Report Cards provide information about each school, including Standards of Learning test scores, attendance rates, school safety, and accreditation ratings. The purpose of these report cards is to directly communicate the academic performance of Virginia's public schools to parents and the public. The goal of this idea was to increase our schools' accountability.

During my campaign for governor, I pledged to reduce class sizes by adding 4,000 new teachers to our public school system—in recognition of the importance of teachers to high-quality education. By the end of my tenure we delivered on that promise. In conjunction with the General Assembly, we also made progress in meeting local school construction needs while not raising taxes. Another pledge made during my gubernatorial campaign was to keep the long-abandoned promise to dedicate all lottery profits to K-12 education. The lottery was passed in 1988, but all the proceeds were dedicated to the General Fund and not earmarked for schools. By directing lottery profits to education, we were able to give localities $245 million in new school funding during my administration. Local flexibility is the best approach to the use of lottery profits, and that commitment to education continues to this day. These proceeds allow schools to spend their share of the state's money on the different educational needs of each locality—to hire new teachers or raise teachers' salaries, to build new schools or renovate old ones, or to enhance teaching of the Standards of Learning.

My wife, Roxane, was also involved with the education initiatives of my administration and assisted teachers with the Standards of Learning. The First Lady's website—"A Commonwealth of Knowledge"—was a resource for teachers to index their lesson plans on-line and help them implement the Standards. Roxane also led an initiative to restore the governor's Mansion to preserve Virginia's history and serve as a working residence for the chief executive and his family.

My education budget also restored full funding for the Early Reading Initiative, which assesses the literacy needs of children in kindergarten and first grade and provides remedial instruction for early reading problems. This is a timely program that works, and I was proud that Gov. Tim Kaine sought to expand it.

Public Safety

A basic responsibility of government is public safety. Perhaps the greatest challenge I faced, or any governor could face, was the terrorist attack on September 11th, 2001. That attack struck Virginia without warning when the terrorists drove the planes they had captured into the Pentagon in Northern Virginia and into the World Trade Center in New York. Local responders faithfully responded to the disaster, and my job was to provide all possible support. Another task was to restore widespread confidence by speaking to the public in a statewide address, by keeping the press informed of our efforts, and to reduce uncertainty. Reagan Airport was subsequently closed, jobs were lost, and the economy of Virginia was dramatically affected. We added economic recovery efforts to traditional law enforcement efforts. Protecting Virginia during this time of upheaval was my principle focus and that of the entire government during the final year of the administration. Virginia came through, as it has come through so many crises of the past, and as it will in the inevitable crises we will all face in the years ahead.

Prior to the 9-11 attack, public safety had not been neglected. As a former commonwealth's attorney and Attorney General, I am aware of the critical importance of public safety in the quality of life of every Virginian. And during my four years as governor, serious crimes declined. One success story is the school resource officer program initiated during my administration as a way to deter our young citizens from being enticed into a life of crime. The program works as a tool of prevention, intervention, and enforcement. The hands-on community policing introduced law enforcement influence and presence in our schools, which are one of the communities that are most crucial to Virginia's future. I offered funding in the budget to immediately hire school resource officers in numerous towns, cities, and counties across Virginia.

Other innovations also strengthened community safety. One new program, Virginia Exile, imposes stiffer sentences for gun-related crimes, including illegal possession of a firearm by a felon, and allows judges to hold these criminals without bail until they're tried. Virginia Exile is based on a federal program, Project Exile, which has been successful in Richmond and Hampton Roads. Virginia placed the responsibility to obey firearms laws on criminals, while not limiting the rights of law-abiding citizens to keep and bear arms.

Deputy sheriffs are essential for protecting citizens at the local level. In some areas of the Commonwealth, sheriffs and their deputies are the only law enforcement officers, yet many earned too little to support their families. Part of my promise of public safety was to make the salaries of deputy sheriffs comparable to other law enforcement professionals, so my budgets provided them with more than a nine percent raise.

Other Initiatives

On another front, it was our responsibility to help the working poor gain access to health care without becoming a permanent part of the welfare system. The Virginia Children's Medical Security Insurance Plan covers uninsured low-income children. The plan provides comprehensive health care benefits for children of working families whose income is too high to be covered by Medicaid but not sufficient to afford insurance on their own. The program we established encouraged parental participation in, and responsibility for, the health of their children. We began reaching out to parents to enroll their children through public service announcements, advertisements, and other efforts.

I was also concerned about improving the quality of care that seniors receive in long-term care facilities. In addition, I worked to ensure that seniors who wish to receive home care are guaranteed a high standard of care. We increased Medicaid reimbursements to nursing homes and earmarked them for better pay for caregivers.

During my campaign, I made it clear that we would work closely with advocates to move environmental quality to the top of our agenda. Improving our water was a major priority, and we undertook an ambitious project to clean up Virginia's streams, rivers, lakes, and the Chesapeake Bay, as well as to enhance wetlands. I budgeted millions of dollars for specific water quality improvement projects throughout Virginia. We developed an award-winning program to improve our state parks. I also proposed significant increases in inspection, monitoring, investigation, and enforcement activities at more than 200 solid-waste facilities.

Additionally, as governor I became concerned about the quality and method of delivering care to Virginians with mental disabilities. Families were in great distress, but new thinking was needed to improve the state's commitment to patients. We proactively initiated reform of Virginia's mental disabilities system. My Commission on Community and Inpatient Care began the long-neglected leadership effort to establish quality care for our most vulnerable citizens. We budgeted an additional $41.5 million to substantially improve the quality of care for our mentally disabled population and allocated much of the funding to community care. As we improve care, we must never forget that the individual and families come first. We never tolerated patient abuse within our system, and I offered legislation to insure that abuses would not occur. I was adamant not to repeat the mistake of the 1970s and place patients on the street with no effective system of community care. Today's patients should not become tomorrow's homeless.

A Four-Year Term of Achieving Goals and Innovation

This summary can only highlight a few initiatives of my term as governor. A chief executive has the opportunity and the duty to use that limited time to set direction for the Commonwealth and to advance initiatives. The credit for the successes goes to the exceptional state employees and appointees who worked tirelessly and unselfishly. During my administration, we recognized and appreciated state employees, and they responded by loyal work on behalf of our citizens. I was proud of those whom I brought to state government to serve in my administration. We helped to move Virginia forward by working with all races and regions of the great Commonwealth. We truly made those four years "a time for all Virginians."

As we go forward, we must govern in a way that helps Virginians to advance, grow, succeed, and define their own lives as free men and women. The 21st century will require that we reach beyond the old shop-worn approaches to governing and seek new ways to respond to the needs of our citizens. Our initiatives during my four years in office, I am confident, furthered that progress that makes us a great Commonwealth today and will make us a great Commonwealth in the years ahead.

James S. Gilmore, III, served as the 68th Governor of Virginia from 1998-2002, Attorney General from 1994-1997, and Henrico County Commonwealth's Attorney from 1987-1993. He is currently the President and CEO of the Free Congress Foundation.

CHAPTER 16
Virginia Leading the Way

By Timothy M. Kaine
Governor of Virginia, 2006-2010

When I was inaugurated in Williamsburg in 2006—becoming the first governor since Thomas Jefferson to be sworn in at the old Governor's Palace—I chose a simple motto for my Administration: "Virginia Leading the Way." Since moving to Richmond in 1984, I had believed strongly in our Commonwealth and wondered why we were not more clearly seen as national leaders in the same way we were in the early years of the American Republic. At the adjournment of my four years in office, despite significant economic, social, and political challenges, I was proud to declare that Virginia had reclaimed that mantle of national leadership.

I didn't run for office with a bumper sticker that said: "Will make more budget cuts than anyone before." But the hand I was dealt as chief executive of Virginia meant I had the difficult task of trimming our state budget by more than $7 billion over four years. It was our task to lead the Commonwealth through the most challenging economic climate since the 1930s—and we did not shrink from the job. We met the challenge through hard work and innovative governance—and established Virginia's position as a leader among states. Virginia's economy today is one of the nation's most vibrant, consistently among the top ten states in median income with one of the ten lowest unemployment rates in the country.

©2009 - Office of the Governor of Virginia

Gov. Timothy M. Kaine walks next to the General Assembly Building with his wife, Anne Holton, right, and staff. Photo by Michaele White, Office of the Governor.

During my time as governor, we recruited five Fortune 500 companies to move their headquarters from other states to the Commonwealth, attained more than $13 billion in new investment even in the midst of recession, and achieved the unparalleled honor of being recognized as the best state for business in America eight times by organizations like Forbes.com and CNBC.

Because of great strides in recent decades, *Education Week* now ranks Virginia among the top five states in overall educational quality, most notably recognizing the Commonwealth in 2007 as "the place where a child born today is most likely to have a successful life." By the end of my term, we had grown career and technical education, our high school students ranked third in the nation in students passing Advanced Placement examinations, and our Latino students led the country in elementary school performance. We expanded pre-Kindergarten education by 40 percent so that thousands more low-income Virginia children can now get a strong start in life. And we passed a $1.5 billion education construction bond package—the largest in state history—that is continuing to improve Virginia schools and expand our facilities to train the next generation of leaders.

Virginia's leadership has extended to governance and politics. My administration was named the best-managed state in America by *Governing Magazine*, and thanks to our strong fiscal management, we were one of only seven states nationwide to hold the coveted Triple-A bond rating from all three major financial agencies—even through the economic crisis. And while we were forced to cut billions of dollars from the state budget due to declining revenues, we made huge steps forward in key areas of state government:

- Cutting our infant mortality rate by almost 15%;
- Dramatically reforming our foster care and community mental health systems;
- Investing more than $1.1 billion in the cleanliness of streams, rivers, and the Chesapeake Bay;
- Restoring more individuals' voting rights than any previous Administration;
- Banning smoking in state buildings, restaurants, and bars;
- And tripling the participation of small-, women-, and minority-owned businesses in state procurement.

At the same time, we vastly exceeded all previous preservation efforts by permanently protecting more than 424,000 acres of open space—largely working forests and farms—and creating three new state parks, five new state forests, 13 new Natural Area Preserves, five new Wildlife Management Areas, and preserving parts of 25 Civil War battlefields.

While we were unable to end the decades-old gridlock in the General Assembly on transportation investments, we made important progress implementing smart growth strategies to mitigate congestion and we made strides advancing rail and public transit solutions—including extending Metro rail to Dulles Airport and expanding Amtrak service between Washington, D.C., and both Richmond and Lynchburg.

Finally, on the political front, Democrats transformed Virginia from a reliably "red" (or Republican) state to one that MSNBC political analyst Chuck Todd has called "the perfect bellwether." During my time in office, we won a majority of the congressional delegation, elected two Democratic United States senators, won a majority in the state Senate, and helped Virginia's electoral votes go Democratic for the first time in 44 years. I can say with confidence now that the Commonwealth is a truly competitive state and that neither political party will take Virginia for granted anytime soon.

Looking back 25 years from now, I will remember my time as governor as a pivotal moment and a pivotal experience. The pivotal moment was the tragic shooting at Virginia Tech in 2007—and the pivotal experience was governing through the worst economic crisis since the Great Depression. Yet even in the toughest of circumstances, there is no higher honor than to serve as the governor of the Commonwealth of Virginia, and I wouldn't trade my four years in office for anything. Reflecting now on my four years as governor, I can honestly say my most significant feelings are those of gratitude for those who supported our work—and pride in the things we were able to accomplish during my time in office.

I served Virginia during the best and worst of times—and I rejoiced on the great days and prayed for strength on the hard days. Then and now, I remain forever humbled and honored to have played my small role in the grand sweep of Virginia history.

Timothy M. Kaine served as the 70th Governor of Virginia from 2006 to 2010. During his tenure, he chaired the Southern Governors Association and the Chesapeake Bay Executive Council. In more than 16 years in public office, he also served as Lieutenant Governor, Mayor of the City of Richmond, and Richmond City Councilman. Prior to his public service career, he spent 17 years as a civil rights attorney, working chiefly on race-based and housing discrimination cases. He is the former Chairman of the Democratic National Committee (DNC).

CHAPTER 17
The Path to Jobs and Prosperity: Economic Development in Virginia

By Hugh D. Keogh
Former President and CEO, Virginia Chamber of Commerce

It is generally accepted that Virginians enjoy an exceptionally high quality of life. That benefit can be attributed to a wide range of factors, including a moderate climate, diverse topography, rich culture, and time-tested traditions. Unmistakably, an essential component of that quality is economic prosperity. We are fortunate to live in a state that has thrived in the post-World War II environment. What accounts for the high level of success? Essentially, it is a phenomenon known as economic development: the vitally important production of wealth through business investments leading to job creation and expansion of the tax base of state and local governments. Virginians have done remarkably well in this endeavor. Let's explore why.

The concept of economic development is not new to Virginia. The founding of the Jamestown settlement in 1607 was a global trade and economic development initiative of the British Crown, and Virginia was a strategic hub for commerce in the American colonies and the nascent United States.

Photo courtesy of the Virginia Chamber of Commerce and Hugh Keogh.

But, in the modern era, the economic development effort in Virginia stems from the gradual evolution of the Virginia economy from an agrarian one to an industrialized one, beginning in the 1940s.[1] As companies began to re-tool and return to commercial production from their wartime efforts, they also began to think about where to operate that would enable them to maximize their profitability. It was during this post-war era that the U.S. Southeast began to emerge as an industrial development haven. The Carolinas and Georgia in particular were ahead of the curve in molding their states into not just receptive but aggressive locations for business. In the 1950s, North Carolina especially stood out, with Gov. Luther Hodges being one of the first statesmen in the region to appreciate the value and impact of workforce development, infrastructure improvements and aggressive marketing and outreach efforts to compete for business. By the time Hodges became President Kennedy's Secretary of Commerce in 1961, North Carolina had a substantial lead in attracting and pursuing new manufacturing industry.

Virginia was playing catch-up in the 1960s and it was not until the administration of Albertis S. Harrison (the Governor of Virginia from 1962 to 1966) that the Virginia program came alive. It was during the first term of the visionary Mills E. Godwin, however, that Virginia put in place the framework of the program that in many respects still exists today for selling the Commonwealth in the highly competitive Southeast. Gov. Godwin instituted the Virginia Division of Industrial Development, complete with a cadre of "Industrial Development Representatives," nominally attached to the Governor's Office and assigned to specific geographic territories across the U.S. The Division also included an economic research section, a public relations and advertising section, and of no mean consequence, a community development component designed to improve the ability of Virginia localities to accommodate the needs of business.

Of particular importance during Godwin's first term was the creation of the Virginia Community College System, which gave Virginians access to higher education and training wherever they resided in the Commonwealth. Also during this timeframe, Virginia became the first state to put in place an overseas office specifically designed to pursue foreign direct investment from Europe, or "reverse investment," as it came to be known. The office was located in neutral Brussels, Belgium, a location that permitted staff easy access to all of the industrialized countries of Western Europe. The tools were thus in place by which to sell Virginia to the industrialized world.

The Framework for Economic Development

The basic ingredients to attracting industry have fluctuated substantially over the last 50 years, but an understanding of these "location factors" is essential to grasping how a state must operate to be successful. A brief look at these factors and an indication of how Virginia rates with them follows.[2]

First is geographic location itself. Geography affects proximity to markets, niche marketing opportunities, access to population clusters and other "God-given" advantages. Virginia finds itself squarely in the middle of the Eastern Seaboard, equidistant from Maine and Florida, equidistant from Boston and Atlanta, coastal with easy access to the Chesapeake Bay and the Atlantic Ocean and, finally, on the doorstep of the nation's capital. The Commonwealth is within a day's drive of two-thirds of the U.S. population. This strategic location has proven to be a huge asset in contributing to Virginia's appeal to business.

Second is infrastructure. Virginia is proud to claim the third largest state-maintained highway network in the U.S. Its network of regional and national airports, the presence of abundant rail access through both CSX and Norfolk Southern (the latter headquartered in Virginia at Norfolk) and the highly sophisticated and accessible Port of Hampton Roads give Virginia impressive credentials in this category. However, significant 21st century investments must be made in both highway construction and maintenance if Virginia is to continue to meet the needs of business.

Third is an even-handed tax policy that does not single out business to bear more than its share of the fiscal burden. Virginia's status as a low-tax state with a balanced posture makes it very attractive. Its 6 percent corporate income tax, for example, is lower than the states around it and has not been increased for nearly 40 years.

Fourth is a generally accepted sense of fiscal discipline. Virginia is required to have a balanced budget. Consequently, even in very severe fiscal times, the state has balanced spending with revenues. While frequently tested, this tight-fisted fiscal discipline has been maintained.

Finally, among fundamental location factors is workforce development. A state's ability to provide the increasingly technically sophisticated supply of workers to meet industry's needs has become a chief determinant of where business locates and where it remains. Workforce in the 21st century has reached the top of the heap among business location factors. Virginia policymakers are increasingly aware of this demand and our capability, largely through the Community College System, is improving.

Hovering over all of these fundamental factors is the less tangible notion of quality of life. While this factor eludes measurement, residents frequently boast about Virginia's unique blend of Yankee assertiveness and Southern pace and demeanor. The change of the seasons and proximity to beaches, mountains, and the nation's capital contribute to Virginia's very positive reputation for livability and tourism.

On balance, Virginia more than meets the test of these basic location factors.

Components of the Virginia Economy

Diversity is the hallmark of the Virginia economy, and its ability to attract new jobs in a wide array of economic sectors has greatly contributed to its success.[3] How Virginia has measured up can be captured in two basic statistics: per capita income and unemployment rate.[4] Virginia's per capita income, most recently measured at more than $44,000 in 2008, is the highest in the Southeast, seventh in the nation and 108 percent of the U.S. national average. As recently as the mid-seventies, that figure was just 85 percent of the national average. So we have come a long way.

Similarly, Virginia's unemployment rate in mid-2009 stood at 6.9 percent, more than 30 percent below the national average of 10 percent. While the Virginia rate was much higher than usual during the recent deep and long-lasting recession, it remained well below that of states around us and the nation as a whole. Why? Because, as noted, we enjoy one of the most diverse economies in the nation.

In this discussion, let's make the distinction between basic employment—that which could locate anywhere—and locally-based employment, such as retail/wholesale, government, health care, and public education. Our interest here is in the basic employment, since that is where we compete with other states. Our basic economic components are these:

1. Business Services/ Technology
2. Defense-related activity
3. Manufacturing
4. Tourism
5. Agribusiness

While Virginia's proximity to Washington, D.C., and the federal establishment has been frequently maligned by politicians, there can be no doubting the fact that the federal government as a customer has played an enormous role in Virginia's economic history and development. The Northern Virginia suburbs of Washington have become a very deep repository for business services—expressly in the technology arena as software developers, systems integrators, Web-based management companies and database manipulators, among others, have flocked to the region. Legions of government contractors have been launched, expanded, and expanded again as the federal government's insatiable appetite for technical assistance and management expertise has matured. In fact, the impact of this phenomenon in Virginia's statewide economic scorecard (high per capita income, low unemployment) is frequently overlooked by policymakers. By any measure the role of Northern Virginia's economic explosion since 1980 has been the lead story of Virginia's economic development and has unmistakably made the region the state's economic powerhouse, or the straw that stirs the drink. Without it, our numbers would look very average.

Similarly, Virginia's strategic role in the nation's defense posture is undeniable. With the Pentagon located in Virginia, the nation's largest naval base in Hampton Roads, in addition to Langley Air Force Base in Hampton, Fort Lee in Petersburg, and Oceana Naval Air Station in Virginia Beach, Virginia's status as a defender of freedom is beyond dispute. Toss in the only shipyard in the world currently capable of constructing a nuclear aircraft carrier (Northrop Grumman Newport News) and you can easily visualize our pre-eminence in this arena. Since the terrorist strikes of September 11th, 2001, that status has become even more acute. More than 100,000 uniformed military are stationed in the state; more than twice that number of public and private sector civilians support them. It is a truly significant phenomenon.

Manufacturing in Virginia has been a bellwether in the state's employment base since World War II. It peeked in the 1990 time frame at about 430,000 Virginians statewide. With the onset of automation, the impact of foreign competition and the inexorability of industrial "right-sizing" in the 21st century, that number shrunk to less than 250,000 by 2009. Nevertheless, the value of goods produced in Virginia has soared in recent years and the sector remains extremely important to Virginia's diversity and economic health. Advanced manufacturing in semi-conductors, aviation components and equipment, environmental controls, and paper and wood products, for example, remain prominent economic generators. Virginia's workforce development capability will remain a key to the state's continued ability to satisfy the demands of this sector.

From left, Rodney Eagle, Mayor Harrisonburg City Council, Dr. Linwood Rose, President James Madison University, Gov. Timothy M. Kaine, William Kyger, Chairman Rockingham County Board of Supervisors, and Walter Moos, SRI Vice-President Biosciences Division, break ground for a new SRI International facility in the Shenandoah Valley. Photo courtesy of Billy Vaughn.

Tourism has long been a chief job-generator in the Commonwealth, and currently more than 220,000 Virginians owe their employment to this sector. Tourism also generates more than $18 billion annually into the Virginia economy. And so it should. Few states enjoy the breadth, depth, and uncanny attractiveness of our Commonwealth as a magnet for visitors from around the country and around the world. It is not an exaggeration to say that Virginia's history is America's history, and the sites have underscored that boast. From Mount Vernon to Monticello, from Colonial Williamsburg to the Blue Ridge Parkway, and from the Shenandoah Valley to the Chesapeake Bay, Virginia has an unbridled array of tourism magnets. Sprinkle in the theme parks and luxurious destinations in both the eastern and western extremities of the state and you can readily appreciate why this sector thrives in our Commonwealth. As our state slogan indicates, Virginia is, indeed, for lovers.

The agribusiness sector is valuable as well. While farming no longer generates the employment of its 20th century heyday, the products produced are world-renowned and contribute mightily to the state's reputation and its coffers. Approximately 550,000 Virginians, both full- and part-time, work in the agribusiness field. The leading products, many of which are exported around the globe, include pork products, tobacco, poultry, forestry products, peanuts, and apples. Wine-making is on a dramatic increase in the state (there are well over 150 wineries operating here) and kudos for the quality of the wine pour in. Additionally, national brand beer is made in Williamsburg and in Rockingham County in the Shenandoah Valley. All of the products combine to make agribusiness an important contributor to the Virginia economy.

Let's reiterate at this juncture that diversity is the hallmark of the Virginia economy and has served us well.

International Trade & Development

By now as we move into the second decade of the 21st Century, the term "Global Economy" has become a very common phrase in American lexicon. But how does a single state immerse itself in that economy and maximize the opportunities? How does the global economy affect everyday Virginians?

There are several answers to those questions. First, let's look at the phenomenon known historically as "reverse investment." As the wounds caused by World War II slowly began to heal and European economies improved, companies in England, Germany, France, and the Netherlands began exporting to the United States. At some point in the late 1960s many of those same companies came to the realization that they would be better served, and their market penetration protected, if they would actually produce their products in the U.S. By the 1970s the attraction of this investment became a very important aspect of Virginia's marketing mix. And, helped enormously by the efforts of the state's European marketing office in Brussels, Virginia fared well. For example, more than 100 German companies and an equal number of British subsidiaries are operating in Virginia. Many of these companies not only produce here for the domestic market but also export from here to destinations around the world.

In 1981, the Commonwealth opened a marketing office in Tokyo to service the Asian markets. The state was admittedly slow to penetrate this region following its European success, and other Southeastern states, especially Florida and Georgia, were clearly outpacing Virginia. Then in 1986, Canon, the copier and camera giant, announced that it would build a state-of-the-art laser beam printer and copier facility in Newport News. Virginia was on the map in pursuit of Japanese industry. Suppliers and vendors followed suit and ultimately other world-class companies such as Mitsubishi Chemical and Sumitomo Heavy Industries followed suit, both locating major plants in the Hampton Roads region.

Today our efforts to attract foreign direct investments have paid great dividends.[5] Cumulatively, Virginia boasts more than 800 companies from overseas that have invested $18 billion and employ at least 150,000 Virginians. We have much to be proud of.

The second component of our international marketing posture is two-way trade—i.e., exports and imports. Virginia's infrastructure for trade is unparalleled, starting with the Virginia port complex in the Hampton Roads region, with its highly sophisticated cargo handling and distribution facilities in Newport News, Portsmouth, and Norfolk. To the northwest is the Virginia Inland Port in Front Royal, a sometimes overlooked asset that has greatly enhanced cargo activity in Hampton Roads. And, of course, there is the inimitable Dulles International Airport, 25 miles from Washington, D.C., which gives Virginia a magnificent gateway to the world.

TOP REGIONAL BUYERS OF VIRGINIA EXPORTS 2010[6]

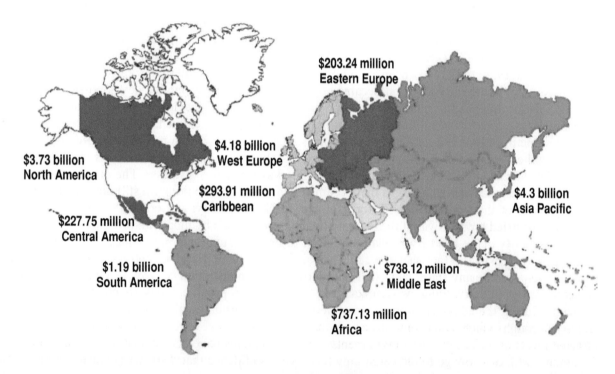

To capitalize on these many assets, Gov. Gerald L. Baliles declared 1987 the "Year of Trade in Virginia" and personally undertook eight overseas business development missions during his administration. The results of those efforts continue to redound to the benefit of the Commonwealth.

So Virginia has a long and distinguished record in penetrating foreign markets. The numbers bear that out. Today at least 4,000 Virginia companies, many of them small firms, have sold goods and services overseas.[7] These exports accounted for $29 billion in revenues and supported more than 300,000 private sector jobs.[8] In fact, one estimate suggests that nearly 17 percent of Virginia's manufacturing workforce owe their jobs to exports.[9]

It's important to note as well in this context that imports create jobs, too—especially in port-related cargo handling capacities and in the array of distribution facilities that have located in the

Hampton Roads region and in the Shenandoah Valley. At the national level, imports do cause concern because of their negative impact on the balance of trade. But make no mistake: They are an important source of prosperity, especially for a centrally located coastal state.

Impact of Policy Decisions on Virginia's Attractiveness

A state government creates the product it represents in the global marketplace and it is that product and its attractiveness to business that determines how successful it will be in economic development. As noted, that policy framework includes many factors, such as tax climate, workplace stability, environmental regulation, and infrastructure development. Let's look at three specific policy actions that serve as excellent examples of Virginia's response to business needs.[10]

In 1947, the U.S. Congress passed a law, the Taft-Hartley Act, that empowered states to enact "Right to Work" laws. These statutes give employees the right to a job without being required to join a labor union to get that job—i.e., the right to work. The Virginia General Assembly passed such a law in 1948. The law not only has served to stabilize Virginia's workplace environment through the years, it has become a symbol of the state's positive attitude toward business. Currently, 22 states have right-to-work laws, including the entire U.S. Southeast, but Virginia is the right-to-work state closest to the Northeast markets. As a result, the law has been an important ingredient to the state's corporate fabric.

Second, in the early 1980s, it became apparent to Virginia's economic development practitioners that too few localities in the state were truly prepared for economic development. They lacked prepared industrial sites served with utilities, they had little or no marketing acumen, and their local government policies sometimes reflected anti-growth sentiments. The Commonwealth reacted to those limitations by fashioning the Virginia Certification Program, which established a broad but clear and well-defined set of criteria that, if met, would certify that the community was ready for business. The program was a huge success and the green and white signs that became the hallmark of the program still dot the interstate and primary roads of the Commonwealth (for example, "Halifax County: A Certified Business Location"). Becoming certified brought with it the ultimate bounty: more visits by industrial prospects.

Similarly in the 1990s, Virginia found itself too often a runner-up in the quest for a new industry, a situation rooted in the fact that the state had not put in place fiscal incentives that would gird its competitiveness, as many states had. In 1992, during the administration of Gov. L. Douglas Wilder, the Governor's Opportunity Fund was capitalized, which would provide funds to close deals. Shortly thereafter during the administration of Gov. George Allen, Virginia embraced the "performance grant" concept through which companies investing in Virginia would receive bonuses when they achieved targeted levels of job creation and investments. Other incentives have been added to the mix, so that the Commonwealth can now go to the bargaining table with confidence that there are adequate arrows in the quiver.[11]

Virginia has for the most part kept pace with 21st century policy demands. Chinks in the armor would include the absence of gubernatorial succession and the cumbersome structure of local government. In general, however, Virginia's tax, workplace, and regulatory framework is balanced and conducive to economic development.

Conclusion

Whether it is the Forbes.com ranking of Virginia as the number one state in the nation for business or *Governing Magazine's* anointing the Commonwealth as the best-managed state in the country,[12] accolades and superlatives continue to roll in. The future is bright. Virginians from all walks of life have been blessed, as borne out by our relatively low unemployment and the highest per capita income in the Southeast. Fiscal discipline and respect for free enterprise remain hallmarks of Virginia's policy framework. But the competition remains severe and serious challenges persist.

Chief among those is the inability or unwillingness of our elected leadership to provide solutions to the need for substantial transportation infrastructure improvements. Long-term, sustainable, and significant sources of revenue to deal with critical needs in both maintenance and construction of highways, mass transit, and intermodal systems are essential.

Further, the shortage of technically skilled workers is the chief inhibitor to Virginia's continued economic progress. Employers need to know that they can find skilled and trainable labor wherever they operate in Virginia. Tied to this problem is the notion of economic disparity in the state, a phenomenon by which much of rural and "remote" Virginia runs the risk of being left behind as structural economic change persists and commercial creativity lags. Our policymakers must come to grips with these challenges; the business community can and will play an inextricable role in meeting them. Technology can be the tool that makes it possible.

Our chief hope for the next century is that Virginia will maintain the regional distinctions that are so much a part of its charm while distributing its largesse in a balanced and even-handed way to all its citizens, regardless of geography, race, or economic status. By doing so, Virginia will indeed achieve a future worthy of its past.

Hugh D. Keogh was the President and CEO of the Virginia Chamber of Commerce from 1992-2010 and Director of the Virginia Department of Economic Development from 1987-1992.

CHAPTER 18
The Attorney General: Virginia's Chief Legal Officer

By Jerry W. Kilgore
Virginia Attorney General, 2002-2005
and Christopher R. Nolen
Chief Counsel to the Attorney General, 2002-2005

Virginia has only three elected executive officers: the governor, lieutenant governor, and attorney general. Initially, the attorney general was appointed by the Virginia General Assembly between 1776 and 1851. Since a change to the Virginia Constitution in 1852, the voters have directly elected the attorney general. The first attorney general for the Commonwealth of Virginia was Edmund Randolph, who served from July, 1776, through November, 1786.

Attorney General Jerry W. Kilgore addresses state lawmakers. Photo courtesy of Jerry Kilgore.

Unlike the office of the governor, there is no limit on the number of terms an attorney general may serve, and many who have held the office have served multiple terms. With the governor's service limited to only four years, attorneys general have frequently vacated the office during the modern era to run for governor after serving one term or less. Should the attorney general resign or die during the term of office, the governor names the replacement unless the General Assembly is in session, when state lawmakers will choose the new attorney general.

Structure of an Attorney General's Office

The attorney general manages one of Virginia's largest law firms. While the office of each attorney general differs in the number of staff and position titles, most offices are generally organized in a similar fashion. Each position in the organizational chart of an attorney general's office is similar to a private sector equivalent.

Offices are organized by division (for example, the "criminal" division) and then by sections within each division (such as criminal appeals, financial crimes, environmental crimes, etc.).

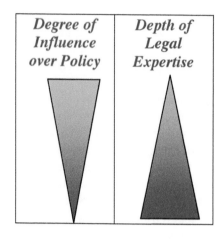

Degree of Influence over Policy	Depth of Legal Expertise

OFFICE OF ATTORNEY GENERAL	PRIVATE SECTOR EQUIVALENT
POSITIONS	POSITIONS
Attorney General	Chief Executive Officer
Chief Deputy	Chief Operating Officer
Chief Counsel	General Counsel
Deputy Attorneys General	Vice-Presidents/ Division Heads
Senior Assistant Attorneys General	Managers
Assistant Attorneys General	Employees

From Obscurity to the Headlines

Long considered the behind-the-scenes offices that simply represent their states in legal disputes, state attorneys general are quickly becoming some of the most powerful state officials—as illustrated by many national headlines. It started with the tobacco lawsuits initiated by attorneys general in 1998 that ultimately brought record dollars to state coffers.[1] Building upon that lawsuit, attorneys general have targeted and regulated financial institutions, tire manufacturers, telemarketers, pharmaceutical companies, lending organizations, credit card companies, accounting firms, and investors, among others.

With the growing willingness of attorneys general to exercise their authority, business practices have often been second-guessed—not in the boardroom, but in state capitals throughout the country. From consumer disclosures to marketing strategies, businesses face the ever-present power of regulators and consumer advocates. However, Virginia's attorneys general tend to move cautiously in the office's dealings with business.

Virginia attorneys general tend to be pro-business, shying away from inquiries on litigation that appear to attack the Commonwealth's businesses. For example, even in the well-renowned tobacco multistate lawsuit, Virginia's attorney general generally supported the tobacco industry until the eve of the tobacco companies' settlement with all the states.[2]

State attorneys general can be active in many realms. Perhaps their most common focus is that of criminal law. Long thought of as the state's "Top Cop," the state attorney general usually has an influence in shaping criminal justice legislation. For example, in Virginia in 2003, we sought and obtained tougher anti-gang legislation following a yearlong study of the problem. Virginia had been facing growing gang violence from criminal street gangs originating in other countries. The legislation not only imposed harsher sentences for gang violence, but created gang prevention and awareness programs throughout the state.

Yet another area of our activism in Virginia involved the challenge of domestic violence. In recognition that few leaders wanted to talk about the issue, let alone push legislation, the office conducted a study of the problem, found glaring loopholes in the state law that unintentionally allowed abuse to continue, and sought passage of tougher laws. The new laws protected victims more aggressively by enforcing harsher penalties and improving the use of protective orders. The office of attorney general also sought to educate the community by creating the "Cut Out Domestic Violence" program that partnered with hair and nail salons to promote awareness of domestic violence. By understanding that, too frequently, the only place a woman got away from her abuser was a salon, the program provided salon employees with information to offer those in abusive situations.

At times, a state attorney general becomes involved in issues that encompass significant national tragedies or events. For our office, the snipers who were terrorizing Washington, D.C., and the Northern Virginia region in 2002 brought a great challenge. The nation's capital and the states of Alabama, Maryland, and Virginia had all suffered at the hands of the snipers, who were randomly shooting victims in the greater region. Schools were on lockdown throughout the area, and the national media were in a frenzy over the shootings. When the two snipers were caught, the jurisdiction issue dominated the discussion: Which state would be the first to try the perpetrators? While meeting with then-U.S. attorney general John Ashcroft, we were able to convince the Department of Justice that Virginia had the criminal justice system in place that could provide seasoned prosecutors to try the snipers and also mete out sound sentences should they be found guilty. Virginia tried the cases, with the adult sniper receiving the death penalty[3] and the juvenile (who was tried as an adult) receiving life in prison without parole.[4]

The Office of Attorney General

The attorney general is a member of the Executive Branch of state government.[5] The sources of the office's power include the following:

1). **The State Constitution:** Virginia's Constitution creates the office of attorney general and declares that he shall have such duties as the legislature may delineate. Article V, § 15 of the Virginia Constitution provides: "He shall perform such duties and receive such compensation as may be prescribed by law…"[6] That section also establishes three eligibility requirements to be elected to the office: "No person shall be eligible for election or appointment to the office of attorney general unless he is a citizen of the United States, has attained the age of thirty years, and has the qualifications required for a judge of a court of record."[7]

2). **State Statutes:** The legislature sets forth in Virginia law the specific duties of the attorney general, who serves as the chief legal officer of the state. Usually, attorneys general nationwide act based on specific authority granted to them in their state's legal code.

3). **Common Law:** Most attorneys general have retained their "common law powers." Their duties and powers typically are not exhaustively defined by either Constitution or statute but included all those exercised at common law. There is no doubt that the legislature may deprive the attorney general of specific powers; but in the absence of such legislative action, he typically may exercise all such authority as the public interests requires and the attorney general has wide discretion in making the determination as to the public interest.[8]

4). *Parens patriae*: A state attorney general may be able to bring a suit under the concept of *parens patriae* if the state is asserting "an injury to what has been characterized as a 'quasi-sovereign' interest."[9] The United States Supreme Court defined "quasi-sovereign interest" by stating that "[t]hey are not sovereign interests, proprietary interests, or private interests pursued by the State as a nominal party. They consist of a set of interests that the State has in the well-being of its populous."[10] The Court went on to indicate that such interests included "the health and well-being—both physical and economic—of its residents in general."[11]

Substantive Responsibility & Areas of Authority

Chief Legal Officer for the State: The attorney general serves as the head of Virginia's Department of Law. In this role, he is responsible for advising state agencies in all legal matters. The office directs the state's litigation strategies and provides agency advice. In several states, the attorney general reviews legislation being considered by the legislature or signed by the governor.[12] In many states, the attorney general also works with state agencies to review proposed regulations.[13]

Virginia's attorney general defends state laws and policies against challenges to their constitutionality and handles related appeals of lower court cases. This may include representing the state's interests before the U.S. Supreme Court. For example, our office defended the Richmond Redevelopment and Housing Authority's anti-trespassing policy that was established to fight crime. In 2003, the High Court upheld Virginia's position after a defendant claimed that the ordinance was too broad under the First Amendment to the U.S. Constitution.[14] Additionally, under my tenure, the office defended Virginia's anti-cross burning statute against claims that it violated the constitutional right to freedom of speech. The Supreme Court upheld Virginia's law in 2003, recognizing that there was no constitutional right to burn a cross when the act was carried out with the intent to intimidate.[15]

In Virginia, the office also represents the Commonwealth's position in appeals of court cases, including criminal justice and death penalty cases.[16]

Consumer Protection: One of the realms in which attorneys general are most active is consumer protection. Most states charge the attorney general with enforcement of their consumer protection laws. Such enforcement includes civil and criminal prosecutions. It is in this area, along with antitrust actions, that the nation's attorneys general do the most work in a coordinated fashion. Examples of consumer protection actions include telemarketing, charitable solicitations, marketing and advertising practices, sweepstakes,[17] and price-gouging. In Virginia, the latter is in response to a relatively new state law. When prices spiked in the Commonwealth in the wake of Hurricane Isabel, our office investigated at least 40 complaints that businesses had unconscionably increased their prices.[18]

The job of protecting consumers has been made more difficult by the rapid development of new technologies. My office established a new Cybercrime Unit to investigate and prosecute computer-related crimes, and we helped to enforce the state laws that were enacted to counter and punish high-tech criminals.[19]

Antitrust: Antitrust violations are another realm in which state attorneys general are particularly active. Except perhaps in larger states, most antitrust enforcement actions brought by attorneys general are coordinated at the national level through the Multistate Antitrust Task Force of the National Association of attorneys general. The national efforts include cooperative investigations and filing multi-state enforcement actions.   Typically, one attorney general will take the lead in coordinating the investigation with other states playing a supporting role.

Securities regulation: Many attorneys general have responsibility for securities regulation in their state. The extent to which the attorney general may prosecute securities issues varies greatly depending on the statutory scheme in each state.

Fraud against government: Increasingly, attorneys general are becoming more active in prosecuting cases involving allegations of fraud in regard to companies contracting with state government. The most recent examples have been in the pharmaceutical and healthcare arenas (for example, pharmacy benefits managers and Medicaid fraud). In 2003, the Medicaid Fraud Control Unit of our office launched an investigation of the company that makes the addictive drug, OxyContin; in 2007, then-Attorney General Bob McDonnell announced that the company had pleaded guilty to felony misbranding for misrepresenting the addictive nature of its product and would pay Virginia $60 million in criminal penalties.[20]

Other substantive areas of responsibility include:

- ✓ Environmental Regulation Enforcement
- ✓ Charitable Trusts and Solicitations
- ✓ Supreme Court Practice/State Constitutional Law
- ✓ Civil Rights
- ✓ Election Law
- ✓ Energy Ratemaking
- ✓ Child Support

Issuance of Advisory Opinions

"Official advisory opinions" are a powerful tool that an attorney general can use to help make policy. Advisory opinions are typically issued to certain state and local officers named in the state's code.[21] The opinions guide agency interpretations of law. Often, courts will rely on such opinions in interpreting state laws, giving such opinions persuasive value. The Supreme Court of Virginia has recognized that "construction of a statute by the attorney general is persuasive and entitled to considerable weight."[22]

Conclusion

State attorneys general continue to exercise greater influence and power over many aspects of our lives—from criminal justice reforms to consumer protection actions. The state attorneys general who tend to be more conservative will focus on serving as the "Top Cop" and seeking ways to influence the criminal justice or legal system. Those who tend to be activists will target business practices under the banner of consumer protection. Citizens can expect to see and hear more from their attorneys general because of their growing power and influence, as these offices spring from obscurity to being obvious influencers of state and national policies.

Jerry Kilgore served as Virginia Attorney General from 2002-2005 and Secretary of Public Safety from 1994-1998. He is a partner with McGuireWoods LLP and a Senior Advisor with McGuireWoods Consulting LLC. Christopher R. Nolen served as Special Counsel to the Attorney General from 2002 to 2003 and as Chief Counsel from 2003-2005. He is a partner with McGuireWoods LLP and a Senior Advisor with McGuireWoods Consulting LLC.

PART IV: THE JUDICIAL BRANCH

Virginia selects its judges very differently from nearly every other state—not through executive appointments or elections, but through its legislature. Part V, *The Judicial Branch*, describes the process of how that is accomplished, as well as Virginia's extensive statewide court system. The author of Chapter 19 is a member of the House of Delegates, chairman of the Courts of Justice Committee, and a longtime veteran of the legislative chore of choosing judges. The author explains *why* Virginia chooses judges through the General Assembly rather than by popular elections where candidates campaign to serve on the bench. He describes the types of judges and justices who must be selected. And, unlike federal judges who are appointed for life, Virginia's judges serve various terms and must be re-elected to stay on the bench.

The delegate also shares his insight into the process by illustrating a variety of scenarios as potential jurists undergo rounds of interviews, legislative scrutiny, and deliberations. Readers may want to note that it is sometimes a bumpy road for them. This may involve partisan disagreements, disputes between houses regardless of party, and even disagreements among caucus members. There may be bipartisan regional accords among the members of local delegations, but other partisans in the General Assembly may not concur. When they are deadlocked, the

Photo by Anne Marie Morgan.

governor selects the judge, as he also does when lawmakers are not in session and a judge retires or dies unexpectedly. Additionally, Virginia has a confidential procedure for investigating judges who face allegations of poor judicial temperament or performance.

Written by the executive secretary of the Supreme Court of Virginia, Chapter 20 further explains the modern organization and functions of the oldest judicial system in America. Virginia's counties and cities have their own local courts, which have names that are similar to the federal courts. Especially noteworthy is the chart that features the court hierarchy and route of appeal. The chapter also delineates the types of cases that are heard at each level. The General District courts are the ones which Virginians encounter most frequently because they hear traffic cases, while the Circuit Courts are the trial courts of general jurisdiction. Only "the courts of record," which are Circuit Courts, the Court of Appeals, and the Supreme Court of Virginia, make and keep transcripts of all proceedings. Additionally, the chapter describes how Virginia's courts hear not only criminal cases, but civil disputes and appeals. Both chapters together are a substantive but concise overview that should help readers become better-acquainted with Virginia's judges and how the courts really work.

CHAPTER 19
Selecting Virginia's Judges

By David B. Albo
Member, House of Delegates

At the time of writing this article, I had served in the Virginia House of Delegates since 1994 and was the Chairman of that chamber's Courts of Justice Committee, which oversees the selection of judges in the Commonwealth. The editors asked me to write about how Virginia chooses judges. Instead of merely explaining what our Constitution and state law require, this chapter will outline how judges are selected in the "real world" of the legislature and politics.

Relationship Between the Branches of Government

Before discussing how judges are appointed, it's important to remember the relationship of judges and the courts to the other branches of government. As many students learn in civics classes, the United States has three branches of government. But this structure also applies to Virginia's state government. The first branch is "legislative" and is comprised of the House of Delegates and State Senate, which write and pass the laws. The second is "executive" and consists of the Governor and related departments and agencies which run the day-to-day operations of the government. The third is the "judicial" branch, which includes all of Virginia's courts with judges who preside over them.

Each branch is a separate and distinct branch. According to Article 3 of the Virginia Constitution, "[t]he legislative, executive, and judicial departments shall be separate and distinct, so that none exercises the powers properly belonging to the others...."[1] In simple terms, this means that each branch has its own specific duties and no other branch can perform the functions of another branch.

For example, the judges in the judicial branch

Delegate David Albo (r) explains legislation on the floor of the House of Delegates, assisted by then-Delegate (now Governor) Robert F. McDonnell. Photo courtesy of David Albo.

are not allowed to pass laws because that is a duty of the legislative branch. And the legislative branch is not allowed to decide cases in court. For instance, no member of the House or Senate should write a letter to a court telling the judge his opinion on whether a criminal is guilty of a crime or which spouse should get custody of a constituent's children. Only a judge can do that. But a judge cannot decide which activities are criminal acts or what the rules are for determining custody. Only the legislature can write laws.

Relationship of the People of Virginia to the Three Branches of Government

In Virginia—and every state of the United States—the government answers to the people. Of course, every one of the nearly 8 million Virginia residents cannot tell the government what to do daily. Instead, on election day, the people cast their votes to designate a representative to tell the government what to do.

The branches of government that write and execute the laws should be chosen by the people of Virginia because these branches are making the rules by which the citizens must live. Thus, the framers of the Virginia Constitution established the provision that the governor who heads the executive branch and the members of the House of Delegates and State Senate who run the legislative branch are to be chosen by the people through their votes on election day.

In Virginia, the branch that interprets and enforces the law—the judicial branch—is not chosen directly by the people. This is not the case in many states, where judges are also elected by the voters. States with this system would argue that this makes the courts responsive to the voters, and that no branch should be "above" the people. In Virginia, the drafters of the state Constitution did not think that this process is a good idea. That is because a court often renders decisions that are not popular, and the whole point of an election is to be popular so that a candidate can get more than 50 percent of the vote. For example, judges must give criminals a fair trial, determine which parent gets custody of a child in a divorce, and decide legal disputes where one person must pay another person. Many of these decisions make one side happy and another side upset. Consequently, the framers of the Virginia Constitution wanted judges to decide cases based *solely* upon the law—and not to decide cases based upon what is popular. Thus, the Virginia Constitution includes Article 6, section 7, which states that the judges shall be chosen by a majority vote of those elected to the House and the Senate[2]—instead of directly by the people.

Here is a clear example of why Virginia's framers did not want the popular election of judges. Let's say there is a criminal case in which a drug dealer had his door kicked down by the police without a proper search warrant. (The U.S. Constitution states that a home cannot be searched unless there is probable cause to believe that there is evidence of a crime in the house.[3] The way that police get a certification that "probable cause" exists is that they go to a court and tell the court their reasons. If a judge agrees, then the court issues a "search warrant" stating that there is a probable cause which justifies the search.)

In this story, the police find a lot of crack cocaine in the house and charge the drug dealer with "distribution of crack." The drug dealer's attorney argues to a judge that the crack should not be admitted into evidence because it was discovered in violation of the constitutional protection against searches of a home without a warrant. The bottom line is that if the large volume of cocaine in the house is not admitted into evidence (and is "thrown out of court"), then there is no evidence of a crime and the drug dealer will have his charge dismissed. In this example, the judge has a tough decision: (1) uphold the constitutional protection against searches without a warrant and, consequently, the drug dealer goes free, or (2) rule that the search was lawful when it was, in fact, not legal, and convict a guy that he knows is guilty. In Virginia, we want judges to decide cases based only on the law. We do not want them to be thinking how popular their decision will be. We do not want judges anxiously wondering how this will look during their next re-election campaign.

Note, however, that the idea that no branch of government should ever be above the people is a paramount concern. So, the framers of the Virginia Constitution solve this problem by requiring the judges of the judicial branch to be selected by the members of the House and State Senate. Therefore, if a really bad or incompetent judge is appointed, then the people of Virginia can complain to the lawmakers who appointed the judge—their representatives to the House of Delegates and State Senate. And if they don't like the answer that the House or Senate member gives them, then the citizen can try and throw the delegate or senator out of office at the next election by voting for the incumbent's opponent.

Types of Courts and Judges in Virginia

To understand how judges are chosen, it is important to know the different types of judges, which are illustrated by the different courts that Virginia has established.

First, there are "trial courts." These are circuit courts where judges preside over cases with an actual trial. They are the types of cases that the public sees on television, where the lawyers present evidence and interview witnesses on the stand.

Another type of court is called an "appellate court." When a person in a trial court thinks that he did not get treated fairly, he can ask for a review—called an "appeal"—of his case to an appellate court. The appellate courts do not retry the case. They read the transcripts of what people said in court. The appellate courts determine if the trial judge applied the law correctly. In the previous drug dealer example, if the trial court had ruled that the search of the house was constitutional and admitted the evidence of the crack, the defendant could appeal his case to an appellate court, and ask the appellate judge to look at whether the trial judge made the correct call on the law regarding searches of homes. In the Commonwealth, appeals are heard by the Court of Appeals and the Supreme Court of Virginia.[4] These two courts examine cases that arose in all localities throughout Virginia.

Both the trial and appellate courts are called "courts of record" because transcripts are made of their proceedings.[5]

All of the trial courts are run by local judges who preside over cases and disputes in their courts' designated areas. For example, local judges in Arlington only hear cases or disputes that come from Arlington, and local judges in Roanoke only hear cases or disputes that come from Roanoke.

There are three types of local judges:[6]

(1) **Juvenile and Domestic Relations Court** judges, who decide cases dealing with crimes committed by people under the age of 18 and matters affecting families, such as temporary custody, child abuse, and truancy;

(2) **General District Court** judges, who decide cases dealing with violations of traffic laws, misdemeanor criminal cases where the punishment is less than one year in jail, and small business disputes where the amount in dispute is $15,000 or less; and

(3) **Circuit Court** judges, who hear original cases for felony crimes where the potential punishment is greater than a year, business disputes that are not originally filed in the General District Court, and divorce and permanent custody cases, to name a few. Circuit Court judges also hear cases from General District or Juvenile and Domestic Relations Courts when the people who were in one of those courts did not like the outcome and appealed (requested a new hearing).

As the justices of the Supreme Court of Virginia watch, Elizabeth A. McClanahan, left, is sworn in by Chief Justice Cynthia D. Kinser as the Court's 101st justice on Sept. 1, 2011. Photo by Bob Brown, *Richmond Times-Dispatch.*

How Judges are Chosen

All of the information on how judges are chosen can be found in more depth in the Virginia Constitution and the state Code. But how does judicial selection work in the "real world"? Let's start with the foundation. Article VI of the Virginia Constitution states that a judge is chosen almost in the same way legislation is passed—by a majority vote of the House and the Senate.[7]

The differences between the passage of a bill and a judge's selection are two-fold. (1) A bill passes by a majority of those *voting*. So if there are only 90 lawmakers present, 46 votes will pass the bill. But a judge has to be appointed by a majority of lawmakers who have been *elected*. So, out of 100 elected delegates, the judge must get 51 votes. In the example where 90 legislators are voting and a potential judge gets 46 votes, that person will not be selected because 51 votes were needed. (2) The governor has no veto power over the selection of a judge. In other words, a person who gets the required votes by the House and Senate becomes a judge, even if the governor does not like it.

The whole process starts when the General Assembly announces that a judge has retired and his job needs to be filled or if an area's population has grown so much that a new judge's seat needs to be created. Only Virginia lawyers (people who have passed the exam to become a lawyer in the Commonwealth) can be judges. Some states allow anyone to be a judge, but we only allow people who have been trained in the law and who have passed the State Bar exam. Also, judges must live in Virginia, and local judges are required to live in that locality. Article VI, section 7 in the Virginia Constitution states: "All justices of the Supreme Court and all judges of other courts of record shall be residents of the Commonwealth and shall, at least five years prior to their appointment or election, have been admitted to the bar of the Commonwealth. Each judge of a trial court of record shall during his term of office reside within the jurisdiction of one of the courts to which he was appointed or elected ... "[8]

When the word gets out that the General Assembly is seeking a lawyer to become a judge in a jurisdiction, anyone who wants to be a judge sends a résumé to the Virginia House of Delegates and Senate and to their local delegate and senator, announcing that this person would like to be considered for appointment to that position. Each individual who wants the job and who can persuade his delegate or senator to invite him for an interview appears before the Senate and House Courts of Justice Committees (panels of delegates and senators who concentrate on bills related to the law, such as criminal law, business law, and divorce law).

These delegates and senators ask the candidates questions about how they will run their courts and how they will make sure that people have a fair hearing in court. One question that delegates and senators always ask is about the separation of powers. The query is often as simple as, "When presiding over a trial, will you make sure that you only interpret the laws and do not make up any laws that do not exist?" The Courts of Justice Committees also search to find out whether the applicants have been convicted of any crimes or have had complaints filed against them as lawyers.

All people who are satisfactory to a Courts of Justice Committee are certified as meeting the minimum qualifications of being a judge. At this stage, the Committee does not decide who gets the job. The members are just certifying that the person is qualified. The final decision is made on the floor of the House and the Senate when all of the members get to vote for the "candidate" whom they like the best. But as one may guess, it's not as simple as it looks on paper!

Here is the way it really works. The House has 100 members and the Senate has 40. In the U.S. and Virginia, there are two major political parties, the Republicans and the Democrats. In the House and Senate, the two parties usually meet before legislative sessions and discuss strategy. This partisan "club" is called a "caucus." Unless there is an actual tie, in nearly all years there will be a majority of either Republicans or Democrats in each body. For example, at the time I wrote this article, the House had a majority of Republicans and the Senate had a majority of Democrats. So, if all the members of the House Republican Caucus and the Senate Democratic Caucus work with those in their parties as a team, they can control what happens. This is because if everyone sticks together, the caucus has a majority of votes in each chamber.

In preparation for the selection of judges, these caucuses have approved among themselves a set of voluntary rules, called the "caucus rules." These are not binding and do not have the force of law. They are more like an agreement among the members to behave in a certain way. Usually, within these rules is an agreement that if the majority of the caucus decides on Judge X, then everyone is encouraged to vote for Judge X. Again, these are not mandatory, so no one is compelled to do it.

But in any large group of people, if there are no parameters upon which everyone agrees, it can be chaos. Imagine the Washington Redskins football playbook. It would be absolute chaos if every time the coach called a run, the players say, "We don't like the run, so we think we will go out for a pass and not block the defense."

The bottom line is that usually—but certainly not always—the person who is approved by the majority of the caucus gets the job. And if both caucuses agree on a single judge, then that person is elected without controversy.

But, once again, it is not that simple. There are hundreds of different scenarios that could arise. I have witnessed many of these events during nearly two decades in the General Assembly. But just to illustrate what can occur, here are some scenarios:

> ➤ **For the Selection of Local Judges:**

(1) The House majority caucus wants Judge X and the Senate majority caucus prefers Judge Y. This is the most common dispute, especially in years when the House and Senate caucuses are controlled by different political parties. And just like any bill, if the House and Senate cannot agree, the bill containing a prospective judge's appointment does not get passed. If this happens, then the seat is not filled. The Constitution allows the governor to appoint someone temporarily until state lawmakers can meet again and give it another try.[9]

(2) Within a caucus there is not agreement on whom to select. This is the second most common cause of conflict. When there is a judge who will serve in a locality with numerous delegates or senators and all of them cannot agree among themselves, frequently no one is selected.

Note that in most caucus rules, delegates and senators agree not to stick their noses in other people's business. We strive to *let* the members from that area choose their judge. I represent Fairfax County, and I really don't want a Delegate from Roanoke telling me who should preside over the Fairfax Courts—and *vice versa.*

But a disagreement can occur, for example, in the House majority caucus when Judge A and Judge B are seeking a position in an area that is served by two delegates who are both majority caucus members. Both judges have great qualifications. Delegate 1 wants Judge A and Delegate 2 wants Judge B. I have seen some angry conversations when this situation takes place! What usually happens is that they reach a compromise. For example, Delegate 2 may say, "I will vote for your judge if you promise next time to support my judge." Or, Delegate 1 may say: "Vote for my judge for General District and I will vote for your judge for the Circuit Court."

(3) The majority caucus wants a certain judge and the minority caucus does not. In this situation, the minority caucus usually does not win the day—unless it can convince enough members of the majority caucus to break with their rules and not follow their own party. This rarely occurs, but I have seen it. For example, a member of the majority caucus wants Judge Z. But the members of the minority caucus point out that Judge Z has a history of making bad rulings. If the minority caucus convincingly states its case on the House floor during arguments on the day of judicial selection, then members of the majority caucus may break with their rules and refuse to vote for the judge that the local delegate has requested.

(4) There are no members of the majority caucus who represent an area. This happens frequently. Here is an example: The House majority is currently Republican, but Arlington County is represented only by Democratic members of the House and the Senate. If a seat opens up in a county such as Arlington, then there is no "local" delegate in the majority caucus to choose the judge. In these cases the majority caucus will defer to the local delegates and senators. We usually say, "You choose—and as long as the person you choose is reasonable, we will agree to vote for that judge." Some might argue that the majority should simply use strong-arm tactics and force their decision on the minority caucus. But the old axiom, "What goes around comes around," applies here. Majority-party legislators usually remember that they may not always be in the majority. Additionally, we all realize that the constituents of that area have designated the delegate or senator as their voice, and our job calls for us to be accommodating.

But to be totally candid, it does not always work this way. Sometimes a local minority caucus will choose a judge who is just unacceptable to the majority. For example, the judge may be perceived as being too lenient in sentencing criminals or has had a history of complaints. The biggest fights in the selection of judges arise when everyone in a certain area is in the minority caucus and wants Judge D, but everyone in the majority—none of whom represent that area—just finds Judge D to be unpalatable.

> ## For the Selection of Statewide Judges:

For the Virginia Supreme Court and the Court of Appeals, all the members of the House and Senate are interested in who will be a justice or judge because those who serve on these courts decide disputes that arise in all areas of the state. Usually, the majority caucus members in the House and the Senate meet and make a selection. If, by chance, they choose the same person, then it's a deal. But in situations where the House majority caucus consists of one party and the Senate's majority is of another, this rarely happens. However, these appellate judges are very important, so the members try their best not to let that occur. Usually, a compromise can be reached, such as allowing each caucus to take turns in selecting the justice or judge—or choosing a completely different person instead of both caucuses' preferred candidates.

Reappointment

Our judges are appointed for limited terms. Some states and the federal government appoint judges permanently, and the only way they can be removed is due to misconduct, illness, or death. The reason behind this permanent appointment method is to prevent judges from making their decisions based upon whether they will be reappointed to another term. The framers of the Virginia Constitution, however, decided that they did not want permanent judges because that may lead to little accountability— where a person does whatever he wants as a judge and does not follow the law. So in Virginia, judges must go through the entire process described above every time their terms are set to expire. In practice, it takes many negative factors for a judge not to be reappointed. The only times that I have seen this happen is when there was misconduct or when a judge's demeanor had become so rude or ill-tempered that the delegates and senators had received many complaints from constituents.

Removal and Complaints

Virginia has a long history of selecting the most honorable people to serve as judges. But there is always "one bad apple in every bushel." In Article VI section 10, the authors of our Virginia Constitution set up a system by which judges can be removed prior to the expiration of their terms. In essence, if anyone (a citizen, legislator, or fellow judge) believes a judge has violated the rules or has become incompetent (for example, sick and unable to understand what is going on in the court), a complaint can be filed with the Judicial Inquiry and Review Commission (JIRC). This commission reviews the allegations, and if the allegations are found to have any merit whatsoever, JIRC can hold hearings. If the hearings show that the allegations are well-founded, JIRC may file a formal complaint before the Virginia Supreme Court:

> Upon the filing of a complaint, the Supreme Court shall conduct a hearing in open court and, upon a finding of disability which is or is likely to be permanent and which seriously interferes with the performance by the judge of his duties, shall retire the judge from office.... If the Supreme Court after the hearing on the complaint finds that the judge has engaged in misconduct while in office, or that he has persistently failed to perform the duties of his office, or that he has engaged in conduct prejudicial to the proper administration of justice, it shall censure him or shall remove him from office. A judge removed under this authority shall not be entitled to retirement benefits, but only to the return of contributions made by him, together with any income accrued thereon.[10]

Conclusion

This has been a long article and maybe a little boring. But there is a more exciting way to learn this: Just go see it in person. The General Assembly is open to the public. We usually select the judges sometime in late January or early February. In addition, courts are open to the public. This is mandated by law so that people can see what is going on and can hold judges accountable who don't follow the law or who are rude and abusive. You are welcome to walk into any General District or Circuit Court at any time during the business day. In addition, most Juvenile and Domestic Relations Court hearings are also open to the public. Take a day and check it out! Seeing it in person is much better than on television.

David B. Albo is a Member of the Virginia House of Delegates, representing the 42nd District since 1994. He is Chairman of the House Courts of Justice Committee and a Member of the Virginia State Crime Commission.

CHAPTER 20
Virginia Courts in Brief

Office of the Executive Secretary,
Supreme Court of Virginia

Virginia has the oldest judicial system in America. The judiciary is an indispensable and integral part of our democratic form of government. As John Marshall, a distinguished Virginian, stated: "The Judicial Department comes home in its effects to every [person's] fireside: it passes on his property, his reputation, his life, his all." Virginia's judiciary will continue to work hard to preserve the rights and freedoms that we as Virginians and Americans cherish, value, and enjoy....
Leroy Rountree Hassell, Chief Justice, 2003-2010

Virginia's Judicial System[1]

The mission of Virginia's judicial system is to assure that disputes are resolved justly, promptly, and economically. The components necessary to discharge this function are a court system unified in its structure and administration, competent, honest judges and court personnel, and uniform rules of practice

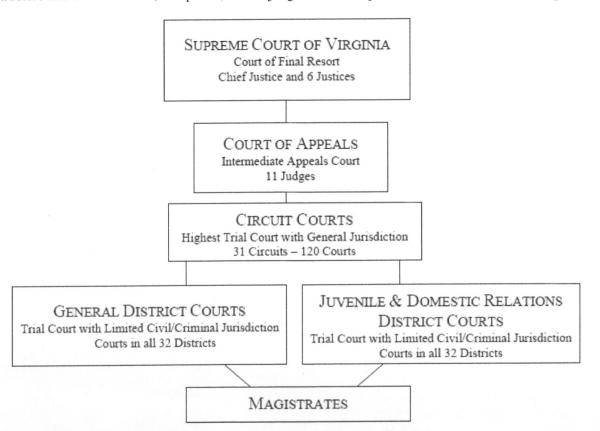

and procedure. This article is offered to promote a better understanding of the operation of the Virginia court system and the manner in which its mission is accomplished.

The present system consists of four levels of courts: the Supreme Court, the Court of Appeals, the circuit courts, and the district courts. In addition, magistrates serve as judicial officers with authority to issue various types of processes. The courts are organized into 31 judicial circuits and 32 similar judicial districts. More than 2,600 people, including judges, clerks, and magistrates, work within the judicial branch of government to provide the citizens of the Commonwealth prompt, efficient service.

Magistrates

In many instances, a citizen's first contact with the judicial system of the Commonwealth comes through the office of the magistrate. A principal function of the magistrate is to provide an independent, unbiased review of complaints brought to the office by police officers, sheriffs, deputies, and citizens. Magistrate duties include issuing various types of processes such as arrest warrants, summonses, bonds, search warrants, subpoenas, emergency mental and medical custody orders, temporary mental and medical detention orders, emergency protective orders and other civil processes. One of the chief duties of the magistrate is conducting bond hearings to set bail in instances in which an individual is charged with a criminal offense. A magistrate may also accept prepayments for traffic infractions and minor misdemeanors.

The Office of the Executive Secretary of the Supreme Court of Virginia provides administrative supervision and training to magistrates. Virginia is divided into eight magisterial regions, and each region is comprised of between three and five judicial districts. A chief magistrate supervises the magistrates serving within each judicial district. Each region has a regional magistrate supervisor who provides direct supervision to the chief magistrates. The eight regional supervisors assist a Magistrate System Coordinator in administering the statewide system. There are magistrate advisors who provide legal and procedural advice to the magistrates.

Each magistrate is authorized to exercise his or her powers throughout the magisterial region for which he or she is appointed. Magistrates provide services on an around-the-clock basis, conducting hearings in person and through videoconferencing systems.

District Courts

Virginia's unified district court system consists of the general district and the juvenile and domestic relations district courts. Within the 32 districts of the state, there are general district courts and juvenile and domestic relations district courts in every city and county.

The general district court hears all criminal cases involving misdemeanors under state law and offenses that are violations of ordinances, laws, and bylaws of the county or city where it is located. A misdemeanor is any charge which carries a penalty of up to one year in jail or a fine of up to $2,500, or both.

The Code of Virginia defines criminal offenses and sets penalties. For many offenses, the penalty described is a fine. Fines collected for violations are paid into the treasury of the city, town, or county whose ordinance has been violated, or into the State treasury for a violation of state law. The district courts do not conduct jury trials. All cases are heard by a judge. Each defendant in a criminal case is presumed innocent until proven guilty beyond a reasonable doubt. Upon consideration of evidence, the judge decides the question of guilt or innocence and on a finding of guilt determines which penalty, if any, is proper and lawful.

The general district court decides civil cases in which the amount in question does not exceed $15,000. Civil cases vary from suits for damages sustained in automobile accidents to suits by creditors to receive payment on past due debts. In Virginia, claims for less than $4,500 can be initiated only in general district courts. A separate small claims division has jurisdiction over civil actions when the amount claimed does not exceed $5,000.

The general district court also hears cases in which a person is charged with a traffic infraction. If convicted of certain traffic violations, the Virginia Department of Motor Vehicles will assess points against the person's driver's license. This is in addition to any fine imposed by the judge.

The general district court holds preliminary hearings in felony cases, that is, any offense which may be punishable by imprisonment of more than one year. At a preliminary hearing, the court determines whether there is sufficient evidence to justify holding the defendant for a grand jury hearing. The grand jury determines whether the accused will be indicted and held for trial in the circuit court.

The juvenile and domestic relations district court in Virginia handles cases involving:

The Augusta County Courthouse. Photo by Pete Giesen.

- juvenile delinquency and status offenses
- juveniles accused of traffic violations
- children in need of services or supervision
- children subjected to abuse or neglect
- children who are abandoned or without parental guardianship
- foster care and entrustment agreements
- children for whom relief of custody or termination of parental rights is requested
- adults accused of child abuse or neglect, or of offenses against family or household members
- adults involved in disputes concerning the custody, visitation, or support of a child
- spousal support
- minors seeking emancipation or work permits
- court-ordered rehabilitation services
- court consent for certain medical treatments

In Virginia, a juvenile is any person under the age of 18. A juvenile is adjudicated "delinquent" when a court finds that the juvenile has committed an act which would be a crime if committed by an adult. A "status offender" is a juvenile who has committed a certain action which, if committed by an adult, would not be considered a criminal offense—such as a curfew violation. A "child in need of supervision" is one who habitually and unjustifiably is absent from school or runs away from home. A "child in need of services" needs treatment, rehabilitation, or services to keep the child or his family safe, and the intervention of the court is required. "Child abuse and neglect" cases involve the improper care or injurious treatment of juveniles.

Juvenile and domestic relations district courts differ from other courts in their duty to protect the confidentiality and privacy of juveniles and their families who have legal matters before the court. In addition to protecting the public and holding delinquent juveniles accountable, the court considers services needed to provide for rehabilitation. As a district court, this court does not conduct jury trials.

As with the general district courts, all parties subject to a juvenile and domestic relations district court order or judgment may appeal the decision to the circuit court. Appeals must be noted with the clerk within 10 days of the court's decision. Cases appealed to the circuit court are reheard de novo (as completely new cases).

Circuit Courts

The only trial court of general jurisdiction in Virginia is the circuit court. The circuit court has jurisdiction over the following:

Civil Actions:
- concurrent jurisdiction with general district courts of monetary claims over $4,500 but not exceeding $15,000
- exclusive original jurisdiction of monetary claims exceeding $15,000
- attachments
- validity of a county or municipal ordinance or corporate bylaw
- divorce proceedings
- wills, trusts, and estate matters
- property disputes
- adoption proceedings

Criminal Cases:
- all felonies, offenses that may be punished by imprisonment of more than one year
- misdemeanor offenses that were appealed from district court or originated from a grand jury indictment
- transfer or certification of felony offenses committed by juveniles

Appeals:
- appeals from the general district court or juvenile and domestic relations district court (heard de novo)
- appeals from administrative agencies.

The circuit court also handles any case for which jurisdiction is not specified in the Code of Virginia.

At the beginning of each term of the circuit court a grand jury is convened. These juries consider bills of indictment to determine whether there is sufficient probable cause to believe that a person accused of having committed a serious crime did commit such crime and should stand trial. The grand jury does not hear both sides of the case and does not determine the guilt or innocence of the accused.

A special grand jury may be convened to investigate any condition which tends to promote criminal activity in the community or which indicates malfeasance of governmental agencies or officials. This grand jury has subpoena powers and may summon persons, documents, or records needed in its investigation.

Court of Appeals

The Court of Appeals of Virginia provides appellate review of final decisions of the circuit courts in domestic relations matters, appeals from decisions of an administrative agency, traffic infractions, and criminal cases, except where a sentence of death has been imposed. It also hears appeals of final decisions of the Virginia Workers' Compensation Commission. While appeals of criminal, traffic, concealed weapons permit, and certain preliminary rulings in felony cases are presented by a petition for appeal, all other appeals to the Court of Appeals are a matter of right. Other civil decisions of the circuit court are appealed directly to the Supreme Court of Virginia by petition for appeal. The Court of Appeals also has original jurisdiction to issue writs of mandamus, prohibition, and habeas corpus in any case over which the court would have appellate jurisdiction, and writs of actual innocence (based on non-biological evidence).

The decisions of the Court of Appeals are final in traffic infraction and misdemeanor cases where no incarceration is imposed, in domestic relations matters, and in cases originating before administrative agencies or the Virginia Workers' Compensation Commission. Except in those cases where the decision of the Court of Appeals is final, any party aggrieved by a decision of the Court of Appeals may petition the Supreme Court for an appeal.

The Court of Appeals consists of eleven judges. The court sits in panels of at least three judges, and the membership of the panels is rotated. The court sits at such locations as the chief judge designates, so as to provide convenient access to the various geographic areas of the Commonwealth.

Supreme Court

Although the Supreme Court of Virginia possesses both original and appellate jurisdiction, its primary function is to review decisions of

The state flag flies over the Supreme Court of Virginia. Photo by Anne Marie Morgan.

lower courts, including the Court of Appeals, from which appeals have been allowed. Virginia does not allow an appeal to the Supreme Court as a matter of right except in cases involving the State Corporation Commission, certain disciplinary actions against an attorney, and review of the death penalty.

The Court's original jurisdiction is limited to cases of habeas corpus (ordering one holding custody to produce the detained person before the Court for the purpose of determining whether such custody is proper), mandamus (ordering the holder of an office to perform his duty), prohibition (ordering a public official to stop an action), and actual innocence (based on biological testing). The Supreme Court also has original jurisdiction in matters filed by the Judicial Inquiry and Review Commission relating to judicial censure and retirement, and removal of judges.

Administration

The Chief Justice of the Supreme Court serves as the administrative head of Virginia's judicial system. The Chief Justice is charged with overseeing the efficient and effective operation of the entire system. Assisting in this task is the Executive Secretary of the Supreme Court, who is the state court administrator.

The Office of the Executive Secretary (OES) provides administrative assistance to the courts of the Commonwealth and to Virginia's magistrates through its eleven departments. The departments within the OES include the Assistant Executive Secretary and Counsel, the Court Improvement Program, Educational Services, Fiscal Services, the Historical Commission, Human Resources, Judicial Information Technology, Judicial Planning, Judicial Services, Legal Research, and Legislative and Public Relations.

The administrative structure of the Supreme Court of Virginia also includes the Clerk of the Court, the Reporter of the Supreme Court, the Chief Staff Attorney, and the Law Librarian.

Each court in the Commonwealth maintains a clerks' office, which receives, processes, and maintains records of all cases brought before that court, as well as other records and papers the court is required by law to maintain. The Clerk of the Supreme Court of Virginia also maintains records of attorneys qualified to practice in the Court, as well as other administrative records.

The Reporter of the Supreme Court, a faculty member of a Virginia law school, is responsible for overseeing the compilation, indexing, printing, and publication of the written opinions of the Supreme Court in the Virginia Reports. The Court of Appeals of Virginia also employs two Virginia law school faculty members who oversee the compilation, indexing, printing, and publication of the written opinions of the Court of Appeals in the Virginia Court of Appeals Reports. One serves as the Court of Appeals Reporter for Civil Cases and the other as the Court of Appeals Reporter for Criminal Cases.

Both the Supreme Court of Virginia and the Court of Appeals of Virginia employ a Chief Staff Attorney. The Chief Staff Attorneys and their staff review petitions for appeal, appeals of right, and petitions in original jurisdiction cases, and prepare written summaries for the justices and judges to aid their decisional process.

The State of Virginia Law Librarian supervises a library of about 100,000 volumes.

Judicial Inquiry and Review Commission

The Judicial Inquiry and Review Commission investigates allegations of judicial misconduct or the serious mental or physical disability of a judge. The Commission has jurisdiction to investigate the justices of the Supreme Court and all judges of the Commonwealth, as well as members of the State Corporation Commission, the Virginia Workers' Compensation Commission, special justices, substitute judges, and retired judges who have been recalled to service. The Commission may file a formal complaint with the Supreme Court against judges for violations of any canon of judicial ethics, misconduct in office, or failure to perform their judicial duties.

The Commission is comprised of seven members who are elected by the General Assembly and serve four-year terms. Membership includes one circuit court judge, one general district court judge, one juvenile and domestic relations district court judge, two lawyers, and two members of the public who are not lawyers. Commission staff receive and investigate allegations of misconduct and present the findings to the Commission.

Judicial Policy-Making Bodies

The Judicial Council is charged with the responsibility of making a continuous study of the organization, rules, and methods of procedure and practice of the judicial system of the Commonwealth. It is responsible for examining the work accomplished and results produced by the system and its individual offices and courts. The Council also studies the need for additional judges in the circuit courts. A report of the proceedings and recommendations of the Council is made to the General Assembly and to the Supreme Court on an annual basis.

The Chief Justice of the Supreme Court is presiding officer for the Council, whose membership includes one Court of Appeals judge, six circuit court judges, one general district court judge, one juvenile and domestic relations district court judge, two attorneys qualified to practice in the Supreme Court of Virginia, and the Chairmen of the Committees for Courts of Justice in the Virginia Senate and House of Delegates. The Committee on District Courts (CDC) was created to assist the Chief Justice in the administrative supervision of Virginia's district courts. Among the statutorily mandated responsibilities of the CDC are recommending new judgeships and certifying the need to fill district court vacancies, and authorizing the number of clerks, magistrates, and personnel in each district, establishing guidelines and policies for court system personnel, and fixing salary classification schedules for district court personnel and magistrates. Membership of this committee includes the Majority Leader of the Senate, the Speaker of the House, the Chairmen of the Committees for Courts of Justice in the Senate and House of Delegates, two members of each of the Courts of Justice Committees appointed by the respective Chairman, one circuit court judge, two general district court judges, and two juvenile and domestic relations district court judges.

The Judicial Conference of Virginia was organized to discuss and consider means and methods of improving the administration of justice in the Commonwealth. Active members include the Chief Justice and justices of the Supreme Court, all judges of the Court of Appeals and the circuit courts, and all retired justices and judges of such courts. The Chief Justice serves as President of the Conference.

The Judicial Conference of Virginia for District Courts is similar to the Judicial Conference of Virginia in its mission and responsibilities. Membership includes the Chief Justice, who serves as its President, and all active judges of the general district and juvenile and domestic relations district courts.

Judges and Court Personnel

The quality of a court system is determined chiefly by the quality of its judges and court personnel. Virginia is fortunate to have a judiciary of the highest competence and integrity. The judges of Virginia's district courts are elected by a majority vote of each house of the General Assembly for terms of six years. Vacancies in district court judgeships occurring when the General Assembly is not in session are filled by the circuit court judges of the corresponding circuit. The judges so appointed must be elected during the next regular session of the General Assembly. Each district has a chief general district court judge and a chief juvenile and domestic relations district court judge elected by peer vote for a two-year term. The chief judge is the administrative head of the respective court in the district and is responsible for its management.

The judges of the circuit courts are also elected by a majority vote of each house of the General Assembly. They serve for eight-year terms. Interim appointments are made by the governor subject to election by the General Assembly at the next regular session. The chief judge of the circuit is elected for a two-year term by a vote of the judges serving in the circuit.

The personnel support for the circuit courts is under the direction of the clerk of the circuit court, who is a constitutional officer and chief administrator of the circuit court, elected for a term of eight years by the voters of the locality. The clerk has authority for the probate of wills, grants of administration, and qualification of guardians. The clerk is the custodian of the court records, and the clerk's office is where deeds are recorded and marriage licenses are issued.

A totally independent judicial personnel system has been established for those support personnel in the district court and magistrate systems. Selection of these employees is on a merit basis with all positions established within a system of uniform job classifications. This insures equal treatment of employees doing similar work throughout the state.

Court personnel are not employed as attorneys and are not permitted to offer legal advice. However, they can provide general procedural information and try to assist the public in any way possible.

The eleven Court of Appeals judges are elected and receive interim appointments in the same manner as the circuit court judges. They serve a term of eight years. The chief judge is elected by a vote of the eleven judges for a term of four years.

The Supreme Court of Virginia is composed of seven justices elected by a majority vote of each house of the General Assembly for a term of twelve years. Interim appointments are made by the governor subject to election by the General Assembly at the next regular session. By law, the Chief Justice is chosen by the majority vote of the seven justices, for a term of four years.

Continuing education for judges and court personnel is essential to maintain a high level of professional competence in the court system. Regularly scheduled educational conferences are held for judges and court personnel.

Uniform Rules and Practices

Uniformity of practice is regarded as a vital element for the development of a sound judicial system. The Constitution of Virginia authorizes the Supreme Court of Virginia to promulgate rules governing the practice and procedures to be used in the courts of the Commonwealth.

The Judicial Council receives and studies all suggestions for rule changes from the bench, bar, and citizens, and makes recommendations on Rules of Court to the Supreme Court of Virginia.

The formulation of the administrative policy for the courts in Virginia, while being ultimately within the authority of the Chief Justice as the administrative head of the system, is vested on a routine basis in the Judicial Council and the Committee on District Courts. These bodies deal with the daily practices of the courts and seek ways to improve their procedures. The rule-making authority and the administrative policy-making authority provide two mechanisms by which uniformity of procedures can be advanced.

General Information for Individuals with Disabilities

The Court System has adopted a policy of non-discrimination in both employment and in access to its facilities, services, programs, and activities. Individuals with disabilities who need accommodation in order to have access to court facilities or to participate in court system functions are invited to request assistance from court system staff. Individuals with disabilities (not employed by the court system) who believe they have been discriminated against in access may file a complaint with local court system officials. Those who need printed material published by the court system in another format or who have general questions about the court system's non-discrimination policies and procedures may contact the Office of the Executive Secretary, Supreme Court of Virginia, 100 North Ninth Street, Third Floor, Richmond, Virginia 23219. The telephone number is (804) 786-6455; communication through a telecommunications device (TDD) is also available at this number.

The Office of the Executive Secretary of the Supreme Court of Virginia provides administrative support for all of the courts and magistrate offices within the Commonwealth.

PART V: THE FOURTH ESTATE

A quick search of the correspondence of preeminent Virginians during the early American republic reveals a conviction that citizens must be well-informed in order to be a self-governing people. They reasoned that a "free press" that enables Americans to know what their elected leaders are doing would be essential to achieving this goal. James Madison is merely one of many leaders of the early Republic who illustrate this concern: "A popular Government, without popular information, or the means of acquiring it, is but a Prologue to a Farce or a Tragedy; or, perhaps both."[1] Thomas Jefferson agreed in a letter to George Washington: "No government ought to be without censors: & where the press is free, no one ever will ... Nature has given to man no other means of sifting out the truth either in ... law, or politics."[2]

The Founders' practical support of a free press extended beyond its guarantee in the First Amendment to their creation of an enumerated Congressional power to establish post offices and postal roads—in part, to enable news distribution in their era. The first postal laws and the Congressional debates surrounding them provide clear evidence of this goal, including the establishment of subsidized delivery of newspapers through the mail, postage-free printers' exchanges to printers in all states to publish one another's news, and creation of a federal crime to punish embezzlement of newspapers during mail delivery.[3] Nationwide, the press flourished and became an essential link between the people and their representatives.

But today, the news media are in a state of flux. Thousands of reporters have lost their jobs over the last decade as broadcast and newspaper outlets fold, downsize, or divert their priorities away from public affairs journalism.[4] In Virginia, the press rooms on Capitol Square were once packed with journalists representing news outlets throughout the Commonwealth, but their numbers are rapidly dwindling. Two prominent reporters who were members of the Virginia Capitol press corps acknowledge the changing state of the industry in Section V, *The Fourth Estate.*

Former Gov. L. Douglas Wilder and broadcast journalist Anne Marie Morgan take a break during a listener call-in radio program. Photo courtesy of Anne Marie Morgan.

One author reported for a Richmond newspaper for 50 years, while the other worked for the sole television outlet that still had a full-time presence at the Capitol. Both chronicle the events that they covered and their daily work to inform the public about what's happening in their state government. As the authors describe this significant role, readers may also want to consider what the impact could be on democratic governance if the current trends to downsize or eliminate such reporting continue.

CHAPTER 21

THE STATE CAPITOL NEWS MEDIA: EYEWITNESSES TO IMPORTANT EVENTS

Tyler Whitley
Former Political Writer, Richmond Times-Dispatch

Often called the Fourth Branch of government, the press corps has been an integral part of state government almost since the time a Virginia governor occupied a corner office on the third floor of the State Capitol in 1790. Without news reporters, it would be much more difficult for Virginians to find out what has actually taken place on Capitol Square.

Through good times and bad, newspapers and, more lately, television and radio stations, have sent reporters to Richmond to cover governors and the Virginia General Assembly, the state legislature. Usually, they have been the most experienced reporters with the ability to develop sources, mine them for news, and assemble stories accurately and fast.

Gov. Robert F. McDonnell walks toward a group of reporters for an impromptu press conference. Photo by Bob Brown, *Richmond Times-Dispatch.*

Of late, as newspapers, radio, and TV stations have retrenched in reaction to Internet competition and slumping advertising, the number of reporters covering state politics has dwindled. After the 2009 General Assembly session, the *Fredericksburg Free-Lance Star* and WDBJ-TV in Roanoke were the latest to shut down their Richmond bureaus after decades of coverage.

Lamenting the decreasing size of the press corps, Anita Kumar, a reporter with *The Washington Post*, said, "The fewer reporters that are here in Richmond, the less accountability there is on our state officials. There are fewer stories being written on fewer topics."

"It hasn't been pleasant seeing some of the most venerated and experienced people in our trade cashiered out through layoffs, buyouts, retirements, or changed beat assignments," the AP's Bob Lewis declared.

Former Gov. Timothy M. Kaine said the diminished press corps makes for more superficial coverage.

"It would be hard for campaigns to get even more superficial, but they might," he told *The Washington Post*.

For example, in 2009, for the first time, reporters did not travel with the candidates for governor on their final weekend campaign swing because of budgetary cutbacks.

But, still, all of the major newspapers in Richmond, Washington, Roanoke, and Norfolk, plus the Associated Press, have reporters in Richmond and other papers send reporters to Richmond for the General Assembly sessions. The *Richmond Times-Dispatch*, based in the seat of government, led the way with four full-time political reporters at the Capitol.

Recognizing the importance of the press, the state has afforded the press corps free accommodations in the Capitol. When the Capitol building was expanded recently, press space was set aside in the addition for print and electronic media.

Reporters also are allowed access to the House of Delegates and State Senate chambers when the General Assembly is in session. The House is more informal. Reporters sit in the rear and banter with the delegates. This is not permitted in the Senate, where the press seats are in the front.

The General Assembly has a long and storied history, dating back to 1619 when it was called the House of Burgesses. Today our legislature generates a great deal of news that is worthy of media coverage and which the public is entitled to know.

The General Assembly usually passes more than 1,500 bills and resolutions in a session. Most of them are minor changes to existing law rather than of far-reaching impacts. The issues can range from the mundane, such as vanity license plates, to the important, such as a smoking ban in most restaurants and a ban on text messaging while driving.

Death—expanding the death penalty—and taxes, whether to raise or lower them, are always hot-button issues. So is the state budget, which now totals about $75 billion for two years.

But along with the routine, the General Assembly has passed such far-reaching measures as allowing branch banking in Virginia, authorizing retail stores to be open on Sunday, abolishing parole, requiring background checks when a firearm is purchased, requiring trucks to cover their loads, raising the speed limit, and establishing a state lottery.

Governors used to hold formal news conferences to answer questions from the press, but, lately, that has given way to more informal "news availabilities," when a group of reporters, known as "a gaggle," converge on the governor, or another state or legislative official, to address issues of the day.

The press room is a lively place when the General Assembly is in session. Bob Lewis, the veteran Capitol reporter for the Associated Press, said, "The widely varied cast of characters, the skepticism and irreverence inherent in their jobs of holding power accountable, and the humor and sometimes outrageous ribaldry that cuts the competitive tensions, make it among the most unusual places in all of journalism."

A major part of that mix is *Times-Dispatch* photographer, Bob Brown, who has been taking photos at the Capitol for more than 40 years. Brown takes pictures of legislators and governors in potentially embarrassing situations, adds a humorous caption and displays the pictures on the press room walls. He also gives them to the subjects, who usually get a good laugh and rarely, if ever, object.

Generally, governors and reporters have had a good working relationship. Governors hire press secretaries to deal with the press, while the two political parties that make up the General Assembly also have press spokesmen. Their job is to "spin"—to give their bosses' side of the story. The reporters' job is to see through this spin and tell the public what really is going on.

Over the past decade, the Capitol press corps has organized itself into an informal association, the Virginia Capitol Correspondents Association. Its job is to allocate space in the press area and file complaints when it feels the press is being put upon. At last count it had 22 members.

Every year during the General Assembly session, the Association sponsors a reception and dinner with a speaker from state government as the main attraction. It has become a sort of state Capitol version of the Gridiron Club with the speakers lampooning the press in light-hearted talks that are not meant to make news.

The press corps gained some notoriety in 1976 when a long-standing gin rummy game in the press room was made public by two reporters. Officials expressed public shock that card-playing for small stakes money was going on in the Capitol, although most officials, including a State Corporation Commission judge and former lieutenant governor, knew about it and even participated. It was a way for the reporters and officials to exchange information and get to know each other. They operated under an elaborate set of rules that reflected Virginia politics.

The topics covered by Capitol reporters include the rough and tumble of politics and electoral decisions, which are now very competitive. Since Linwood Holton in 1969 became the first Republican elected governor since Reconstruction, the balance of power has shifted back and forth between the two political parties, and there have been an equal number of Democratic and Republican governors.

In 1989 Virginia, once the Capitol of the Confederacy, made history by becoming the first state to elect an African-American governor, L. Douglas Wilder. In a ringing inaugural address, the Democrat said, "I am a son of Virginia." His election was just one of the many newsworthy events where Capitol reporters have been eyewitnesses.

Barack Obama carried Virginia in 2008, making him the first Democrat to carry the state in a presidential election since Lyndon B. Johnson in 1964. But another long streak continued in 2009 when Republican Robert F. McDonnell was elected governor. Since 1976, Virginians have elected a governor from the opposite party that carried the White House the year before.

McDonnell's victory margin of 17.36 percentage points was the second highest since the two parties became competitive. Only George Allen, with a winning margin of 17.4 percentage points in 1993, finished higher.

Professor Larry J. Sabato, political scientist at the University of Virginia and one of the nation's most frequently quoted pundits, has postulated "10 Keys" to winning the Governor's Mansion. By evaluating such indicators as the economy, party unity, whether a scandal emerges, campaign money and organization, personality, and presidential popularity, reporters (and the public) can make an educated guess about who will win each election.

Capitol reporters also cover the political candidates' campaign finances whenever there is an election—which, in Virginia, is every year. Money is important in the Commonwealth's politics and it is easy to raise, because, unlike in federal elections and in many other states, there is no limit on how much money an individual or corporation can donate to a campaign. Virginia excuses this by claiming that those donations must be disclosed in public filings with the State Board of Elections.

McDonnell spent more than $19 million in 2009, winning election, while his Democratic opponent, R. Creigh Deeds, spent more than $12 million. The money goes to television advertising, direct mail, robo-calls to voters, and campaign staff salaries.

Many in the Capitol press corps also write stories about voter turnout and other electoral dynamics. Virginia's voting record is spotty. Presidential elections are always the biggest draw—Obama received more than 2 million votes in 2008 and 74 percent of registered voters cast ballots. The next year, in the gubernatorial race, 43 percent voted. Only about two million total votes were cast.

The image of Gov. Timothy M. Kaine is mirrored in a camera as he reacts to a reporter's question in 2009. Photo by Bob Brown, *Richmond Times-Dispatch.*

Increasingly, the key to winning elections in Virginia is capturing the majority of the vote in populous Northern Virginia, particularly Fairfax County, the largest jurisdiction in Virginia. An influx of newcomers seeking government jobs has turned that once conservative bastion into a moderate battleground that goes back and forth among the parties.

Northern Virginia went heavily for Obama in 2008 and the Democratic candidates for governor in 2005 and 2001. It helped elect Democrat Mark R. Warner to the U.S. Senate in 2008 and Jim Webb to the Senate in 2006. But it swung back to the Republican camp in 2009.

In winning elections, Democrats have two reliable voting blocs, African-Americans and labor unions. Republicans rely on white suburban voters. The Shenandoah Valley remains the most reliably Republican area of the state, while Democrats win handily in African-American-dominated cities.

A huge African-American turnout in 2008, boosted by the Obama campaign, helped Democrats score upset victories in the 2nd and 5th congressional districts. That gave Democrats a 6-5 majority among the state's 11 congressmen for the first time in decades. But the trend was reversed in 2010, when three of the Democratic Congressmen lost to Republican challengers. The swift partisan turnaround underscores the highly competitive nature of Virginia politics.

Once known as "the mother of Presidents," Virginia has not had a native-born President since Woodrow Wilson, in 1920. But in recent years several Virginia politicians have explored a presidential candidacy, traveling to Iowa and New Hampshire and generating some interest. Wilder made a futile try in 1992. Republican George Allen's hopes were derailed in 2006 when he was defeated in his bid for re-election to the U.S. Senate. Former Gov. and now Sen. Mark R. Warner abandoned a presidential bid in 2007, but remains a potential future candidate.

Gov. McDonnell won such a huge landslide victory in 2009 by concentrating on jobs creation that he is being touted as future presidential material in the Republican Party.

Republicans gained control of the legislature in 2001. But as of 2008, the State Senate was controlled by Democrats and the House of Delegates by Republicans.

Because Republicans controlled both the House of Delegates and the Governor's Mansion, they had an advantage when the General Assembly drew new districts in 2011, following the Census that measured Virginia's population changes. Through a process known as gerrymandering, legislators can draw up districts that tend to protect themselves and their political party. There have been recent calls for bipartisan redistricting reform, and Gov. McDonnell established an independent bipartisan commission in 2011 to draw new district boundaries and advise the General Assembly, although its advice was not binding.

But Virginia also is under the federal Voting Rights Act because of a past history of racial discrimination. This requires legislators to create districts with an African-American majority, when possible. There are 12 such districts in the House of Delegates and five in the Senate. All are represented by Democrats, as is the black-majority 3rd congressional district, which stretches along the James River from Richmond to Portsmouth.

Democrats believe that by "packing" African-Americans who vote for their party into these districts, Republicans have created neighboring districts that tend to be more Republican.

When the redistricting of the General Assembly district boundaries was completed in 2011, the remaining members of the press were on hand to see which legislator artfully drew a line around his house to keep him in a safe district. These and many other state government-related topics will continue to be under scrutiny and reported to Virginians by the State Capitol press corps.

Tyler Whitley is a political writer and reporter who worked at the Richmond Times-Dispatch *and the former* Richmond News Leader *for 50 years. He has written about politics since 1980 and the General Assembly since 1972. He also covered 14 national political conventions and nine governors.*

CHAPTER 22
The Broadcast Perspective

By Adam Rhew
Former State Capitol Bureau Chief, WVIR TV

Throughout the two press rooms on Virginia's Capitol Square, there are dozens of plug-ins which broadcast journalists use to record the audio and video from the floors of the House of Delegates and the State Senate.
Most of those outlets stand empty.

From left, Adam Rhew with former Govs. George F. Allen, James S. Gilmore, III, Timothy M. Kaine, and L. Douglas Wilder (background) in the Executive Mansion, 2009. Photo by Michaele White, Office of the Governor.

Like our friends in the newspaper industry, broadcasters have been whittled away by a tough economy. Years ago, television and radio stations from across the state had permanent bureaus at the State Capitol, with correspondents and photographers dedicated to covering state issues year-round.

I have had the dubious distinction of being the only television reporter in Virginia based full-time at the Capitol. Virginia Public Radio keeps a full-time presence here, too. Other stations, even the Richmond affiliates, "parachute in" for big stories but do not maintain a bureau.

During the legislative session, broadcast reporters work side-by-side with our print colleagues. Unlike many cities, where newspaper and television journalists clash, there is a sense of camaraderie among those of us on the politics beat, regardless of how our stories are published.

We cover the same issues—committee hearings, press conferences, and budget negotiations.

Unlike newspaper reporters, broadcasters typically do not sit in the House and Senate chambers to watch the floor proceedings. Instead, we monitor both chambers from the press room, recording the audio and video to use in our stories later that night.

What Happens on a News Day

On a typical day, if there is such a thing, I am in the office by 8:15 a.m. I read the newspapers and blogs, check-in with my producers, and decide what stories I'll cover that day. Often, I'll attend a meeting or press conference in the morning and conduct other interviews in the afternoon. By 3:00 p.m., I'm writing the stories and editing the video for the evening newscasts. Two hours later, it's air time. After filing a couple of live reports, I'll write a version of my stories for the 11 p.m. news, make plans for the next day, and leave for home around 7:00 p.m.. Somewhere along the way, I maintain my own political blog, follow the conversation on Twitter, and work on developing long-form, investigative pieces.

Of course, all that can change on a moment's notice since significant news events can occur at all hours. It's what makes this job both fun and challenging.

Here's an example of an actual workday during the 2011 legislative session:

We were in the waning days of the session and budget negotiations were underway behind closed doors. In the morning, I spent a couple of hours tracking down budget conferees to understand the latest iterations of their talks. Those negotiations would evolve by the time my deadline rolled around. Then, I poked my head in a committee meeting, flagging down a legislator who promised to give me a tip on a bill I was monitoring. The lawmaker promised to give me some information "on background"—that is, not for attribution—later in the day. When the House and Senate floor sessions convened, I was monitoring the progress of no less than a half-dozen bills, which meant listening to both chambers at once, taking notes, and processing the information. When the legislature approved a controversial abortion bill, I immediately was on the phone with my producer, telling her the significance of the measure, and pushing to be the lead story in the newscast. Finally, with my deadline looming, I sat down to write eight stories—on the abortion bill, budget negotiations, and the six other bills that we were following.

One of the most significant hurdles for broadcast reporters who cover politics and government is the difficulty of explaining incredibly complex policies and legislation in 90 seconds or less. Some stories earn just 20 seconds. Many debates at the General Assembly are nuanced, and in order to be fair to both sides, broadcasters often are forced to cram as much into our allotted time as possible. It means some details are left on the cutting room floor. My job is to figure out what's most important, most relevant, and most powerful.

Reporting the Truth

The governor and legislators maintain a complicated relationship with the media, particularly with broadcasters. Many lawmakers dislike being "ambushed" by a television crew and do not care to be put on the spot with cameras rolling. Legislators simply are more comfortable with print reporters, an old school politician once told me. Yet, savvy governors and members of the General Assembly know that were it not for television coverage—when people across Virginia can put a face to a name—many elected officials would be unknown to their constituents.

But above all, government reporters have a simple responsibility—to work for the truth. That is our only obligation to our viewers: to report the truth without bias.

One of the most important facets of that obligation is investigating government spending. It is our job to be watchdogs of government, to make sure leaders are being good stewards of taxpayer dollars.

This is not the typical "if it bleeds, it leads" news coverage, where newscasts begin with reports on the latest local murders. In fact, many consultants recommend against full-time political coverage because of the belief that state government isn't "sexy enough" for viewers.

I disagree.

Political reporters—especially those of us in broadcast news—must present the information in a way that our viewers, listeners, and readers can understand. But ultimately, it is not our job to make the stories any more or less interesting.

Indeed, even if no one read and no one watched, it still would be critical to have reporters at the Capitol, asking tough questions, witnessing history unfolding, and holding our politicians accountable.

_____

Adam Rhew worked as the chief political reporter and manager for the State Capitol Bureau for WVIR-TV, the NBC affiliate in Charlottesville.

PART VI: LOCAL GOVERNMENTS IN VIRGINIA: A UNIQUE ARRANGEMENT

The units of government that deliver the greatest amount of direct services to Virginians are the Commonwealth's counties, cities, and towns. Public schools, police, courts, libraries, jails, and social services are but a handful of the enormous plethora of activities undertaken by localities. But as they provide these services, they are also required to comply with hundreds of state and federal mandates that may or may not be funded. When they do receive grants from those entities, it is frequently with strings attached. These are just a few of the challenges described by our experts in Part VI, *Local Governments in Virginia*.

Chapter 23 introduces readers to another exigency, the Dillon Rule, which is a municipal law doctrine that generally restricts the types of decisions that localities can make. As defined in a Virginia Supreme Court ruling,

> Virginia follows the Dillon Rule of strict construction concerning the legislative powers of local governing bodies. The Dillon Rule provides that local governing bodies have only those powers that are expressly granted, those that are necessarily or fairly implied from expressly granted powers, and those that are essential and indispensable.[1]

Richmond City Hall. Photo by Anne Marie Morgan.

This practice is in contrast to the doctrine known as "home rule," which authorizes more local governing discretion.[2] Without home rule, localities must depend on the General Assembly even for such parochial decisions as revisions to their own charters.

While describing counties as an "arm of the state" created to execute the state's policies, the chapter also outlines the historical development of Virginia's counties, their powers, relationships with other governing entities, and the potential for regional cooperation. But as Chapter 24 adds, Virginia's counties and cities are politically and geographically separate from one another, and the Commonwealth's system of independent cities is one of the most unique features of Virginia's localities.

Chapter 24 also provides an overview of the governing structure of cities and towns, municipal functions, and expenditures, with a special focus on public education.

Additionally, readers should note the sources of revenues that finance local operations. Funding is another great challenge faced by counties, cities, and towns. Although localities possess revenue options that the state does not, such as property taxes, they receive a substantial portion of their funds from the state. As a result, when an economic downturn occurs, the state usually cuts its aid to counties and cities, which are also reaping declining revenues from local sources. Nevertheless, the state adds new, often costly requirements and mandates for localities nearly every year. Thus, it is reasonable to ask: How independent are cities and counties in reality? It's a question that merits further contemplation when reading about Virginia's local governments.

CHAPTER 23
Virginia's Counties:
Governing Close to Home

By James D. Campbell
Executive Director, Virginia Association of Counties

L ocal government institutions are more the creations of custom, common law, and legislative acts than of grand constitutional designs.[1] Accordingly, the constitutional development of Virginia counties represents a blending of unwritten English constitutional traditions, legislation, and Virginia's six written Constitutions. Developments in this constitutional tradition reflect major change as well as continuity in Virginia county government institutions.[2]

The first counties in America were established in 1634 by an act of the Grand Assembly that divided the Virginia colony into eight shires, much like their counterparts in England. The new system of local government was created by an order of King Charles I, and the House of Burgesses named the eight original shires and assigned each their own local officer. The eight original shires were:

- Accomac Shire (now Accomack County)
- Charles City Shire (now Charles City County)
- Charles River Shire (now York County)
- Elizabeth City Shire (extinct)
- Henrico Shire (now Henrico County)
- James City Shire (now James City County)
- Warwick River Shire (extinct)
- Warrosquyoake Shire (now Isle of Wight County)

These shires were designated as counties a few years later. These early counties served as convenient territorial divisions for administering justice, collecting taxes, and otherwise establishing royal influence and the institutions of civil government within the colony. As units of local government, each county was served by: a governing body, the county court, which held legislative and administrative as well as judicial powers; a number of civil and military officers; and the church parish structure. The sheriff, appointed by the governor on the recommendation of the county court, performed a variety of executive functions for the colonial and county governments. The extensive authority of the county court and the sheriff helped to establish the Virginia tradition of strong county government that served as a model for American counties, particularly in the South.[3]

Although the American Revolution and the period of state- and nation-building that followed brought important changes to Virginia state government, Virginians held closely to the local government institutions of the colonial period. In fact, Virginia county government underwent few changes until the

190

last half of the 19th century, when the doctrines of representative government and separation of powers were applied to local governments. Popularly elected local officials first took office under the Constitution of 1861. The Constitution of 1870 converted the county court to essentially a judicial entity and transferred its function as the county governing body to the newly established board of supervisors.[4]

Virginia entered the twentieth century with a new Constitution, designed to restrain the power of state and local governments and to limit the influence of large corporate interests on public decision-making. The local government provisions of the Constitution of 1902 prescribed the organization of county and city governments in exacting detail. A number of restrictive provisions, which also proved to be more appropriate subjects for statutory law than for the Constitution, were contained in sections regulating the power of local governments to borrow money and levy taxes and establishing the duties of local officials. In addition, the 1902 Constitution prohibited the General Assembly from using special acts to provide for the organization, government, or powers of counties. These provisions built a rigid constitutional framework around county government that the General Assembly was powerless to change.

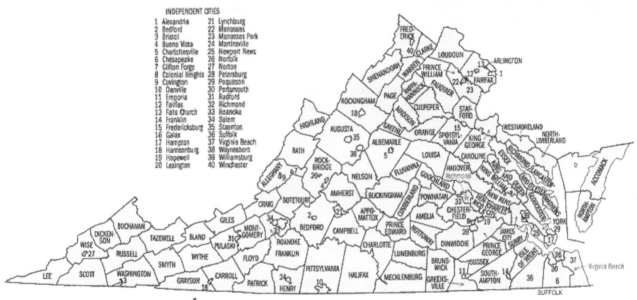

Source: Virginia Association of Counties[5]

Soon after the adoption of the 1902 Constitution, however, it became evident that a key challenge of the twentieth century would be to develop flexible, efficient, and responsive approaches to governmental management. The Constitution was revised in 1928 to respond to this need. Amendments were adopted to permit the General Assembly to enact, by general law, optional forms of county government that would provide alternatives to the system established in the Constitution.

Beginning in 1932, the General Assembly enacted a series of laws establishing several complete forms of government that are available to counties in which the voters have approved a change of government. In addition, many of the most important features of the optional forms of government gradually were made available, as a matter of local option, to counties that want to modify, but not replace, the constitutional form of government. Today, all questions of local government management and organization are within the province of the General Assembly, which has turned many of them over to the localities themselves for solution.

Population growth and an enormous expansion in the scope of government have created new challenges for Virginia county governments. The state's present Constitution, adopted in 1971, allows the General Assembly and Virginia localities substantial freedom to experiment with new techniques for strengthening local self-government and encourages cooperation among interdependent local governments.

Three important themes of the current Constitution set out in Article VII, which deals with local government, significantly affect Virginia counties. First, the Constitution recognizes the similarity of counties and cities in Virginia by treating these units of government similarly, although not identically. Second, by permitting either general or special laws to be used in establishing the organization, powers, and government of localities, the Constitution makes it easier for local governments to be designed according to local needs and desires. Third, the Constitution makes possible a wide range of alternative approaches to problems that cut across local boundaries, including such options as interlocal agreements for sharing powers and functions, consolidating governments, and establishing regional governments.[6]

Important to the development of local government law in Virginia is the application of the "Dillon Rule" to construing powers given to localities by the Virginia General Assembly. This concept is addressed at length in the "County Powers" section of this chapter.

Intergovernmental Relations

Federal, state, and local governments are linked together by a complicated network of intergovernmental relationships. Public policy objectives often are accomplished through the cooperative efforts of two or more units or levels of government. Regulations and mandated programs also contribute to the complexity. Governments have become more interdependent, with the result that decisions made on one level of government often have far-reaching effects on other levels and in other jurisdictions.

Federal-Local Relations

Cooperative efforts between national, state, and local governments have been built upon the growth of federal programs providing financial and technical assistance for state and local services. Although in the past federal grants-in-aid were distributed primarily to state governments (sometimes for redistribution among local governments), in recent years a growing proportion of federal aid has been channeled directly to city and county governments. Thus, the state in many cases serves as a clearinghouse for federal grants to local governments. In fiscal year 2005, state and federal funds paid to local governments in Virginia totaled more than $10.4 billion, plus $4.8 billion to local school divisions.[7]

Federal regulations and mandated programs also are important factors in the day-to-day operations of local governments. The decisions of local governing bodies and administrators must take into account important, and often complicated, federal rules for protecting the environment, nondiscriminatory personnel plans, equal employment requirements, and other policy objectives of national significance. Even so, the federal policies with which local governments are most concerned are often not those directed exclusively, or even primarily, at local governments. Federal approaches to problems like inflation, unemployment, and energy shortages, which cannot be solved locally, are sometimes more important to localities than legislation designed with local governments in mind.

One factor that has haunted local governments in recent years is the federal government's deficit. In addition to the deficit's negative impact on the economy, localities suffer because of the federal budget cuts designed to control spending and to reduce the debt. Funds for social programs of all types have been cut to stem the rising deficit. Federal grants-in-aid have been reduced. Budget reductions and tax cuts at the federal and state level have increased the pressure on local governments, which must both make up the reduction in revenue and manage the consequences.

Recognizing the significant impact of federal policies on state and local government in Virginia, the General Assembly in 1978 established the Virginia Liaison Office in Washington, D.C., "to serve as an institutional and organizational link" between the Commonwealth and various agencies of the federal government. Among the responsibilities of the office are monitoring and analyzing federal legislation and regulations, as well as alerting local governments to early opportunities for federal grants.[8]

Other state agencies are responsible for intergovernmental relations as well. For example, the Department of Planning and Budget is charged with the duty of "[a]ssessment of the impact of federal funds on state government by reviewing, analyzing, monitoring and evaluating the federal budget."[9] In addition, the Department of Housing and Community Development is responsible for "[i]dentifying and disseminating information to local governments about the availability and utilization of federal and state resources."[10]

State-Local Relations

Shared Goals

Dependence of local governments on the General Assembly for their powers is an important element in state-local relationships, but it is not the only one. In fact, when state and local governments cooperate to accomplish shared goals, their fundamental legal relationship is often not immediately apparent. Many contacts between state and local governments occur through mutual assistance agreements, shared administrative responsibilities and other cooperative arrangements in which the participants may function more like equal partners than like superior and subordinate levels of government.

The state, like the federal government, provides assistance to localities, most of it in the form of direct services, technical assistance, and financial assistance. Direct services are services provided to individuals or to local governments by state agencies, such as the Department of Transportation, the Department of Social Services, and the Department of Health. Almost all state agencies provide technical information, advice, and training to local governments. Financial assistance to localities consists of state revenues distributed to local governments. State funds are disbursed primarily as shared revenue, for which no programmatic purpose is specified, or categorical aid, which is earmarked for specific programs. As mentioned earlier, state agencies serve as "pass through" agents for federal funds that are devoted to local programs and services. State-local relationships are strengthened further by the participation of representatives from local governing bodies and local government associations on state boards and commissions.[11]

State Regulation

Local governments must also comply with state regulations. For example, the state establishes professional qualifications for school superintendents and teachers, directors of social services, and local health officials. Moreover, the state requires that local governments provide certain services, such as building inspections, and establishes standards for education, water and wastewater treatment, auditing of public accounts, filing of uniform fiscal reports, and other activities.

The County as an Agent of the State

The concept of the county as an "administrative district of the state" or as an "arm of the state" is the oldest and most frequently cited description of a county. According to this concept, the county is a political subdivision created to execute the policies of the state and is, in fact, a branch of the general administration for those policies. The state, acting through the General Assembly, establishes counties "without the particular solicitation, consent, or concurrent action of the people who inhabit them ...." These units then serve as local units for the administration of the state's functions and duties.[12]

Cities generally are recognized as municipal corporations "called into existence either at the direct request or by consent of the persons composing them and created principally for the advantage and convenience of the people of the locality."[13] Moreover, because of the Virginia practice of city-county separation, the Virginia city often performs functions that in other states would be performed by counties alone. In this respect, the city is a political subdivision of the state in much the same way as a county.

Rockingham County's Courthouse is located in a 19th-century building in the city of Harrisonburg. Photo by Pete Giesen.

The difference between "cities" and "counties" has, in many ways, blurred in recent years. As noted in a legislative report:

From the time of Virginia's first Constitution through the first half of this century, distinctions between cities, towns, and counties were clear. Cities and towns were urban centers for work and shopping. They had relatively high population densities. Counties, on the other hand, were the agricultural, less densely populated areas of the state. As rural localities, counties required fewer powers since they did not face the problems associated with urbanization. "Suburbs" had not gained the level of prominence they hold today.

"City" and "county" titles were appropriate during the early 1900s because they accurately identified different locality types of urban and rural. However, the accurate descriptors of 1900 serve as artificial distinctions today.[14]

As federal and state budgets have been reduced and adjusted, counties have been expected to shoulder a higher proportion of costs of various government programs, although increased control over program operations has not always come with the increased financial responsibilities. Thus, the distinction between the county acting on behalf of the state and the county directly providing "state" services is increasingly artificial. The dual, sometimes blurred, role of the county is the key.

The County as a Unit of Local Government

In addition to serving as territorial and political subdivisions for the administration of state duties and functions, counties perform certain functions exclusively for the benefit of their residents. These local services often include water and wastewater treatment, trash collection and disposal, landfill operation, and fire protection. In Virginia counties, functions like these can be performed directly by the county government or through locally established sanitary districts or public authorities. Such functions are local in nature, although the authority to perform them must be granted by the General Assembly. The similarity between counties and cities as units of local self-government has led the courts to refer to counties as quasi-municipal corporations.[15]

Several developments illustrate the continuing evolution of counties as providers of local services. As the number and complexity of local functions performed by county governments have increased, the traditional distinction between counties and cities as separate types of government for rural and urban areas has become more difficult to apply. In many cases, this distinction has disappeared altogether under the pressure of demands for services that are neither urban nor rural, but suburban in nature. Thus, in 1966 the General Assembly granted to counties all the powers and authority of cities and towns except, according to the Virginia Supreme Court, the powers delegated to municipal corporations through the Uniform Charter Powers Act. In 1969, the Commission on Constitutional Revision, citing the fact that Virginia's counties and cities are on a par with each other, proposed a single local government article to replace the separate articles of the 1902 Constitution. The General Assembly and the voters adopted this recommendation as well as one that grants counties the option to incur long-term general obligation debt in the same manner as cities.[16]

In 1985, the General Assembly granted counties the authority to apply to the General Assembly for a charter. The provisions of the Uniform Charter Powers Act were made available to a chartered county. Since that time, Roanoke, Chesterfield, and James City counties have adopted charters that have been enacted by the General Assembly.[17]

The potential capacity of county governments to provide local services has been enhanced by constitutional changes that permit the General Assembly to give local governments greater powers of self-determination. The powers and organizational forms of county government can be prescribed through special acts or through charters that attempt to meet the particular needs of individual counties, as well as through general laws that apply either to all counties or to a group of counties. Other constitutional provisions and enabling statutes permit a county or other locality to abolish one or more of its public offices, to change the procedure by which some public officers are appointed and to make other arrangements affecting the county's organization or procedures. Usually such alterations are made only after a referendum, but a few can be made by resolution or ordinance passed by the board of supervisors.[18]

Finally, Virginia, as well as a number of other states, has established statutes intended to facilitate the sharing of services and revenues between cities and counties and to permit the consolidation of city and county governments. These legal provisions give implicit support to the notion that counties and cities are equal providers of local services.[19]

County Powers

Under the Virginia Constitution, all county powers are delegations of authority granted by the General Assembly and, unless otherwise indicated by statute or the Constitution, are vested in the board of supervisors. Except to the extent that the General Assembly is limited by the Constitutions of Virginia and the United States, there are no restraints on the powers it may grant to localities. It is clear, however, that these limitations do not impair to any significant degree the discretion of the legislature in conferring powers on county governments.[20]

The following sections discuss several of the broadest and most important grants of power to counties.

Rules of Construction

Two important rules of judicial construction (how the courts interpret the Constitution and statutes) control the use of county powers. One restriction is that the measure adopted must not be inconsistent with the general laws of Virginia or of the United States.[21] This means, of course, that actions taken under any of the county's grants of authority must not be contrary to the provisions of state or federal law, or the Virginia or U.S. Constitutions. It also means that the subject of the proposed action must not have been preempted exclusively by the state. County ordinances paralleling state laws may be held invalid unless it is shown that the state is sharing its jurisdiction on a given subject and intends for authority to be exercised concurrently with local governments.[22]

Another significant restriction on the use of county powers in Virginia is a rule of statutory construction known as the "Dillon Rule," which is stated in full as follows:

> It is a general and undisputed proposition of law that a municipal corporation possesses and can exercise the following powers, and no others: First, those granted in express words; second, those necessarily or fairly implied in or incident to the powers expressly granted; third, those essential to the accomplishment of the declared objects and purposes of the corporation not simply convenient, but indispensable. Any fair, reasonable, substantial doubt concerning the existence of power is resolved by the courts against the corporation, and the power is denied.[23]

Thus, according to this rule, all county actions must be supported by unambiguous grants of authority. If there is reasonable doubt as to whether or not authority has been granted, the question is likely to be construed against the county. First advanced in the 19th century, the Dillon Rule is still followed by Virginia courts.[24]

General Police Power

The broadest grant of authority that has been made to Virginia county governments is contained in the general police power, which states that "any county may adopt such measures as it deems expedient to secure and promote the health, safety and general welfare of its inhabitants, which are not inconsistent with the general laws of the Commonwealth." Application of the rule of strict construction has made it difficult, in many instances, for counties to rely solely on the police power for authority to act. Where the subject of proposed county legislation is not clearly within the police power, this power is used in conjunction with another, more specific, authorization.[25]

The U.S., Virginia, and Henrico County flags are flown next to Henrico's courthouse. Photo by Anne Marie Morgan.

Cities' Powers Conferred on Counties

The General Assembly has granted to county governing bodies the same powers and authority as those allowed city and town councils, except those contained in the Uniform Charter Powers Act. As noted earlier, however, a county may apply to the General Assembly for a charter and if the charter is granted, the county may exercise all the powers of municipal corporations under the Uniform Charter Powers Act unless otherwise provided in the charter.[26]

Power to Tax, Appropriate and Spend

The board of supervisors is authorized by statute to annually set the amount of county and district taxes. Revenues that are thus collected cannot be spent, however, without a specific appropriation of the funds by the board. No money may be paid out for any expenditure unless and until the governing body has made an appropriation for the expenditure. The board is required, however, to appropriate funds to pay the principal and interest on bonds and to pay the obligations of the county arising under contracts approved by the board of supervisors.[27]

Interlocal Relations

While Virginia has a relatively streamlined state and local governmental structure, the relationships between counties, cities, and towns are complicated by issues of development, revenues, and services. Examples abound of both cooperation and competition. Since the problems of local governments do not necessarily respect jurisdictional boundaries, legally distinct political subdivisions are often economically and socially interdependent. Common problems and scarce resources can create compelling reasons for intergovernmental cooperation and, at the same time, provide grounds for interlocal jealousy and conflict. As separate units of local government, independent of county jurisdiction, Virginia cities face many of the same problems as counties in providing services and managing growth.

Towns, unlike cities, share part of the county's tax base. Town citizens receive county services, help to elect the county's constitutional officers and governing body, and generally are subject to county ordinances. Yet one of the continuing problems of town-county relations has been an equitable balance between a town's contribution of revenues and the benefits it receives from the county.[28] Despite these obstacles, Virginia local governments have found a number of ways to make more effective use of their combined resources.

Authority to Cooperate

The General Assembly has given Virginia localities broad authority to cooperate with one another. The most frequently used grant of authority for interlocal cooperation permits any powers, privileges, or authority of any political subdivision of the state to be exercised jointly with any other political subdivision of Virginia or another state.[29] The General Assembly also has enacted numerous statutes that authorize interlocal and regional cooperation in specific areas.[30] Cooperating localities have considerable flexibility in implementing this authority to suit their needs.

A variety of administrative arrangements have been developed, including formal and informal mutual assistance agreements; parallel enactment of ordinances; designation of a single existing agency to provide a service while billing participating localities for their shares; establishment of a joint authority or board; contracts for provision of services; and, contributions of money, equipment, or personnel. The highest number of cooperative undertakings among Virginia localities relate to services pertaining to public safety, general and financial administration, jails, animal control, assessment of real property, building code enforcement, and libraries.[31]

Local governments also have joined in cooperative associations that work to improve local government and to advance its interests through research, training, and representation before the legislative and executive branches of the federal and state governments.[32] Planning district commissions have proven to be another important mechanism for interlocal cooperation.[33] Localities also may choose, by referendum, to share one or more of their constitutional officers or offices, a practice that can result in substantial savings even if the functions of the office are such that they must be handled separately for each locality.[34] Consolidated governments, regional councils and service districts offer additional opportunities for localities to operate jointly in providing some or all of their services.

State and Federal Encouragement of Cooperation

Federal and state governments encourage cooperation among local governments through financial incentives that offer increased levels of funding for joint activities and projects. In addition to authorizing financial assistance to planning district commissions, state laws and administrative regulations authorize grants for regional libraries, jails and mental health, mental retardation, and substance abuse programs.[35] Among the federal assistance programs that emphasize regional cooperation are grants for sewage treatment facilities, juvenile delinquency programs, criminal justice training, and airport development. In many instances, the federal government further encourages local cooperation and policy coordination by requiring that local grant applications be submitted to regional and state agencies for review and that some local projects be given federal financial assistance only if they conform to a state or regional plan.

Regional Cooperation

Planning District Commissions

Legislation was adopted by the General Assembly in 1995 amending the prior statutes on planning district commissions. These statutes continue to provide a means for localities to work together on state and local issues of a regional nature.[36]

Counties, cities, and towns which together comprise at least 45 percent of the population within a planning district (the boundaries of which are established by the Virginia Department of Housing and Community Development) may organize a planning district commission simply by developing a written agreement to that effect. The commissions have general powers under the law to make and enter into contracts; apply for, accept, and disburse state financial assistance, and other loans, grants, and property; to employ such staff as necessary; issue bonds; form nonprofit corporations; and related powers. In addition, each commission must file an annual report with the Department of Housing and Community Development.[37]

As noted in the Code of Virginia, the purpose of planning district commissions is:

… to encourage and facilitate local government cooperation and state-local cooperation in addressing on a regional basis problems of greater than local significance. Functional areas warranting regional cooperation may include … (i) economic and physical infrastructure development, (ii) solid waste, water supply and other environmental management, (iii) transportation, (iv) criminal justice, (v) emergency management, (vi) human services and (vii) recreation.[38]

Each planning district commission is required to prepare a regional strategic plan, including regional goals and objectives, strategies to meet those goals and objectives and mechanisms for measuring progress. The plan must be submitted to the Virginia Department of Housing and Community Development, as well as to the governing body of each locality within the district.[39] Once the strategic plan becomes effective, the planning district commission may not establish any policies or take any actions inconsistent with the plan.[40]

State Funding for Regional Cooperation

The General Assembly has established two funding sources to promote regional cooperation. One is called the Regional Cooperation Incentive Fund, which requires a minimum 25 percent match from the planning district commission or member localities. The second fund derives from the Regional Competitiveness Act and requires no local matching funds. Both funds are administered by the Virginia Department of Housing and Community Development.

The Code of Virginia establishes the Regional Cooperation Incentive Fund for the purpose of encouraging interlocal strategic and functional area planning and other regional cooperative activities.[41] This provides state funding for the operation of the planning district commissions, as well as for any priority functional areas which the Governor or General Assembly select and fund. Unfortunately, no monies have ever been appropriated by the General Assembly for the Regional Cooperation Incentive Fund.

The Regional Competitiveness Act, adopted in 1996, establishes an incentive fund to encourage regional strategic planning and cooperation.[42] Under these provisions, "regional partnerships" consisting of government, business, education and civic leaders, approved by the local governing bodies of the region, develop a strategic economic development plan. The focus of the plan must be to increase the region's economic competitiveness based on increasing median family income and job creation, while reducing differences in median family income levels among the region's localities, and to identify joint activities aimed at improving these and related factors.

Regions have broad latitude in determining the projects that will have the greatest impact. Eligibility for state funding is determined by the type of activity involved in the project.[43] The Code of Virginia assigns weights to various activities, with higher point values to job creation, economic development, regional revenue and growth sharing agreements, and education. The Virginia Department of Housing and Community Development makes the point assignments, determines eligibility for funding, and administers the program.

Although initially funded by the General Assembly in 1996, appropriations for the Regional Competitiveness Act were finally terminated in 2002.

Annexation

Urban Expansion by Annexation

One traditional method for providing urban governmental services in densely populated areas beyond the boundaries of cities and towns has been to extend municipal services to these areas. An area's need for services, as well as a municipality's desire for additional land for development and increased tax resources, can prompt the municipality to consider annexation. Over the years, however, the authority of county governments to provide urban services directly or through sanitary districts or authorities has been steadily expanded, thereby eroding much of the rationale for municipal annexation. At the same time, the social and fiscal problems of most Virginia local governments have intensified in past years, making the localities more dependent on continued growth in order to survive economically. As a result of these trends, annexation proceedings have become increasingly protracted and costly in both dollar and political terms, especially in the most urbanized areas of the state.[44]

In 1987, the General Assembly enacted a temporary moratorium on annexation proceedings in the Commonwealth. The moratorium took effect on Jan. 1, 1987, and has been extended to July 1, 2018. Annexation actions initiated by towns as well as municipal boundary expansions by agreement are not subject to the moratorium.[45]

Consolidation[46]

In 1972, Nansemond County consolidated with its two small towns (Holland and Whaleyville) as the city of Nansemond. Two years later, in 1974, the cities of Nansemond and Suffolk merged as the city of Suffolk. Although those were the last times they were successfully used, the general consolidation statutes remain. This portion of the Code of Virginia authorizes any two or more local governments to consolidate, or merge, into a single political subdivision.[47]

According to the Virginia Supreme Court, the purpose of the consolidation statutes is to advance the consolidation of political subdivisions by the respective governing bodies, but if not, by proceedings initiated by engaged citizens. Although it does not remedy all interlocal problems, consolidation is sometimes recommended as a means to cultivate local governments capable of extracting on a broader tax and manpower base, distributing services equally over wider areas, and creating greater economies and efficiency in administration.[48]

Virginia's merger laws are relatively flexible, although the procedural requirements are fairly detailed. A special court is required to review proposals to consolidate two or more local governments if the proposal involves unlike governmental entities (e.g., a county and a city), or change to a different form (e.g., consolidation of a county and city into a city). No special court or petition review is required, however, if consolidation is of like units of government.[49]

Local governments that wish to consolidate enter into a merger agreement that specifies such matters as the proposed name of the new government, the disposition of the jurisdiction's property and debts, the time for the election of new officers, and other terms. Consolidation can also be initiated by a petition of at least 10 percent of the voters in the affected locality. A referendum on the consolidation question must be held, if citizen-initiated or if one of the affected jurisdictions is a county. A majority of voters voting in each jurisdiction must agree to the question of consolidation.[50]

Special Authorities

Other Governmental Entities

In addition to general-purpose local governments, Virginia has numerous special-purpose political subdivisions that serve a broad range of statewide, regional, or local interests. Most of these subdivisions are established to perform a single function or several related functions. The list below indicates some of the functions served by these authorities and districts. These subdivisions may serve either all or part of only one local government, or their operations may extend into two or more jurisdictions, in which case they become a means for interlocal cooperation.

The U.S. Census Bureau counted 196 special districts in Virginia in 2002.[51] Most of these were single-function districts, focusing on soil and water conservation, libraries, and airports. Some of these may be chartered under federal law. The Code of Virginia also authorizes various special districts and authorities. Examples of other governmental entities include:

1. Agricultural and forestal districts;
2. Transportation improvement districts;
3. Industrial development authorities;
4. Water and waste authorities;
5. Hospital or health center commissions;
6. Hospital authorities;
7. Electric authorities;
8. Tourism development authorities;
9. Redevelopment and housing authorities;
10. Community and development authorities;

11.   Public recreational facilities authorities; and
12.   Park authorities.

In general, special districts are established to provide services that other levels of government either cannot or will not perform, or to escape debt limitations or cumbersome preconditions to assuming debt. For example, Article X of the Virginia Constitution requires that all taxes must be uniform upon the same class of subjects within the territorial limits of the authority levying the tax. By forming a new district, sanitary districts are able to meet the service needs of the more densely populated areas of a county (particularly the towns) without spreading the burden of taxation to other areas that do not require the same services. Water and sewer authorities provide similar flexibility, since they are able to select those areas for which it is economically feasible to provide services and facilities on a paying basis. Authorities have their own distinct and separate governing bodies; sanitary districts, on the other hand, are unique in that the county board of supervisors or city council of the locality creating the district also serves as the district's governing board.

In a number of cases, the existence of federal programs has prompted the establishment of special districts as the most readily available means of meeting local needs and satisfying the organizational requirements for federal assistance. Special districts have an added advantage in that the local share of the program costs can be met without requiring a general tax increase or adding to the debt of the general government of the community. In addition, some special districts have been created to handle projects or services that certain areas of a county do not need or want and thus oppose funding through the county's general budget. The special district bears the responsibility of making the program pay for itself.

Conclusion

Local governments have evolved over the centuries and today provide an enormous variety of services to their citizens. In fact, they deliver the largest portion of domestic services in the nation. But localities often have little discretion in how they can use federal or state grants and must comply with sometimes costly federal and state mandates that require them to take prescribed actions. Many county officials in Virginia would like additional flexibility in how they deliver services—especially during difficult budget times—and a gubernatorial reform commission has advanced that idea with a recommendation that state agencies review local mandates. The commission found that "[t]here are 570 state and federal mandates placed on Virginia's localities. 456 are subject to assessment by state agencies."[52] It also found that mandates on local governments have been added every year since 2000, but "efforts to review and eliminate mandates have led to the suggested striking of only two mandates. Neither has been eliminated, hindering the ability for state and local government to find operational efficiencies or innovate."[53] The commission recommended that "[a]gencies should justify the continuation of mandates with an eye towards cost-benefit analysis and performance-based metrics to determine the value of the mandate relative to the output required."[54]

The outcome of that process could make a profound difference in the way counties govern in the future.

James D. Campbell, AICP, CAE, has 40 years of service to local governments in Virginia, including more than 20 as the Executive Director of the Virginia Association of Counties.

CHAPTER 24
Virginia's Municipal Governments: Independent Cities—or Are They?

By Mary Jo Fields
Director of Research, Virginia Municipal League

Virginia's Constitution and laws are not particularly enlightening in defining the terms "city" and "town." The Constitution and Code of Virginia declare that a city is an independent incorporated community that was a city as of July 1, 1971, or that has a population of 5,000 or more and becomes a city as allowed under general law. A town similarly is defined as any existing town that became a town before the same date or that has a population of 1,000 or more and becomes a town.[1] State general law establishes a process for the incorporation of cities and towns, although there is a moratorium on the creation of new cities, except through consolidation.[2]

Important Characteristics of Virginia Local Governments

There are only two forms of municipal government in Virginia: cities and towns. Virginia is unique among the 50 states in having a statewide system of independent cities. Thus, the state's 39 cities are *geographically* and, for the most part, *politically,* separate from counties. The cities serve as administrative arms of the state in the same way as counties in Virginia and other states. But this is not a role assigned to most cities in other states. City residents in the Commonwealth do not pay local taxes to the county, and with the exception of some court officials (see the section under "Overview of Governing Structure") do not vote for county officeholders. The 190 towns in Virginia, on the other hand, are much like municipal governments in other states. Towns are part of one (or more) counties, town residents pay town taxes and county taxes, and town residents vote for town officials and county officials.[3] According to U.S. Bureau of the Census data, in July 2009, Virginia's cities ranged in size from Norton with 3,713 residents to Virginia Beach with a population of 433,575. Towns ranged in size from 56 in Columbia to Blacksburg with a population of 42,885.[4]

Virginia local government is also unusual when compared to local governments nationwide due to its reliance on the council-manager form of government in all but one city and most of the towns of any size. Under the council manager form of government, the elected governing body—the city or town council—hires a professional administrator to supervise the staff. Typically, the council or board will directly hire and supervise only a few individuals, which usually are the manager, the attorney, and the clerk.[5]

Another important characteristic of a local government in Virginia is that it has relatively fewer local units than in many states. Virginia has 324 counties, cities, and towns—a smaller number of general purpose local governments than in 31 other states. Virginia has been even stingier in its use of special district forms of government: Forty-three states have more special purpose districts than does the Commonwealth.[6]

Two cities, South Boston and Clifton Forge, reverted—that is, went from being a city to a town. This process is governed by sections 15.2-4100 through 15.2-4120 of the Code of Virginia.[7]

History of Municipal Government in Virginia[8]

Municipal governments were slow to develop in colonial times. The colonial government tried to encourage the development of towns through general acts that required that a town be established in each county and by special acts that established particular towns. These towns were not governmental units but, instead, were defined areas in which trustees were charged with surveying the land, establishing lots and streets, and selling lots. The towns otherwise had no governmental authority, although they formed the centers where many municipalities developed.

By the time of the American Revolution, two municipalities with governmental powers had been incorporated through charters granted by the Royal Governor in the name of the English Crown. Williamsburg was granted a city charter in 1722. The charter created a governing body and granted the city the authority to regulate trade, hold court, operate prisons, and perform other functions. The borough of Norfolk was issued a charter with similar powers in 1736.

Following the Revolution, the General Assembly continued the practice of incorporating towns and cities through special acts. Towns and cities continued to exercise similar powers, although the Constitution of 1870 required that municipalities (with no distinction between cities and towns) with more than 5,000 in population elect constitutional officers and have a separate court. In 1887, the General Assembly defined cities as incorporated areas with populations of 5,000 or more and towns as those with populations of less than 5,000. This distinction was included in the Constitution of 1902 and in the current Constitution.

Overview of Governing Structure

Virginia's cities and towns are governed by an elected council and mayor. In about half of the cities[9] and many of the towns, the mayor is directly elected by the voters. The mayor in about half of the cities and a smaller number of towns is elected by the council members from among themselves. The mayor is the official and ceremonial head in municipalities operating under the council-manager form of government. Richmond is the only city in which the mayor is also the chief executive; in that city, the mayor hires a chief administrative officer to handle day-to-day operations. While the office of mayor may appear to be largely ceremonial in council-manager municipalities, mayors serve as the political leaders of their communities and, depending on their personalities, have more influence than might be suggested from a mere reading of duties in the charter or state law.

While local elections are officially nonpartisan in Virginia (since the names of political parties do not appear on the ballots for local offices),[10] the political parties in some cities traditionally nominate candidates. In some localities, the charters specify that candidates for council may get their names on the ballot only through the petition process or prohibit identification of candidates by political party.[11]

Outside of the broad outline of authority in the state Constitution, Virginia's municipalities derive their authority from two primary sources: their charters and statutory provisions in the Code of Virginia. The charters are in effect local constitutions that lay out the municipalities' organization, powers and duties.[12] Most counties derive their authority from state general law, although three counties (Chesterfield, James City, and Roanoke) have been issued charters. In addition, some counties are organized according to special forms of government contained in state law. For example, the Fairfax

County government operates under the urban county executive form of government[13] and Henrico County under the county manager form.[14]

Five "constitutional officers" are elected in most of Virginia's cities (and counties). These officers are the sheriff, the Commonwealth's attorney, the circuit court clerk, the commissioner of the revenue, and the treasurer.[15] In some of the special forms of county government (such as Henrico County and Fairfax County), the offices of the commissioner and treasurer are eliminated and those functions are performed by a director of finance appointed by the manager. Further, some smaller cities share three constitutional officers (sheriff, Commonwealth's attorney, and circuit court clerk) with their neighboring county. Finally, individual offices in some cities—such as the commissioner of revenue in the city of Richmond—have been eliminated through referenda.

What Municipalities Do

Title 15.2 of the Code of Virginia focuses exclusively on local governments, but numerous other chapters of the state Code also place requirements on municipalities or contain language that authorizes municipalities to perform particular functions.

Cities, like counties, operate as administrative arms of the state and are required by the state to provide (and to pay a share of) numerous services. Some of these services are governed by boards over which cities and counties have limited control. Some of them are delivered through regional agencies. Services that the state requires cities and counties to offer include: public education, public health, social services, services for troubled youth, building code enforcement, election administration, jails, behavioral health (primarily through regional community services boards), and planning, including development of a comprehensive plan.[16]

In addition, cities and towns with populations of 3,500 or more are responsible for maintaining streets and bridges, including general repairs and resurfacing, snow removal, litter pickup, maintenance of traffic signs, and pavement markings. These cities and towns also are responsible for funding a portion of the cost of new construction of urban roads.[17] Arlington and Henrico counties also maintain their own roads. Even though the state is officially responsible for road construction and maintenance in other jurisdictions, some counties have undertaken road projects as they have become increasingly frustrated by state underfunding of road construction.

For each of these functions, state statutes and administrative regulations prescribe a minimum level of service to greater or lesser degrees depending on the function, how the service is to be delivered, and qualifications of personnel.

Cities and counties devote a large part of the revenue they raise from local taxes and fees to help pay for services that they are required by the state to provide.

While cities serve as administrative arms of the state, both cities and towns undertake a number of other functions designed to secure the general welfare and safety of its citizens. Many municipal functions are authorized under either specific laws covering discrete topics (as narrowly defined as the regulation of tattoo parlors) to the broad authority granted under § 15.2-1102 of the Code of Virginia that allows municipalities "to secure and promote the general welfare of the inhabitants of the municipality and the safety, health, peace, good order, comfort, convenience, morals, trade, commerce and industry of the municipality and the inhabitants thereof ..."[18] Municipal governments (and many counties) clean and distribute water, collect storm water, collect and dispose of sewage, collect and dispose of trash, operate parks and libraries, provide street lights, run or contract for shelters for the homeless, regulate nuisance activities, operate airports and ports, undertake economic development activities, and perform numerous other functions affecting the everyday lives of residents.

Chart 1 shows expenditures by cities, counties, and larger towns by functional area. By far, the largest expenditures are for public education, followed by public safety, and health and welfare services. (The larger towns are those with populations of 3,500 or more. These towns are required to report financial information to the state Auditor of Public Accounts.)

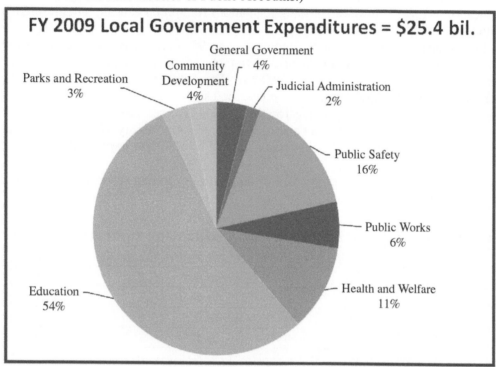

CHART 1: [19]   Source: "2009 Amended Comparative Report of Local Government," Auditor of Public Accounts, Commonwealth of Virginia.

A Closer Look at Public Education

Public education is deserving of a closer look because it accounts for such a large portion of local and state expenditures. It is also one of the few services specifically mentioned in the state Constitution (in Article VIII).[20] The General Assembly is required to provide for the compulsory education of every eligible child, and to "seek to ensure" that an educational program of high quality is maintained. The Board of Education is required to establish Standards of Quality (SOQ), which can be revised only by the General Assembly, while the General Assembly is charged with determining where the money comes from to meet the SOQ. Under Section 2, the General Assembly also has the responsibility of determining how costs are to be shared between the state and localities, and local governments are required to meet their share of the costs of the SOQ. The State Board of Education has the authority to generally supervise the school divisions and has the primary authority to establish educational policy. The supervision of local schools is placed under the hands of the local school boards.

Educational programs are governed by federal and state laws and regulations. Federal legislation such as the No Child Left Behind Act and the Individuals with Disabilities Education Act place numerous requirements on states and school divisions.

At the state level, the Standards of Quality set staffing ratios and prescribe other components that drive funding for public education. The Standards of Accreditation prescribe accountability standards that schools and school divisions must meet in order to attain accreditation, and the Standards of Learning prescribe the content of courses. The State Board of Education adopts regulations governing other facets of public education— ranging from establishing regulations for special education to prescribing scoliosis exams for students.[21]

By far the largest portion of state funding—some 90 percent—is for meeting the SOQ. The annual Appropriation Act adopted by the General Assembly establishes what the state will recognize as costs to meet the SOQ and how much the state will pay. Examples of programs outside the SOQ include those directed at students at-risk of educational failure, food services, and preschool, to name a few.

The state shares the cost of paying for the SOQ and other educational programs with local governments. The local share is based on a composite index of local "ability to pay," which is a statistical measure that is supposed to measure the need and ability of a locality to pay for education in relation to other localities.

Local governments pay the largest share of the cost of operating schools, and virtually all of the capital costs (see Table 1).

TABLE 1: Sources of financial support for education operating expenditures

(Expressed as percentage of total operating expenditures)					
	FY09	FY08	FY07	FY06	FY05
Local	48.6	49.9	48.6	50.2	49.3
State	44.9	43.6	44.7	42.8	43.5
Federal	6.4	6.5	6.7	7.1	7.1

Source: "Table 15," in "Annual Report, Superintendent of Public Instruction," for the fiscal years indicated. The state share includes the state sales tax dedicated to public education.[22] Totals may not equal 100 percent due to rounding.

Local Revenue Sources

Municipalities and counties finance their local operations through local taxes and fees as well as from revenues received from the state and federal governments. Table 2 shows the breakdown of revenues derived from local, state, and federal sources.

TABLE 2: Sources of Local Revenues, FY 2009

Local Revenues from Own Sources	$17,065,626,792	61.5%
State Aid	$ 9,187,075,950	33.1%
Federal Aid	$ 1,490,170,705	5.4%
Total Local Resources	$27,742,873,447	100.0%

Source: "Exhibit A," in "2009 Amended Comparative Report of Local Government," Auditor of Public Accounts, Commonwealth of Virginia.[23] The data reflect financial reports from 39 cities, 94 counties, and 36 towns. One county did not report its data.

Table 3 shows local revenue sources for cities, counties, and the 36 towns reporting to the Auditor of Public Accounts.

TABLE 3: Local Revenues from Own Sources, FY 2009

Real property taxes	$ 8,858,451,612	52.3%
Other property taxes	$ 2,118,985,647	12.5%
Other local taxes	$ 3,452,569,061	20.4%
Permits, fees, regulatory licenses	$ 154,410,897	0.9%
Fines & forfeitures	$ 96,651,478	0.6%
Charges for services	$ 739,208,248	10.3%
Revenue from use of money & property	$ 306,368,843	1.1%
Miscellaneous	$ 338,981,006	2.0%
Total	$17,065,626,792	

Source: "Exhibit B," in "2009 Amended Comparative Report of Local Government," Auditor of Public Accounts, Commonwealth of Virginia.[24] The data reflect financial reports from 39 cities, 94 counties, and 36 towns. One county did not report its data.

Table 4 outlines the primary local tax sources available to cities, towns and counties.

TABLE 4: Local Governments Taxing Authority Overview

Tax	Local Governments With Authority to Levy	Any Restrictions?
TAXES ON PROPERTY:		
Real property	Cities, counties, & towns	Unrestricted
Tangible personal property ('car tax')	Cities, counties, & towns	Yes
Machinery & tools	Cities, counties, & towns	Yes
Merchants' capital	Cities, counties, & towns	Yes
TAXES ON INDIVIDUALS:		
Sales and use	Cities & counties, *Not towns*	Yes
Motor vehicle license	Cities, counties, & towns	Yes
Utility consumers (electric, gas and water)	Cities, counties, & towns	Yes
		Note: Consumer utility on phones was repealed effective Jan. 2007 as part of the statewide communications tax reforms*

Continued on next page

Meals	Cities & towns; certain counties by unanimous approval of board; any county by referendum.	No city or town restrictions; county rate capped at 4%.
Income	Certain cities & counties (Northern Virginia: Alexandria, Arlington, Fairfax City, Fairfax County, Falls Church, Loudoun, Manassas, Manassas Park, & Prince William; & Norfolk & Virginia Beach).	Yes Maximum of 1%; approved by referendum; for transportation only; 5 year sunset. This authority has not been used because of the many restrictions on it.
Cigarettes	Certain cities & towns (those with authority prior to 1977). Certain counties (Arlington & Fairfax).	No limit on cities & towns; Arlington & Fairfax counties may levy to 5-cents per pack or state levy.
Transient occupancy (lodging)	Cities, counties, & towns	No restrictions on cities & towns; Several restrictions on county rates and dedication of revenues.
Admissions	Cities & towns; certain counties	No restrictions on cities & towns; several restrictions on county rates and application.
Recordation	Cities & counties	Yes
Probate	Cities & counties	Yes
TAXES ON BUSINESSES:		
Business, professional, & occupational license	Cities, counties, & towns	Yes Capped rates. Counties cannot levy in towns that use the tax without town permission.
Daily rental property	Cities, counties, & towns	Yes
Coal severance	Cities & counties	Yes
Gas Severance	Cities & counties	Yes
Coal & gas road improvement	Cities & counties	Yes
Oil severance	Cities & counties	Yes

Continued on next page

Utility license	Cities, counties & towns	Yes Capped rates. Counties cannot levy in towns that use the tax without town permission. Note: Except for specific grandfathered localities, the Utility License on phones was repealed effective Jan. 2007 as part of the statewide communications tax reforms*
Alcohol license	Cities & towns; certain counties	Yes Maximum taxes are set by state; counties may not levy in towns that levy.
Bank franchise	Cities, counties, & towns	Yes Capped at 80% of state rate; county tax does not apply in towns.
Cable TV franchise	Cities, counties, & towns	As part of Jan. 2007 statewide communications tax reforms, localities continue to negotiate franchise agreements including in kind and extra revenues. However, cable companies charge taxpayers the 5 percent sales & use tax and remit the dollars to the state. The state subsequently apportions the funds to localities.*
Virginia Communications Sales & Use Tax	Cities, counties & towns	*Beginning in Jan. 2007, the Communications Sales & Use Tax of 5 percent replaced several local taxes including cable, E-911 and consumer utility. Communications companies – phone, wireless, cable and satellite – charge taxpayers the 5 percent Sales & Use Tax and remit the dollars to the state. The state subsequently apportions the funds to localities.

Source: Updated from "Table 11.1" in "Municipal Revenue Sources," *Handbook for Virginia Mayors and Council Members.* Charlottesville: University of Virginia and Virginia Municipal League, 2004.[25]

Cities, towns, and counties also have the authority to levy a variety of service charges (such as for refuse collection or recycling), collect permits, fines, and forfeitures, and earn interest on the use of money and property.

Municipalities and counties derive their authority to levy property taxes from the state Constitution and general law. The Constitution states that property taxes are subject to local taxation only.[26]

Cities and towns also exercise some taxing powers[27] under § 15.2-1104 of the Code of Virginia, which states that a "municipal corporation may raise annually by taxes and assessments on property, persons and other subjects of taxation ...."[28] This section allows cities and towns to levy taxes on meals, cigarettes, admissions, and lodgings. (Counties, on the other hand, are not included in this section, and for the most part may levy these taxes only if approved in a referendum.)

The next section will give additional details on five important local revenue sources.

Real Property Tax

The state Constitution requires that all property be taxed, that taxes be uniform on the same class or subject, and that assessment be made by fair market value.[29] The Constitution also allows the General Assembly to make some exceptions, however. For example, the General Assembly has used its authority under the Constitution to allow localities to defer or exempt real estate devoted to agricultural, horticultural, forest, or open space uses.[30]

An important issue for real estate taxation is determining the value of the property. Having accurate assessments of the value of real property helps ensure that real estate taxes are fair—that the taxes are assessed on the appropriate value of the real estate. In general, larger cities are required to reassess their property every two years, although they are allowed to have an annual reassessment. Cities with less than 30,000 in population may elect to reassess every four years.[31] Town property is typically included in the county reassessment process (counties reassess property on a one- to six-year process).[32]

Real estate taxes are the largest source of revenue for cities and counties, and are one of the few sources that have not been capped or unlimited by action of the General Assembly.

Tangible Personal Property

Tangible personal property also is subject to local taxation. The personal property tax is the second largest source of revenues for localities (including the amount received from the state under the car tax reimbursement program). The tax is applied on motor vehicles, business furniture and fixtures, boats, recreational vehicles, and farming equipment. The same constitutional provisions that cover real property also require that uniformity in the assessment of personal property.[33] The state Constitution allows the General Assembly to create classifications of personal property that allow for differentials in tax rates.[34]

In 1999, the state instituted the personal property tax relief program, in which the state pays a portion of the personal property tax on personal-use vehicles. Total state reimbursement cannot exceed $950 million a year.[35]

Local Sales and Use Tax

The state of Virginia first levied a sales tax in 1966. Prior to that time, some cities had begun imposing a local sales tax. With the adoption of the state sales and use tax, the General Assembly assumed authority over this revenue source but granted all cities and counties the authority to levy a one-cent local option tax. All the cities and counties took advantage of that option. The one-cent local option tax is collected by the state along with the remainder of the state tax. The one-cent local option tax is returned to cities and counties based on the point of sale. Counties are required to share a portion of their one-cent collections with towns based on the proportion of the school-age population in the town compared to the county.[36]

Communications Sales and Use Tax

In response to complaints about the number and variety of local taxes relating to the telecommunications industry and differences in taxation of the "wired" and "wireless" industries, the General Assembly in 2006 adopted the Virginia Communications Sales and Use Tax. This tax replaced a number of other taxes and fees previously levied by local governments. The state collects the tax and returns most of it monthly to cities, counties, and towns.[37] However, the state takes a portion of the revenue to operate a telephone relay service center and has taken a larger share over the past few years to offset state costs.

Business, Professional, and Occupational License Tax

Counties, cities, and towns may levy a business, professional, and occupational license tax on "businesses, trades, professions, occupations and callings."[38] A county tax does not apply in a town unless authorized by the town council. Some businesses are exempt from the license and there are numerous statutory restrictions on the administration and tax rates for this tax. All cities, many towns, and about half of the counties levy the BPOL tax. Those counties that do not levy BPOL generally impose a merchants' capital tax (which is a form of personal property taxation).

State Revenues

Most state aid distributed to cities and counties is designed to pay a share of the costs of programs that these localities are required to offer. The largest categorical state aid program is for education. Other important state aid programs including funding for constitutional officers, human services programs, and public safety programs. Towns, on the other hand, receive little state aid except in the form of urban street maintenance (for towns of at least 3,500 residents) and law enforcement assistance (for towns with police departments). The two towns (West Point and Colonial Beach) that operate independent school systems also receive state education aid.

Federal revenues

Local governments receive federal funding primarily in the form of categorical grants for specific types of activities such as education, community development, public safety, and public works.

The Future of Local Governments

Local governments face a myriad of challenges, primarily focused on how to finance services required by either the state or federal government or demanded by citizens. Local governments are restricted in their ability to raise revenues and are hamstrung by rules and regulations that dictate what they do and how they do it. Reductions in state and federal funding play out primarily at the local level, as the state has chosen to deliver most of its services through local or regional agencies. Balancing demands for services and demands for tax relief and government reform will be challenges faced by virtually all local governments in years to come.

Mary Jo Fields is Director of Research at the Virginia Municipal League. She is a VML lobbyist and also coordinates program planning for the league's annual conferences, mayors' institutes, and conferences for newly elected officials. She is a co-editor of the "Handbook for Virginia Mayors and Council Members."

Part VII: Elections and Politics

Elections and the activities that impact their outcomes are vehicles that many Americans use to participate in the governance of their nation. One of the easiest ways to take part is by voting to select officials who will make federal, state, and local governing decisions. Virginia is unique among most states in that it holds elections every year, so it is important to understand their critical role in the Commonwealth's political system. In Section VII, *Elections and Politics,* a former state official who helped oversee a series of elections describes Virginia's electoral process. It is clear that the system and procedures that undergird voting must be fair and honest if representative government is to work properly, and the author explains the steps that Virginia takes to ensure the integrity of its elections.

One component of this administration is making sure that people have the ability to register to vote and that they are, in fact, eligible to do so in the Commonwealth.[1] The author explains Virginia's eligibility requirements, which include never having been convicted of a felony (unless the individual's rights have been restored through the Governor's office). Virginia utilizes state and federal databases in an effort to confirm whether applicants are American citizens and residents of the Commonwealth. Chapter 25 also highlights other policies that affect voting in Virginia. To make registration more accessible, state law permits applications to be made at the offices of local registrars and at numerous public agencies. Citizens who want to vote in a primary or general election must register before the records are closed 21 days before an election. Additionally, Virginia permits approved categories of citizens, such as college students who are away from home, deployed military personnel, and individuals who are out of town on business, to vote absentee. Unlike some other states, the Commonwealth does not allow registration in the days just prior to an election, mail-in registration, or permissive early voting options before election day.[2]

Contributing money to political campaigns is another way that citizens participate. Chapter 26 is written by the executive director of a nonprofit watchdog organization that monitors the flow of money in Virginia politics. In the arena of election-related contributions, the Commonwealth uses an approach that is different from that of the federal government. As the author explains, Virginia does not cap donations to candidates or parties, preferring instead to require public disclosure of donors and recipients throughout the year on prescribed dates. Citizens can access this information through the State Board of Elections or on-line through the Virginia Public Access Project. Through this method of accountability, readers can form their own opinions about the significance of specific donations, as well as the role of money in influencing candidates and outcomes.

Political parties are tools for direct citizen activism in electoral politics, and Chapter 27 outlines how they work in Virginia. The parties are defined by state law and are especially important in nominating the candidates who will be on the ballot for general elections and in galvanizing votes on behalf of their nominees. However, they lose a measure of control over the nomination process in the Commonwealth when candidates are chosen through primaries instead of conventions. This is because unlike many states, Virginia does not require voter registration by political party, so when candidates are nominated through elections, anyone can vote in its open primaries regardless of party identification.

The Commonwealth began to have a vigorous two-party system in the 1970s and since then, Virginia voters have chosen an equal number of Democratic and Republican governors in state elections and produced thriving partisan competition in the General Assembly. The Commonwealth also has become a contested battleground state in federal elections. As the author explains, Virginia's two major parties articulate governing visions in order to rally like-minded citizens to their causes. They organize through city and county committees, which meet on a larger scale occasionally for district and statewide conventions. Democrats and Republicans dominate the Commonwealth's elections, and although minor or third parties do exist, their efforts have not resulted in the same level of electoral success. But ultimately, while every voter does not identify with partisans of one stripe or another, the political parties still play an essential role in selecting the people who govern Virginia.

Members of the Patriot Guard Riders line the steps to the State Capitol in May, 2010, during a ceremony honoring Virginians in the Armed Forces who have died fighting global terrorism.   Photo by Bob Brown, *Richmond Times-Dispatch*.

CHAPTER 25
Voting in Virginia:
Ensuring Integrity of Elections

By Nancy Rodrigues
Secretary of the State Board of Elections, 2007-2011

Our nation's election process is the cornerstone of America's democratic republic, but it is actually a complex system that requires a great deal of work behind the scenes to keep it running well. The legendary Speaker of the U.S. House of Representatives, Thomas "Tip" O'Neill, once observed that "all politics are local."[1] For all intents and purposes, he could have been talking about elections in Virginia. That's because the Commonwealth has 134 localities, each with a local electoral board that conducts its own elections. They are overseen by a nonpartisan agency, the State Board of Elections (SBE), which watches over the Commonwealth's election community and provides guidance, resources, and citizen education. And with the ever-changing landscape of local, state, and federal laws, technology, employees, and political officials, it is challenging for any government agency to stay at the forefront.

When Virginians think of the State Board, they often view it as merely a repository of information, rather than the infrastructure that provides a great breadth of services for the Commonwealth's democratic system. Our modern election process is not without its faults, but the mere fact that it is the conduit through which decisions occur at the local, state, and federal levels makes it imperative for the State Board to serve as an effective portal for the public. Accessible to citizens and candidates of the Commonwealth, SBE's mission is to ensure the uniformity, accuracy, and purity of all elections.

Local Boards

The Virginia Constitution establishes in each county and city an electoral board composed of three citizen members.[2] These individuals, though selected by a local circuit court judge, are nominated by the two major

Nancy Rodrigues "referees" on election day, 2008. Photo courtesy of Nancy Rodrigues.

political parties. Following a gubernatorial election the majority of those on the board are selected based on the governor's political affiliation.

Electoral boards play a vital election role. These boards appoint the general registrar for their counties or cities, as well as all the officers of election who run the polling places on Election Day. They are also charged with responsibility for everything from the security of voting equipment to reviewing provisional ballots.[3]

It is the general registrar who manages the day-to-day operations on a local level. This individual adds and deletes voter names from the rolls and helps the electoral board carry out its responsibilities, such as training officers of election and sending out absentee ballots.[4]

State Board of Elections[5]

Established in 1946, the State Board of Elections' mission is to supervise and coordinate the work of the county and city electoral boards and the general registrars, to obtain uniformity in practices and proceedings, and to achieve a legal and uncorrupted process in all elections. It is a bit like the unwieldy chore of "herding cats" since each county and city is also operating independently.

However, this small, three-member State Board provides guidance through its policies.[6] The staff of a state agency by the same name assists the Board in carrying out its responsibilities. Together they work to ensure adherence to election laws and fair treatment of voters.

According to Virginia law, the State Board members are appointed by the governor and subject to confirmation by the General Assembly. The appointments to the Board are determined by the outcome of the last election for governor. The political parties of the winner and the runner-up will be represented on the Board. Two of the three Board members must be of the political party that cast the most votes for governor at this election. The governor designates one member of the board as the Secretary.

Elections

Virginia elections run on a four-year cycle. Virginia is one of the few states in the country that has a major election annually, with federal elections in even years and state elections in odd years. The Commonwealth also has a propensity for special elections, which are held when public offices are vacated. During the last several years there were more than 20 special elections, including one for Congress, eight primaries to nominate candidates, three May general elections, and three statewide November general elections. They added up to more than 30 elections with at least ten million voters casting their ballots.[7]

Each election year is unique. Although federal elections are generally held in even years, a special election for a federal office such as a congressional seat can be held in an odd year in case of a vacancy due to death or a resignation. Therefore, due to special elections, state and local elections are often held every year.

Federal, state, and special elections each have specific laws that must be followed with different deadlines and/or identification requirements.[8] The deadline for sending absentee ballots to voters is 45 days before a general election, but an exception is made for a special election because the latter are held on a condensed timetable. However, special elections can run at the same time as a general election. Confusing? Yes, but somehow it seems to all come together before an election. And the variety makes it important for voters to check what type of election is taking place.[9]

Voter Registration[10]

One of the key roles the election community plays is ensuring that only eligible citizens are allowed to register to vote. Both federal and state laws agree on the eligibility factors, which require that a voter in the Commonwealth:

> - is a United States citizen, either by birth or naturalized;
> - is a resident of Virginia;
> - is 18 years old or 17 under some circumstances;
> - does not claim the right to vote in any other state;
> - is not currently declared mentally incompetent by a court of law; and
> - if convicted of a felony, must have had the right to vote restored.[11]

Any person who is 17 years old and will be 18 at the next general election is permitted to register in advance and also vote in any intervening primary or special election. So a citizen who turns 18 in October can vote in the preceding June primary for the candidates competing to be on the November ballot.

The Virginia Department of Motor Vehicles and other state agencies such as Social Services allow citizens the opportunity to complete a voter application while performing a separate transaction. An application is also available on-line.[12] However, only general registrars can approve the applications. So it is not possible to "register to vote at the DMV."

By law, general registrars must notify anyone who is denied. That individual then has an opportunity to appeal or correct mistakes on the voter application.[13] More than five million Virginians are registered to vote, and monthly statistics on voter registration are available to the public.[14]

SBE works proactively to ensure the integrity of the voter list by routinely comparing other government databases against the voter registration list. Such lists include non-citizen drivers from the DMV, the Bureau of Vital Statistics, the Social Security Administration, and convicted felons from the Virginia State Police. In 2009, more than ten million records from these databases were compared to the voter list and affected 56,972 voters. In each case, the local registrar reviewed the data and if there was a true match, then the applicant received a letter of voting rights or a request for additional information. Since 2007, we have significantly increased the frequency of database checks and, in some cases, switching from once a year to monthly reviews.

According to state and federal law, the SBE is responsible for maintaining the Voter Registration and Election Management System (VERIS) used by agency employees and general registrars to register voters, administer absentee voting and elections, and report election results. Since its implementation in early 2007, the central voter registration database has experienced close to 4.6 million changes. In 2008 the VERIS implementation was put through its most robust test to date because of record-setting voter registration and turnout. Some notable accomplishments as a result of the work of the electoral community and implementing VERIS include:

- The Commonwealth of Virginia exceeded 5 million registered voters;
- More than 500,000 were new voters;
- 1.8 million voter registration forms were processed through VERIS;

- 500,000 voters' absentee applications were processed through VERIS;
- Virginia's election results website experienced more than 8 million hits on election night on November 4, 2008. In June of 2009, NBC News Political Director Chuck Todd noted that "the Virginia State Board of Elections handles returns better than any state in the union."[15]
- Hundreds of thousands of voters across Virginia used SBE's website, powered by VERIS to verify their registration status, locate their polling place, review the candidates on their ballot, or confirm the status of their absentee ballots.

The implementation of VERIS has allowed the SBE to be more responsive to voters' needs, speed up the processing of registration forms and absentee applications, and provide more data accountability and accuracy. Also, general registrars are now more connected to the data and can provide better service to citizens.

Absentee Voting

A growing number of Virginians are taking advantage of absentee balloting to exercise their right to vote. The Virginia General Assembly has added several excuses in recent years to allow Virginians to vote before Election Day.[16] Most recently, Congress has enacted sweeping legislation, known as the Military and Overseas Voter Empowerment (MOVE) Act, which works to ensure that our military and oversea voters will not miss out on opportunities to have their ballots counted.[17]

Provisional Voting

It is imperative that every legitimate vote cast on or by Election Day be counted. As a result, a safeguard is built into the system to ensure that qualified voters can exercise the franchise. In 2008, more than 3.7 million voters cast their full ballots, of which 2,578 were provisional ballots. Human errors can occur, such as the omission of a name from the voter roll at the polls (referred to as a pollbook). The provisional ballot permits a potential voter to exercise the right to vote on Election Day while affording more time to check on the voter's eligibility status. Sadly, many provisional ballots are not counted because the voters failed to update their voter registration information.

Campaign Finance

Virginia is a "disclosure" state. This means that we do not have restrictions on who can donate—or how much—to a political race; however, we require candidates, political action committees (PACs), political parties, and inaugural committees to disclose how they received their donations and spent every dollar. The State Board of Elections administers the Campaign Finance Disclosure Act. This law requires the State Board to review campaign finance disclosure reports for completeness and compliance with filing deadlines. Additionally, the State Board administers a computer system to collect electronic campaign finance reports and track violations. All reports are available on-line.[18]

We also work with the Virginia Public Access Project (VPAP) to produce an interactive election results map. The following map was used by media outlets and other entities statewide on Election Day in 2009.[19]

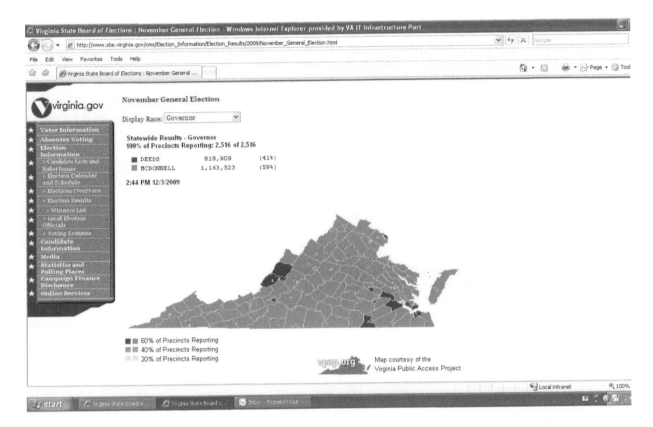

Voting Accessibility: Americans with Disability Act Compliance

The SBE continues to work with general registrars and electoral boards to ensure every polling place in the Commonwealth is accessible to individuals with disabilities and the aging population. The Board continually audits Virginia's polling places to ensure compliance with ADA and other laws regarding accessibility. In addition, SBE staff is available to assist localities in overcoming barriers by providing guidance and obtaining grant funding to minimize the cost impact.

Polling places are equipped to accommodate voters who are physically impaired or unable to clearly use the voting equipment. Virginia election law also provides "curbside" voting that enables voters to cast ballots outside the polling place—such as in a parking lot—to assist voters who have mobility restrictions.[20]

Voter Rights and Responsibilities

On Election Day every year, Virginia's polling places all display a poster called "Voter Rights and Responsibilities." Despite being displayed in more than 2,400 precincts, many voters do not take the time to read it. Here is the important information from that poster:

As a Virginia Voter, you have the following *rights:*

- To be treated with courtesy and respect by the election officials.
- To be notified if your voter registration has been accepted or denied.

- To vote if you have registered at your current address at least 22 days before Election Day.
- To seek help from the election officials if you are unsure about anything relating to the voting process.
- To be given a demonstration of how the voting equipment works.
- To have your paper or optical scan ballot voided before it is cast and be given a new one if you want to change your vote.
- To change your touch screen ballot before it is cast.
- To enter the full name of a write-in candidate if the candidate of your choice is not on the ballot (except in party primaries).
- To have a ballot brought to your vehicle instead of entering the polling place if you are 65 years of age or older, or if you are physically disabled.
- To have an officer of election or other person help you vote if you are physically disabled or unable to read or write (or need the ballot translated into another language). Blind voters may have any person assist them. Other voters may have anyone who is not their employer or union representative assist them. Note: The officer of election or other person who assists you must follow your instructions, without trying to influence your vote, and shall not tell or signal how you voted on any office or question.
- To vote even if you have no identification with you at the polling place. You must sign the "Affirmation of Identity" statement before voting if you have no ID. Exception: Voters who registered by mail for the first time in Virginia on or after January 1, 2003, and who did not mail in a copy of their ID at that time, and who fail to show one of the federally required forms of ID when voting for the first time in a federal election must vote by Provisional Ballot in that election. They may not use the "Affirmation of Identity" statement at that election.
- To vote a Provisional Ballot if your status as a qualified voter is in question, and to be present when the Electoral Board meets to determine if your ballot will be counted. See "Provisional Ballots" below.
- To bring your minor child (age 15 or younger) into the voting booth with you to observe you vote.
- To vote if you are in line by 7:00 p.m. when the polls close.
- To cast an absentee ballot if you are qualified to vote absentee.
- To register to vote absentee in Virginia if you are a U.S. citizen overseas and your last residence in the U.S. was in Virginia, or you are a Virginia resident away in the military.
- You cannot be denied the right to vote if you are legally qualified to do so.
- Government officials must not apply standards or practices which deny or abridge the right to vote on account of race, and must not deny any individual the right to vote on account of errors or omissions in registration applications which are not material to determining whether such individual is qualified to vote. Officials must not apply different standards and procedures to voters in the same circumstances in determining whether they are qualified to vote.

As a Virginia Voter, you have the following *responsibilities:*

- To treat the election officials with courtesy and respect.
- To keep your voter registration information up-to-date with your current address. (If not, you may be eligible to vote at your prior precinct for a limited time under a legal exception. You must tell the election officials when and where you moved. Contact your voter registration office or the State Board of Elections if you have questions about your eligibility to vote.)

- To show your identification (ID) at the polls. If you do not have an ID with you at the polling place, you may still vote if you sign an "Affirmation of Identity" statement, depending on your registration status. See "Provisional Ballots" below.
- If party nominating primaries are being held, to tell the officials which primary you want to vote in. You may vote in either primary, but not both primaries held on the same day.
- To request assistance if you do not know how to use the voting equipment or have other questions about the voting process, or need assistance preparing your ballot because of a physical disability or inability to read or write.
- To follow the instructions on how to mark your ballot.
- To understand that once your ballot is cast, you cannot be given another ballot.
- To ask the election official to call the General Registrar's office before you leave the polling place if you have problems regarding your eligibility to vote or the casting of your ballot.

In conclusion

Throughout my tenure as Virginia's Chief Election Officer, I have chosen to wear a referee shirt and a whistle on the numerous Election Days over which I presided. I have done so because I believe that it symbolized the role of the Secretary, the Board, and the agency: to keep election participants on a level playing field. Yes, I have blown the whistle to signal a foul a few times. But, most importantly, the candidates who were certified as winners by the Board actually received the majority of votes cast. In the end, that's what honest elections are really all about.

———————————

Nancy Rodrigues served as Chief Election Officer from September of 2007 to January of 2011. She oversaw the historic 2008 Presidential election when Virginia became a battleground state for the first time in 44 years and the number of voters topped five million.

CHAPTER 26
Money in Virginia Politics

By David Poole
Executive Director, Virginia Public Access Project

When it comes to money in politics, Virginia goes its own way. Most states seek to curb the influence of money in politics by erecting legal firewalls (usually in the form of contribution limits) between elected representatives and powerful interests. Virginia is one of only a handful of states with absolutely no limits. Candidates for state and local offices can accept donations in any amount, as long as they disclose the identity of any donor who gives more than $100.

For decades, the prevailing view in the Virginia General Assembly has been that disclosure is more effective than federal-style regulations. Advocates of the Virginia system have pointed across the Potomac River for examples of how campaign-finance limits have failed to stem the flow of money into politics. Contribution limits, the argument goes, tend to drive money into unregulated channels and make it more difficult for the public to understand who is underwriting campaigns. Advocates of the Virginia way say disclosure is a more straightforward approach to give citizens the information they need to determine if a politician is being more responsive to donors than to constituents who elect her.

However, disclosure did not always work well in Virginia. The problem is that the public had no practical way to monitor campaign donations. Candidates filed periodic disclosure reports, but the paper documents were stored in file cabinets at the State Board of Elections. The public had no meaningful access to the information to know who was funding whom. The rare citizen who showed up during normal business hours to inspect the campaign finance disclosure reports was overwhelmed with paperwork. Even journalists often gave up and reported only summary numbers.

In 1997, the nonprofit Virginia Public Access Project bought together what, at the time, were two recent technological innovations—powerful desktop computers and the Internet—to organize the campaign finance information in ways that people can understand. By distilling the information into a database, VPAP made it possible to sort and filter hundreds of thousands of transactions within a few seconds. With the data posted on VPAP.org, citizens for the first time had the ability to sort donations by donor name, occupation, locality, and ZIP Code. Virginia now has the nation's most transparent system of monitoring money in state elections.

The absence of limits has led to some very expensive races:

o In 2009, House of Delegates candidates who won at least 40 percent of the vote spent an average of $305,000.[1]
o In 2007, Senate candidates who won at least 40 percent of the vote spent an average of $811,623.[2]
o In 2007, Gerald Connolly spent $1.4 million to win re-election as chairman of the Fairfax County Board of Supervisors.[3]
o In 2009, candidates for Governor spent a combined $53 million.[4]

Critics of the Virginia system say disclosure is not enough to preserve the public's faith in the political system. The system, they say, discourages people of modest means from seeking office and gives too much power to wealthy individuals, large corporations, and labor unions that have the means to spread around hundreds of thousands of dollars.

Photo courtesy of Anne Marie Morgan.

Defenders of the Virginia system simply point to Washington, D.C., to make the point that limits don't work—and often prove counterproductive. The 2002 McCain-Feingold bill culminated years of effort to reduce the influence of money on politics and Congress. But the bill has done nothing to stem the flow of money, much of it now beyond the regulatory reach of the Federal Election Commission. During the 2010 midterm congressional elections, the big story was a torrent of money funneled to not-for-profit corporations engaging in electioneering while shielding disclosure of donors' names. "It is too late for a new law to have any effect on the dark swamp of this year's elections," *The New York Times* editorial page said, "but there is still hope that Congress will allow the sun to shine on the elections of 2012 and beyond.[5]

In Virginia's state and local elections, candidates can accept donations in any amount and from virtually any source. Corporations, partnerships, unions and, of course, individuals can give. Virginia law contains a single ban: anyone who holds a license to conduct pari-mutuel wagering on horse races cannot make a political contribution. The only other prohibition—which is an extension of federal law—is donations by foreign corporations or nationals.

In terms of disclosure, candidates are required to file periodic campaign finance reports. The frequency is semi-annual (July and January) in non-election years and eight times a year during election years. As Election Day draws near, the reports are more frequent. In the final week of a campaign, candidates must report "large" contributions by 5:00 p.m. the next day. The thresholds for large contributions are: $500 for local candidates, $1,000 for General Assembly candidates, and $5,000 for statewide candidates.

Local candidates file campaign finance disclosure reports with the office of the local voter registrar. Local candidates have a choice of filing on paper or electronically. The vast majority file on paper. A growing number (in 2010, the number was about 100) file electronically through a centralized server at the State Board of Elections. General Assembly candidates also have a choice of filing on paper or e-filing. Nearly all of them e-file; those who file on paper must provide a copy to both the State Board of Elections and the voter registrar in the locality where they reside. E-filing is mandatory for candidates for statewide office.

In General Assembly elections, approximately half of all money raised comes from companies and trade associations that are registered to lobby the legislature. Virtually all of the lobbyist money goes to incumbents. Consider these figures from fundraising by State Senate incumbents during an 18-month period starting in January, 2009. Of the $4.4 million raised by incumbent senators, companies and trade associations that lobby or from firms that represent multiple lobbying clients gave a total of 65 percent.[6] The incumbents' lock on lobbyist money makes it very difficult for anyone who seeks to challenge a sitting legislator.

In 2009, there were 68 candidates who ran against an incumbent member of the House of Delegates. There were eight winners, which compared to past years was an unusually high number. The data from the post-election reports show a correlation between the amount of money a challenger spent and the percentage of votes received:[7]

Average Spent	Outcome
$ 5,493	Received < 20% of vote
$ 20,533	Received between 20% and 30% of vote
$137,146	Received between 30% and 40% of vote
$261,731	Received > 40 %
$483,357	Won Election

However, money does not ensure success at the ballot box. There are many examples of candidates who outspent their opponents but came up short when the votes were counted. At the same time, the numbers suggest that legislative candidates who raise little money have little chance of success.

With all this money being raised, how are candidates spending it? In calendar year 2009, candidates for the House of Delegates spent a total of $25.6 million. The money broke down this way:[8]

Staff/Consultants	19.8 %
TV/Radio	19.2 %
Donations to Other Committees	17.4 %
Mail/Postage	15.3 %
Misc. Campaign Expenses	5.1 %
Fundraising Costs	3.7 %
Signs/Bumper Stickers	3.5 %
Polling/Phone Calls	2.4 %
All other	13.8 %

The Virginia Public Access Project's mission is to empower citizens to know who is funding the candidates and to draw their own informed conclusions from the data. The listings on VPAP.org provide a unique way for voters to get to know the candidates before Election Day and to help assure voters about their choices.

David Poole founded the nonprofit Virginia Public Access Project in 1997. He worked as a newspaper reporter from 1983 to 1997. His last assignment was state capital correspondent for The Roanoke Times *and* Virginian-Pilot.

CHAPTER 27
Political Parties in Virginia: Organizing to Win Elections

By Charles E. Judd
Chairman, State Board of Elections

At the advent of the United States, Virginia's leaders were trailblazers in forging many aspects of American political life, including Thomas Jefferson's authorship of the Declaration of Independence,[1] James Madison's role in crafting the U.S. Constitution and Bill of Rights,[2] and George Washington's influence in shaping the office of the presidency.[3]

This leadership also applies to the creation of political parties: "Virginia has exercised a unique role in US politics as the birthplace not only of representative government but also of one of America's two major parties. The modern Democratic Party traces its origins to the original Republican Party (usually referred to as the Democratic-Republican Party, or the Jeffersonian Democrats), led by two native sons of Virginia, Thomas Jefferson and James Madison."[4]

However, the term "political party" is not used at all in the U.S. Constitution. George Washington was elected as the first President without a partisan affiliation[5] and, in fact, warned against political parties in his farewell address to the nation in 1796:

> They serve to organize faction; to give it an artificial and extraordinary force; to put in the place of the delegated will of the nation the will of a party, often a small but artful and enterprising minority of the community, and, according to the alternate triumphs of different parties, to make the public administration the mirror of the ill-concerted and incongruous projects of faction rather than the organ of consistent and wholesome plans, digested by common councils and modified by mutual interests.[6]

Notwithstanding such caution, political parties were formed because members of the first Congress found them to be useful in achieving their objectives.[7] They still play an integral role in the rough-and-tumble politics of America today.

A political party can be defined as "a coalition of people seeking to control the government by contesting elections and winning office."[8] A party is different from an interest group in that its primary focus typically is electoral politics. The many functions of a party include recruiting and nominating candidates to run for office, waging electoral contests, mobilizing voters, coordinating public policies, and providing accountability to voters.[9]

In Virginia, a political party is defined by state law as: "An organization of citizens of the Commonwealth which, at either of the two preceding statewide general elections, received at least 10 percent of the total vote cast for any statewide office filled in that election. The organization shall have a state central committee and an office of elected state chairman, which have been continually in existence for the six months preceding the filing of a nominee for any office."[10]

The Code of Virginia also delineates the activities that political parties may perform: "Each political party shall have the power to (i) make its own rules and regulations, (ii) call conventions to proclaim a platform, ratify a nomination, or for any other purpose, (iii) provide for the nomination of its candidates, including the nomination of its candidates for office in case of any vacancy, (iv) provide for the nomination and election of its state, county, city, and district committees, and (v) perform all other functions inherent in political party organizations."[11]

Political parties exist and function as a focal point for certain ideologies and beliefs. For example, one party may espouse the belief that the role of government is merely to provide national defense, while another party may believe that government should provide benefits that individuals cannot provide for themselves. And yet another may advocate that the less government intervention in the lives of its citizens, the better.

Political parties also provide the vehicle through which individuals can become involved in the electoral process and elect candidates to office. The party recruits members, communicates with them regularly about the party's (and candidates') positions on issues, keeps them informed of the progress of the campaigns, and encourages members to inform and involve other like-minded voters. While not everyone will always agree on every issue or position, party leaders will find the most common issues of interest and focus on those where there is a consensus among a majority of the members. The most successful election victories are those where the party works in concert with the individual candidate's campaign operation.

State lawmakers organize and are seated in the House and Senate chambers by party caucus. Here, the House Democratic Leader, Del. Ward Armstrong, speaks from the Democratic "side of the aisle" on the floor of the House of Delegates. Photo by Bob Brown, *Richmond Times-Dispatch*.

Two parties dominate the political process in the United States, as well as in the Commonwealth of Virginia: the Republican Party and the Democratic Party. Each party has its statement of purpose—usually published and made readily available to the public—that is intended to define the tenets of the organization.

For example, the Republican Party of Virginia (RPV) statement is called the "Republican Creed" and outlines these principles:

> We believe: That the free enterprise system is the most productive supplier of human needs and economic justice,
> That all individuals are entitled to equal rights, justice, and opportunities and should assume their responsibilities as citizens in a free society,
> That fiscal responsibility and budgetary restraints must be exercised at all levels of government,
> That the Federal Government must preserve individual liberty by observing Constitutional limitations,
> That peace is best preserved through a strong national defense,
> That faith in God, as recognized by our Founding Fathers is essential to the moral fiber of the Nation.[12]

The Democratic Party of Virginia (DPVA) has its "Statement of Common Purpose," which declares:

> The Democratic Party of Virginia is united in its efforts to elect Democratic leaders of character, integrity, ability, vision, and commitment to delivering results for Virginians. The Democratic Party of Virginia is the party that commits to delivering fiscal responsibility, ensuring excellence in education, reinvesting in our infrastructure, preserving a social safety network, providing accessible healthcare and creating economic opportunity for all Virginians. We are dedicated to protecting our inalienable rights and constitutional freedoms that provide us the opportunity to improve the lives of others. We will work to elect leaders that will provide change through leadership that is both commonsense and results-oriented. As Democrats we know there is more that unites us rather than divides us. Working together, we make this Commonwealth and nation a stronger and better place for all.[13]

The governing document for both the RPV and the DPVA is called the Party Plan and sets forth the rules and organizational structure, which includes the various governing committees that conduct the business of that party. These governing documents can be amended (as spelled out within the document) and, because of the federal Voting Rights Act passed by the U.S. Congress in 1964, must be pre-approved by the U.S. Department of Justice before being implemented.[14] The Party Plans can be found on each party's website.[15]

Each party is organized by political subdivision—governing committees at the local unit (county and city), legislative district, congressional district, and state levels. Membership is defined by each committee's plan or bylaws. Membership in each of the committees varies in numbers but may include as many as 300 members or as few as 15—depending on the size of the political subdivision. However, when all committee members are included in a total count, the numbers are in the thousands.

The parties organize, conduct business, and can nominate candidates for office through a process conducted by the local unit party (according to the party plan). The nomination may take place using one of several methods: a "mass meeting," which often takes the form of a miniature convention; a "party canvass" which usually is conducted in one or more locations where voters drop by to cast their votes; or a "convention" attended by delegates selected by a mass meeting or canvas. The cost of this nomination process is borne by the party. But instead of one of these methods, the party can choose to nominate candidates for office through a primary election, which is open to all qualified voters and is conducted by the State Board of Elections at government expense.

During even-numbered years, local county or city parties hold mass meetings in the spring to elect members and officers, and elect delegates to the congressional district convention. The congressional district convention elects officers of the district committee and delegates to the state convention, and nominates the party's congressional candidate (unless a primary was chosen as the nominating process). During presidential election years the district convention will elect delegates to the national convention (based on a formula determined by the national committee). The state convention also nominates its candidate for U.S. Senate (unless a primary for the Senate nomination was chosen by the state party). It also elects at-large delegates to the national convention (which nominates the party's candidate for president and vice president), the state party chairman, and members of the national party committee.

During the odd-numbered years, local unit parties hold mass meetings in the spring to conduct business, elect members, elect representatives to the legislative district committees, and elect delegates to the congressional district and state conventions (if the state party chose a convention over a primary election to nominate candidates for governor, lieutenant governor, and attorney general).

Political party activities are funded by dues and/or voluntary contributions from party members, organizations, and individuals who share their political ideals. There is no limit on political contributions in Virginia. However, ALL contributions over $100 must be reported and are a matter of public record.

Political parties are influenced by—and linked to—political ideals and ideologies. Many voters become involved in interest groups or political action committees based on a particular issue or ideology, such as fiscal policy, taxes, defense, abortion, education reform, or judicial restraint, etc. These voter groups have grown in importance to the success of elections, and both political parties and individual campaigns often cultivate the support of these groups and form coalitions with them.[16] Virginians who belong to these organizations will endorse candidates, communicate with their membership or the general public, publish voter guides that list the candidates' positions on their issues, and initiate other get-out-the-vote efforts to elect the candidates of their choice.[17]

Virginia Republicans have often formed coalitions with members of organizations that advocate fiscal restraint, gun rights, social conservatism, and more.[18] Virginia Democrats have frequently coalesced with union members, social justice organizers, pro-choice activists, and others.[19] But candidates and interest groups also make exceptions, such as when the National Rifle Association's political action committee endorsed Democratic Sen. Creigh Deeds in his 2005 bid for Attorney General[20] or when the National Treasury Employees Union gave campaign contributions to Republican Rep. Tom Davis before he retired from office in 2009.[21]

Generally, each state political party aligns with the national party ideologically. However, in some instances, Virginia partisans have differed from their national counterparts. For example, many—although not all—Democrats in the General Assembly voted in 2010 for the Virginia Health Care Freedom Act.[22] This state law sought to block the federal mandate in the Patient Protection and Affordable Care Act (passed by a Democratic majority in Congress and signed by Democratic Pres.

Barack Obama) that required most Americans to buy health insurance or pay a penalty. At the same time, Virginia's former Democratic governor, Timothy M. Kaine, was chairman of the Democratic National Committee and a strong advocate for the federal law.[23]

According to some observers, the differences between the two major parties have become obscured in the last few election cycles[24]—even though the parties often attempt to draw attention to their differences. In 1856, the national Democratic and Republican Party platforms were each only three pages in length; but by 2008, their platforms were at least 20 pages, suggesting that more words are required to convey an ever-expanding statement of purpose.[25] Yet, the perception that the two major parties are alike has persisted.

This obscurity of political views and the issues for which the two major parties stand have resulted in the rise of grassroots activities by some voters who feel that they have been disenfranchised by the dominant political parties. Often, these voters begin to identify with a *third* party that they feel better represents their ideology.

The rise of the "Tea Party" beginning in 2009 is the most recent example of this type of voter thinking. It was named after the Boston Tea Party protest in 1773 against the Tea Act passed by the British Parliament. But today's Tea Party is not a formal political party but a catch-all title for independent groups of citizens who often work together, support candidates, and even run for office to advance their causes.[26]

However, other third parties have also been active in Virginia over the years, including (alphabetically): the American Party, Constitution Party, Green Party, Independent Green Party, Libertarian Party, Reform Party, and Workers Reform Party. While there is no formally organized Independent Party by title, candidates may also stand for election as "Independent" candidates by meeting qualification requirements, which include circulating petitions to gather the signatures of registered voters. The number of signatures required depends on whether it is a statewide or district election.[27]

The two major political parties dominate elections in Virginia, but these other political parties have engaged in various levels of participation, albeit with mixed success at actually winning office.

Political parties in Virginia strive to be inclusive, and although the process described here may seem complicated, it is designed and intended to be the most open process possible as a vehicle for citizen participation in our representative form of government.

Charles E. Judd was appointed Chairman of the State Board of Elections in 2011. He has extensive experience in political party operations, having served as Executive Director for the Ohio Republican Party, Deputy Director for the Republican National Committee, and Executive Director for the Republican Party of Virginia. He previously held elective office and is currently an active instructor in campaign schools and workshops around the country.

Epilogue:
The Virginia Way

By John Chichester
Former State Senator and Chairman, Virginia Senate Finance Committee

Every last chapter is given the task of either wrapping up or bringing the past to closure or, alternatively, offering up a glimpse of what is to come.

This author's musings will reflect both on the past and on what is to come because our past and our future are inextricably linked. In so doing, the bias of the author will appear again and again throughout the chapter, driven by a strong affection for our rich history. Those who were born in Virginia know of this bias instinctively; those who have come to Virginia have acquired it.

We cannot talk about the Old Dominion and its future without turning the pages back to see from whence we came. From early Williamsburg to the present, Virginia has led the nation not only through its personal "giants" but with its ideas. Who today in a position of leadership could stray permanently from a common-sense philosophy when one need only to look over one's shoulder and see the likes of eight presidents, any number of national leaders, and those with international prestige?

A Virginian makes the proper choice—and he feels compelled to do so, even if that choice is contrary to his own personal philosophy or unpopular with his constituency. Oftentimes, unpopular decisions are made, only to be found later to be correct and applauded by historians. But, Virginia leaders don't make decisions on the basis of how they think history will treat them. They use history as a guide and eventually settle on the right course. That's another way of saying that Virginians are reflective, not reactive.

Those who study the political process in the Commonwealth and the evolution of public policy will never be caught off guard by sudden change because that is not the Virginia way. Every major policy change in Virginia's history has followed years of discourse and debate. That is perfectly logical when you consider that Virginia, as the matriarch of this great nation, is expected to lead with a steady hand.

The words "moderate" and "methodical" flow from that expectation, and they form the basis of the Virginia philosophy. We do not embrace change because of ideological fancy or simply for the sake of change. We consider and weigh change when there is a compelling case to do so.

In large part, the "Virginia way" is rooted in the deep sense of responsibility that goes with occupying the space of our founding fathers—those who shaped this great nation with a bold vision that continues to inspire the world. Virginia's citizens intuitively feel the weight of that responsibility and honor our extraordinary past by taking a studied and deliberative approach to our future.

The success of the "Virginia way" should be obvious. The accolades of best fiscal management, best business environment, and best education system are not the result of a beauty pageant. They are the result of deliberate choices about Virginia's future—choices that often are accompanied by considerable controversy.

And so, while our patience sometimes is tested by the time that it takes for the "Virginia way" to play out, we should be heartened by the fact that the "Virginia way" does work and will continue to work.

House of Delegates Chamber. Photo by Bob Brown, *Richmond Times-Dispatch.*

The success that we enjoy today is a direct result of fortitude and courage and the willingness of the Commonwealth's leaders to make unpopular, but necessary choices at pivotal crossroads along the way. There are numerous examples, but a few come readily to mind.

For 40 years, which spanned the 1920s through the mid-1960s, the powerful "Byrd organization" (with U.S. Sen. Harry F. Byrd, Sr., at its helm) controlled politics in Virginia. That organization reflected the staunchly conservative views of the day, with one of its most notable campaigns being Massive Resistance to school desegregation. In 1956, Virginia's General Assembly passed a series of laws to implement Massive Resistance and, thereby, thwart the U.S. Supreme Court decision in *Brown v. Board of Education.*

Two years later, lawsuits filed around the state resulted in federal orders to integrate certain schools. Newly-elected Gov. James Lindsay Almond, Jr., instead moved to close those schools, which set the stage for further legal action. A year into Almond's term, a federal court ruled that the action of school closure violated the equal protection clause of the Constitution.

Thereupon, Almond stepped away from the Byrd organization's still hard-line position on Massive Resistance, setting in motion a series of steps that eventually led to the integrated school system that we know today. Change did not occur overnight, but it did occur because a Virginia leader had the courage and fortitude to step up to the plate and do what was right, notwithstanding substantial political pressure to the contrary.

Virginia's path to desegregation was a reflection of the "Virginia way." There was no calling out of the National Guard … no mustering of local police to escort children to school. Rather, there was a gradual conditioning of Virginians, and schools over time were fully integrated.

A second pivotal point in Virginia's history flows from the Byrd organization's view that the Commonwealth should invest in its transportation system only to the degree that it had cash to do so. Again, that was a philosophy which was very consistent with conservative Virginia tradition. It was a notion that nearly all embraced. However, it was a notion that became out-of-step with the times.

As the Interstate highway system was created and expanded, with the resulting growth in commerce, it became obvious that Virginia could not keep pace and thrive economically with a transportation system that was based solely on pay-as-you-go. Something needed to change. Someone needed to step out of the comfort zone and advocate for Virginia's future.

That someone was Gov. Mills Godwin, who advocated for changes to Virginia's Constitution that would loosen restrictions on state-issued bonds and borrowing. The 1968 General Assembly authorized a Commission on Constitutional Revision, which was appointed by Godwin, to undertake the fifth complete revision of Virginia's fundamental law since 1776. In the fall of 1970, four questions were placed on the ballot to be decided by the people: a general question containing the main body of the revised Constitution and three separate questions, two of which dealt with borrowing by the Commonwealth. All four questions passed.

The less restrictive debt provisions included in the 1971 Constitution represented a major step for the Commonwealth's future. Yet, without a doubt, this change was a wrenching decision for the state's conservative political leaders. But, as was demonstrated, Virginia leaders can and do set aside personal preferences and take unpopular votes when they are pivotal for Virginia's future.

Yet another example of courage and fortitude involved Godwin, and this one was even more controversial because it involved the dreaded "t" word: taxes. Virginia's tax system was virtually unchanged from its inception until 1966, when Godwin convinced the legislature that a sales tax was needed to establish the community college system and place higher education within the reach of every Virginian.

A tax increase is never something that one wants to embrace.

However, when a compelling case is made that Virginia's future success rests on additional investment, and that investment can be made only through a tax increase, history shows that Virginia leaders marshal the strength needed to produce that change. I don't think any Virginian regrets the decision to make higher education a priority. In fact, we take great pride in our public higher education system, which is arguably the best in the nation.

More recent history provides similar examples of courage from both sides of the political aisle as Republican Gov. John Dalton and Democratic Gov. Gerald Baliles asked for and won unpopular votes on the gasoline tax, and in 2004 when Gov. Mark Warner proposed comprehensive tax reform. In the latter case, after much debate, a vote was taken, and a fragile coalition enacted a compromise.

In these examples, the requisite number of General Assembly members took a vote they did not want to take, subordinating their own personal preferences to the need to invest in Virginia's future.

These actions did not result in a mass "firing" of legislators who made the unpopular votes because Virginia voters are forgiving when the motive is pure. Most Virginia voters lean toward the middle. They are fiscally conservative, traditionally moderate, and fiercely independent—that's part of our heritage. It goes back to the notion that Virginians are mindful of their past and recognize that the Commonwealth we know is inextricably linked to the courage and fortitude and sacrifice of past generations. The link can't be broken.

Fountain on the grounds of the State Capitol. Photo by Anne Marie Morgan.

And so, I am confident that Virginia and her leaders will continue the tradition of careful reflection and methodical, calculated action at those inflection points where it is absolutely clear that our future is at stake.

Every choice won't be perfect. There will be times when we falter. We all can think of examples where we tried to go down a path that sounded too good to be true—and it was. In other words, pressures on those handling the oars of Virginia's ship of state may cause the ship to quiver to the right or left momentarily. However, we should all take comfort in the fact that her keel is so deep in the ocean of history that it will always right itself.

As time goes on, many will be asked or will feel compelled to pick up those oars and be part of Virginia's ship of state. That choice of public service will involve making hundreds and hundreds of decisions, some of which may measure zero on the Richter scale of thought. But, there will come a time, or perhaps more than one time, when the decision to be made truly is generational in scope. At that point, one must sit alone and decide what is best for all, not what is popular with a few. One must decide what in the long term will keep Virginia on the path that was set so long ago by our forefathers.

The decision will come down to common sense. It will flow from a philosophy that has roots firmly planted in Virginia's earth and, if self-service is set aside, it will be the right decision for the time.

This soul-searching has occurred on a number of occasions in Virginia. We can all think of crucial junctures in our history. And while by today's standards, all of the original choices were not correct, they were ultimately corrected so that our way of life did not depart significantly from the traces in which we walk.

We can take comfort from the lessons of Virginia history. At those truly crucial points in our journey, Virginia's political leaders will reach deep and find fortitude and courage. They will coalesce and make that unpopular choice, if it truly is necessary to preserve the treasure that is our Commonwealth.

John Chichester represented the 28th District in the Virginia Senate from 1978-2007. He served as President Pro Tempore of the Senate and as Chairman of the Senate Finance Committee.

Bibliography

1850-51 Virginia Convention Documents, Statement by First Auditor respecting Census.

1901-02 Convention Debates, II.

1902 Virginia Constitution, secs. 65 and 110, *Report of the Commission on Constitutional Revision.*

1945 Virginia Convention Journal.

1956 Virginia Convention Journal.

Acts of Assembly, 1849-50. Richmond: Library of Virginia.

Acts of Assembly, 1928. Richmond: Library of Virginia.

Acts of Assembly, May 1862 Ex. Sess. Wheeling. Richmond: Library of Virginia.

AFL-CIO. "Virginia Legislators," accessed Apr. 13, 2011, http://southeastvirginia.blogspot.com/ 2010/08/2010-virginia-afl-cio-constitutional.html.

Alfred L. Snapp & Son, Inc. v. Puerto Rico, 458 U.S. 592, (1982).

Allen, W.B., ed. The Online Library of Liberty, accessed May 6, 2011, http://oll.libertyfund.org /?option=com_staticxt&staticfile=show.php%3Ftitle=848&chapter=101778&layout=html&Itemi d=27.

Ambler, Charles Henry. *A History of West Virginia*. New York, 1933.

Ambler, Charles Henry. *Sectionalism in Virginia from 1776 to 1861*. Chicago, 1910.

Andrews v. Shepherd, 201 Va. 412, 415, 111 S.E.2d 279, 282 (1959).

Associated Press, "Republican McDonnell wins Va. governor's race," MSNBC, accessed May 2, 2011, http://www.msnbc.msn.com/id/33609733#.

Atkinson, Frank B. *The Dynamic Dominion*. Fairfax: George Mason University Press, 1992.

Atkinson, Frank B. *Virginia in the Vanguard: Political Leadership in the 400-Year-Old Cradle of American Democracy, 1981-2006*. Lanham: Rowman & Littlefield Publishers, 2006.

Auditor of Public Accounts, Commonwealth of Virginia, "2009 Amended Comparative Report of Local Government Revenues and Expenditures," accessed Oct. 28, 2010, http://www.apa.state.va.us/ ComparativeReport.cfm.

Badenhausen, Kurt. "The Best States For Business," Sept. 23, 2009, *Forbes*, accessed Nov. 26, 2010, http://www.forbes.com/2009/09/23/best-states-for-business-beltway-best-states_lander.html.

Bailyn, Bernard, ed. *Pamphlets of the American Revolution, 1750-1776*. Cambridge: 1965.

Bain, Chester W. *A Body Incorporate: The Evolution of City-County Separation in Virginia*. Charlottesville: University Press of Virginia, 1967.

Barone, Michael, and Richard E. Cohen. *The Almanac of American Politics 2006*. Washington, D.C.: National Journal Group, 2005.

Bartel, Bill. "NRA switches to McDonnell; firefighters endorse Deeds," *The Virginian-Pilot*, Sept. 15, 2009, accessed Apr. 13, 2011, http://hamptonroads.com/2009/09/nra-switches-mcdonnell-firefighters-endorse-deeds.

Bemiss, Samuel M., ed. *Three Charters of the Virginia Company of London*. Williamsburg: 1957.

Billings, Warren M. *A Little Parliament*. Richmond: Library of Virginia, 2004.

Billings, Warren M., ed. *The Old Dominion in the Seventeenth Century: A Documentary History of Virginia*, 1606-1700. Chapel Hill: University of North Carolina Press, 2007.

Biographical Directory of the United State Congress, 1774 – Present, "Leslie Larkin Byrne," accessed August 17, 2010, http://bioguide.congress.gov/scripts/biodisplay.pl?index =b001213.

Board of Supervisors v. Corbett, 206 Va. 167, 142 S.E.2d. 504 (1965).

Bearss, Sara B., et al, "Sallie Cook Booker" and "Nancy Melvinia Caldwell," *Dictionary of Virginia Biography*. Richmond: Library of Virginia, 2001.

Boyd, Julian P., et al, eds. *The Papers of Thomas Jefferson*. Volume 1. Princeton: Princeton University Press, 1950.

Braxton, A. C. "The Virginia State Corporation Commission," 38 *Am. L. Rev.* 483, 498 (1904).

Brown v. Board of Education of Topeka, Kansas, 347 U.S. 483 (1954).

Buni, Andrew. *The Negro in Virginia Politics, 1902-1965*. Charlottesville: The University Press of Virginia, 1967.

Burch, Adam. "Eva Scott: Visions of Amelia," *Virginia Capitol Connections* 4 (Autumn 1998).

Burch, Adam. "The Great Worth of a Gentle Woman: Helen Timmons Henderson and Buchanan County," *Virginia Capitol Connections* 14 (Winter 2008).

Byrd, Governor Harry F. "Address to the General Assembly, Simplification of Government in Virginia," February 3, 1926.

Byrd, Harry F. *A Discussion of the Amendments Proposed to the Constitution of Virginia: Proposals 3, 4, and 5*. Richmond, 1928.

Cable News Network. "CNN Exit Polls—Virginia Governor," accessed Apr. 14, 2011, http://i2.cdn.turner.com/cnn/2009/images /11/04/2009.exit.polls.-.va.gov.pdf.

Cable News Network. "Sniper Muhammad sentenced to death," March 09, 2004, accessed Oct. 22, 2010, http://articles.cnn.com/2004-03-09/justice/sniper_1_muhammad-and-malvo-sniper-killings-lee-boyd-malvo?_s=PM:LAW.

Camp v. Birchett, 143 Va. 686, 126 S.E. 665 (1925).

Carper, Elsie. "A Lonely Voice at Richmond: Kathryn Stone Won Respect in House of Men and Became Spokesman for Virginia's Conscience," *Washington Post*, August 8, 1965.

Center for American Women and Politics, Rutgers University. "Women in Elective Office- Virginia," accessed April 10, 2011, http://www.cawp.rutgers.edu/.

Charter of the city of Lexington. Section 8, accessed Oct. 28, 2010, http://www.ecode360.com /documents/LE2692/LE2692-C.pdf.

Charter of the city of Portsmouth. Section 3.02, accessed Oct. 28, 2010, http://library1.municode.com/default-now/home.htm?infobase=13866&doc_action =whatsnew.

City Council v. Newsome, 226 Va. 518, 311 S.E.2d. 761 (1984).

City of Richmond v. Board of Supervisors, 199 Va. 679, 101 S.E.2d. 641 (1958).

Code of Virginia, http://leg1.state.va.us/cgi-bin/legp504.exe?000+cod+TOC.

Colbourn, H. Trevor. *The Lamp of Experience: Whig History and the Intellectual Origins if the American Revolution*. Chapel Hill, 1965.

Commission on Constitutional Revision. *The Constitution of Virginia: Report of the Commission on Constitutional Revision to His Excellency, Mills E. Godwin, Jr., Governor of Virginia, the General Assembly of Virginia and the People of Virginia*. Charlottesville: The Michie Company, 1969.

Commonwealth of Virginia, Department of Housing and Community Development, *Local Government Information 1985 Survey Report*. Richmond, December 1, 1985.

Cook County v. City of Chicago, 142 N.W. (Illinois) 512 (1924).

Cook, Stanley A. "The Role of Judges in Virginia Local Government: A Historical Overview and Virginia's Local Executive Constitutional Officers in Historical Perspective," *University of Virginia Newsletter*. Charlottesville: Institute of Government, University of Virginia, June 1981 and September 1981.

Council of State Government, *The Book of the States 2004*. Lexington: Council of State Government, 2004.

County of Fairfax v. Southern Iron Works, Inc., 242 Va. 435, 410 S.E.2d. 674 (1991).

Cunard, Robert and Ramos, Sharon. "Other Voices: Car Tax Relief Slights Virginia's Rural Areas," *Daily Press*, February 28, 2003, accessed Apr. 14, 2011, http://articles.dailypress.com/2003-02-28/news/0302280041_1_car-tax-tax-relief-tax-bills.

Cushing, Harry A. "History of the Transition from Provincial to Commonwealth Government in Massachusetts," in Columbia University, *Studies in History, Economics and Public Law*, VII (1896).

Cushing, Luther Stearns. *Elements of the Law and Practice of Legislative Assemblies in the United States of America*. Ninth Edition. Boston: Little, Brown and Company, 1874.

Dabney, Virginius. *Virginia: The New Dominion*. Doubleday and Company, Inc., 1971.

Daily Press Article Collections. Political System, "Gov. Mills E. Godwin Jr.: 1914-1999," Gerald L. Baliles, "Godwin A Helmsman Who Steered State Into The 21st Century," February 07, 1999, accessed on Nov. 26, 2010, http://articles.dailypress.com/1999-02-07/news/9902090123_1_mills-e-godwin-virginia-democratic-party-political-system/3.

Danville Register & Bee. "Former AG Reflects on Leadership," February 21, 2008.

Davis v. County School Board of Prince Edward County, 103 F. Supp. 337 (1952).

de Tocqueville, Alexis. *Democracy in America*, Volume I, Henry Reeve Translation, circa 1839, revised and corrected in 1899. University of Virginia: American Studies Programs, accessed May 29, 2011, http://xroads.virginia.edu/~HYPER/DETOC/1_ch02.htm.

de Voursney, Robert M. "Powers & Responsibilities of Municipal Government," *Handbook for Virginia Mayors and Council Members*. Charlottesville: University of Virginia and Virginia Municipal League, 2004.

Deans, Bob. *The River Where America Began: A Journey Along the James*. Lanham: Rowman & Littlefield Publishers, 2008.

Democratic Party of Virginia. "Virginia Democratic Party Plan," accessed October 11, 2010, http://va-dems.vanwebhost.com/sites/va-dems.vanwebhost.com/files/TheDPVAPartyPlan.pdf.

Democratic Party of Virginia. "The Party Platform," accessed October 11, 2010, http://www.vademocrats .org/party-platform.

Department of Education. "Table 12 of the Superintendent's Annual Report for Virginia Receipts by Division and Regional Program (in dollars) Fiscal Year 2009," accessed Oct. 28, 2010, http://www.doe.virginia.gov/statistics_reports/supts_annual_report/2008_09/table12.pdf.

Dixon, Donald C. "Local Government in Colonial Virginia: A Prelude to Constitution Making," *The University of Virginia News Letter*, March 15, 1973.

Duncombe, Herbert S. *County Government in America*. National Association of Counties Research Foundation, 1966.

Eckenrode, Hamilton James. *The Political History of Virginia During the Reconstruction*. Baltimore, 1904.

Exec. Order No. 4, May 9, 1865, 13 Stat. 777.

Fields, Mary Jo, and Sandra H. Wiley, "Town-County Relations in Virginia," *University of Virginia Newsletter*. Charlottesville: Institute of Government, University of Virginia, June 1980.

FindLaw. "First Amendment—Religion and Expression," accessed May 11, 2011, http://caselaw.lp .findlaw.com/data/constitution/amendment01/.

Fineman, Howard. "The Virginians," *Newsweek*, December 26, 2005 – January 2, 2006.

Fiske, Warren. "Charge dropped against former Va. game department director," *The Virginian-Pilot*, June 5, 2008, accessed Nov. 20, 2010, http://hamptonroads.com/2008/06/charge-dropped-against-former-va-game-department-director.

Florida Ex Rel. Shevin v. Exxon Corporation, 526 F.2d 266, 268-69 (5th Cir. 1976).

Force, Peter, ed. *American Archives* (4th ser.), I. Washington, D.C., 1837).

Fry v. County of Albemarle, 86 Va. 195, 198 S.E. 1004 (1889).

Ferguson v. Board of Supervisors, 133 Va. 561, 113 S.E. 860 (1922)

Gaines, Jr., Francis Pendleton. "The Virginia Constitutional Convention of 1850-51: A Study in Sectionalism." U.Va. Ph.D. dissertation, 1950.

Geary, James J. Unpublished notes, January 17, 2007.

Giesen, Jr., Arthur R. "Pete. "Charlotte Giesen: A Southwestern Virginia Trailblazer," *Virginia Capitol Connections* 4, Autumn 1998.

"Gerald E Connolly," accessed Oct. 20, 2010, http://www.vpap.org/candidates/profile/elections/21224.

Godwin, Jr., Mills E. "Leadership in Crisis: Selected Statements and Speech Excerpts of The Honorable Mills E. Godwin, Jr., Governor of Virginia, 1974-1978."

Godwin, Jr., Mills E. "Oral History Interview with Mills E. Godwin, Jr., Norfolk, Virginia," Old Dominion University Libraries, Special Collections, Oral History in the Perry Library, April 1, 1981, accessed on Nov. 26, 2010, http://www.lib.odu.edu/special/oralhistory/politics/godwintranscript.html.

Gooch, Robert K. "The Recent Limited Constitutional Convention in Virginia," *3 Virginia Law Review.* 70 8 (1945).

Governor of Virginia. "Executive Order No. 1 (2010), Establishing the Chief Job Creation Officer and the Governor's Economic Development and Job Creation Commission," accessed Sept. 30, 2010, http://www.governor.virginia.gov/Issues/ExecutiveOrders/2010 /EO-1.cfm.

Green, Elna C. *Southern Strategies: Southern Women and the Woman Suffrage Question.* Chapel Hill: University of North Carolina Press, 1997.

Green, Frank. "Forbes to serve 10 years in $4 million fraud case," *Richmond Times-Dispatch*, November 24, 2010, accessed Dec. 2, 2010, http://www2.timesdispatch.com/news/virginia-news/2010/nov/24/frau24-ar-673560/.

Greene, Jack P. *Colonies to Nation*, 1763-1789 (New York, 1967), II, 202;

Griffin v. School Board of Prince Edward County, 377 U.S. 218 (1964).

H.J. Res. 3, Acts of Assembly, 1968.

Hannon, Kelly. "Education group grades gubernatorial candidates," *Fredericksburg Free-Lance Star,* Aug. 23, 2005, Apr. 13, 2011, http://fredericksburg.com/News/FLS/2005/082005/08232005/124103.

Hardin, Peter. "Reclaiming History: The Struggle of Virginia's Indians," *Richmond Times-Dispatch*, March 5-6, 2000.

Harrison, Jr., Albertis S. "Albertis S. Harrison, Jr. Oral History Interview," College of William and Mary, W&M Digital Archive, Swem Library, Oral History Collection, accessed on Nov. 26, 2010, http://hdl.handle.net/10288/2118 and http://digitalarchive.wm.edu/bitstream/10288/2118/1/AlbertisSHarrisonJr.pdf.

Heinemann, Ronald L. *Old Dominion, New Commonwealth: A History of Virginia 1607-2007.* Charlottesville: University of Virginia Press, 2007.

Hening, William Waller. *The Statutes at Large Being a Collection of All the Laws of Virginia, Volume 1* (New York: R. & W. & G. Bartow, 1823).

Henry, William Wirt. *Patrick Henry*. New York, 1891.

Holton, Jr., A. Linwood. *Opportunity Time*, Charlottesville: University of Virginia Press, 2008.

Hoover's, Inc. "Build A List-Virginia," accessed Apr. 6, 2011, http://subscriber.hoovers.com/H/search/buildAList .html?_target0 =true.

House Appropriations Committee. "Approved 2010-2012 GF Operating Budget," accessed Nov. 30, 2010, http://hac.virginia.gov/documents/2010/Post-Session/PieChart4-GFOperating.pdf.

House Appropriations Committee. "FY 2010-12 Nongeneral Fund Revenues," accessed Nov. 30, 2010, http://hac.virginia.gov/documents/2010/Post-Session/PieChart2-NGFRevenues.pdf.

House Appropriations Committee. "FY 2010-12 Total Revenues," accessed Nov. 30, 2010, http://hac.virginia.gov/documents/2010/Post-Session/PieChart3-RevenueSources.pdf.

House Appropriations Committee. June 30, 2010. "FY 2010-12 General Fund Revenues," accessed Nov. 30, 2010, http://hac.virginia.gov/documents/2010/Post-Session/PieChart1-GFRevenues.pdf.

House Journal, 1862 Ex. Sess., Doc. No. I.

House Journal, 1874 Sess.

Howard, A. E. Dick. "Constitutional Revision: Virginia and the Nation," 9 *U. Richmond L. Rev.* I (1974).

Howard, A. E. Dick. *Commentaries on the Constitution of Virginia*. Charlottesville: The University Press of Virginia, 1974.

Howard, A. E. Dick. *Road from Runnymede: Magna Carta and Constitutionalism in America*. Charlottesville: University Press of Virginia, 1968.

Howard, A. E. Dick. *The George Mason Lectures: Honoring the Two Hundredth Anniversary of the Virginia Declaration of Rights*. Williamsburg: Colonial Williamsburg Foundation, 1976.

Howard, A. E. Dick, and Tim Finchem. *Virginia Votes for a New Constitution*. Roanoke, Va., 1973.

Jefferson, Thomas. "A Bill for the More General Diffusion of Knowledge," accessed May 5, 2011, http://www.monticello.org/site/research-and-collections/bill-more-general-diffusion-knowledge#footnote2 _th4wdx0.

Jeffries, J. L. *Virginia's Native Son: The Election and Administration of Governor L. Douglas Wilder*. West Lafayette: Purdue University Press, 2000.

Joint Legislative Audit and Review Commission. *1993 Update: Catalog of State and Local Mandates on Local Governments*, House Document No. 2. Richmond, 1994.

Joint Legislative Audit and Review Commission. *Intergovernmental Mandates and Financial Aid to Local Governments*, House Document No. 56. Richmond, 1992.

Joint Legislative Audit and Review Commission. *Review of State Spending: December 2004 Update*, House Document No. 19. Richmond, 2005.

Joint Legislative Audit and Review Commission. *State/Local Relations and Service Responsibilities*, Senate Document No. 37. Richmond, 1993.

Journals of the House of Burgesses of Virginia, 1761-1765.

Kamper v. Hawkins, 3 Va. (I Va. Cas.) 20 (1793).

Kennedy, John Pendleton, ed. *Journals of the House of Burgesses of Virginia, 1761-1765*. Richmond, 1907.

Key, Jr., V.O. *Southern Politics in State and Nation*. New York: Alfred A. Knopf, Inc., 1949.

Kingsbury, Susan Myra, ed. *Records of the Virginia Company of London*. Washington: Government Printing Office, 1905.

Kirk, Russell. *John Randolph of Roanoke*. Chicago, 1964.

Kumar, Anita. "Veterans Groups Support Gilmore," *The Washington Post*, Oct. 17, 2008, accessed Apr. 13, 2011, http://voices.washingtonpost.com/virginiapolitics/2008/10/veteran_groups_support _gilmore.html.

Lapa, Tracy. "Raw Data: State-By-State Voter Registration Requirements." Fox News, Aug. 17, 2006, accessed June 20, 2011, http://www.foxnews.com/story/0,2933,209070,00.html.

Lebsock, Suzanne. "A Share of Honour: Virginia Women 1600-1945." Richmond: Virginia Women's Cultural History Project, 1984.

Letter from Jefferson to John Taylor, July 21, 1816, in *Writings of Thomas Jefferson* edited by Paul Leicester Ford. New York: G. P. Putnam's Sons, 1892.

Lewis, Bob. "Virginia Gets Nation's Top Grade in Management," March 31, 2005, Associated Press and WTOP, accessed Nov. 26, 2010, http://www.wtopnews.com /index.php?sid=405474&nid=25.

Library of Congress. "A Century of Lawmaking for a New Nation: U.S. Congressional Documents and Debates, 1774 – 1875," Annals of Congress, 4th Congress, Pages 2873 & 2874 of 2966, accessed Oct. 20, 2010, http://memory.loc.gov/cgi-bin/ampage?collId=llac&fileName=006/llac006 .db&recNum=679.

Library of Virginia. "Mary Marshall (1921-1992)," "Online Voices of Arlington" exhibit sponsored by the Arlington Bicentennial Celebration Task Force, Online exhibit, *Dictionary of Virginia Biography*.

Library of Virginia. "Mary Sue Terry," Virginia Women in History 2009, accessed August 17, 2010, http://www.lva.virginia.gov/public/vawomen/2009/honoree.asp?bio=6.

Lieutenant Governor of Virginia. "History of the Office of the Lieutenant Governor," accessed Oct. 25, 2010, http://www.ltgov.virginia.gov/educational/aboutOffice.cfm.

Lieutenant Governor of Virginia. "Interesting Facts," accessed Oct. 25, 2010, http://www.ltgov.virginia.gov/educational/aboutOffice.cfm.

Locke, Mamie E. "Women's Leadership in the Virginia State Senate," *Virginia Capitol Connections* 14 (Winter 2008), 2.

Long, Betty. "Municipal Revenue Sources," Updated from Table 11.1, *Handbook for Virginia Mayors and Council Members*. Charlottesville: University of Virginia and Virginia Municipal League, 2004.

Lowe, Richard G. "Virginia's Reconstruction Convention: General Schofield Rates the Delegates," 80 *Va. Mag. Hist. & Biog.* 341 (1972).

Madison, James. *The Federalist Papers,* "Federalist No. 47," February 1, 1788. Library of Congress, accessed May 30, 2011, http://thomas.loc.gov/home/histdox/fed_47.html.

Manarin, Louis. *Officers of the Senate of Virginia 1776-1996*. Richmond: Carter Printing Company, 1997.

Manarin, Louis H., and Jon Kukla. *The General Assembly of Virginia 1619-1978: A Bicentennial Register of Members*. Richmond: Library of Virginia, 1978.

Marbury v. Madison, 5 U.S. (1 Cranch) 137 (1803).

McClellan, James. *Liberty, Order, and Justice*. Third Edition. Indianapolis: Liberty Fund, 2000.

McDanel, Ralph Clipman. *Virginia Constitutional Convention of 1901-1902*.

McIlwaine, Henry Read, ed. *Journals of the House of Burgesses of Virginia*. 1695-1696, 1696-1697, 1698, 1699, 1700-1702. Richmond: The Colonial Press, E. Waddey Co., 1913.

McQuillen, Eugene. *A Treatise on the Law of Municipal Corporations*. 3d ed. Chicago: Callaghan & Company, 1911.

Michie, Jr., Thomas J., and Marcia S. Mashaw. "Annexation and State Aid to Localities: A Compromise is Reached," *University of Virginia Newsletter*. Charlottesville: Institute of Government, University of Virginia, July 1979.

Michie's Jurisprudence of Virginia and West Virginia. The Michie Company, 1949.

Moger, Allen Wesley. *Virginia: Bourbonism to Byrd.*

Morgan, Edmund S. *Prologue to Revolution: Sources and Documents on the Stamp Act Crisis, 1764-1766.* Chapel Hill: The University of North Carolina Press, 1959.

Morris, Thomas. *Virginia's Lieutenant Governors: The Office and the Person.* Charlottesville: University of Virginia, 1970.

Murray v. Roanoke, 192 Va. 321, 64 S.E.2d. 804 (1951).

National Archives. "Bill of Rights, Amendment IV," accessed Oct. 22, 2010, http://archives.gov/exhibits/charters/bill_of_rights_transcript.html.

National Archives. "Declaration of Independence," accessed October 11, 2010, http://www.archives.gov/exhibits/charters/declaration.html.

National Archives. "Differences in Course Offerings," Davis v. Prince Edward County, United States District Court, Eastern District of Virginia, RG 21, National Archives Mid Atlantic Region, accessed Oct. 20, 2010, http://www.archives.gov/midatlantic/education/desegregation/davis.html.

National Archives. "The Founding Fathers: Virginia," accessed October 11, 2010, http://www.archives.gov/exhibits/charters/constitution_founding _fathers_virginia.html.

National Archives. "The Virginia Declaration of Rights," accessed May 29, 2011, http://www.archives.gov/exhibits/charters/virginia_declaration_of_rights.html.

National Association of Attorneys General. "The Master Settlement Agreement" (1998), accessed Oct. 22, 2010, http://www.naag.org/backpages/naag/tobacco/msa/msa-pdf/MSA%20with%20Sig %20Pages%20and%20Exhibits.pdf/file_view.

National Association of Secretaries of State. "Voter Registration: Get Registered or Check Your Registration Info," accessed June 20, 2011, http://www.canivote.org.

National Lieutenant Governor's Association, "About NLGA," accessed Sept. 30, 2010, http://www.nlga.us/web-content/AboutNLGA/About.html.

National Public Radio. "A Lobbyist by Any Other Name?," January 22, 2006, accessed May 11, 2011, http://www.npr.org/templates/story/story.php?storyId=5167187.

Newton, Blake Tyler. "The Governor of Virginia As Business Manager." Richmond: The General Assembly of Virginia, 1942.

Niles' Weekly Register 20-21 (1816).

Office of the Attorney General of Virginia, "McDonnell, Brownlee Announce Maker of OxyContin Pleads Guilty to Felony Misbranding," May 10, 2007, accessed Oct. 22, 2010, http://www.vaag.virginia.gov/PRESS_RELEASES/NewsArchive/051007_OxyContin .html.

Office of the Executive Secretary, Supreme Court of Virginia, "Canons of Judicial Conduct for the State of Virginia," accessed Nov. 11, 2010, http://www.courts.state.va.us/agencies/jirc/canons_112398.html.

Office of the Executive Secretary, Supreme Court of Virginia, accessed Oct. 5, 2010, http://www.courts .state.va.us/courts/cib.pdf.

Old Dominion Land Company v. Warwick County, 172 Va. 160, 200 S.E. 619 (1939).

Page, Susan and Jagoda, Naomi. "What is the Tea Party? A growing state of mind," *USA TODAY*, July 8, 2010, accessed Apr. 13, 2011, http://www.usatoday.com/news/politics/2010-07-01-tea-party_N.htm#.

Peden, William, ed. *Notes on the State of Virginia*, Chapel Hill, N.C., 1955.

Peterson, Merrill D. *Democracy, Liberty, and Property: The State Constitutional Conventions of the 1820's*. Indianapolis: MacMillan Publishing Company, 1966.

Plaisance, Patrick Lee. "Realities Of Car Tax Cut Emerge In Public Meeting," *Daily Press*, December 17, 1997, accessed Apr. 14, 2011, http://articles.dailypress.com/1997-12-17/news/9712170041_1_car-tax-personal-property-tax-jim-gilmore.

Porter, Albert Ogden. *County Government in Virginia: A Legislative History, 1607-1904*. Columbia: University Press, 1947.

Proceedings and Debates of the Virginia State Convention of 1829-30. Richmond: S. Shepherd & Co. for Ritchie & Cook, 1830.

Quotation from John F. Dillon, *Commentaries on the Law of Municipal Corporations*, 5th Edition. Little, Brown and Co., 1911.

Report of the Commission on Public Education to the Governor of Virginia, accessed Mar. 31, 2011, http://www2.vcdh.virginia.edu/civilrightstv/documents/images/commissionreport onpubliceducation.pdf.

Republican Party of Virginia. "Republican Party of Virginia," accessed October 11, 2010, http://www.rpv.org/docLib/20100121_PartyPlanNovUpdatesNotes.pdf.

Republican Party of Virginia. "Republican Party of Virginia Creed," accessed October 11, 2010, http://www.rpv.org/about/page/republican-party-of-virginia-creed.

Reese, George H., ed. *Proceedings of the Virginia State Convention of 1861: Feb. 13-May 1, 1861.* Richmond, 1965.

Rich, Richard. "News from Virginia," in *Virginia Reader: A Treasury of Writings from the First Voyages to the Present*, edited by Francis Coleman Rosenberger. New York: E. P. Dutton and Company, 1948.

Richmond Enquirer, Jan. 25, 1817, 3, col. 5; Feb. 13, 1817, 3, col. 1.

Richmond Times-Dispatch. "Ex-Delegate for 23 Years Dies at 71," October 16, 1992.

Richmond Times-Dispatch. "Kaine's Two Jobs: Juggling Act," July 10, 2009, accessed Apr. 14, 2011, http://www2.timesdispatch.com/news/2009/jul/10/ed-timk10_20090709-195203-ar-37800/.

Richmond Whig, Nov. 24, 1851.

Robert, Joseph C. *The Road from Monticello: A Study of the Virginia Slavery Debate of 1832.* Durham: Duke University Press, 1941.

Robertson, Alexander F. *Alexander Hugh Holmes Stuart 1807-1891: A Biography.* Richmond, 1925.

Rosenberg, Alyssa. "Federal employee groups step up political efforts as fall elections approach," Government Executive.com, July 14, 2008, accessed Apr. 1, 2011, http://www.govexec.com/dailyfed/0708/071408ar1.htm.

Ross, Lynne M. *State Attorneys General Powers and Responsibilities.* Washington: Bureau of National Affairs Books, 1990.

Rowland, Kate Mason. *Life of George Mason,* 1725-1792. New York, 1892.

Rutland, Robert Allen, ed. *Papers of George Mason.*

Saxon, Wolfgang. "Mills Godwin Jr., 84; Ruled Virginia as Democrat and Republican," February 02, 1999, *The New York Times,* accessed May 31, 2011, http://www.nytimes.com/1999/02/02/us/mills-godwin-jr-84-ruled-virginia-as-democrat-and-republican.html.

Salmon, Emily J. *A Hornbook of Virginia History.* Third Edition. Richmond: Library of Virginia, 1983.

Schuyler, Lorraine Gates. *The Weight of Their Votes: Southern Women and Political Leverage in the 1920s.* Chapel Hill: University of North Carolina Press, 2006.

Secretary of the Commonwealth of Virginia. "Clemency," accessed September 23, 2010, http://www.commonwealth.virginia.gov/JudicialSystem/Clemency/clemency.cfm.

Secretary of the Commonwealth, "Virginia Organization of State Government," accessed Dec. 2, http://www.commonwealth2010,virginia.gov/StateGovernment/StateOrgChart/OrgChart 2009rev.pdf.

Seraile, Brian G. "Ex-Delegate's Causes Keep McDiarmid Busy in Retirement," *Richmond Times-Dispatch*, December 30, 1990; Ellen Robertson and John Lyle, "Dorothy McDiarmid Dies: Longtime Delegate Broke Barriers, Headed Budget Panel," *Richmond Times-Dispatch,* June 10, 1994.

Sherwood, Tom. "National Attention Follows Va. Governor," *The Washington Post*, January 2, 1986, Final Edition, A1.

Shanks, Henry T. *The Secession Movement in Virginia, 1847-1861.* Richmond: Garrett and Massie, 1934.

Spicer, Jr., Robert E. "Annexation in Virginia: The 1979 Amendments Usher in a New Era in City-County Relations," 17 *University of Richmond Law Review* 819 (1983).

Squire, Peverill, James Lindsay, Cary R Covington, and Eric Smith, *Dynamics of Democracy.* Fourth Edition. Atomic Dog Publishing, 2005.

Squire, Peverill, James Lindsay, Cary R Covington, and Eric Smith, *Dynamics of Democracy.* Fifth Edition. Mason: Thomson Custom Publishing, 2008.

Staples v. Gilmer, 183 Va. 613, 33 S.E.2d 49 (1945).

State Board of Elections. "Absentee Voting," accessed September 23, 2010, http://www.sbe .virginia.gov/cms/Absentee_Voting/Index.html.

State Board of Elections. "Election Calendar and Schedule," accessed September 23, 2010. http://www.sbe.virginia.gov/cms/Election_Information/Election_Calendar_Schedule.html.

State Board of Elections. "Forms and Publications," accessed September 23, 2010, http://www.sbe .virginia.gov/cms/Forms_Publications/Index.html.

State Board of Elections. "Local Election Officials," accessed September 23, 2010, http://www.sbe .virginia.gov/cms/Election_Information/Local_Election_Officials/Index.html.

State Board of Elections. "Overview of the Election Process, Who Conducts the Elections in Virginia?" accessed September 23, 2010, http://www.sbe.virginia.gov/cms/Election_Information/Election_ Procedures/Index.html.

State Board of Elections. "Petition for Appeal of Denial of Virginia Voter Registration," accessed September 23, 2010, http://www.sbe.virginia.gov/cms/documents/Petitionforappealofdenial.pdf.

State Board of Elections. "References and Election Laws," accessed August 20, 2010, http://www.sbe .virginia.gov/cms/Misc/Election_Laws.html.

State Board of Elections. "Registering To Vote," accessed September 23, 2010, http://www.sbe.virginia.gov/cms/Voter_Information/Registering_to_Vote/Index.html.

State Board of Elections. "Registration Statistics," accessed September 23, 2010, http://www.sbe.virginia.gov/cms/Statistics_Polling_Places/Index.html.

State Board of Elections. "Virginia State Board of Elections: Voter ID Requirements in Virginia," accessed September 23, 2010, http://www.sbe.virginia.gov/cms/Voter_Information/Voter_ID_Requirements_in_Virginia_text.html.

State Board of Elections. "Voters With Special Needs," accessed September 23, 2010, http://www.sbe.virginia.gov/cms/Voter_Information/Voters_with_Special_Needs/Index.html.

State Board of Elections. "Welcome to Virginia's Campaign Finance Website," accessed September 23, 2010, http://www.sbe.virginia.gov/cms/Campaign_Finance_ Disclosure/Index.html.

Statement by Philip Doddridge, of Brooke County, in *1829-30 Convention Debates*.

Statement of Jerry W. Kilgore, Attorney General Commonwealth of Virginia, On Virginia's Anti-SPAM Law Before the Subcommittee on Crime, Terrorism, and Homeland Security, House Committee on the Judiciary United States House of Representatives, July 8, 2003, accessed Oct. 22, 2010, http://judiciary.house.gov/legacy/kilgore070803.htm.

Stuart, Alexander H. H. *A Narrative of … the Restoration of Virginia to the Union.* Richmond, 1888.

Supreme Court Record No. 730695.

Tabler v. Fairfax County, 221 Va. 200, 202, 269 S.E. 2nd, 358, 359 (1980), quoted in de Voursney, Raben M. "The Dillon Rule in Virginia: What's Broken? What Needs to be Fixed?" University of Virginia Newsletter, Vol. 68, No. 7, July/August 1992.

Tansill, Charles C. "Documents Illustrative of the Formation of the Union of the American States," House Document No. 398, Government Printing Office, 1927, accessed May 11, 2011, http://avalon.law.yale.edu/18th_century/resolves.asp.

Temple, David G. *Merger Politics: Local Government Consolidation in Tidewater Virginia.* Charlottesville: Institute of Government, University of Virginia, by the University Press of Virginia, 1972.

The New York Times. "The Secret Election," accessed Oct. 20, 2010, http://www.nytimes.com/2010/09/19/opinion/19sun1.html?_r=1&ref=editorials.

Thomas P. O'Neill, Jr. Papers. Biographical Note, John J. Burns Library, Boston College, accessed September 23, 2010, http://www.bc.edu/bc_org/avp/ulib /oneill_findingaid2.html.

Thorpe, Francis Newton, ed. *The Federal and State Constitutions: Colonial Charters, and Other Organic Laws of the States, Territories, and Colonies Now or Heretofore Forming the United States of America.* Volumes: I, III, VII. Washington, D.C.: U. S. Government Printing Office, 1909.

Todd, Chuck. "Deeds wins big," NBC News, accessed September 23, 2010, http://firstread.msnbc.msn.com/_news/2009/06/09/4424904-deeds-wins-big.

Treadway, Sandra Gioia. "'A Most Brilliant Woman': Anna Whitehead Bodeker and the First Woman Suffrage Association in Virginia," *Virginia Cavalcade* 43. Spring 1994.

Treadway, Sandra Gioia. "Sarah Lee Fain: Norfolk's First Woman Legislator," *Virginia Cavalcade* 30. Winter 1981.

USA Today. "Lee Malvo, the D.C. sniper's teen accomplice, remains imprisoned for life," Nov. 11, 2009, accessed Oct. 22, 2010, http://content.usatoday.com/communities/ondeadline/post/2009/11/lee-malvo-the-dc-snipers-teen-accomplice-remains-imprisoned-for-life/1.

U.S. Bureau of the Census, "Local Governments and Public School Systems by Type and State: 2007," accessed Oct. 28, 2010, http://www.census.gov/govs/cog/GovOrgTab03ss.html.

U.S. Bureau of the Census, "Population Division, Table 4, Annual Estimates of the Resident Population for Incorporated Places in Virginia: April 1, 2000 to July 1, 2009," (SUB-EST2009-04-51), June 2010.

U.S. Census Bureau, "2002 United States Census of Federal, State and Local Governments," accessed Oct. 24, 2010, http://www.census.gov/govs/www/gid2002.html.

U. S. Justice Department. "About Section 5 of the Voting Rights Act," accessed October 11, 2010, http://www.justice.gov/crt/voting/sec_5/about.php.

Van Schreeven, William J. *The Conventions and Constitutions of Virginia, 1776-1966.* Richmond: 1967.

Van Schreeven, William J., and George H. Reese, ed. *Proceedings of the General Assembly of Virginia, July 30-August 4, 1619.* Jamestown: 1969.

Virginia Association of Counties. *Virginia Map*, accessed Aug. 25, 2010, http://www.vaco.org/VaMap.html.

Virginia Association of Counties. *Virginia County Supervisors' Manual.* Seventh Edition. Richmond: Virginia Association of Counties, 2006.

Virginia Association of Professional Lobbyists. "The VAPL Code of Ethics," accessed Nov. 11, 2010, http://vaplonline.org.

Virginia Association of Professional Lobbyists. "Virginia Lobbyist Standards of Professional Practice and Competency," accessed Nov. 11, 2010, http://vaplonline.org/whowe.htm#standards.

Virginia Association of Realtors. "RPAC endorses congressional candidates," Oct. 18, 2010, accessed Apr. 13, 2011, http://www.varealtor.com/news/2010/10/rpac-endorses-congressional-candidates.

Virginia Constitution. Virginia General Assembly Legislative Information System, http://legis.state.va.us/Constitution/ConstitutionTOC.htm.

Virginia Democratic Party. "Virginia Democratic Party Plan," accessed October 11, 2010, http://va-dems.vanwebhost.com/sites/va-dems.vanwebhost.com/files/TheDPVAPartyPlan.pdf.

Virginia Democratic Party. "The Party Platform," accessed October 11, 2010, http://www.vademocrats.org/party-platform.

Virginia Department of Education. "Table 12 of the Superintendent's Annual Report for Virginia Receipts by Division and Regional Program (in dollars) Fiscal Year 2009," accessed Oct. 28, 2010, http://www.doe.virginia.gov/statistics_reports/supts_annual_report/2008_09/table12.pdf.

Virginia Economic Development Partnership. "Compare Virginia," accessed Nov. 26, 2010, http://reports.yesvirginia.org /HVC/hvcAllies.php.

Virginia Economic Development Partnership. "Business Incentives," accessed Nov. 26, 2010, http://www.yesvirginia.org/whyvirginia /financial_advantages/Business_Incentives.aspx.

Virginia Department of Planning and Budget. 2005 Executive Budget Document. Richmond, 2005.

Virginia Gazette, March 21, 1766. In *Documents of American History*, edited by Henry Steele Commager. Third Edition. New York: F.S. Crofts & Co., 1943.

Virginia General Assembly. HD No. 22, "Report of the Joint Subcommittee to Study The Appropriate Balance of Power between the Legislative and Executive Branches to Support a Two-Term Governor in the Commonwealth." Richmond: Commonwealth of Virginia, 2005, accessed May 31, 2011, http://leg2.state.va.us/dls/h&sdocs.nsf/By+Year/HD222005/$file/HD22.pdf.

Virginia General Assembly Division of Legislative Services. "An Inventory of Local-level Incentives." Richmond: Commonwealth of Virginia, 2004, accessed Nov. 26, 2010, http://dls.state.va.us/GROUPS/incentives/meetings/062308/Inventory.pdf.

Virginia Lawyers Weekly. "Southside smoker files class-action lawsuit," Sept. 28, 1998, accessed Apr. 17, 2011, http://valawyersweekly.com/blog/1998/09/28/southside-smoker-files-classaction-lawsuit/.

"Virginia - Political parties," accessed October 11, 2010, http://www.city-data.com/states/Virginia-Political-parties.html.

Virginia Public Access Project. "Disclose Virginia." Richmond: Spring, 2010.

Virginia Public Access Project. "Gerald E Connolly," accessed Oct. 20, 2010, http://www.vpap.org/candidates/profile/elections/21224.

Virginia Public Access Project. "Governor, 2009," accessed Oct. 20, 2010, http://www.vpap.org/elections/election_seat/1?year=2009.

Virginia Public Access Project. "Lobbyist Disclosures, Top Spenders," accessed April 25, 2011, http://www.vpap.org/lobbyists/top?expense_type=total_amount&order=amount&page=1&period=2009-2010.

Virginia Public Access Project. "State Board of Elections and VPAP Team Up to Display Election-Night Results," accessed September 23, 2010, http://www.vpap.org/updates/show/416.

Virginia Public Access Project. "Top Vendors," accessed Oct. 20, http://www.vpap.org/vendors/top_services12010,?end_year=2009&start_year=2009&lookup_type=year&filing_period=all&filter_cmte_radio=1&filter_cmte=1.

Virginia v. Black (01-1107) 538 U.S. 343 (2003).

Virginia v. Hicks (02-371) 539 U.S. 113 (2003).

Virginia Electoral Board Association. "Welcome to the Virginia Electoral Board Association," accessed August 20, 2010, http://vebanews.org/Welcome.html.

"Virginia - Political parties," accessed October 11, 2010, http://www.city-data.com/states/Virginia-Political-parties.html.

Walker, Julian. "Candidate Kaine says he's crisis-tested," *The Virginian-Pilot*, Apr. 7, 2011, accessed Apr. 13, 2011, http://hamptonroads.com/2011/04/candidate-kaine-says-hes-crisistested?page=1.

Washington Times, "Price-gouging accusations linger," Nov. 16, 2003, accessed Oct. 22, 2010, http://www.washingtontimes.com/news/2003/nov/16/20031116-111210-6127r/?page=2.

Weldon Cooper Center for Public Service, University of Virginia. "2009 Tax Rates," accessed Oct. 28, 2010, http://www.coopercenter.org/econ/2009-tax-rates.

Wheeler, Marjorie Spruill. *New Women of the New South: The Leaders of the Woman Suffrage Movement in the Southern States.* New York: Oxford University Press, 1993.

Whitmer, Clair. "What the Move Act Means For You," Overseas Vote Foundation, accessed September 23, 2010, https://www.overseasvotefoundation.org/node/282.

Wiltrout, Kate. "Virginia's Few Female Senators Rise to the Occasion," *Virginian-Pilot,* February 4, 2008.

Woolley, John T. and Gerhard Peters. *The American Presidency Project*, accessed Apr. 12, 2011, "Democratic Party Platform of 1856," http://www.presidency.ucsb.edu/ws/index.php?pid=29576 #axzz1JSGVb0SV; "2008 Democratic Party Platform," http://www.presidency.ucsb.edu/ws/index.php?pid=78283#axzz1J3YMsQw6; "Republican Party Platform of 1856," http://www.presidency.ucsb.edu/ws/index.php?pid=29619#axzz1J3YMsQw6; "2008 Republican Party Platform," http://www.presidency.ucsb.edu/ws/index.php?pid=78545#axzz1J3YMsQw6.

"Women in the General Assembly," *Virginia Capitol Connections* 14. Winter 2008.

Yancey, Dwayne. *When Hell Froze Over*. Roanoke: Taylor Publishing Co., 1988, quoted in Atkinson, Frank. *The Dynamic Dominion*. Fairfax: George Mason University Press, 1992.

Constitution of Virginia - Table of Contents[1]

ARTICLE I - Bill of Rights
Section 1. Equality and rights of men.
Section 2. People the source of power.
Section 3. Government instituted for common benefit.
Section 4. No exclusive emoluments or privileges; offices not to be hereditary.
Section 5. Separation of legislative, executive, and judicial departments; periodical elections.
Section 6. Free elections; consent of governed.
Section 7. Laws should not be suspended.
Section 8. Criminal prosecutions.
Section 9. Prohibition of excessive bail and fines, cruel and unusual punishment, suspension of habeas corpus, bills of attainder, and ex post facto laws.
Section 10. General warrants of search or seizure prohibited.
Section 11. Due process of law; obligation of contracts; taking of private property; prohibited discrimination; jury trial in civil cases.
Section 12. Freedom of speech and of the press; right peaceably to assemble, and to petition.
Section 13. Militia; standing armies; military subordinate to civil power.
Section 14. Government should be uniform.
Section 15. Qualities necessary to preservation of free government.
Section 15A. Marriage.
Section 16. Free exercise of religion; no establishment of religion.
Section 17. Construction of the Bill of Rights.

ARTICLE II - Franchise and Officers
Section 1. Qualifications of voters.
Section 2. Registration of voters.
Section 3. Method of voting.
Section 4. Powers and duties of General Assembly.
Section 5. Qualifications to hold elective office.
Section 6. Apportionment.
Section 7. Oath or affirmation.
Section 8. Electoral boards; registrars and officers of election.
Section 9. Privileges of voters during election.

ARTICLE III - Division of Powers
Section 1. Departments to be distinct.

ARTICLE IV - Legislature
Section 1. Legislative power.
Section 2. Senate.
Section 3. House of Delegates.
Section 4. Qualifications of senators and delegates.

Section 5. Compensation; election to civil office of profit.
Section 6. Legislative sessions.
Section 7. Organization of General Assembly.
Section 8. Quorum.
Section 9. Immunity of legislators..
Section 10. Journal of proceedings.
Section 11. Enactment of laws.
Section 12. Form of laws.
Section 13. Effective date of laws.
Section 14. Powers of General Assembly; limitations.
Section 15. General laws.
Section 16. Appropriations to religious or charitable bodies.
Section 17. Impeachment.
Section 18. Auditor of Public Accounts.

ARTICLE V - Executive
Section 1. Executive power; Governor's term of office.
Section 2. Election of Governor.
Section 3. Qualifications of Governor.
Section 4. Place of residence and compensation of Governor.
Section 5. Legislative responsibilities of Governor.
Section 6. Presentation of bills; powers of Governor; vetoes and amendments.
Section 7. Executive and administrative powers.
Section 8. Information from administrative officers.
Section 9. Administrative organization.
Section 10. Appointment and removal of administrative officers.
Section 11. Effect of refusal of General Assembly to confirm an appointment by the Governor.
Section 12. Executive clemency.
Section 13. Lieutenant Governor; election and qualifications.
Section 14. Duties and compensation of Lieutenant Governor.
Section 15. Attorney General.
Section 16. Succession to the office of Governor.
Section 17. Commissions and grants.

ARTICLE VI - Judiciary
Section 1. Judicial power; jurisdiction.
Section 2. Supreme Court.
Section 3. Selection of Chief Justice.
Section 4. Administration of the judicial system.
Section 5. Rules of practice and procedure.
Section 6. Opinions and judgments of the Supreme Court.
Section 7. Selection and qualification of judges.
Section 8. Additional judicial personnel.
Section 9. Commission; compensation; retirement.
Section 10. Disabled and unfit judges.

254

Section 11. Incompatible activities.
Section 12. Limitation; judicial appointment.

ARTICLE VII - Local Government
Section 1. Definitions.
Section 2. Organization and government.
Section 3. Powers.
Section 4. County and city officers.
Section 5. County, city, and town governing bodies.
Section 6. Multiple offices.
Section 7. Procedures.
Section 8. Consent to use public property.
Section 9. Sale of property and granting of franchises by cities and towns.
Section 10. Debt.

ARTICLE VIII - Education
Section 1. Public schools of high quality to be maintained.
Section 2. Standards of quality; State and local support of public schools.
Section 3. Compulsory education; free textbooks.
Section 4. Board of Education.
Section 5. Powers and duties of the Board of Education.
Section 6. Superintendent of Public Instruction.
Section 7. School boards.
Section 8. The Literary Fund.
Section 9. Other educational institutions.
Section 10. State appropriations prohibited to schools or institutions of learning not owned or exclusively controlled by the State or some subdivision thereof; exceptions to rule.
Section 11. Aid to nonpublic higher education.

ARTICLE IX - Corporations
Section 1. State Corporation Commission.
Section 2. Powers and duties of the Commission.
Section 3. Procedures of the Commission.
Section 4. Appeals from actions of the Commission.
Section 5. Foreign corporations.
Section 6. Corporations subject to general laws.
Section 7. Exclusions from term "corporation" or "company."

ARTICLE X - Taxation and Finance
Section 1. Taxable property; uniformity; classification and segregation.
Section 2. Assessments.
Section 3. Taxes or assessments upon abutting property owners.
Section 4. Property segregated for local taxation; exceptions.
Section 5. Franchise taxes; taxation of corporate stock.

Section 6. Exempt property.
Section 7. Collection and disposition of State revenues.
Section 8. Limit of tax or revenue.
Section 9. State debt.
Section 10. Lending of credit, stock subscriptions, and works of internal improvement.
Section 11. Governmental employees retirement system.

ARTICLE XI - Conservation
Section 1. Natural resources and historical sites of the Commonwealth.
Section 2. Conservation and development of natural resources and historical sites.
Section 3. Natural oyster beds.
Section 4. Right of the people to hunt, fish, and harvest game.

ARTICLE XII - Future Changes
Section 1. Amendments.
Section 2. Constitutional convention.

SCHEDULE
Section 1. Effective date of revised Constitution.
Section 2. Officers and elections.
Section 3. Laws, proceedings, and obligations unaffected.
Section 4. Qualifications of judges.
Section 5. First session of General Assembly following adoption of revised Constitution.

Endnotes

Introduction: The Diffusion of Knowledge

[1] Thomas Jefferson, "A Bill for the More General Diffusion of Knowledge," Monticello, accessed May 5, 2011, http://www.monticello.org/site/research-and-collections/bill-more-general-diffusion-knowledge#footnote2 _th4wdx0.

[2] George Washington, letter to James Warren, March 31, 1779, The Online Library of Liberty, *George Washington: A Collection,* "Chapter: 43: To James Warren," compiled and edited by W.B. Allen (Indianapolis: Liberty Fund, 1988), accessed May 6, 2011, http://oll.libertyfund.org/?option=com_staticxt&staticfile=show.php%3Ftitle=848&chapter=101778&layout=html&Itemid=27.

[3] Va. Constitution, Bill of Rights, Article I, Sec. 2, accessed May 6, 2011, http://legis.state.va.us/Constitution/Constitution.htm.

[4] James Madison, State of the Union Address, December 5, 1810, "A Century of Lawmaking for a New Nation: U.S. Congressional Documents and Debates 1774 – 1875," *Annals of Congress, Senate, 11th Congress, 3rd Session,* Library of Congress, accessed May 6, 2011, http://memory.loc.gov/cgi-bin/ampage?collId=llac&filename=022/llac022.db&recNum=4.

Part I: Virginia's Metamorphosis

[1] James McClellan, *Liberty, Order, and Justice,* Third Edition (Indianapolis: Liberty Fund, 2000), 122.

[2] Alexis de Tocqueville, *Democracy in America,* 1835, Volume I, Chapter II, "Origin of the Anglo-Americans, and Importance of This Origin in Relation to Their Future Condition," from the Henry Reeve Translation, circa 1839, revised and corrected in 1899, University of Virginia, American Studies Programs, accessed May 29, 2011, http://xroads.virginia.edu/~HYPER/DETOC/1_ch02.htm.

[3] "The Virginia Declaration of Rights," National Archives, accessed May 29, 2011, http://www.archives.gov/exhibits/charters/virginia_declaration_of_rights.html.

Chapter 1: Virginia in the Vanguard

[1] This essay was adapted by the author from his 2006 book on Virginia government and politics. See Frank B. Atkinson, *Virginia in the Vanguard: Political Leadership in the 400-Year-Old Cradle of American Democracy, 1981-2006* (Lanham, MD: Rowman & Littlefield Publishers, 2006), xiii-xxiv, 307-309.

[2] Richard Rich, "News from Virginia," in *Virginia Reader: A Treasury of Writings from the First Voyages to the Present,* ed. Francis Coleman Rosenberger (New York: E. P. Dutton and Company, 1948), 109-114.

[3] "Virginia … was the indispensable creator of the Republic and the Constitution that has held together the world's greatest democracy." Michael Barone and Richard E. Cohen, *The Almanac of American Politics 2006* (Washington, D.C.: National Journal Group, 2005), 1705.

[4] The state-sponsored discrimination faced by Virginia Indians in the first half of the twentieth century is chronicled in Peter Hardin, "Reclaiming History: The Struggle of Virginia's Indians," *Richmond Times-Dispatch,* March 5-6, 2000. Eight Virginia Indian tribes were formally recognized by the Commonwealth of Virginia in the 1980s. Although recognized by the English Crown via a 1677 treaty, the Virginia Indian tribes still await long-overdue federal tribal recognition at this writing.

[5] V.O. Key, Jr., *Southern Politics in State and Nation* (New York: Alfred A. Knopf, Inc., 1949), 19.

[6] Virginia's nickname as the "Old Dominion" derives from colonial times. In the mid-17th century, King Charles II of England, who was especially fond of the colony, elevated Virginia to the "dominion" status enjoyed by England,

Scotland, Ireland, and France. The "old" adjective was added by Virginians to reflect their status as the first of the King's settlements in the New World.

[7] Virginia was the locus of the Internet traffic because America Online (AOL) and more than 1,300 other Internet service providers and technology companies were based in Northern Virginia. Computer memory chips briefly became the state's top manufactured export in 2005-2006, less than a decade after they were first produced in the state and before the worldwide recession gutted demand for personal computers.

[8] "Review of State Spending: December 2004 Update," Joint Legislative Audit and Review Commission, Commonwealth of Virginia, December 13, 2004, 51.

[9] Howard Fineman, "The Virginians," *Newsweek*, December 26, 2005 – January 2, 2006, 70.

[10] *Leadership in Crisis: Selected Statements and Speech Excerpts of The Honorable Mills E. Godwin, Jr., Governor of Virginia, 1974-1978,* vii.

[11] Va. Constitution, Article I, §15 (from the Virginia Declaration of Rights), "Qualities necessary to preservation of free government," accessed on Dec. 5, 2010, http://legis.state.va.us/Constitution/Constitution.htm#1S15.

Chapter 2: Virginia Transformed

[1] Deans, Bob, *The River Where America Began: A Journey Along the James* (Lanham, Maryland: Rowman & Littlefield Publishers, 2008), xv.

[2] Jeffries, J.L., *Virginia's Native Son: The Election and Administration of Governor L. Douglas Wilder* (West Lafayette, Indiana: Purdue University Press, 2000), 71.

[3] Ibid.

[4] Ibid.

[5] Ibid.

Chapter 3: The Six Constitutions of Virginia

[1] *Three Charters of the Virginia Company of London,* ed. Samuel M. Bemiss (Williamsburg, Va., 1957), 9. The text of the first Virginia charters may also be found in Thorpe, VII, 3783-3810. For provisions, like that quoted in the text, in the letters patent of 1578 to Sir Humfrey Gilbert and the charter of 1584; to Sir Walter Raleigh, see Thorpe, I, 51, 55.

[2] Thorpe, III, 1856-57. Similar language appeared in the charters of colonies that followed. See *id.,* III, 1681 (Maryland, 1632); III, 1635 (Maine, 1639); I, 533 (Connecticut, 1662); V, 2747 (Carolina, 1663); VI, 3220 (Rhode Island, 1663); V, 2765 (Carolina, 1665); III, 1880-81 (Massachusetts Bay, (691); II, 773 (Georgia, 1732).

[3] *Three Charters of the Virginia Company of London,* 52; Thorpe, VII, 3801.

[4] Thorpe, VII, 3806 (Virginia, 1612); III, 1833 (New England, 1620); III, 1853 (Massachusetts Bay, 1629); III, 1680 (Maryland, 1632); III, 1628 (Maine, 1639); I, 533 (Connecticut, 1662); V, 2746 (Carolina, 1663); VI, 3215 (Rhode Island, 1663); III, 1638, 1639 (Maine, 1664); V, 2764, 2765 (Carolina, 1665); III, 1642 (Maine, 1674); V, 3038 (Pennsylvania, 1681); III, 1882 (Massachusetts Bay, 1691).

[5] See Howard, *Road from Runnymede,* 20-22.

[6] Not all of the 1618 document survives. For the text of the extant portion, see *Three Charters of the Virginia Company of London,* 95-108; Susan Myra Kingsbury, ed., *Records of the Virginia Company of London* (Washington, D.C., 1906-35), III, 98.

[7] See *Proceedings of the General Assembly of Virginia, July 30-August 4, 1619,* ed. William J. Van Schreeven and George H. Reese (Jamestown, Va., 1969).

[8] 1 Hening 363-64.

[9] See Bernard Bailyn, ed., *Pamphlets of the American Revolution, 1750-1776* (Cambridge, Mass., 1965), I, 292. Bland later wrote *Inquiry into the Rights of the British Colonies*, opposing the Stamp Act. See H. Trevor Colbourn, *The Lamp of Experience: Whig History and the Intellectual Origins if the American Revolution* (Chapel Hill, N.C., 1965), 145-47.

[10] *Journals of the House of Burgesses of Virginia, 1761-1765*, ed. John Pendleton Kennedy (Richmond, 1907), 302-04.

[11] William Wirt Henry, *Patrick Henry* (New York, 1891), I, 86.

[12] *Journals of the House of Burgesses of Virginia, 1761-1765*, 360.

[13] Edmund S. Morgan, *Prologue to Revolution: Sources and Documents on the Stamp Act Crisis, 1764-1766* (Chapel Hill, N.C., 1959), 62-65.

[14] 14 Kate Mason Rowland, *Life of George Mason, 1725-1792* (New York, 1892), I, 124-25.

[15] 15 Virginia Gazette, March 21, 1766. The text of the court's order is reprinted in Henry Steele Commager,.ed., *Documents of American History* (3d ed.; New York, 1943), 59.

[16] 5 U.S. (1 Cranch) 137 (1803).

[17] See Jack P. Greene, *Colonies to Nation, 1763-1789* (New York, 1967), II, 202; Harry A. Cushing, "History of the Transition from Provincial to Commonwealth Government in Massachusetts," in Columbia University, *Studies in History, Economics and Public Law,* VII (1896), 1.

[18] *American Archives* (4th ser.), Ed. Peter Force, I (Washington, D.C., 1837), 350.

[19] *Id.,* I, 350-51.

[20] See Howard, *Road from Runnymede,* 188-202, Chapter X, "The Colonists' Case: The Rights of Englishmen or the Rights of Man?".

[21] *Papers of George Mason* (Rutland ed.), I, 201.

[22] *Papers of Thomas Jefferson* (Boyd ed.), I, 290-91.

[23] Ibid.

[24] For a discussion of the various plans, see Howard, "For the Common Benefit," 816.

[25] In 1774 Mason had written the Fairfax County Resolves. See *Papers of George Mason* (Rutland ed.), I, 201-15.

[26] See Introduction to Art. I, *infra* 34-36.

[27] *Notes on the State of Virginia*, ed. William·Peden (Chapel Hill, N.C., 1955), 118.

[28] *Id.,* 120.

[29] *Id.,* 121-25.

[30] Kamper v. Hawkins, 3 Va. (I Va. Cas.) 20 (1793).

[31] See generally, Charles Henry Ambler, *Sectionalism in Virginia from 1776 to 1861* (Chicago,1910); Howard, "For the Common Benefit," 838-40.

[32] See Howard, "For the Common Benefit," 841-46.

[33] 11 Niles' Weekly Register 20-21 (1816).

[34] A resolution favorable to calling a convention passed in the House of Delegates but was defeated in the Senate. Richmond Enquirer, Jan. 25, 1817, 3, col. 5; Feb. 13, 1817, 3, col. I.

[35] Howard, "For the Common Benefit," 846.

[36] See *id.,* 848-49.

[37] Merrill D. Peterson, *Democracy, Liberty, and Property: The State Constitutional Conventions of the 1820'S* (Indianapolis, 1966), 271.

[38] See statement by Philip Doddridge, of Brooke County, in *1829-30 Convention Debates*, 476.

[39] *Id.,* 687.

[40] *Id.,* p 492, 790, 321. For a vivid portrait of Randolph, see Russell Kirk, *John Randolph of Roanoke* (Chicago, 1964).

[41] For the compromise resolution, see 1829-30 *Convention Debates*, 455.

[42] See *id.,* p 641, 647, 650, 651-52.

[43] See *id.,* p 485, 596, 709, 822, 856.

[44] 44 Letter from Jefferson to John Taylor, July 21, 1816, in *Writings of Thomas Jefferson* (Ford ed.), X, 53.

[45] 1829-30 *Convention Debates*, 724.

[46] *Id.*, 90 3.

[47] See 1850-51 *Convention Documents*, Statement by First Auditor respecting Census.

[48] The slavery debate in the General Assembly in 1832 reveals ' clearly the difference between the two sections. See Joseph C. Robert, *The Road from Monticello: A Study of the Virginia Slavery Debate of 1832* (Durham, N.C., 1941).

[49] Ambler, *Sectionalism in Virginia from 1776 to 1861*, 175-218,238-50, 273-78; Henry T. Shanks, *The Secession Movement in Virginia, 1847-1861* (Richmond, 1934), 1-17.

[50] Acts of Assembly, 1849-50, ch. 8, 9-12.

[51] Francis Pendleton Gaines, Jr., "The Virginia Constitutional Convention of 1850-51: A Study in Sectionalism" (U. Va. Ph.D. dissertation, 1950), 91-93.

[52] On the Convention of 1850-51, see generally Ibid.

[53] Richmond Whig, Nov. 24, 1851.

[54] *Proceedings of the Virginia State Convention of 1861: Feb. 13-May I, 1861*, ed. George H. Reese (Richmond, 1965), IV, 144. For the county represented by each delegate, see *id.*, I, 783-87.

[55] House Journal, 1862 Ex. Sess., Doc. No. I, xii.

[56] Charles Henry Ambler, *A History of West Virginia* (New York, 1933), 317-22.

[57] Acts of Assembly, May 1862 Ex. Sess. (Wheeling), ch. I, 3-4.

[58] Hamilton James Eckenrode, *The Political History of Virginia During the Reconstruction* (Baltimore, 1944), 22. The text of the 1864 Constitution appears in Thorpe, VII, 353-7.

[59] Exec. Order No. 4, May 9,1865,13 Stat. 777.

[60] Act of Mar. 2, 1867, ch. 153, 14 Stat. 428.

[61] Act of Mar. 23, 1867, ch. 6, 15 Stat. 2; Act of July 19, 1867, ch. 30, 15 Stat. 14.

[62] On the composition of the 1867-68 Convention, see Richard G. Lowe, Virginia's Reconstruction Convention: General Schofield Rates the Delegates," 80 *Va. Mag. Hist. & Biog.* 341 (1972).

[63] On these events, see Alexander H. H. Stuart, *A Narrative of the Restoration of Virginia to the Union* (Richmond, 1888), Alexander F. Robertson, Alexander Hugh Holmes Stuart, 1807-1891 (Richmond, 1925), 266-79.

[64] The vote on the main body of the Constitution was 210,585 for, 9,136 against; on the test oath clause, 83,458 for, 124,715 against; on the disfranchisement clause, 84.410 for, 124,360 against. McDanel, *Virginia Constitutional Convention of 1901-1902*, 6.

[65] On this period, see Moger, *Virginia: Bourbonism to Byrd*, 32-7.

[66] McDanel, *Virginia Constitutional Convention of 1901-1902*, 11.

[67] *Id.*, 16.

[68] 1901-02 *Convention Debates*, II, 3076. See McDanel, *Virginia Constitutional Convention of 1901-1902*, 24.

[69] Andrew Buni, *The Negro in Virginia Politics, 1902-1965* (Charlottesville, Va., 1967), 24.

[70] Moger, *Virginia: Bourbonism to Byrd*, 98.

[71] 1901-02 *Convention Debates*, II, 2170.

[72] A. C. Braxton, "The Virginia State Corporation Commission," 38 *Am. L. Rev.* 483, 498 (1904).

[73] McDanel, *Virginia Constitutional Convention of 1901-1902*, 113-15.

[74] 1901-02 *Convention Debates*, II, 3258-60.

[75] 101 Va. 829,831, 44 S.E. 754 (1903).

[76] Moger, Virginia: *Bourbonism to Byrd*, 334-442. The Commission was appointed under authority of Acts of Assembly, 1926, ch. 481.

[77] In 1874 Governor James L. Kemper made such a suggestion, though it was not acted upon. See House Journal, 1874 Sess., 482, 484.

[78] Staples v. Gilmer, 183 Va. 613, 33 S.E.2d 49 (1945).

[79] Prentis Comm'n Rep., 7.

[80] Acts of Assembly, 1928, ch. 205.

[81] Harry F. Byrd, *A Discussion of the Amendments Proposed to the Constitution of Virginia: Proposals 3, 4, and 5* (Richmond, 1928), 4.

[82] The general revision passed by a vote of 74,109 to 60,531. Votes on the "short ballot" proposals were 69,034 to 65,176 (Commissioner of Agriculture and Immigration), 68,756 to 65,695 (Superintendent of Public Instruction), and 68,665 to 65,816 (Treasurer). William J. Van Schreeven, *The Conventions and Constitutions of Virginia, 1776-1966* (Richmond, 1967), 19-20.

[83] 1945 *Convention Journal*, 113-15.

[84] Staples v. Gilmer, 183 Va. 613, 33 S.E.2d 49 (1945). See the critical appraisal in Robert K. Gooch, "The Recent Limited Constitutional Convention in Virginia," *3 Va. L. Rev.* 70 8 (1945).

[85] *1956 Convention Journal*, 69-71.

[86] S. Doc. No. I, 1968 Sess., 10-11.

[87] H.J. Res. 3, Acts of Assembly, 1968, 1568.

[88] For a list of the Commission's members, see CCR, i.

[89] For a description of the Commission's procedures, see *id.,* 2-5.

[90] *Id.,* 9-12.

[91] For an account of the events leading to the adoption of the Constitution of 1971 and an analysis of the vote in the 1970 referendum, see A. E. Dick Howard and Tim Finchem, *Virginia Votes for a New Constitution* (Roanoke, Va., 1973). A fuller analysis, comparing Virginia's experience to that of other states, appears in Howard, "Constitutional Revision: Virginia and the Nation," 9 *U. Richmond L. Rev.* I (1974).

Chapter 4: The Emergence of Modern Virginia Politics

[1] V.O. Key, Jr., *Southern Politics in State and Nation* (New York: Alfred A. Knopf, Inc., 1949), 19.

[2] See A.E. Dick Howard, *Commentaries on the Constitution of Virginia* (Charlottesville: University of Virginia Press, 1974).

[3] Frank B. Atkinson, *The Dynamic Dominion* (Fairfax: George Mason University Press, 1992), 4.

[4] Ibid., 4-5.

[5] For a general historical overview of Byrd, his administration, and his political organization, see Atkinson, *The Dynamic Dominion*, and Alden Hatch, *The Byrds of Virginia, An American Dynasty, 1670 to the Present* (New York: Holt, Rinehart and Winston), 1969.

[6] Ibid.

[7] Ibid., 8.

[8] Ibid., 15.

[9] Brown v. Board of Education of Topeka, Kansas, 347 U.S. 483 (1954).

[10] Private conversation between Gov. Mills Godwin and the author in the Governor's office, March, 1974.

[11] This was one of the main thrusts of the stump speech which M. Caldwell Butler used when campaigning for Republican House of Delegate nominees in 1967.

[12] Tom Sherwood, "National Attention Follows Va. Governor," *The Washington Post*, January 2, 1986, Final Edition, A1.

[13] The Hon. Richard C. Cranwell's presentation to the James Madison University Political Science 351 class, Nov. 16, 2011.

[14] Patrick Lee Plaisance, "Realities Of Car Tax Cut Emerge In Public Meeting," *Daily Press*, December 17, 1997, accessed Apr. 14, 2011, http://articles.dailypress.com/1997-12-17/news/9712170041_1_car-tax-personal-property-tax-jim-gilmore; Robert Cunard and Sharon Ramos, "Other Voices: Car Tax Relief Slights Virginia's Rural Areas," *Daily Press*, February 28, 2003, accessed Apr. 14, 2011, http://articles.dailypress.com/2003-02-28/news /0302280041_1_car-tax-tax-relief-tax-bills.

[15] "CNN Exit Polls – Virginia Governor," CNN, accessed Apr. 14, 2011, http://i2.cdn.turner.com/cnn/2009/images/11/04/2009.exit.polls.-.va.gov.pdf.

[16] "Kaine's Two Jobs: Juggling Act," *Richmond Times-Dispatch*, July 10, 2009, accessed Apr. 14, 2011, http://www2.timesdispatch.com/news/2009/jul/10/ed-timk10_20090709-195203-ar-37800/.

[17] Associated Press, "Republican McDonnell wins Va. governor's race," MSNBC, accessed May 2, 2011, http://www.msnbc.msn.com/id/33609733#.

Chapter 5: Commemorating the Anniversary of Public School Closings in Virginia

[1] Davis v. County School Board of Prince Edward County, 103 F. Supp. 337 (1952).

[2] Brown v. Board of Education of Topeka, Kansas, 347 U.S. 483 (1954).

[3] *Report of the Commission on Public Education to the Governor of Virginia*, Senate Document 1, Richmond, Virginia, 1955, 7, accessed Mar. 31, 2011, University of Virginia, http://www2.vcdh.virginia.edu/civilrightstv/documents/images/commissionreportonpubliceducation.pdf.

[4] Griffin v. School Board of Prince Edward County, 377 U.S. 218 (1964).

[5] National Archives, "Differences in Course Offerings," Davis v. Prince Edward County, United States District Court, Eastern District of Virginia, RG 21, National Archives Mid Atlantic Region, accessed Oct. 20, 2010, http://www.archives.gov/midatlantic/education/desegregation/davis.html.

Part II: The Legislative Branch

[1] James Madison, *The Federalist Papers*, Federalist No. 47, "The Particular Structure of the New Government and the Distribution of Power Among Its Different Parts," From the New York Packet, Friday, February 1, 1788, the Library of Congress, accessed May 30, 2011, http://thomas.loc.gov/home/histdox/fed_47.html.

[2] Ibid.

Chapter 6: The Virginia General Assembly and the Process of Making State Laws

[1] Luther Stearns Cushing, *Elements of the Law and Practice of Legislative Assemblies in the United States of America,* Ninth Edition (Boston: Little, Brown and Company, 1874), 2.

[2] Louis H. Manarin and Jon Kukla, *The General Assembly of Virginia 1619-1978: A Bicentennial Register of Members* (Richmond: Library of Virginia, 1978), ix.

[3] Warren M. Billings, ed., *The Old Dominion in the Seventeenth Century: A Documentary History of Virginia, 1606-1700* (Chapel Hill: University of North Carolina Press, 2007), 52.

[4] Ibid., 48.

[5] Emily J. Salmon, *A Hornbook of Virginia History,* Third Edition (Richmond: Library of Virginia, 1983, 11-12; Ronald L. Heinemann, *Old Dominion, New Commonwealth: A History of Virginia 1607-2007* (Charlottesville: University of Virginia Press, 2007), 28.

[6] Salmon, 11.

[7] Billings, 10-11.

[8] A.E. Dick Howard, *Commentaries on the Constitution of Virginia, Volume I* (Charlottesville: University Press of Virginia, 1988), 451.

[9] Billings, 10-11.

[10] From a presentation by Sanford W. Peterson, Ph.D., at the Professional Development Seminar for the American Society of Legislative Clerks and Secretaries, Austin, Texas, September 21, 2006.

[11] Ibid.

[12] Heinemann, 32.

[13] Heinemann, 42.

[14] Billings, 58-59.

[15] Henry Read McIlwaine, ed., *Journals of the House of Burgesses of Virginia*, 1695-1696, 1696-1697, 1698, 1699, 1700-1702 (Richmond: The Colonial Press, E. Waddey Co., 1913), xxx.

[16] Louis H. Manarin, *Officers of the Senate of Virginia 1776-1996* (Richmond: Carter Printing Company, 1997), 13.

[17] Maps adapted from the Virginia Division of Legislative Services. For the most up-to-date information on redistricting, see Virginia Division of Legislative Services, "Redistricting Virginia," accessed Dec. 2, 2010, http://dlsgis.state.va.us/.

[18] For information about the General Assembly, see Article IV of the Va. Constitution, "Legislature," accessed Dec. 6, 2010, http://legis.state.va.us/Constitution/Constitution.htm#4S1.

[19] This motion is only applicable to the meetings of House of Delegates committees.

[20] The daily calendar includes the chamber's agenda or order of business and references the stages of legislation as it passes through the process.

Chapter 7: Virginia's Budget Process

[1] For a history of the House of Burgesses, including appropriations and tax policies, see Warren Billings, *A Little Parliament*, (Richmond: Library of Virginia, 2004).

[2] Va. Constitution, "Article, X, Section 7, Collection and disposition of State revenues," accessed Nov. 30, 2010, http://legis.state.va.us/Constitution/Constitution.htm#10S7.

[3] House Appropriations Committee, June 30, 2010, "FY 2010-12 General Fund Revenues," accessed Nov. 30, 2010, http://hac.virginia.gov/documents/2010/Post-Session/PieChart1-GFRevenues.pdf.

[4] Ibid., "FY 2010-12 Nongeneral Fund Revenues," accessed Nov. 30, 2010, http://hac.virginia.gov /documents/2010/Post-Session/PieChart2-NGFRevenues.pdf.

[5] Ibid., "FY 2010-12 Total Revenues," accessed Nov. 30, 2010, http://hac.virginia.gov/documents/2010/Post-Session/PieChart3-RevenueSources.pdf.

[6] Ibid., "Approved 2010-2012 GF Operating Budget," accessed Nov. 30, 2010, http://hac.virginia.gov /documents/2010/Post-Session/PieChart4-GFOperating.pdf.

Chapter 8: A Lady's Place is in the House (of Delegates)

[1] Sandra Gioia Treadway, "'A Most Brilliant Woman': Anna Whitehead Bodeker and the First Woman Suffrage Association in Virginia," *Virginia Cavalcade* 43 (Spring 1994), 166-177; Elna C. Green, *Southern Strategies: Southern Women and the Woman Suffrage Question* (Chapel Hill: University of North Carolina :Press, 1997), 152-156; Marjorie Spruill Wheeler, *New Women of the New South: The Leaders of the Woman Suffrage Movement in the Southern States* (New York: Oxford University Press, 1993), 17.

[2] Suzanne Lebsock, *A Share of Honour: Virginia Women 1600-1945* (Richmond: Virginia Women's Cultural History Project, 1984), 134-136, 155; Green, *Southern Strategies*, 157-164.

[3] Lebsock, *Share of Honour*, 136-138; Lorraine Gates Schuyler, *The Weight of Their Votes: Southern Women and Political Leverage in the 1920s* (Chapel Hill: University of North Carolina Press, 2006), 3-9, 39-59, 166-177.

[4] Lebsock, *Share of Honour*, 138; Schuyler, *Weight of Their Votes*, 145-149, 172-173.

[5] Sandra Gioia Treadway, "Sarah Lee Fain: Norfolk's First Woman Legislator," *Virginia Cavalcade* 30 (Winter 1981), 125-130; Adam Burch, "The Great Worth of a Gentle Woman: Helen Timmons Henderson and Buchanan County," *Virginia Capitol Connections* 14 (Winter 2008), 4, 6.

[6] Treadway, "Sarah Lee Fain," 130-132.

[7] "Sallie Cook Booker" in Sara B. Bearss, et. al., *Dictionary of Virginia Biography* (Richmond: Library of Virginia, 2001), 2:86-87.

[8] "Nancy Melvinia Caldwell" in Bearss, et. al, *Dictionary of Virginia Biography*, 2:505-506.

[9] For a list of women who served in the General Assembly between 1924 and 2008, see "Women in the General Assembly," *Virginia Capitol Connections* 14 (Winter 2008), 7.

[10] Elsie Carper, "A Lonely Voice at Richmond: Kathryn Stone Won Respect in House of Men and Became Spokesman for Virginia's Conscience," *The Washington Post*, August 8, 1965.

[11] Arthur R. "Pete" Giesen, Jr., "Charlotte Giesen: A Southwestern Virginia Trailblazer," *Virginia Capitol Connections* 4 (Autumn 1998).

[12] Brian G. Seraile, "Ex-Delegate's Causes Keep McDiarmid Busy in Retirement," *Richmond Times-Dispatch*, December 30, 1990; Ellen Robertson and John Lyle, "Dorothy McDiarmid Dies: Longtime Delegate Broke Barriers, Headed Budget Panel," *Richmond Times-Dispatch*, June 10, 1994.

[13] "Ex-Delegate for 23 Years Dies at 71," *Richmond Times-Dispatch*, October 16, 1992; "Mary Marshall (1921-1992)," "Online Voices of Arlington" exhibit sponsored by the Arlington Bicentennial Celebration Task Force; Print-out of online exhibit in files of the *Dictionary of Virginia Biography*, Library of Virginia.

[14] Adam Burch, "Eva Scott: Visions of Amelia," *Virginia Capitol Connections* 4 (Autumn 1998), 10, 17.

[15] "Leslie Larkin Byrne" in *Biographical Directory of the United State Congress, 1774 –Present*, accessed August 17, 2010, http://bioguide.congress.gov/scripts/biodisplay.pl?index=b001213; "Mary Sue Terry," Virginia Women in History 2009, accessed August 17, 2010, http://www.lva.virginia.gov/public/vawomen/2009/honoree.asp?bio=6; "Former AG Reflects on Leadership," *Danville Register & Bee*, February 21, 2008.

[16] Mamie E. Locke, "Women's Leadership in the Virginia State Senate," *Virginia Capitol Connections* 14 (Winter 2008), 2; Kate Wiltrout, "Virginia's Few Female Senators Rise to the Occasion," *Virginian-Pilot*, February 4, 2008.

[17] Statistics for "Women in Elective Office," Virginia, compiled by the Center for American Women and Politics, Rutgers University, accessed April 10, 2011, http://www.cawp.rutgers.edu/.

[18] Wiltrout, "Virginia's Few Female Senators Rise to the Occasion."

Chapter 10: The Lieutenant Governor

[1] National Lieutenant Governor's Association, "About NLGA," accessed Sept. 30, 2010, http://www.nlga.us/web-content/AboutNLGA/About.html.

[2] Va. Constitution, "Section 14. Duties and compensation of Lieutenant Governor," accessed Sept. 30, 2010, http://legis.state.va.us/Constitution/Constitution.htm#5S14.

[3] Ibid., "Section 16. Succession to the office of Governor," accessed Sept. 30, 2010, http://legis.state.va.us /Constitution/Constitution.htm#5S16.

[4] See, for example, Va. Code, accessed Sept. 30, 2010, § 2.2-306, "Secure Commonwealth Panel; membership; duties; compensation; staff," http://leg1.state.va.us/cgi-bin/legp504.exe?000+cod+2.2-306; § 2.2-2235, "Board of directors; members and officers; Chief Executive Officer," http://leg1.state.va.us/cgi-bin/legp504.exe ?000+cod+2.2-2235; § 2.2-2721, Center for Rural Virginia Board of Trustees established...," http://leg1.state.va.us/cgi-bin/legp504.exe?000 +cod+2.2-2721.

[5] "Executive Order No. 1 (2010), Establishing the Chief Job Creation Officer and the Governor's Economic Development and Job Creation Commission," accessed Sept. 30, 2010, http://www.governor.virginia .gov/Issues/ExecutiveOrders/2010/EO-1.cfm.

[6]. For historical background, see Louis Manarin, *Officers of the Senate of Virginia 1776-1996* (Richmond: Carter Printing Company, 1997); Thomas Morris, *Virginia's Lieutenant Governors: The Office and the Person* (Charlottesville: University of Virginia, 1970); and Office of the Lieutenant Governor, "Interesting Facts," accessed Oct. 25, 2010, http://www.ltgov .virginia.gov/educational/aboutOffice.cfm.

[7]Ibid. See also Office of the Lieutenant Governor, "History of the Office of the Lieutenant Governor," accessed Oct. 25, 2010, http://www.ltgov.virginia.gov/educational/aboutOffice.cfm.

Chapter 11: Lobbying in Virginia

[1] "Declaration and Resolves of the First Continental Congress," October 14, 1774, The Avalon Project, Yale Law School, Lillian Goldman Law Library, from Charles C. Tansill, "Documents Illustrative of the Formation of the Union of the American States," House Document No. 398, Government Printing Office, 1927, accessed May 11, 2011, http://avalon.law.yale.edu/18th_century/resolves.asp.

[2] "First Amendment - Religion and Expression," FindLaw, accessed May 11, 2011, http://caselaw.lp.findlaw.com /data/constitution/amendment01/.

[3] Liane Hansen, transcript of a broadcast with Jesse Sheidlower, editor-at-large for the *Oxford English Dictionary*, "A Lobbyist by Any Other Name?," National Public Radio, January 22, 2006, accessed May 11, 2011, http://www .npr.org/templates/story/story.php?storyId=5167187.

[4] "A Century of Lawmaking for a New Nation: U.S. Congressional Documents and Debates, 1774 – 1875," *Annals of Congress,* House of Representatives, 10th Congress, 1st Session, pages 1535-1538, Library of Congress, accessed May 11, 2011, http://memory.loc.gov/cgi-bin/ampage?collId=llac&fileName=018/llac018.db&recNum=48 and http://memory.loc.gov/cgi-bin/ampage?collId=llac&fileName=018/llac018.db&recNum=49.

[5] Va. Code, § 2.2-419, "Definitions," accessed April 25, 2011, http://lis.virginia.gov/cgi-bin/legp604.exe?000+cod +2.2-419.

[6] Virginia Public Access Project, "Lobbyist Disclosures, Top Spenders," accessed April 25, 2011, http://www.vpap .org/lobbyists/top?expense_type=total_amount&order=amount&page=1&period=2009-2010.

[7] Ibid., http://www.vpap.org/lobbyists/top?expense_type=total_amount&order=amount&period=2007-2008.

[8] Ibid., http://www.vpap.org/lobbyists/top?expense_type=total_amount&order=amount&page=1&period=2009-2010.

Chapter 11-Part 2: The Role and Ethics of Lobbying

[1] Peverill Squire, James Lindsay, Cary R Covington, and Eric Smith, *Dynamics of Democracy*, Fifth Edition (Mason, Ohio: Thomson Custom Publishing, 2008), 321.

[2] Ibid., 307-324.

[3] Va. Code, § 2.2-419 "Definitions," accessed Nov. 11, 2010, http://leg1.state.va.us/cgi-bin/legp504.exe?000 +cod+2.2-419.

[4] Ibid, § 2.2-426, "Lobbyist reporting; penalty," accessed Nov. 11, 2010, http://leg1.state.va.us/cgi-bin /legp504.exe?000+cod+2.2-426, and § 2.2-420, "Exemptions," http://leg1.state.va.us/cgi-bin/legp504.exe?000+cod +2.2-420.

[5] Ibid., § 2.2-426.

[6] Office of the Executive Secretary, Supreme Court of Virginia, "Canons of Judicial Conduct for the State of Virginia," accessed Nov. 11, 2010, http://www.courts.state.va.us/agencies/jirc/canons_112398.html.

[7] Virginia Association of Professional Lobbyists, "The VAPL Code of Ethics," accessed Nov. 11, 2010, http://vaplonline.org/.

[8] Ibid. "Virginia Lobbyist Standards of Professional Practice and Competency," accessed Nov. 11, 2010, http://vaplonline.org/whowe.htm#standards.

Part III: The Executive Branch

[1] Wolfgang Saxon, "Mills Godwin Jr., 84; Ruled Virginia as Democrat and Republican," February 02, 1999, *The New York Times,* accessed May 31, 2011, http://www.nytimes.com/1999/02/02/us/mills-godwin-jr-84-ruled-virginia-as-democrat-and-republican.html.

[2] For an interesting study that provides more details and a variety of perspectives, see a General Assembly document produced by a joint panel of delegates and senators on the issue of allowing governors to run for a second, consecutive term: HD No. 22, "Report of the Joint Subcommittee to Study The Appropriate Balance of Power between the Legislative and Executive Branches to Support a Two-Term Governor in the Commonwealth" (Richmond: Commonwealth of Virginia, 2005), accessed May 31, 2011, http://leg2.state.va.us/dls/h&sdocs.nsf/By+Year/HD222005/$file/HD22.pdf.

Chapter 12: The Governor and His Cabinet

[1] Va. Constitution, "Article V, Executive, Section 3. Qualifications of Governor," accessed Nov. 18, 2010, http://legis.state.va.us/Constitution/Constitution.htm#5S3.

[2] Ibid., "Section 4. Place of residence and compensation of Governor," accessed Nov. 18, 2010, http://legis.state.va.us/Constitution/Constitution.htm#5S4.

[3] Ibid., "Section 1. Executive power; Governor's term of office," accessed Nov. 18, 2010, http://legis.state.va.us/Constitution/Constitution.htm#5S1.

[4] Ibid., "Section 7. Executive and administrative powers," accessed Nov. 18, 2010, http://legis.state.va.us/Constitution /Constitution.htm#5S7.

[5] Ibid., "Section 5. Legislative responsibilities of Governor," accessed Nov. 18, 2010, http://legis.state.va.us/Constitution/Constitution.htm#5S5.

[6] Ibid., "Section 6. Presentation of bills; powers of Governor; vetoes and amendments," accessed Nov. 18, 2010, http://legis.state.va.us/Constitution/Constitution.htm#5S6. This section also describes the governor's powers in taking action on legislation during the lawmaking process and related legislative procedures.

[7] Ibid.

[8] Ibid., Section 7.

[9] Ibid., "Section 12. Executive clemency," accessed Nov. 18, 2010, http://legis.state.va.us/Constitution/Constitution.htm#5S12.

[10] Ibid., Section 1.

[11] However, Virginia Governors may sit out for at least one term and later serve a second term. Only one modern Governor, Mills Godwin, has done so.

[12] Ibid., "Section 10. Appointment and removal of administrative officers," accessed Nov. 18, 2010, http://legis.state.va.us/Constitution/Constitution.htm#5S10.

[13] Va. Code, § 2.2-2905, "Certain officers and employees exempt from chapter," accessed Nov. 18, 2010, http://legis.state.va.us/Constitution/Constitution.htm#12S1.

[14] Va. Code, § 2.2-103, "Authority to formulate executive branch policies; chief officer for personnel administration and planning and budget," accessed No. 18, 2010, http://leg1.state.va.us/cgi-bin/legp504.exe?000+cod+2.2-103.

[15] Ibid., "Title 2.2 – Administration of Government. Chapter 29 - Virginia Personnel Act," accessed Nov. 18, 2010, http://leg1.state.va.us/cgi-bin/legp504.exe?000+cod+TOC02020000029000000000000.

[16] Ibid., "§ 2.2-104. Delegation of powers," accessed Nov. 18, 2010, http://leg1.state.va.us/cgi-bin/legp504.exe?000+cod+2.2-104.

[17] Ibid. See "Title 2.2 – Administration of Government" for cabinet positions and secretariats, accessed Nov. 18, 2010, http://leg1.state.va.us/cgi-bin/legp504.exe?000+cod+TOC02020000002000000000000.

[18] See, for example, "Executive Order No. 1 (2010), Establishing the Chief Job Creation Officer and the Governor's Economic Development and Job Creation Commission," accessed Nov. 18, 2010, http://www.governor.virginia.gov/Issues/ExecutiveOrders/2010/EO-1.cfm.

[19] Va. Code, § 2.2-200, "Appointment of Governor's Secretaries; general powers; severance," accessed Nov. 18, 2010, http://leg1.state.va.us/cgi-bin/legp504.exe?000+cod+2.2-200.

[20] Ibid., § 2.2-201, "Secretaries; general; compensation," accessed Nov. 18, 2010, http://leg1.state.va.us/cgi-bin/legp504.exe?000+cod+2.2-201.

[21] Warren Fiske, "Charge dropped against former Va. game department director," *The Virginian-Pilot*, June 5, 2008, accessed Nov. 20, 2010, http://hamptonroads.com/2008/06/charge-dropped-against-former-va-game-department-director.

[22] Va. Code, § 2.2-208, "Position established; agencies for which responsible; powers and duties," accessed Nov. 20, 2010, http://leg1.state.va.us/cgi-bin/legp504.exe?000+cod+2.2-208.

[23] Ibid., § 2.2-203, "Position established; agencies for which responsible," accessed Nov. 20, 2010, http://leg1.state.va.us/cgi-bin/legp504.exe?000+cod+2.2-203.

[24] Secretary of the Commonwealth, "VIRGINIA Organization of State Government," accessed Dec. 2, 2010, http://www.commonwealth.virginia.gov/StateGovernment/StateOrgChart/OrgChart2009rev.pdf.

[25] See the prior chapter by L. Douglas Wilder, where he uses this phrase.

[26] Information obtained from unpublished notes provided on Jan. 17, 2007, by James J. Geary, retired Associated Press Virginia Capitol Reporter.

[27] Blake Tyler Newton, *The Governor of Virginia As Business Manager* (Richmond: The General Assembly of Virginia, 1942).

[28] Governor Harry F. Byrd, address to the General Assembly, "Simplification of Government in Virginia," February 3, 1926.

[29] Historical background about the reorganization of the executive branch during the Holton administration can be found in A. Linwood Holton, Jr., Opportunity Time, (Charlottesville: University of Virginia Press, 2008).

[30] Frank Green, "Forbes to serve 10 years in $4 million fraud case," *Richmond Times-Dispatch*, November 24, 2010, accessed Dec. 2, 2010, http://www2.timesdispatch.com/news/virginia-news/2010/nov/24/frau24-ar-673560/.

Chapter 17: The Path to Jobs and Prosperity

[1] For historical background on mid-20th century Virginia Governors who advanced economic development in the Commonwealth, see, for example: College of William and Mary, W&M Digital Archive, Swem Library, Oral History Collection, "Albertis S. Harrison, Jr. Oral History Interview," accessed on Nov. 26, 2010, http://hdl.handle.net/10288/2118 and http://digitalarchive.wm.edu/bitstream/10288/2118/1/AlbertisSHarrisonJr.pdf, 16-17; Old Dominion University Libraries, Special Collections, Oral History in the Perry Library, "Oral History Interview with Mills E. Godwin, Jr., Norfolk, Virginia," April 1, 1981, accessed on Nov. 26, 2010, http://www.lib.odu.edu/special/oralhistory/politics/godwintranscript.html; *Daily Press* Article Collections, Political System, "Gov. Mills E. Godwin Jr.: 1914-1999," Gerald L. Baliles, "Godwin A Helmsman Who Steered State Into The 21st Century," February 07, 1999, accessed on Nov. 26, 2010, http://articles.dailypress.com/1999-02-07/news/9902090123_1_mills-e-godwin-virginia-democratic-party-political-system/3.

[2] More details on factors that affect Virginia's business and economic climate can be found at: Virginia Economic Development Partnership, accessed Nov. 26, 2010, "Why Virginia?," http://www.yesvirginia.org/whyvirginia/default.aspx; "Robust Economy," http://www.yesvirginia.org/whyvirginia/Robust_Economy.aspx; "Pro-Business Climate," http://www.yesvirginia.org/whyvirginia/probusiness_climate.aspx; and "Virginians are the Advantage," http://www.yesvirginia.org/whyvirginia/quality_workforce/Virginians_are_the_advantage.aspx.

[3] Ibid., "Virginia's Key Business Sectors," accessed Nov. 26, 2010, http://www.yesvirginia.org/businesssectors/default.aspx; Virginia Tourism Corporation, "Tourism $$ in Virginia," accessed Nov. 26, 2010,

http://www.virginia.org/pressroom/tourism.asp and "Economic Impact," http://www.vatc.org/research/economicimpact.asp.

[4] Virginia Economic Development Partnership, "Compare Virginia," accessed Nov. 26, 2010, http://reports.yesvirginia.org/HVC/hvcAllies.php.

[5] For general Virginia international trade information, see Ibid. and Virginia Economic Development Partnership, "Fast Facts, Virginia Trade Overview," accessed Nov. 26, 2010, http://www.exportvirginia.org/fast_facts/FastFacts_2008/FF_Issues_Virginia_Trade_Overview_08.pdf.

[6] Virginia Economic Development Partnership Division of International Trade, "Fast Facts: Virginia Trade Overview," "Top Regional Buyers of Virginia Exports," Mar. 2011, 4.

[7] Hoover's, Inc., "Build A List-Virginia," accessed Apr. 6, 2011, http://subscriber.hoovers.com/H/search/buildAList.html?_target0=true.

[8] Virginia Economic Development Partnership Division of International Trade, "Fast Facts: Virginia Trade Overview," Mar. 2011, accessed Apr. 20, 2011, http://www.exportvirginia.org/fast_facts/Current/FF_Issues_Virginia_Trade_Overview.pdf.

[9] Ibid.

[10] For some examples of gubernatorial economic development initiatives in the 1980s and 1990s, see for Gov. Gerald L. Baliles: *Daily Press* Article Collections, "Where The Newspaper Stands," June 10, 2007, accessed Nov. 26, 2010, http://articles.dailypress.com/2007-06-10/news/0706080313_1_world-trade-trade-and-investment-new-economic-development; for Gov. L. Douglas Wilder: Donald P. Baker, "Wilder Given Funds to Attract Business; Va. Governor Also Plans to Appoint Defense Conversion Panel," *The Washington Post,* March 25, 1992, C3; for Gov. George F. Allen: "Comprehensive Economic Development Strategic Plan" (Richmond: Commonwealth of Virginia Secretary of Commerce and Trade, 1994), accessed Nov. 26, 2010, http://leg2.state.va.us/dls/h&sdocs.nsf/By+Year/HD581994/$file/HD58_1994.pdf.

[11] "An Inventory of Local-level Incentives," Va. General Assembly Division of Legislative Services, 2008, accessed Nov. 26, 2010, http://dls.state.va.us/GROUPS/incentives/meetings/062308/Inventory.pdf; Virginia Economic Development Partnership, "Business Incentives," accessed Nov. 26, 2010, http://www.yesvirginia.org/whyvirginia/financial_advantages/Business_Incentives.aspx.

[12] Kurt Badenhausen, "The Best States For Business," Sept. 23, 2009, *Forbes,* accessed Nov. 26, 2010, http://www.forbes.com/2009/09/23/best-states-for-business-beltway-best-states_lander.html; Bob Lewis, "Virginia Gets Nation's Top Grade in Management," March 31, 2005, Associated Press and WTOP, accessed Nov. 26, 2010, http://www.wtopnews.com/index.php?sid=405474&nid=25.

Chapter 18: The Attorney General

[1] National Association of Attorneys General, "The Master Settlement Agreement" (1998), accessed Oct. 22, 2010, http://www.naag.org/backpages/naag/tobacco/msa/msa-pdf/MSA%20with%20Sig%20Pages%20and%20Exhibits.pdf/file_view.

[2] "Southside smoker files class-action lawsuit," *Virginia Lawyers Weekly,* Sept. 28, 1998, accessed Apr. 17, 2011, http://valawyersweekly.com/blog/1998/09/28/southside-smoker-files-classaction-lawsuit/.

[3] "Sniper Muhammad sentenced to death," March 09, 2004, accessed Oct. 22, 2010, http://articles.cnn.com/2004-03-09/justice/sniper_1_muhammad-and-malvo-sniper-killings-lee-boyd-malvo?_s=PM:LAW.

[4] "Lee Malvo, the D.C. sniper's teen accomplice, remains imprisoned for life," Nov 11, 2009, accessed Oct. 22, 2010, http://content.usatoday.com/communities/ondeadline/post/2009/11/lee-malvo-the-dc-snipers-teen-accomplice-remains-imprisoned-for-life/1.

[5] Lynne M. Ross, *State Attorneys General Powers and Responsibilities* (Washington, D.C.: BNA Books, January, 1990), 15-26.

[6] Va. Constitution, "Section 15. Attorney General," accessed Oct. 22, 2010, http://legis.state.va.us/Constitution/Constitution.htm#5S15.

[7] Ibid.

[8] Florida Ex Rel. Shevin v. Exxon Corporation, 526 F.2d 266, 268-69 (5th Cir. 1976) (emphasis added).

[9] Alfred L. Snapp & Son, Inc. v. Puerto Rico, 458 U.S. 592, 601 (1982).

[10] Ibid., 602.

[11] Ibid., 607.

[12] Council of State Government, *The Book of the States 2004* (Lexington, KY: Council of State Government, 2004), 208.

[13] Ibid.

[14] Virginia v. Hicks (02-371) 539 U.S. 113 (2003).

[15] Virginia v. Black (01-1107) 538 U.S. 343 (2003).

[16] Va. Code § 2.2-511, "Criminal cases," accessed Oct. 22, 2010, http://leg1.state.va.us/cgi-bin/legp504.exe?000+cod+2.2-51.

[17] Council, 204.

[18] *Washington Times*, "Price-gouging accusations linger," Nov. 16, 2003, accessed Oct. 22, 2010, http://www.washingtontimes.com/news/2003/nov/16/20031116-111210-6127r/?page=1.

[19] "Statement of Jerry W. Kilgore, Attorney General Commonwealth of Virginia, On Virginia's Anti-SPAM Law Before the Subcommittee on Crime, Terrorism, and Homeland Security," House Committee on the Judiciary, United States House of Representatives," July 8, 2003, accessed Oct. 22, 2010, http://judiciary.house.gov/legacy/kilgore070803.htm.

[20] Office of the Attorney General of Virginia, "McDonnell, Brownlee Announce Maker of OxyContin Pleads Guilty to Felony Misbranding," May 10, 2007, accessed Oct. 22, 2010, http://www.vaag.virginia.gov/PRESS_RELEASES/NewsArchive/051007_OxyContin.html.

[21] See, for example, Va. Code § 2.2-505, "Official opinions of Attorney General," accessed Oct. 22, 2010, http://leg1.state.va.us/cgi-bin/legp504.exe?000+cod+2.2-505.

[22] Andrews v. Shepherd, 201 Va. 412, 415, 111 S.E.2d 279, 282 (1959).

Part IV: The Judicial Branch

Chapter 19: Selecting Virginia's Judges

[1] Va. Constitution, "ARTICLE III, Division of Powers, Section 1. Departments to be distinct," accessed Oct. 22, 2010, http://legis.state.va.us/Constitution/Constitution.htm#3S1.

[2] Ibid., "ARTICLE VI, Judiciary, Section 7. Selection and qualification of judges," accessed Oct. 22, 2010, http://legis.state.va.us/Constitution/Constitution.htm#6S7.

[3] National Archives, "Bill of Rights, Amendment IV," accessed Oct. 22, 2010, http://archives.gov/exhibits/charters/bill_of_rights_transcript.html.

[4] Va. Constitution, "ARTICLE VI, Judiciary, Section 1. Judicial power; jurisdiction," accessed Oct. 22, 2010, http://legis.state.va.us/Constitution/Constitution.htm#6S1.

[5] Ibid.

[6] Va. Code, accessed October 28, 2010, § 16.1-69.5, "Meaning of certain terms," http://leg1.state.va.us/cgi-bin/legp504.exe?000+cod+16.1-69.5; § 17.1 "Courts of Record, Chapter 1 - General Provisions," http://leg1.state.va.us/cgi-bin/legp504.exe?000+cod; "Chapter 3 - Supreme Court," http://leg1.state.va.us/cgi-bin/legp504.exe?000+cod+TOC17010000003000000000000; "Chapter 4 - The Court of Appeals," http://leg1.state.va.us/cgi-bin/legp504.exe?000+cod+TOC17010000004000000000000; "Chapter 5 - Circuit Courts," http://leg1.state.va.us/cgi-bin/legp504.exe?000+cod00000000+TOC170100000050000.

[7] Va. Constitution, ARTICLE VI, Judiciary, Section 7.

[8] Ibid.

[9] Ibid.

[10] Ibid., "ARTICLE VI, Judiciary, Section 10. Disabled and unfit judges," accessed Oct. 22, 2010, http://legis .state.va.us/Constitution/Constitution.htm#6S10.

Chapter 20: Virginia Courts in Brief

[1] Office of the Executive Secretary, Supreme Court of Virginia, "Virginia Courts in Brief," accessed Oct. 5, 2010, http://www.courts.state.va.us/courts/cib.pdf. For more details about the Judiciary, see Article VI of the Virginia Constitution, http://legis.state.va.us/Constitution/Constitution.htm#6S1.

Part V: The Fourth Estate

[1] James Madison, "Letter to W. T. Barry, August 4, 1822," *The Writings of James Madison*, Gaillard Hunt, ed., The James Madison Papers, The Library of Congress, accessed June 6, 2011, http://memory.loc.gov/cgi-bin/query/r ?ammem/mjmtext:@field%28DOCID+@lit%28jm090034%29%29.

[2] Thomas Jefferson, "Letter to George Washington, September 9, 1792," Library of Congress, *The Works of Thomas Jefferson in Twelve Volumes*, Federal Edition, Paul Leicester Ford, accessed June 16, 2011, http://memory.loc.gov /cgi-bin/query/r?ammem/mtj:@field%28DOCID+@lit%28tj070029%29%29.

[3] See the congressional debates on the Post Office law at: House of Representatives, Post Office Bill, 6-7 Dec. 1791, 3, 5 Jan. 1792 *Annals of Congress* 3:229-41, 303-10, accessed June 16, 2011, http://press-pubs.uchicago.edu /founders/documents/a1_8_7s3.html; and *United States Statutes at Large*, Volume 1 by United States Congress: Public Acts of the Second Congress, 1st Session, Chapter 7, "An Act to establish the Post-Office and Post Roads within the United States," Feb. 20, 1792, accessed June 16, 2011, http://en.wikisource.org/wiki/United_States_ Statutes_at_Large/Volume_1/2nd_Congress/1st_Session /Chapter_7.

[4] See University of Virginia, Miller Center of Public Affairs, "Old Media, New Media, and the Challenge to Democratic Governance," March, 2010, accessed June 16, 2011, http://web1.millercenter.org/publications /mediagovt.pdf.

Part VI: Local Governments in Virginia: A Unique Arrangement

[1] Tabler v. Fairfax County, 221 Va. 200, 202, 269 S.E. 2nd,358, 359 (1980), quoted in Raben M. de Voursney, "The Dillon Rule in Virginia: What's Broken? What Needs to be Fixed?" University of Virginia Newsletter, Vol. 68, No. 7, July/August 1992, 2.

[2] de Voursney, 2.

Chapter 23: Virginia's Counties

[1] Portions of this chapter are from the *Virginia County Supervisors' Manual 7th Edition* (Richmond: Virginia Association of Counties, 2006), reproduced with permission of the Virginia Association of Counties.

[2] The six Constitutions were adopted in 1776, 1830, 1851, 1869, 1902, and 1971. The Constitutional revision of 1928 is sometimes considered another. The Virginia Constitution of 1864 is not generally recognized. For historical development of Virginia local government and the constitutional setting in which it occurred, see

Virginius Dabney, *Virginia: The New Dominion* (Doubleday and Company, Inc., 1971); A.E. Howard, *Commentaries on the Constitution of Virginia* (Charlottesville: University Press of Virginia, 1974); Albert Ogden Porter, *County Government in Virginia: A Legislative History, 1607-1904* (Columbia University Press, 1947); and, Chester W. Bain, *A Body Incorporate: The Evolution of City-County Separation in Virginia* (Charlottesville: University Press of Virginia, 1967).

[3] Herbert S. Duncombe, *County Government in America* (National Association of Counties Research Foundation, 1966), 19-22. For an overview of the historical development of the county court and the constitutional officers, see Stanley A. Cook, "The Role of Judges in Virginia Local Government: A Historical Overview and Virginia's Local Executive Constitutional Officers in Historical Perspective," *University of Virginia Newsletter* (Charlottesville: Institute of Government, University of Virginia), June 1981 and September 1981, respectively.

[4] Howard, *Commentaries*, 1:2-8.

[5] Virginia Association of Counties, accessed Aug. 25, 2010, http://www.vaco.org/VaMap.html.

[6] Howard, *Commentaries*, 2:792.

[7] Virginia Department of Planning and Budget, 2005 Executive Budget Document.

[8] Va. Code, §§ 2.2-300-2.2-302, "Title 2.2 - Administration of Government. Chapter 3 - Virginia Liaison Office," accessed Aug. 25, 2010, http://leg1.state.va.us/cgi-bin/legp504.exe?000+cod+TOC02020000003000000000000. The duties of office are at Va. Code, § 2.2-302.

[9] Va. Code, § 2.2-1501(9), "Duties of Department," accessed Aug. 25, 2010, http://leg1.state.va.us/cgi-bin/legp504.exe?000+cod+2.2-1501.

[10] Va. Code, § 36-139(16), "Powers and duties of Director," accessed Aug. 25, 2010, http://leg1.state.va.us/cgi-bin/legp504.exe?000+cod+36-139.

[11] Virginia General Assembly, Joint Legislative Audit and Review Commission (JLARC), *Intergovernmental Mandates and Financial Aid to Local Governments*, House Document No. 56 (Richmond, 1992). See also JLARC's 1993 update: *Catalog of State and Local Mandates on Local Governments*, House Document No. 2 (Richmond, 1994).

[12] *Michie's Jurisprudence of Virginia and West Virginia* (The Michie Company, 1949), Counties, secs. 3 and 4, and cases cited therein. See also Fry v. County of Albemarle, 86 Va. 195, 198 S.E. 1004 (1889).

[13] Cook County v. City of Chicago, 142 N.W. (Illinois) 512 (1924); Camp v. Birchett, 143 Va. 686, 126 S.E. 665 (1925); and, Murray v. Roanoke, 192 Va. 321, 64 S.E.2d. 804 (1951).

[14] JLARC, *State/Local Relations and Service Responsibilities,* Senate Document No. 37 (Richmond, 1993), 49.

[15] Fry v. County of Albemarle, 86 Va. 195, 9 S.E. 1004 (1899); Ferguson v. Board of Supervisors, 133 Va. 561, 113 S.E. 860 (1922); and, Camp v. Birchett, 143 Va. 686, 126 S.E. 665 (1925).

[16] Board of Supervisors v. Corbett, 206 Va. 167, 142 S.E.2d. 504 (1965). See also Commission on Constitutional Revision, *The Constitution of Virginia: Report of the Commission on Constitutional Revision to His Excellency, Mills E. Godwin, Jr., Governor of Virginia, the General Assembly of Virginia and the People of Virginia* (The Michie Company, 1969), 215 and Va. Const. Art. VII, sec. 10.

[17] Va. Code, §§ 15.2-200, et seq., "Required procedure for obtaining new charter or amendment," accessed Aug. 25, 2010, http://leg1.state.va.us/cgi-bin/legp504.exe?000+cod+15.2-200; and §§ 15.2-1100, et seq., "Powers conferred; exercised by council," http://leg1.state.va.us/cgi-bin/legp504.exe?000+cod+15.2-1100.

[18] Va. Const. Art. VII, sec. 2, "Section 2. Organization and government," accessed Aug. 25, 2010, http://legis.state.va.us/Constitution/Constitution.htm#7S2. See also 1902 Va. Const., secs. 65 and 110; *Report of the Commission on Constitutional Revision,* 216; Va. Const. Art. VII, sec. 4; and, Va. Code, § 15.2-1602. The power to abolish constitutional offices, pursuant to special legislation by the General Assembly, was upheld for the City of Alexandria in 1973. See Supreme Court Record No. 730695. No written opinion was delivered.

[19] See 1 McQuillen Municipal Corporations (3d ed.), sec. 2.46.

[20] Va. Code, § 15.2-1401, "Powers granted localities vested in their governing bodies," accessed Aug. 25, 2010, http://leg1.state.va.us/cgi-bin/legp504.exe?000+cod+15.2-1401.

[21] Ibid., § 1-248, "Supremacy of federal and state law," accessed Aug. 25, 2010, http://leg1.state.va.us/cgi-bin/legp504.exe?000+cod+1-248.

[22] Old Dominion Land Company v. Warwick County, 172 Va. 160, 200 S.E. 619 (1939).

[23] The Dillon Rule is named after Judge John F. Dillon of the Iowa Supreme Court, who advanced the rule in Clark v. City of Des Moines, 19 Iowa 199, 212, 87 Am. Dec. 423 (1865). See also County of Fairfax v. Southern Iron Works, Inc., 242 Va. 435, 410 S.E.2d. 674 (1991). The quotation is from John F. Dillon, *Commentaries on the Law of Municipal Corporations,* 5th Ed. (Little, Brown and Co., 1911), I, sec. 237.

[24] City of Richmond v. Board of Supervisors, 199 Va. 679, 101 S.E.2d. 641 (1958). See also JLARC, *State/Local Relations and Service Responsibilities,* 9.

[25] Va. Code, § 15.2-1200, "General powers of counties," accessed Aug. 25, 2010, http://leg1.state.va.us/cgi-bin/legp504.exe?000+cod+15.2-1200.

[26] Va. Code, § 15.2-1201, "County boards of supervisors vested with powers and authority of councils of cities and towns; exceptions," accessed Aug. 25, 2010, http://leg1.state.va.us/cgi-bin/legp504.exe?000+cod+15.2-1201; and 15.2-1100, et seq., "Powers conferred; exercised by council," http://leg1.state.va.us/cgi-bin/legp504.exe?000+cod+15.2-1100.

[27] Va. Code, § 15.2-2506, "Publication and notice; public hearing; adjournment; moneys not to be paid out until appropriated," accessed Aug. 25, 2010, http://leg1.state.va.us/cgi-bin/legp504.exe?000+cod+15.2-2506; and § 58.1-3001, "When boards of supervisors to fix and order county and district taxes; funds not available, allocated, etc., until appropriated," http://leg1.state.va.us/cgi-bin/legp504.exe?000+cod+58.1-3001.

[28] Mary Jo Fields and Sandra H. Wiley, "Town-County Relations in Virginia," *University of Virginia Newsletter* (Charlottesville: Institute of Government, University of Virginia, June 1980).

[29] Va. Code, § 15.2-1300, "Joint exercise of powers by political subdivisions," accessed Aug. 25, 2010, http://leg1.state.va.us/cgi-bin/legp504.exe?000+cod+15.2-1300.

[30] The specific authorizations to cooperate often duplicate the general authority granted in Ibid.; For examples, see Va. Code § 15.2-1726 (consolidation or cooperation in furnishing police protection) and § 42.1-34 (libraries).

[31] Commonwealth of Virginia, Department of Housing and Community Development, *Local Government Information 1985 Survey Report* (Richmond: December 1, 1985), 4.

[32] Va. Code, § 15.2-1303, "Associations to promote welfare of political subdivisions," accessed Aug. 25, 2010, http://leg1.state.va.us/cgi-bin/legp504.exe?000+cod+15.2-1303.

[33] Va. Code, § 15.2-4201, "Powers granted localities vested in their governing bodies," accessed Aug. 25, 2010, http://leg1.state.va.us/cgi-bin/legp504.exe?000+cod+15.2-1401.

[34] Va. Const. Art. VII, sec. 4, "Section 4. County and city officers," accessed Aug. 25, 2010, http://legis.state.va.us/Constitution/Constitution.htm#7S4; and Va. Code, § 15.2-1602, "Sharing of such officers by two or more units of government," http://leg1.state.va.us/cgi-bin/legp504.exe?000+cod+15.2-1602.

[35] Va. Code, § 15.2-4216, "State aid," accessed Aug. 25, 2010, http://leg1.state.va.us/cgi-bin/legp504.exe?000+cod+15.2-4216; § 42.1-48, "Title 42.1 – Libraries," http://leg1.state.va.us/cgi-bin/legp504.exe?000+cod+TOC4201000; 53.1-80, "Title 53.1 - Prisons and Other Methods of Correction," http://leg1.state.va.us/cgi-bin/legp504.exe?000+cod+TOC5301000; and 37.2-500, "Purpose; community services board; services to be provided," http://leg1.state.va.us/cgi-bin/legp504.exe?000+cod+37.2-500.

[36] Ibid., §§ 15.2-4200, et seq., "Title 15.2 - Counties, Cities and Towns," accessed Aug. 25, 2010, http://leg1.state.va.us/cgi-bin/legp504.exe?000+cod+TOC1502000004200000000000.

[37] Ibid., § 15.2-4205, "Powers of commission generally," accessed Aug. 25, 2010, http://leg1.state.va.us/cgi-bin/legp504.exe?000+cod+15.2-4205; 15.2-4206, "Additional powers of planning district commissions," http://leg1.state.va.us/cgi-bin/legp504.exe?000+cod+15.2-4206; 15.2-4207(C), "Purposes of commission," http://leg1.state.va.us/cgi-bin/legp504.exe?000+cod+15.2-4207; and 15.2-4215, "Annual report required," http://leg1.state.va.us/cgi-bin/legp504.exe?000+cod+15.2-4215.

[38] Ibid., § 15.2-4207, "Purposes of commission," accessed Aug. 25, 2010, http://leg1.state.va.us/cgi-bin/legp504.exe?000+cod+15.2-4207.

[39] Ibid., § 15.2-4209, "Preparation and adoption of regional strategic plan," accessed Aug. 25, 2010, http://leg1.state.va.us/cgi-bin/legp504.exe?000+cod+15.2-4209; 15.2-4211, "Amendment of regional strategic plan," http://leg1.state.va.us/cgi-bin/legp504.exe?000+cod+15.2-4211; and 15.2-4212, "Review of regional strategic plan by commission," http://leg1.state.va.us/cgi-bin/legp504.exe?000+cod+15.2-4212.

[40] Ibid., § 15.2-4209(C), "Preparation and adoption of regional strategic plan," accessed Aug. 25, 2010, http://leg1.state.va.us/cgi-bin/legp504.exe?000+cod+15.2-4209.

[41] Ibid., § 15.2-4217, "Preparation and adoption of regional strategic plan," accessed Aug. 25, 2010, http://leg1.state.va.us/cgi-bin/legp504.exe?000+cod+15.2-4209.

[42] Ibid., § 15.2-1306, et seq., "Policy of General Assembly," accessed Aug. 25, 2010, http://leg1.state.va.us/cgi-bin/legp504.exe?000+cod+15.2-1306.

[43] Ibid., § 15.2-1310, "Assignment of weights for functional activities," accessed Aug. 25, 2010, http://leg1.state.va.us/cgi-bin/legp504.exe?000+cod+15.2-1310.

[44] For historical treatment of annexation, see Robert E. Spicer, Jr., "Annexation in Virginia: The 1979 Amendments Usher in a New Era in City-County Relations," 17 *University of Richmond Law Review* 819 (1983). See also Thomas J. Michie, Jr. and Marcia S. Mashaw, "Annexation and State Aid to Localities: A Compromise is Reached," *University of Virginia Newsletter* (Charlottesville: Institute of Government, University of Virginia, July 1979).

[45] Va. Code, § 15.2-3201, "Temporary restrictions on granting of city charters, filing annexation notices, institutions of annexation proceedings and county immunity proceedings," accessed Aug. 25, 2010, http://leg1.state.va.us/cgi-bin/legp504.exe?000+cod+15.2-3201; For voluntary settlements, see Va. Code, § 15.2-3400, "Voluntary settlements among local governments," http://leg1.state.va.us/cgi-bin/legp504.exe?000+cod+15.2-3400.

[46] Ibid., §§ 15.2-3500, et seq., "Title 15.2 - Counties, Cities and Towns. Chapter 35 - Consolidation of Localities," accessed Aug. 25, 2010, http://leg1.state.va.us/cgi-bin/legp504.exe?000+cod+TOC1502000003500000000000.

[47] For general law provisions governing consolidation, see Ibid.; See also City Council v. Newsome, 226 Va. 518, 311 S.E.2d. 761 (1984).

[48] City Council v. Newsome, 226 Va. 518, 311 S.E.2d. 761 (1984).

[49] Va. Code, §§ 15.2-3501, et seq., "Authority to consolidate counties, cities or towns," accessed Aug. 25, 2010, http://leg1.state.va.us/cgi-bin/legp504.exe?000+cod+15.2-3501.

[50] Va. Code, § 15.2-2903, General powers and duties of Commission," accessed Aug. 25, 2010, http://leg1.state.va.us/cgi-bin/legp504.exe?000+cod+15.2-2903; For a discussion of some successful consolidation attempts in Virginia, see David G. Temple, *Merger Politics: Local Government Consolidation in Tidewater Virginia* (Charlottesville: Published for the Institute of Government, University of Virginia, by the University Press of Virginia, 1972).

[51] See U.S. Census Bureau, "2002 United States Census of Federal, State and Local Governments," accessed Oct. 24, 2010, http://www.census.gov/govs/www/gid2002.html.

[52] Governor McDonnell's Commission on Government Reform & Restructuring, "Report to the Governor, December 1, 2010," "Local Mandate Review," accessed on Dec. 2, 2010, http://www.reform.virginia.gov/docs/12-01-10_GovernorsCommissionReport.pdf, 46.

[53] Ibid.

[54] Ibid.

Chapter 24: Virginia's Municipal Governments

[1] Va. Constitution, Article VII, Sect. 1, "Section 1. Definitions," accessed Sept. 25, 2010, http://legis.state.va.us/Constitution/Constitution.htm#7S1.

[2] Va. Code, accessed Sept. 25, 2010, §§ 15.2-3600-15.2-3605, "Title 15.2 - Counties, Cities and Towns. Chapter 36 - Incorporation of Towns by Judicial Proceeding," http://leg1.state.va.us/cgi-bin/legp504.exe?000+cod+TOC1502000003600000000000; §§ 15.2-3800-15.2-3834, Title 15.2 - Counties, Cities and Towns. Chapter 38 -

Transition of Towns to Cities"; §15.2-3201, "Temporary restrictions on granting of city charters, filing annexation notices, institutions of annexation proceedings and county immunity proceedings," http://leg1.state.va.us/cgi-bin /legp504.exe?000+cod+15.2-3201.

[3] Robert M. de Voursney, "Powers & Responsibilities of Municipal Government," *Handbook for Virginia Mayors and Council Members* (Charlottesville: University of Virginia and Virginia Municipal League, 2004), 13-15.

[4] U.S. Bureau of the Census, "Population Division, Table 4, Annual Estimates of the Resident Population for Incorporated Places in Virginia: April 1, 2000 to July 1, 2009," (SUB-EST2009-04-51), June 2010.

5 de Voursney, 14.

6 U.S. Bureau of the Census, "Local Governments and Public School Systems by Type and State: 2007," accessed Oct. 28, 2010, http://www.census.gov/govs/cog/GovOrgTab03ss.html.

7 Va. Code, "Title 15.2 - Counties, Cities and Towns. Chapter 41 - Transition of City to Town Status," accessed Oct. 28, 2010, http://leg1.state.va.us/cgi-bin/legp504.exe?000+cod+TOC150200000041000000000000.

[8] General histories of county and municipal government that reference numerous other sources are contained in A. E. Dick Howard, *Commentaries on the Constitution of Virginia* (Charlottesville: The University Press of Virginia), 782-876; and Chester Bain, *A Body Incorporate: The Evolution of City-County Separation in Virginia* (Charlottesville: The University Press of Virginia, 1967). See also Donald C. Dixon, "Local Government in Colonial Virginia: A Prelude to Constitution Making," *The University of Virginia News Letter*, March 15, 1973.

[9] de Voursney, 22-23.

[10] Va. Code, § 24.2-613, "Form of ballot," accessed Sept. 25, 2010, http://leg1.state.va.us/cgi-bin/legp504.exe ?000+cod+24.2-613.

[11] See Section 3.02 of the charter of the city of Portsmouth, accessed Oct. 28, 2010, http://library1.municode .com/default-now/home.htm?infobase=13866&doc_action=whatsnew, or Section 8 of the charter for the city of Lexington, accessed Oct. 28, 2010, http://www.ecode360.com/documents/LE2692/LE2692-C.pdf.

[12] de Voursney, 15.

[13] Va. Code, §§15.2-800-15.2-858, "Title 15.2 - Counties, Cities and Towns. Chapter 8 - Urban County Executive Form of Government," accessed Sept. 25, 2010, http://leg1.state.va.us/cgi-bin/legp504.exe?000+cod +TOC150200000008000000000000.

[14] Ibid., §§ 15.2-600-15.2-642, Title 15.2 - Counties, Cities and Towns. Chapter 6 - County Manager Form of Government," accessed Sept. 25, 2010, http://leg1.state.va.us/cgi-bin/legp504.exe?000+cod+TOC15020000006 000000000000.

[15] Va. Constitution, Article VII, Sect. 4, "County and city officers," accessed Sept. 25, 2010, http://legis.state .va.us/Constitution/Constitution.htm#7S4.

[16] See the Code of Virginia or the Va. Constitution for the following responsibilities: Public education-Va. Constitution, Article VIII and Va. Code, Title 22.1; Public health-Va. Code, § 32.1-30 and other sections in Va. Code, Title 32.1; Social services-Va. Code, Chapter 3, Title 63.2, Services for troubled youth (Comprehensive Services Act for At-Risk Youth and Families)-Va. Code, Chapter 52, Title 2.2; Building code enforcement-Va. Code, § 36-105 and other sections in Title 36; Towns also are required to enforce the building code, although many towns contract with their county for this service; Election administration-Va. Code, Title 24.2; Jails- Va. Code, § 53.1-71 and other sections in Title 53; Behavioral health, primarily through regional community services boards-Va. Code, § 37.2-500 and other sections primarily in Chapter 5, Title 37.2; Planning (development of a comprehensive plan)-Va. Code, § 15.2-2223.

[17] Road construction and maintenance is governed by Va. Code, Title 33.1, "Highways, Bridges, and Ferries," accessed Sept. 25, 2010, http://leg1.state.va.us/cgi-bin/legp504.exe?000+cod+TOC3301000. See in particular § 33.1-23.3 and § 33.1-41.1, Code of Virginia, for provisions relating to cities and towns.

[18] Va. Code, § 15.2-1102, "General grant of power; enumeration of powers not exclusive; limitations on exercise of power," accessed Sept. 25, 2010, http://leg1.state.va.us/cgi-bin/legp504.exe?000+cod+15.2-1102.

[19] Auditor of Public Accounts, Commonwealth of Virginia, "2009 Amended Comparative Report of Local Government Revenues and Expenditures," accessed Oct. 28, 2010, http://www.apa.state.va.us/ComparativeReport.cfm.

[20] Va. Constitution, "Article VIII, Education, accessed Sept. 25, 2010, http://legis.state.va.us/Constitution/Constitution.htm#8S1.

[21] For the Standards of Quality and other requirements, see Va. Code, "Title 22.1 – Education," accessed Sept. 25, 2010, http://leg1.state.va.us/cgi-bin/legp504.exe?000+cod+TOC2201000.

[22] See, for example, "Table 12 of the Superintendent's Annual Report for Virginia Receipts by Division and Regional Program (in dollars) Fiscal Year 2009," accessed Oct. 28, 2010, http://www.doe.virginia.gov/statistics_reports/supts_annual_report/2008_09/table12.pdf.

[23] Auditor of Public Accounts, "Exhibit A."

[24] Ibid., "Exhibit B."

[25] Betty Long, "Municipal Revenue Sources," Updated from Table 11.1, *Handbook for Virginia Mayors and Council Members* (Charlottesville: University of Virginia and Virginia Municipal League, 2004), 137-138.

[26] Va. Constitution, "Section 4. Property segregated for local taxation; exceptions," accessed Sept. 25, 2010, http://legis.state.va.us/Constitution/Constitution.htm#10S4.

[27] The Weldon Cooper Center at the University of Virginia annually publishes *Virginia Local Tax Rates*, a compilation of tax rates in Virginia cities, counties, and selected towns. Tax Rates includes extensive information on local taxes and fees, including summaries of legislative changes. See, for example," 2009 Tax Rates," accessed Oct. 28, 2010, http://www.coopercenter.org/econ/2009-tax-rates.

[28] Va. Code, § 15.2-1104, "Taxes and assessments," accessed Sept. 25, 2010, http://leg1.state.va.us/cgi-bin/legp504.exe?000+cod+15.2-1104.

[29] Va. Constitution, "Article X, Taxation and Finance, Section 1. Taxable property; uniformity; classification and segregation," accessed Sept. 25, 2010, http://legis.state.va.us/Constitution/Constitution.htm#10S1.

[30] Ibid., also Va. Code, §§ 58.1-3230-58.1-3244, "Title 58.1 – Taxation. Chapter 32 - Real Property Tax," accessed Sept. 25, 2010, http://leg1.state.va.us/cgi-bin/legp504.exe?000+cod+TOC58010000032000000000000.

[31] Va. Code, § 58.1-3250, "General reassessment in cities," accessed Sept. 25, 2010, http://leg1.state.va.us/cgi-bin/legp504.exe?000+cod+58.1-3250.

[32] Ibid., § 58.1-3252, "In counties," accessed Sept. 25, 2010, http://leg1.state.va.us/cgi-bin/legp504.exe?000+cod+58.1-3252.

[33] Long, 125.

[34] Va. Code, § 58.1-3503, "General classification of tangible personal property," accessed Sept. 25, 2010, http://leg1.state.va.us/cgi-bin/legp504.exe?000+cod+58.1-3503.

[35] Ibid., §§ 58.1-3523-58.1-3536, "Title 58.1 - Taxation. Chapter 35.1 - Personal Property Tax Relief," accessed Sept. 25, 2010, http://leg1.state.va.us/cgi-bin/legp504.exe?000+cod+TOC58010000035000010000000.

[36] Ibid., "Title 58.1 - TAXATION. Chapter 6 - Retail Sales and Use Tax," accessed Sept. 25, 2010, http://leg1.state.va.us/cgi-bin/legp504.exe?000+cod+TOC58010000006000000000000.

[37] Ibid., "Title 58.1 – TAXATION. Chapter 6.2 - Virginia Communications Sales and Use Tax," accessed Sept. 25, 2010, http://leg1.state.va.us/cgi-bin/legp504.exe?000+cod+TOC58010000006000020000000.

[38] Ibid., § 58.1-3703, "Counties, cities and towns may impose local license taxes and fees; limitation of authority," accessed Sept. 25, 2010, http://leg1.state.va.us/cgi-bin/legp504.exe?000+cod+58.1-3703.

Part VII: Elections and Politics

[1] For all of the details on qualifications, registration, absentee voting, and other election-related processes, see Va. Code, "Title 24.2 – Elections," accessed on June 20, 2011, http://leg1.state.va.us/cgi-bin/legp504.exe?000+cod+TOC2402000.

[2] For more information on voting requirements in the 50 states, see the National Association of Secretaries of State, "Voter Registration: Get Registered or Check Your Registration Info," accessed June 20, 2011, http://www.canivote .org; and Tracy Lapa, "Raw Data: State-By-State Voter Registration Requirements," Fox News, Aug. 17, 2006, accessed June 20, 2011, http://www.foxnews.com/story/0,2933,209070,00.html.

Chapter 25: Voting in Virginia

[1] "Thomas P. O'Neill, Jr. Papers" | Biographical Note, John J. Burns Library, Boston College, accessed September 23, 2010, http://www.bc.edu/bc_org/avp/ulib/oneill_findingaid2.html.

[2] Va. Constitution, "Article II - Franchise and Officers," accessed August 20, 2010, http://legsearch.state.va.us /smb/198.246.238.222/dlas/constitution/a2s8.htm.

3 Virginia Electoral Board Association "Welcome to the Virginia Electoral Board Association," accessed August 20, 2010, http://vebanews.org/Welcome.html.

[4] State Board of Elections, "Local Election Officials," accessed September 23, 2010, http://www.sbe.virginia.gov /cms/Election_Information/Local_Election_Officials/Index.html.

[5] Ibid., "Overview of the Election Process, Who Conducts the Elections in Virginia?" accessed September 23, 2010, http://www.sbe.virginia.gov/cms/Election_Information/Election_Procedures/Index.html.

[6] Ibid., "References and Election Laws," accessed August 20, 2010, http://www.sbe.virginia.gov/cms/Misc /Election_Laws.html.

[7] Ibid., "Election Calendar and Schedule," accessed September 23, 2010, http://www.sbe.virginia.gov /cms/Election_Information/Election_Calendar_Schedule.html.

[8] Ibid., "Virginia State Board of Elections: Voter ID Requirements in Virginia," accessed September 23, 2010. http://www.sbe.virginia.gov/cms/Voter_Information/Voter_ID_Requirements_in_Virginia_text.html.

[9] Ibid., "Absentee Voting," accessed September 23, 2010, http://www.sbe.virginia.gov/cms/Absentee_Voting /Index.html.

[10] Ibid., "Registering To Vote," accessed September 23, 2010, http://www.sbe.virginia.gov/cms/Voter_Information /Registering_to_Vote/Index.html.

[11] Secretary of the Commonwealth of Virginia, "Clemency," accessed September 23, 2010, http://www .commonwealth.virginia.gov/JudicialSystem/Clemency/clemency.cfm.

[12] State Board of Elections, "Forms and Publications," accessed September 23, 2010, http://www.sbe .virginia.gov/cms/Forms_Publications/Index.html.

[13] Ibid., "Petition for Appeal of Denial of Virginia Voter Registration," accessed September 23, 2010, http://www .sbe.virginia.gov/cms/documents/Petitionforappealofdenial.pdf.

[14] Ibid., "Registration Statistics," accessed September 23, 2010, http://www.sbe.virginia.gov/cms/Statistics_Polling _Places/Index.html.

[15] Chuck Todd, "Deeds wins big," NBC News, accessed September 23, 2010, http://firstread.msnbc.msn.com/_news /2009/06/09/4424904-deeds-wins-big.

[16] "Absentee Voting," accessed September 23, 2010, http://www.sbe.virginia.gov/cms/Absentee_Voting/Index.html.

[17] Clair Whitmer, "What the Move Act Means For You," Overseas Vote Foundation, accessed September 23, 2010, https://www.overseasvotefoundation.org/node/282.

[18] State Board of Elections, "Welcome to Virginia's Campaign Finance Website," accessed September 23, 2010, http://www.sbe.virginia.gov/cms/Campaign_Finance_Disclosure/Index.html.

[19] Virginia Public Access Project, "State Board of Elections and VPAP Team Up to Display Election-Night Results," accessed September 23, 2010, http://www.vpap.org/updates/show/416.

[20] State Board of Elections, "Voters With Special Needs," accessed September 23, 2010, http://www.sbe .virginia.gov/cms/Voter_Information/Voters_with_Special_Needs/Index.html.

Chapter 26: Money in Virginia Politics

[1] *Disclose Virginia*, a newsletter of the Virginia Public Access Project (Richmond: Spring, 2010).
[2] Ibid.
[3] "Gerald E Connolly," accessed Oct. 20, 2010, http://www.vpap.org/candidates/profile/elections/21224.
[4] "Governor, 2009," accessed Oct. 20, 2010, http://www.vpap.org/elections/election_seat/1?year=2009.
[5] "The Secret Election," *The New York Times,* September 8. 2010, accessed Oct. 20, 2010, http://www.nytimes.com/2010/09/19/opinion/19sun1.html?_r=1&ref=editorials.
[6] This figure is not found in a link on the VPAP site. It is a query of VPAP data.
[7] Ibid.
[8] "Top Vendors," accessed Oct. 20, 2010, http://www.vpap.org/vendors/top_services1?end_year=2009&start_year=2009&lookup_type=year&filing_period=all&filter_cmte_radio=1&filter_cmte=1.

Chapter 27: Political Parties in Virginia

[1] National Archives, "Declaration of Independence," accessed October 11, 2010, http://www.archives.gov/exhibits/charters/declaration.html.
[2] Ibid., "The Founding Fathers: Virginia," accessed October 11, 2010, http://www.archives.gov/exhibits/charters/constitution_founding_fathers_virginia.html.
[3] Ibid.
[4] "Virginia - Political parties," accessed October 11, 2010, http://www.city-data.com/states/Virginia-Political-parties.html.
[5] Peverill Squire, James Lindsay, Cary R Covington, and Eric Smith, *Dynamics of Democracy,* Fourth Edition (Atomic Dog Publishing, 2005), 257, A-19.
[6] "A Century of Lawmaking for a New Nation: U.S. Congressional Documents and Debates, 1774 – 1875," *Annals of Congress, 4th Congress*, Pages 2873 & 2874 of 2966, accessed Oct. 20, 2010, http://memory.loc.gov/cgi-bin/ampage?collId=llac&fileName=006/llac006.db&recNum=679.
[7] Squire, 265.
[8] Ibid., 256.
[9] Ibid., 257-258.
[10] Va. Code, § 24.2-613, "Form of ballot. The ballots shall comply with the requirements of this title and the standards prescribed by the State Board," accessed October 11, 2010, http://leg1.state.va.us/cgi-bin/legp504.exe?000+cod+24.2-613.
[11] Ibid., § 24.2-508, "Powers of political parties in general," accessed October 11, 2010, http://leg1.state.va.us/cgi-bin/legp504.exe?000+cod+24.2-508.
[12] Republican Party of Virginia, "Republican Party of Virginia Creed," accessed October 11, 2010, http://www.rpv.org/about/page/republican-party-of-virginia-creed.
[13] Democratic Party of Virginia, "The Party Platform," accessed October 11, 2010, http://www.vademocrats.org/party-platform.
[14] U.S. Justice Department, "About Section 5 of the Voting Rights Act," accessed October 11, 2010, http://www.justice.gov/crt/voting/sec_5/about.php.
[15] DPVA, "Virginia Democratic Party Plan," accessed October 11, 2010, http://va-dems.vanwebhost.com/sites/va-dems.vanwebhost.com/files/TheDPVAPartyPlan.pdf; RPV, "Republican Party of Virginia," accessed October 11, 2010, http://www.rpv.org/docLib/20100121_PartyPlanNovUpdatesNotes.pdf.

[16] The interest groups and voting coalitions are illustrated by contributions to political candidates of each political party. For example, see the Virginia Public Access Project, "Top Donors By Industry," accessed Apr. 14, 2011, http://www.vpap.org/donors/top_industries1, and "State PACs," http://www.vpap.org/committees.

[17] See these examples of interest group involvement, which are a fraction of their many activities: Kelly Hannon, "Education group grades gubernatorial candidates," *Fredericksburg Free-Lance Star*, Aug. 23, 2005, http://fredericksburg.com/News/FLS/2005/082005/08232005/124103; Virginia Association of Realtors, "RPAC endorses congressional candidates," Oct. 18, 2010, http://www.varealtor.com/news/2010/10/rpac-endorses-congressional-candidates; Anita Kumar, "Veterans Groups Support Gilmore," *The Washington Post*, Oct. 17, 2008; http://voices.washingtonpost.com/virginiapolitics/2008/10/veteran_groups_support_gilmore.html; AFL-CIO, "Virginia Legislators," http://southeastvirginia.blogspot.com/2010/08/2010-virginia-afl-cio-constitutional.html, all accessed Apr. 13, 2011.

[18] Virginia Public Access Project, "Top Donors By Industry," accessed Apr. 14, 2011, http://www.vpap.org/donors/top_industries1.

[19] Ibid.

[20] Bill Bartel, "NRA switches to McDonnell; firefighters endorse Deeds," *The Virginian-Pilot*, Sept. 15, 2009, accessed Apr. 13, 2011, http://hamptonroads.com/2009/09/nra-switches-mcdonnell-firefighters-endorse-deeds.

[21] Alyssa Rosenberg, "Federal employee groups step up political efforts as fall elections approach," Government Executive.com, July 14, 2008, accessed Apr. 1, 2011, http://www.govexec.com/dailyfed/0708/071408ar1.htm.

[22] See the votes of delegates and senators in the Virginia General Assembly on SB 417, "Individual health insurance coverage; resident of State shall not be required to obtain a policy," accessed Apr. 13, 2011, http://leg1.state.va.us/cgi-bin/legp504.exe?101+sum+SB417.

[23] Julian Walker, "Candidate Kaine says he's crisis-tested," *The Virginian-Pilot*, Apr. 7, 2011, accessed Apr. 13, 2011, http://hamptonroads.com/2011/04/candidate-kaine-says-hes-crisistested?page=1.

[24] Susan Page and Naomi Jagoda, "What is the Tea Party? A growing state of mind," *USA TODAY*, July 8, 2010, accessed Apr. 13, 2011, http://www.usatoday.com/news/politics/2010-07-01-tea-party_N.htm#.

[25] John T. Woolley and Gerhard Peters, The American Presidency Project, accessed Apr. 12, 2011, "Democratic Party Platform of 1856," http://www.presidency.ucsb.edu/ws/index.php?pid=29576#axzz1JSGVb0SV; "2008 Democratic Party Platform," http://www.presidency.ucsb.edu/ws/index.php?pid=78283#axzz1J3YMsQw6; "Republican Party Platform of 1856," http://www.presidency.ucsb.edu/ws/index.php?pid=29619#axzz1J3YMsQw6; "2008 Republican Party Platform," http://www.presidency.ucsb.edu/ws/index.php?pid=78545#axzz1J3YMsQw6.

[26] Examples of this activism can be found at: "The Federation of Virginia Tea Party Patriots," accessed Apr. 13, 2011, http://virginiateapartypatriots.com; "Jamie Radtke: Tea Party 'Wouldn't Exist Today If Republicans Hadn't Failed Under Bush Years,'" *The Huffington Post*, Jan. 30, 2011, accessed Apr. 13, 2011, http://www.huffingtonpost.com/2011/01/30/jamie-radtke-tea-party-wo_n_815969.html.

[27] Va. Code, § 24.2-506, "Petition of qualified voters required; number of signatures required; certain towns excepted," accessed October 22, 2010, http://leg1.state.va.us/cgi-bin/legp504.exe?000+cod+24.2-506.

Constitution of Virginia

[1] The entire Constitution of Virginia can be found at the Virginia General Assembly's Legislative Information System Website: http://legis.state.va.us/Constitution/ConstitutionTOC.htm.